Absolute Equality
An Early Feminist Perspective

INFLUENCIAS DE LAS IDEAS MODERNAS

BY / POR **Luisa Capetillo**

ENGLISH TRANSLATION AND INTRODUCTION BY /
TRADUCCIÓN AL INGLÉS E INTRODUCCIÓN DE
LARA WALKER

Arte Público Press
Houston, Texas

Absolute Equality: An Early Feminist Perspective / Influencias de las ideas modernas is made possible through grants from the City of Houston through the Houston Arts Alliance and the Exemplar Program, a program of Americans for the Arts in collaboration with the LarsonAllen Public Services Group, funded by the Ford Foundation.

Recovering the past, creating the future

Arte Público Press
University of Houston
452 Cullen Performance Hall
Houston, TX 77204-2004

Cover design by James E. Brisson
Cover photo courtesy of Biblioteca Nacional
José Martí, La Habana, Cuba

9 0 1 2 3 4 5 6 7 8   10 9 8 7 6 5 4 3 2 1

CONTENTS

INTRODUCTION[1]

U p until the last two decades of the twentieth century, most of what had been written about Luisa Capetillo had focused on two incidents of her life. One, that she was the first Puerto Rican woman to wear pants and two, that she was subsequently arrested for that transgression in 1915 while in Havana, Cuba. The photograph of Capetillo dressed in men's clothing—a suit and Panama hat that documents these events—has become emblematic of her work and ideology. As we enter the twenty-first century and begin to mark one hundred years since Capetillo's work was first published, it is poignant that we re-discover her writing as well as her contributions as a historical figure.

Capetillo participates in the early-twentieth-century Puerto Rican diaspora along with other working-class exiles, immigrants, and activist nomads who were the result of the social movements of the 1890s; they left behind significant bodies of work.[2] Although a few of her contemporaries, such as Bernardo Vega and Jesús Colón, have been categorized as the *pionero* generation of Latino working-class writers and activists in the United States, others (and their work) have received less study or have been ignored.[3] Additionally, other early-twentieth-century, working-class exile, immigrant, and activist work from the Latino diaspora, as well as from native Latino writers, has been left unstudied or at least "under"-studied, leaving a space for their recovery and re-construction work to be done.[4]

The recovering and re-reading of Capetillo's texts is part of the need for a renewed critical and historical recovery and exploration of women's working-class literature and the subsequent "discovery" of a working-class intellectual community of Latinas in the United States allowing connections with other working-class intellectuals, literatures, and feminisms. In this sense I group Capetillo with other Latina[5] working-class women writers and activists whose political and literary work flourished at the turn of the twentieth century in the United States.[6] In doing so, I hope that her work can be explored along with other different forms of struggle that will add to the voices, as well as the study of, early Latina working-class feminist practices. Through this recovery and re-reading, I believe that Capetillo's texts, along with others, provide historical grounding for later generations of Latina writing and cultural production in the United States.[7]

Capetillo, as a working-class intellectual and writer, assumes and appropriates the power and authorization of writing, intellectual, and artistic production. During her life she published four books that contain a variety of propaganda, essays, speeches, fiction, letters, plays, experimental prose, journal entries, and translations of anarchist principles: *Ensayos libertarios*, written between 1904 and 1907, published in 1907 in Arecibo, Puerto Rico; *La humanidad en el futuro*, published in 1910 in San Juan, Puerto Rico; *Mi opinión sobre las libertades, derechos y deberes de la mujer*, published in 1911 in San Juan, Puerto Rico, and an expanded version published in Tampa, Florida in 1913; and *Influencias de las ideas modernas*, published in 1916 in San Juan, Puerto Rico. The texts cover topics that range from marriage to free love, from child-rearing to sexuality, from education to women's roles in society, social justice, and relations of power. In all situations she offers critical examples of corruption and exploitation from the elite and dominant class fractions. She denounces the ideologies generated by hegemonic social and cultural forces as she lays bare the ironies present in their exploitative logic and beliefs. Hegemony, as Stuart Hall indicates, "is accomplished through the agencies of the superstructure—the family, education systems, the church, the media, and cultural institutions, as well as the coercive side of the state—the law, police, army, . . . " (Hall 333). Therefore, Capetillo strives to make her public—the working-class and women—cognizant of these power relations, offering them an alternate vision of social justice and equality. For Capetillo, subversion of any and all hegemonic interests is clear throughout her writing and practice.

Capetillo's *Influencias de las ideas modernas* (*IIM*) has never been republished in its entirety until now as *Absolute Equality: An Early Feminist Perspective*. Several excerpts of *IIM* were printed in Norma Valle Ferrer's seminal biography of Capetillo, *Luisa Capetillo. Historia de una mujer proscrita* (1990), and in her recent edition in English with Gloria Waldman, *Luisa Capetillo, Pioneer Puerto Rican Feminist* (2006).[8] Additionally, Julio Ramos' groundbreaking study and anthology of Capetillo's writing, *Amor y anarquía* (1992), incorporates a variety of Capetillo's work, including several selections from *Influencias de las ideas modernas*.[9] Other anthologies that feature selections of Capetillo's writing from *Influencias de la ideas modernas*, are Rubén Dávila Santiago's anthology of working-class Puerto Rican theater

1900-1920, *Teatro obrero en Puerto Rico 1900-1920: Antología* (1985) which contains two short plays, "Cómo se prostituyen las pobres" and "En el campo, amor libre," and Nicolás Kanellos' editions of *En otra voz: Antología de la literatura hispana de los Estados Unidos* (2002) and *Herencia: The Anthology of Hispanic Literature of the United States* (2002), which both include the two short plays, "Cómo se prostituyen las pobres" and "Cómo se prostituye una rica" published in Spanish and then translated into English, respectively.[10]

This edition is an important contribution to Caribbean, Latin American, Latina/o, Women's, Working-Class, and Anarchist studies. For the first time, Capetillo's hybrid-genre text will be accessible to scholars and students in both English and Spanish.

Luisa Capetillo (1879-1922)

Luisa Capetillo was born in Arecibo, Puerto Rico, in 1879 to immigrant working-class parents and grew up in the center of radical working-class culture. Her mother, Luisa Margarita Perone, was of French descent and she immigrated to Puerto Rico during her youth to work as a governess for the wealthy Zeno family in Arecibo and later as a domestic (Valle Ferrer, *Historia* 39). Luisa Capetillo's father, Luis Capetillo Echevarría, was a Spanish immigrant from the Basque Country who arrived in Puerto Rico around the same time as Margarita Perone to seek his fortune as a director and promoter of traveling amusement fairs. He was unsuccessful and then became a migrant worker of sorts (Valle Ferrer, *Historia* 40, 44). Both Luis and Margarita, who never married (Valle Ferrer, *Historia* 39), were influenced by the lingering revolutionist ideologies present in Europe after the French Revolution of 1848 and brought those ideologies with them to Puerto Rico (Valle Ferrer, *Historia* 41).

Margarita instilled in her daughter a sense of self, a passion for learning, and a knowledge of work as a reality for daily survival. As a young girl she accompanied her mother who was working as a domestic in the homes of wealthy families in the area. Her mother also taught her French and encouraged her to read and study. It has been documented that Margarita attended *tertulias* or literary gatherings to discuss the pertinent news and topics of the day, even though she was the only woman among a group of all men (Valle Ferrer, *Historia* 45). Luis was also an avid reader and political thinker who consistently gathered with friends in their homes or in cafés to discuss politics, ideology, and current events (Valle Ferrer, *Historia* 44-45).

Needless to say, education and learning were important aspects of Luisa Capetillo's upbringing: they are frequently mentioned throughout her work. Capetillo was taught by her parents and later attended a private school for girls under the direction of María Sierra Soler in Arecibo (Valle Ferrer, *Historia* 45). Even though she received this formal education, the majority of her instruction came from her parents. There she was encouraged to read the great literary works of authors such as Tolstoy, Victor Hugo, Emile Zola, and George Sand, the political philosophy of Kropotkin and John Stuart Mill, among many others (Valle Ferrer, *Historia* 46).

While accompanying her mother in her domestic work, Luisa Capetillo met Manuel Ledesma, the son of a wealthy family in Arecibo. In 1898, Capetillo gave birth to her first child, Manuela Ledesma, and in 1900 they had a second child, Gregorio (Valle Ferrer, *Historia* 54). They never married, and Luisa was never accepted by Ledesma's wealthy family. Their illicit relationship proved difficult for Capetillo who was censured by the social and class norms of the times (Valle Ferrer, *Historia* 54). Later, after each went their separate ways, Capetillo and her two young children went to live with her mother. The children were recognized legally by the Ledesma family, and Manuel provided financially for his children in some way. Manuel later went on to become mayor of Arecibo and continued to have contact with his two children. While living with her mother, Luisa Capetillo supported her children as a worker in the garment industry and later, during her activist years, entrusted their care to her mother (Valle Ferrer, *Historia* 56, 59).

Capetillo's ideology, development, and historical context

At the turn of the twentieth century, Capetillo began to collaborate and write for some of the local newspapers in Arecibo as she was further developing her political thought, which was especially steeped in socialism and anarchism (Valle Ferrer, *Historia* 59). The changes and unrest at the end of the nineteenth century and the first decades of the twentieth century in the international context had particular effects in Puerto Rico, specifically with regard to the U.S. invasion in 1898. Therefore, although Puerto Rico was no longer a Spanish colony after the Spanish American War, the U.S. involvement was still problematic, to say the least. These changes caused the working class to question their rights and even their understanding of democracy as it had been ambiguously laid out by the United States. The importance of organized labor was coming to a head, and in late 1898 Puerto Rico's working class formed the Federación Libre de Trabajadores (FLT or the Free Federation of Workers), which came to be the largest labor movement organization on the island and eventually the leading labor organization into the first part of the twentieth century; Capetillo became an active member (Suárez Findlay 138; Matos Rodríguez xv). The FLT was not without internal and even external conflicts with other labor organizations, but it was still able to create alliances on and beyond the island with other groups, such as the U.S. Socialist Labor Party and the American Federation of Labor (Matos Rodríguez xv). The first decade of the labor movement created a space for working women and men to articulate their ideologies and express their own political discourse (Ramos; Suárez Findlay 139). It was during this time that two important areas of intellectual and artistic production came to the forefront for working-class political organizing, the Centros de estudios (Study Centers) and the tradition of readers in the tobacco factories. The Centros de estudios worked with both men and women, as well as study groups on worker's issues, and included a cross-section of workers such as unionists, anarchists, and socialists (Suárez Findlay 139; Dávila Santiago 201). Artistic production was combined with activism as the workers "wrote essays, novels, poetry, and plays, which they read out loud and performed to large, enthusiastic audiences across the island in theaters, union halls, worker demonstrations, and town squares" (Suárez Findlay 139).

Ángel Quintero Rivera's detailed study of the tobacco economy in Puerto Rico describes the formation of an intellectual working class by way of readers, *lectores*, who introduced workers to political ideologies and literatures. Bakunin, Kropotkin, Tolstoy, Dostoievsky, Nietzsche, and Zola were only some of the many authors who were read to the workers in the factories (Ramos 27; Valle Ferrer 43). This provided a source of access to education and intellectualism for workers. Political working-class leaders and intellectuals such as Bernardo Vega, Jesús Colón, and José Santana, were also "schooled" in the tobacco factories.[11] Capetillo began her intellectual work as a *lectora* in a tobacco factory in Arecibo in 1906 (Sánchez González, *Luisa Capetillo* 151). The factory was, among other things, a cultural space where artisans —many with anarchist and socialist tendencies—received an alternate education from a very young age.[12] The significance of Capetillo's role as a reader in the tobacco factories is not to be overlooked. As Matos-Rodríguez has pointed out, "being a reader was an extremely presti-

gious public role for a worker and one that immediately placed them
among the worker's elite" (xvi).

In addition to her work as a reader in the factories, Capetillo participated in protests, strikes, and organizing meetings locally and around
the island. She participated in strikes, affiliated with FLT (1905) and
also with La Cruzada del Ideal (The Crusade of the Ideal) which strove
to involve workers in union politics (1909). Through these public manifestations she, as well as others, were met by police opposition and
attacks (Matos Rodríguez xvii).

From 1912-1916 Capetillo traveled from Puerto Rico to New York
City and Ybor City/Tampa, Florida, to work with the *tabaquero* groups
in the tobacco factories, to advocate union organizing, and to work with
other working-class Hispanics. It is during this time that Capetillo participates in the Caribbean diaspora and in expanding her transnational
vision in New York and Ybor City (Tampa's Latino enclave), as well as
Cuba. Perhaps coupled with her international vision was also the sup-
pression of anarchists in Puerto Rico by U.S. colonial officials during
1911-1912 (Suárez Findlay 165). This self-imposed exile and emigration in the United States had a great impact on her writing, activism, and
personal life. The majority of texts included in *Influencias de las ideas
modernas* were written during her time in U.S. cities. It is of interest and
important to note that Capetillo, unlike many of her compatriots, was
not a nationalist nor did her writing reflect a nationalist project, despite
nationalism's heightened strength at the turn of the twentieth century
(Hewitt 2; Ramos; Sánchez-González, *Luisa Capetillo* 156). Her vision
of *patria* was more closely aligned to a global imagined community of
workers, where freedom and equality reigned (Sánchez González, *Luisa
Capetillo* 155).

In Tampa, Capetillo worked again as a reader in the tobacco factories and continued her propaganda for anarcho-syndicalism and
women's freedom. Tampa, as Hewitt has pointed out, "was not a typical
southern city" (6). A plethora of conditions had created an immigrant
and industrial city, as well as a creative and intellectual epicenter for
progressive thought (Dworkin y Méndez; Hewitt; Pozzetta). Due to
U.S. intervention in Puerto Rico, many tobacco factories had moved to
southern Florida to escape taxation and to be closer to buyers
(Rodríguez Matos xxi).

Capetillo also traveled to New York City where she collaborated
and organized with other working-class Hispanics, wrote articles for
Hispanic and unionist newspapers, owned and operated a vegetarian

restaurant, and continued her anarcho-feminist writing and praxis. Her mission and ideology remained the same no matter where she went: to fight for women and workers' equality and freedom. Capetillo claimed that "the present social system, with all its errors, is held in place by the ignorance and the slavery of women" [el actual sistema social, con todos sus errores, se sostiene, por la ignorancia y la esclavitud de la mujer] (*Mi opinión* viii). To create social change and "correct" these problems and ills she employed didactic, artistic, and activist practices.

This culture of informal education and real-life praxis formed her intellect and thought. In her texts Capetillo writes about this alternative form of education in opposition to the formal, university education of the upper classes as a way to legitimize her knowledge and intellectual participation. Always aware of the various structures of power that are constantly in play, she addresses issues of access to learning and knowledge and the hegemonically accepted sites of such activities. Capetillo elucidates this position by stating:

> I speak with perfect understanding of that which I say, with a profound intuition that guides me. I have not been able to study anything according to the precepts of the schools, universities, or halls of higher learning [. . .] Now I have introduced myself as a propagandist, journalist, and writer, without any authorization other than my own vocation and initiative, without any recommendation other than my own, or any help other than my own effort. I care little about the criticism from those who have been able to procure a formal education that allows them to present their written observations, protests, or literary narrations . . . (*Absolute Equality* 60)

Capetillo's writing, like other texts of working-class literature, employs bourgeois literary conventions and elements, subverting not only elite culture, but also anarchism and anarcho-syndicalism's phalologocentrism and orthodox Marxism. In this sense Capetillo's "literature of resistance" in this context signifies writing directed not only against dominant culture, but also against restrictive elements within a subculture —in this instance, the working-class and union organizing. Urban growth and modernization brought both sexes into the factories and sweatshops and consequently increased the number of women in urban labor; however, as Asunción Lavrín points out, "at the turn of the twentieth century most changes in the social and political structure were defined and undertaken by men" (4).

Another important concept tied to anarchism that Capetillo discussed in her work and in her life experiences was that of nature and the natural way of life. The anarchist idea believes in man's natural state and that the closer she can be to this "natural" state, the closer man comes to creating a just society—a belief rooted in romanticism and utopianism (Horowitz 63; Valle Ferrer 47). Throughout Capetillo's text Mother Nature is humankind's perfect example.

Capetillo, in accord with many anarchists, does not believe in religious rites or dogmas. She sees them as another form of enslavement and oppression. Many times she writes against the institution of the Church, its hypocrisy and enslavement. This theme is not new to her 1916 text; it was also seen in her previous writings. In her first book, *Ensayos libertarios* (1907), she exhorts her public not to baptize children; she asks, if it were really necessary, why then are there millions of beings that don't do it or believe in it (19). Later in her book, *Mi Opinión* (1911), in a letter she wrote to her daughter, Manuela, she tells her that "she never taught her to pray . . . " and that she didn't baptize her in any religion (83). In *Influencias de las ideas modernas*, she continues denouncing the problems and social ills of the Church and anticlericism. At one point she reflects back on her life and refers to Catholicism stating that she "protested that degrading mark, because I was not a slave, I did not carry my children to the infected baptismal font" (63).

However, Capetillo was not an atheist; to the contrary, she believed in a Supreme God, in Jesus Christ and even in certain passages of the Bible. In her play, "Influences of Modern Ideas," the protagonist, Angelina, comments that even though "true anarchists will find the history of the Bible doubtful and will reject institutions with selfish objectives," she footnotes that statement saying, "in the Bible there are written sublime truths, let us practice them" (30). Capetillo's spirituality is rooted in Spiritism, influenced by the teachings of Allan Kardec from France, reincarnation, Christianity, and Asian beliefs that created a syncretic and unique belief system. For Capetillo, spirituality should be something that enables human beings to love one another and is synonymous with anarchism. In the same play the protagonist explains that by studying spiritism she became a revolutionary:

> I was studying Spiritism [. . .] I felt a desire to know something of the afterlife [. . .] and to understand the diversity of inhabited worlds and to fully accept diverse existences. This made me

a revolutionary, because it explained to me that all men are brothers, that no one has the right to hurt others, misery or to impose their ideas on them or to enslave them, and that luxury was a crime as long as there was misery. (29)

The protagonist later continues by saying, "The word 'religion' has been confused. The least religious have been the priests" (29). After discussing the important teachings regarding brotherly love taught by Krishna, Jesus, Yao, Confucius, and Philon, she states that they were "true anarchists," because they were "'humane,' in every sense of the word" (*IIM* 34). As Matos-Rodríguez has noted, Kardec's Spiritism was taught in Puerto Rico at the turn of the twentieth century (xix) and Hergiz Shannon's study of Spiritism in early twentieth-century Puerto Rico underscores its important impact on women and their role in society. "Based on the beliefs and philosophies of the French educator Hippolyte Léon Denizard Rivail (1804-1869), better known by his *nom be plume* Allan Kardec (a name supposedly based on previous reincarnations ascertained from mediumistic communications), Spiritism was a moral philosophy rather than a religion, incorporating the ideas of Romanticism and the scientific revolution to bridge the gap between the material and spiritual worlds" (Fernández Olmos 172). In this sense it inscribes a Christian morality, the importance of charitable acts, and the Christian golden rule, and simultaneously rejects other key precepts, such as the divinity of Christ. For Kardec, Spiritism "bridged the gap between science and religion, provided a rational basis for faith, linked social progress to spiritual progress and equilibrated natural laws with moral laws," (Fernández Olmos 173) especially during this era of scientific breakthroughs, such as Darwin's theory of evolution,[13] which contested traditional Christian beliefs.

Capetillo's ideas and writing about spirituality and what she termed "true Christianity" make her quite different from other anarchists (Valle Ferrer 48). In one of her reflections on politics and religion she states, "being a Christian is not to hate one another, or offer Mass and charge for it, or baptize and do the same. These are simply rites invented in order to speculate in the name of Christianity" (45). Later in another reflection, she writes about religion being solely based on the teaching "to love one another." She explains by saying that when humankind can truly understand that concept and do it, then there will be no borders or distance between anyone and justice can be attained (47). She ends by saying that "the idea of Jesus was the most revolutionary idea that the human mind ever could conceive" (45). Capetillo invokes Christ as an example many times in her writing, calling attention to his life and teachings. In a reflection written while looking out over the cityscape of a small town with a silver domed church she questions the need for churches if people can keep Christ's teaching in their hearts, minds, and actions (57-58). As Valle Ferrer has pointed out, Capetillo's understandings of Christianity and religion also stemmed from a Russian writer, Tolstoy, who in the latter part of his life had a spiritual crisis and from then on believed in a Christianity that was founded upon brotherly love and non-resistance (50).[14]

Capetillo was often attacked for her antireligious ideas. While in New York City in 1912, she writes an autobiographical sketch of her attacks and discrimination for her ideology and propaganda. In it she compares the situation to Christ and says, "you don't need redeemers, you yourselves can be them . . . search for the truth, do not worship anyone, explore nature, study its effects, and you will see the cause. We are Gods and sinners. Let us endeavor to be gods and the sinners will disappear" (64).

The beginning of the twentieth century marks an era of social unrest and turmoil. Immigration and subsequent urbanization and industrialization lent themselves to the denouncement of oppression and injustice and the search for social movements that facilitated, although not without struggle, minority voices with a space in which to insert themselves in dialogue with the hegemony. These social movements challenged hegemony's status quo and by extension also challenged the relationship between authority and power. Angel Rivera Quintero posits:

> It is fascinating to explore how a conflictive situation such as was produced in the first decade of the century could give rise to new forms of relationships between men and women of the working class, forms which began to break old patterns of domination/subordination. (5)

Analysis of writing and texts from the early twentieth-century working class allow for exploration of rupture, change, and struggle. A particularly fascinating and complex site of investigation is that of migration between the Caribbean and the United States. Historical research of working-class migration (both voluntary and forced)[15] illustrates that Cuban and Puerto Rican workers brought with them to the United States "an activist tradition" and that by the end of the nineteenth century they had organized workers in both Tampa and New York (Poyo and Díaz-Miranda 310). In Tampa, the first three decades of the twentieth century were replete with conflict and "confrontation between management and labor" in the flourishing tobacco industry (Poyo and Díaz-Miranda 311). It is within, and because of, this historical context that we find the texts and writings of Luisa Capetillo. A militant feminist anarchist, labor leader and strong proponent of social justice, Capetillo dedicated her life to fighting for women's rights and anarcho-syndicalist principles. She was a respected voice in the worker's movement at the beginning of the twentieth century and a passionate defender of women's agency.

Influencias de las ideas modernas (1916)

Influencias de las ideas modernas / Absolute Equality: An Early Feminist Perspective is a hybrid-genre and genre-defying text.[16] It includes long and short plays, fiction, essays, propaganda, letters, poems, philosophical reflections, and journal entries. The title piece is a long theatrical play that was written in 1907 in Arecibo, Puerto Rico, while the other writings were written between 1912 and 1916 in Tampa and Ybor City, Florida; New York City; and Havana, Cuba. They are divided into sections and the next one entitled, "Philosophical, Naturalist, Psychological and Moralist Notes, Annotations, Thoughts, Concepts, Definitions, Maxims, and Reflections," was begun in Ybor City on July 24, 1913. In addition to all the items mentioned in this section's title, there are also short fictional writings and fragments of letters, all of which articulate Capetillo's ideology and propaganda of women and workers' rights. The following section is entitled, "Interesting Letters from a Panamanian Anarchist," which contains letters written to Capetillo while she was union organizing and disseminating propaganda in Tampa, Florida. It is interesting to note that this section only contains "one side" of their correspondence, as Capetillo's responses are not included here. These are followed by five short plays and a poem.

Before providing a more detailed examination of these texts, it is interesting to explore the hybridity of the book's composition. According to Iris Zavala's study of modernist writers:

> It is significant that since the turn of the [twentieth] century some women modernists were consciously elaborating and repositioning language and discourse. Poetry, letters, and diary writing, which used to reflect the previous forms of hegemonic

private literary practices, no longer constitute the main and sole activity to verbalize women's ideas, as more and more women begin to intervene in the cultural struggle to transform hegemonies. (187)

Ramos, as well, argues that Capetillo's writing consists of heterogeneous "minor" literary genres because those styles (letters, translations, proclamations, autobiographical notes, fragments of speeches, short articles and essays) fit the lifestyle of an emerging working-class propagandist and writer (39), many times due to not having the time to dedicate solely to one project or book-length literary text. Additionally, the text as a whole can be read as an insight into Capetillo's activities: writing essays and propaganda for the union newspapers, writing correspondence to both her supporters and attackers, writing due to a creative spirit that almost compels her to do so, writing plays for the union halls and mutualist clubs, and so on.

In her play, "Influences of Modern Ideas," Capetillo employs many of the tenets of her ideology and propaganda. Anarchism, socialism, free love, feminism, anti-clericism, disillusion of class structures, and philosophical ideals based on modernity and progress, among others.

This "Three-Act Play" as she calls it, is a long, multi-character piece with stage directions and scenery descriptions. The protagonist is a young, bourgeois woman who lives with her widowed father. In Capetillo's writing the moment of becoming conscious of the social system is always described, whether it be someone from the bourgeoisie or from the working class. She includes protagonists from various levels of social class, thus emphasizing her belief that social change will involve all levels of society. The protagonist, Angelina, is made conscious of society's inequalities, both of class and gender, through her own personal study of European writers, philosophers and anarchists such as Tolstoy, Zola, Malestesta, Malato, and Kropotkin, to name a few. The play opens with Angelina reading *The Slavery of Our Times* by Tolstoy.

The first scene presents the ideological thought that will continue throughout the drama. A dialogue between the protagonist, Angelina, the daughter of a rich businessman and landowner, and the house servant, Ramón, presents the explicitly didactic nature of the play.

RAMÓN: Miss, do you not remember that today is your birthday?
ANGELINA: Actually, I didn't remember I've been concentrated these past few days on reading Tolstoy's *The Slavery of Our Times*, which has convinced me that the slavery of our

times is the inflexible wage law. (SHE *takes the cards, looks at them, and leaves them on the table.*)

RAMÓN : (*Winks an eye to obtain the young woman's opinion.*) And how could we live without receiving a wage?

ANGELINA: By educating the poor that no one has the right to place a value on one's work, nor should fixed working hours be established; work should be free and spontaneous, and there should be equal consumption. Each individual should work according to their potential and consume according to their needs.

RAMÓN : That is an anarchist maxim, but how do we put it into practice . . . through violence?

ANGELINA: No, through instruction and education; the majority of injustices and crimes are committed through ignorance. The capitalist class, for its own sake, should have tried to suppress the crimes and diseases created by the misery born of exploitation. (9)

And thus the stage is set. The problem is presented with promises of not only solutions, but concrete examples of how to put theories into practice. Angelina will cross all social class divisions between herself, the servant Ramón, and the peasants that cultivate the land owned by her father. At one point the protagonist asks, "Do you agree with those ideas? Would you dare to break from tradition?" (14). The question places the "tradition" of capitalism and the exploitation of workers at the forefront of concern. The final line of the scene is a call for action, "The working class will have to gain their freedom themselves" (15). This statement made by the wealthy landowner, after he shrinks from commencing a social revolt, not only indicts the dominant culture but also suggests the complicity of the working class in its social and economic subjugation when it does not resist. The working-class audience members are to be inspired to rise up and act for themselves.

The female protagonist even breaks class barriers to the point of falling in love with Carlos Santana, the labor strike and union leader. At each other's side, *compañeros* and equals, Angelina and Carlos lead the workers in revolution. As Ramos has indicated, "one of the key projects that forwards Capetillo's writing is that of producing contacts, intersections between classes, almost always achieved through the intervention of the woman" (53; my translation). Capetillo's feminist practice and class equality propose places of contact,[17] alliances between women and men of heterogeneous backgrounds, which in turn are corollary to her keen observation of the oppressive effects of social difference. Capetillo consistently creates characters who incorporate her political ideals and utopian visions, forging female working-class subjectivities that are leaders and instruments for change and equality.

As signifying and resignifying practices, Capetillo's dramas reinforced the values and beliefs of the anarcho-syndicalist movements and created a space for women and gender issues while directing the audience to take social action. As with later generations of social protest theater, Capetillo intended her plays to be transformative and regenerative. They affirmed cultural and class unity while demonstrating that the spectators' own oppressive social circumstances were ultimately transformable. The subversive action of these social protest dramas was to revitalize the struggles of the working class and to confirm the urgency and logic of their cause.

The next section, entitled "Philosophical, Naturalist, Psychological, and Moralist Notes, Annotations, Thoughts, Concepts, Definitions, Maxims, and Reflections," states that it was started in Ybor City (Florida) on July 24, 1913. It is here where the reader can see Capetillo's thought processes and how she connects her ideas and philosophies to create her unique ideology. As she articulates her thoughts on capitalist exploitation, women and children's rights, the need for moral and ethical parenting, motherhood, respect for all living organisms and Mother Nature, even the irony of a society that cares more for animal rights than protecting children, the elderly, and the sick. Through these reflections, ponderings, and exercises in creating her own ideology and beliefs, Capetillo begins a process of unraveling monolithic or hegemonic thought in order to expose the inherent flaws and false logic present in these systems of domination. She then reconstructs a world in which all persons are respected and sexism, classism, racism, ageism, and all other forms of discrimination are abolished. Humankind and Mother Nature work as one in a utopian eco-friendly society and where "life in its diverse and various manifestations is governed by love" (54).

The act of writing and what it means to be a writer is a topic of great importance to Capetillo and the basis of many essays and letters included in this text. While claiming for herself the titles of "propagandist, journalist, and writer" (60) and referring to the desires of her "poetic mind" (70), she inscribes all women into the creative, intellectual space of writers and creators. The female characters she creates in her fiction and plays espouse the maxim of woman as artist and intellectual.

Angelina, the protagonist of the play "Influences of Modern Ideas," studies anarchist and socialist theory, theology, and literature. Esmeralda, the protagonist of the play "Marriage Without Love, Consequence, Adultery," refers to her "artistic imagination." Gizelda, the dead mother of the orphaned youth in the short story, "Loves," was a great artist and diva of the theater. The absent-present protagonist of the play, "After her Death," is a poet. She argues with those who would claim that writers, artists, and philosophers are not producers, pointing out the primordial role of creativity as the necessary beginning for all forms of production from agriculture to architecture to poetry. She contests those who would not take her social ideas seriously or would dismiss them because they weren't popular with the majority (51-52). She writes that she must continue in the struggle, which is both artistic and activist, even though she is being attacked, rejected, and misunderstood. In the essay entitled, "I" which is directed to an artist friend, Manuel García, Capetillo calls herself "una equivocada" (66), which I translate to mean "a woman out of place," "misunderstood," and "mistaken." As Capetillo tries to negotiate between her marginalization as female artist and activist and her desire to create real social change, she often becomes frustrated. She writes, "in spite of all my frankness, I have not been understood, but instead, slandered, and misinterpreted" (66). This title she gives herself, "una equivocada," is representative of her writing and praxis, especially its use in the context of her essay, "I," and read in conjunction with daily activist "performances."[18] As she asserts her "right to enjoy" (66) all that nature and mankind have to offer, she places those rights within a capitalist society based on commodities, exchange, and inherent exploitation. As such Capetillo remarks that clothing and style of dress can be forms of female artistry, but are too tightly enmeshed in the monetary system. Capetillo then relates her strategic and manipulative processes of public image and use of the body, especially the female body, to "speak" to her audiences in order to disrupt certain spaces and subvert power structures.

> Sometimes, in order that they don't forget that I possess an artist's soul, like most women, I dress up without ostentation. And if I were not such an anarchist, that is to say, such a "Christian," I would dress splendidly, with true art, and with exquisite taste; but, the unfortunate who lack all necessities? The hungry and the naked? . . . What cruelty! What sarcasm! (66)

This use of the body and clothing as artist and activist expression is then situated against the capitalist system and those who are disenfranchised through this system of exchange.[19] Additionally, this artistic act of fine taste and beauty can also be read against Capetillo's notorious cross-dressing habit in a suit and tie.[20] Echevarría posits that Capetillo, "in claiming for herself both the identity of the artist and the identity of the woman, in uniting both identities with her claim that all women are potential artists, Capetillo is redefining the traditional understanding of the 'artist' and the 'woman.'"

Creativity and power are not reserved for men only, and Capetillo takes aim at those who would disregard any and all female artists, writers, and scholars. While referencing George Sand she denounces those men who give little regard to the French writer or who think of her as an immoral or "loose" woman. She refutes these comments stating that these men must be intimidated by women as artists, thinkers, and creators and that it is only with exaggerated flattery that they console themselves into thinking that women are not capable of original intellectual work. It is significant that Capetillo reinforces the notion that women are a locus of power, creativity, and intellect. She must continually assert herself as a participant in the artistic and intellectual discourses of the time. Woman as artist and intellectual was not embraced by the literary elite. Such characterizations as French sculptor Pierre-Auguste Renoir's "I consider women writers, lawyers, and politicians (such as George Sand, Mme. Adam and other bores) as monsters and nothing but five-legged calves. . . . The woman artist is merely ridiculous" (Ctd. in Chadwick 215), or of Latin American modernist poet, Rubén Darío referring to French suffragists as "ugly" and as unwomanly and even masculine, in the most pejorative sense,[21] are indicative of the disdain and resistance toward women as creative intellectuals. Perhaps this is why Capetillo repeatedly writes of herself, famous women, and her female characters as artists and intellectuals—to counter those who would attack and dismiss any and all women in these roles.

Restrictive gender roles, societal norms, and gendered imaginaries are again questioned and contested in the essay entitled "The Opinion of Many Men and My Opinion." In this short essay, through a strategic, creative use of hegemonic thought and a clever interpretation of power, Capetillo blurs the borders and spaces of gendered social roles while unmasking their inherent problems. The essay begins with remarks and opinions regarding women, their role and place in society. She lists the patriarchal, societal norms and opinions of men regarding women in order to then deconstruct them and thus subvert and change society's structures of power. Capetillo's style to use logic and common sense are seen throughout this piece which begins:

> Women should be women! Women's work is in the home! They shouldn't be macho! Mend stockings and underwear! Doze by the heartwarming fire knitting socks! Who asks them for their opinions, or to become involved in politics, or to aspire to be an elected candidate? This cannot be tolerated! Haven't we already permitted them to enter the lecture halls to become lawyers and doctors? But they are not satisfied: now they want to be judges, mayors, chiefs of police, legislators. Is that why we have allowed them to study, so they can cast us aside, aspiring to monopolize our positions and desiring to surpass us? I do not know how these women forget their weakness and their indiscretion; one cannot trust them at all, or teach them anything because immediately they want to take over. But how can a woman imitate a man? She can't, she's inferior! Even Mother Nature condemns her to be secluded during childbirth and breastfeeding! (66-67)

Through the act of writing, by putting these opinions and concepts on the page, by creating a textual space she is able to demystify their power, the power of the male, patriarchal opinion and, in turn, create her own interpretation of power. The working class and especially working-class women participate in public spaces differently than other social classes, and it is important that the public spheres referred to in the essay are othered. That is, they are not only leadership positions but also governing institutions. The hegemonically marginalized public space of the factory, the streets and even the schools have already been "sexed." It is the threat of women in other public spaces and the desire to protect that space that becomes an urgent necessity. In the title of the piece Capetillo states that there will be (at least) two opinions presented, but the reader is unaware (at the onset) as to who is voicing the first opinion. The opening line, "Women should be women," could just as well encapsulate Capetillo's feminist stance. It is this sort of strategic manipulation of hegemonic thought that characterizes Capetillo's discourse. As she unravels the patriarchal argument, she counters the opening remark in the second part of the essay with "A woman will *always* be a woman" (my emphasis). It is this unraveling of binary logic that pushes Capetillo's argument beyond a "he says, she says," to a theoretical and revolutionary paradigm for social change. She continues to explain by stating that "being a woman isn't only being powdered and covered in ribbons and lace," just as a man does not stop being a man when he "learns to cook, mend, sweep, and sew" (67). Again, Capetillo refers to the body, adornments, sexed and gendered activities, and spaces. In doing so, she performs another act that shifts boundaries and projects the possibility for something different.

Critic Lisa Sánchez-González claims that Capetillo's writing:

> undoes the binary logic that her essentialist method implies, because she derives her theory from the scene of practice, despite her positivist impulses. She cannot help but to de-essentialize and de-romanticize social constructs, because her feminist and anarchist epistemes require that she dwell on the very seams of the binary split; and dwelling on these overlapping edges, the contractions become apparent, even glaring. ("Luisa Capetillo" 160)

The remainder of the essay is devoted to this "de-essentializing." In the end, women will supersede men because of their superior moral conduct and sense of duty. And it will be because of men's own weakness and vices that they are replaced by women. Women will replace them in the workplace and in politics due to their better judgment and strength against vice. Capetillo offers as example the woman who replaced a man in the position of a stoker in a steamer because the boss acknowledged that the woman did a better job, plus she didn't drink whiskey (67). From this example Capetillo supposes that "in the future, woman will be preferred and men will have to abandon their vices in order to obtain employment" (67).

The essay ends making mention of many great women from history in various professions and areas who have brought about important change and betterment for society, including Joan of Arc, Madame Curie, the empress of Egypt Semiramis, Diana of Poiters, Saint Teresa, and Mary Magdalene, among many others. Capetillo, while reminding her audience of strong and important women also performs an (en)gendering of history, of (re)writing women into the field in the same way that contemporary historians and critics such as Emma Pérez and others have done.[22] Capetillo's approach of integrating women into the past, present, and future insists that a "sexing" occur and that it "will benefit the human race" (67). By offering her opinion to create change in the "opinion of many men," in society in general, Capetillo endeavors to revolutionize social structures.

The questioning of the status quo and social norms is continued in a quick-paced fictional stichomythia-style dialogue about free love, blatant inequalities in the prevailing honor and fidelity codes between the sexes, female sexuality and autonomy, men's sexual ownership of women, and inequitable child care and responsibility. Capetillo presents the story from various perspectives. It begins with a dialogue between the young couple, Elena and Andrés, and then moves to a dialogue between two "busybodies" who discuss what they have seen. As in many of Capetillo's texts, she is able to capture the opinions of contrasting views in order to unveil the double standards and illogical, restrictive social norms. Capetillo clearly hears her public and her critics, she presents those voices through her characters and essays, ultimately demonstrating the "logic" of her ideology while simultaneously displaying the ridiculousness of her opponents' arguments.

The story begins with a man driving down the street and, upon seeing a woman he knows, stops to ask her if she needs a lift. The dialogue ensues and he presents her with the option of living with him in a free love union. After discussing the situation he drops her off at her destination with plans to meet each other the next day. The next section introduces two busybodies who see Elena waiting on the street corner. It seems strategic that the busybodies are male and not the stock characters of neighborhood female gossips. Not only does it dismantle that stereotype, but it also allows the argument about women's rights and social inequalities to take place between men. One of those men is in favor of the social change that would free women from patriarchal, social, and sexist oppressions. They begin to question her actions, and, after watching her get in the car with Andrés, the sexist and patriarchal assumptions begin. The busybodies don't have names but rather are only referred to as "one" and "the other one." Their argument stems from the dominant belief that women are to remain virgins until marriage, that she should not express any sort of sexuality or engage in physical intimacies, that she should not work outside the home, and that a man is not required to adhere to any of those standards. Each of the sexist statements is questioned and countered, allowing the reader to do the same. In the end Elena and Andrés have united together in a free love, happily surrounded by nature and the children who are the fruits of their union, free from the social systems that bind and oppress. Elena acted in accordance with her own desires—physical, emotional, and mental—and was better off for having done so.

Free love unions are present in all Capetillo's texts as well as in her own life experiences. As previously mentioned, her parents never married, nor did Capetillo marry Manuel Ledesma, her lover and the father of her two children. This concept of mutually monogamous relationships is detailed in her 1911 text, *Mi opinión*, and is a reoccurring theme in *Influencias de las ideas modernas* as well. Suárez Findlay has noted that "Capetillo's vision of free love coincided in many ways with that advanced by her fellow male anarchists. Unlike her male comrades, however, Capetillo was careful to point out that conflict within couples arose not only because of the permanence and coldly contractual nature of marriage but also because of men's failure to treat women properly on a consistent basis" (158). Although Capetillo insisted on the rights of both men and women to end a relationship that was no longer viable, she did understand that within the patriarchal and capitalist system women were more susceptible to economic, as well as social, obstacles. She therefore demanded male and paternal responsibility for children while advocating the importance of self-sufficiency, financial, and otherwise, on the part of women.

Economic trappings are not the only oppressive barriers women may face in asserting their independence and emancipation. Throughout her text Capetillo creates female characters from bourgeois and elite social classes. They must overcome and demand equal rights and participation in society, the right to explore and pursue their desires as subjects and not mere objects, and become a locus of power and a catalyst for change. If they don't, they continue to be subjugated to the sexist and patriarchal systems with no hope for revolution. Capetillo recalls an American movie she once saw about a princess; she uses it as a point of departure for the short fictional piece she titles "Two Cages" to stress her point saying, "[we] fear freedom. We run from it as if it were a disease, even though we desire it" (58). For Capetillo, desire was meant to be acted upon, not repressed. One could not, should not shrink from their "duty"; one must act, continually reminding her audience that indeed, "desire is power!" (Capetillo, *Mi opinión* vii). Her characters (both female and male, both working-class and bourgeois) are applauded for asserting themselves, acting on desire, and appropriating power. At the end of the long play "Influences of Modern Ideas" a chorus of workers chants, "Long live free union! Down with exploitation!" while the young, bourgeois, but enlightened Angelina is united with her lover,

Carlos, the union organizer and strike leader (42). When Marina runs off with her lover instead of obeying her parents and marrying the young marquis, the play ends with a member of the community saying, "Excellent for valiant women!" (33).

In addition to Capetillo's discourse on feminism and female emancipation, she also articulates notions of modernity and its relationship to progress and civilization. Moreover, Capetillo elaborates on the "backwardness" (Sánchez-González, "Luisa Capetillo" 159) of so-called "modern" and "civilized" society. She emphasizes that the positivist view of "progress" and "civilization" has been tainted and manipulated by the social system of the bourgeoisie. It represents a classist view of society that excludes and moralizes through hypocrisy and ignorance coupled with the widely accepted idea that "progress" is to "civilize" the unruly or savage. According to Capetillo, "progress" is to strip away hypocrisy and hierarchies of power in the name of freedom and liberty. Her project and purpose is to displace and dismantle the hierarchies and hegemonies that oppress and undermine human life. In a way that recalls her own use of cross-dressing, perhaps because she understands its strategy, she is able to see through it and unmask it. In one of her reflections she writes:

> There are well-dressed thieves that they call gentlemen and thieves dressed in rags that they call beggars. Some rob from the stock exchange and others from businesses; others pickpocket in the streets, plazas, or houses due to poverty or vagrancy, which the present social system engenders, while others speculate because of selfish ambition. The second ones mentioned are more admissible than the first." (45)

In a capitalist society, crimes are disguised and "admissible" through class markers such as clothing and occupation.

Modernity and civilization are similarly masked as she describes in an essay on hygiene or the lack thereof, as practiced by the middle classes entitled, "Exaggerations":

> An infinite number of people believe that to be civilized is to wear patent leather shoes, a new collared shirt, and tie even though the undergarments stink of sweat, and one doesn't bathe not even once a week, and furthermore they overeat like cannibals, and they lose control like satyrs. (75)

Clothing, therefore, according to Capetillo is a strategic vehicle of masking and unmasking. Hygiene and its importance to modern-ness and civilization becomes the message of the essay. In fact she goes so far as to say, "in order to call oneself or believe oneself to be civilized, one must be clean" and "civilization, modern progress rests upon hygiene" (76).

Other ruminations on civilization, progress, modernity, and hygiene are present in her autobiographical or journal entry-style writings where Capetillo explains her daily routine of calisthenics, bathing, vegetarian diet, and intellectual production. Civilization and social change are themes espoused in her experimental prose and visions of future society.

Capetillo returns to the themes of exploitation, desire, social change in her short fictional piece, "The Cashier," which is, as Ramos has indicated, both the story of the perfect anarchist robbery and an allegory of the role of money in a capitalist society (44). Capetillo's astute manipulation of fiction and narration allow her to express her ideological beliefs through various levels of storytelling and symbolization. According to Sánchez-González it is through fiction that Capetillo finds her "best method for coming to grips with the ineluctable modality of revolutionary praxis" ("Luisa Capetillo" 161). Written while in Ybor City in 1913, "The Cashier" presents Ricardo, a young man whose mother, Ramona, is sick and dying after having almost worked herself to death in order to raise her son on her own. Ramona wants her son to receive an education in order to live a productive life without the poverty and misery that she had experienced working as a piecework seamstress and at other low-paying jobs. She is able to convince Don Castro, a local wealthy businessman, to sponsor Ricardo's education. He agrees and sends Ricardo to New York where he will study accounting.[23] In the meantime, Ramona dies of tuberculosis after too much work and exploitation, while Ricardo secures a middle-class job in New York at a bank. The trope of the orphaned adolescent as commonly seen in nineteenth-century European literature is presented here in Capetillo's writing, but instead of overcoming all odds to attain access to the middle class and in so doing, happiness, Capetillo's characters are aware of the social ills and emptiness of the bourgeoisie.[24] Therefore, Ricardo is not satisfied, aware that he is still an exploited worker in the capitalist system, just as his mother was. In a moment of consciousness and realization (a moment shared by all of Capetillo's protagonists) he sees how the system had institutionalized the mechanization of human life, how capitalism had turned him (and the rest of society) into a slave to the all-important dollar, unable to enjoy any profits from it—always working with no time left to spend with loved ones or family.

> Ricardo says, "What a life!" He passes money from one side to other, millions of dollars without being able to make use of one cent. He is corralled, muzzled, made into a counting machine without no aspirations other than to be careful not to make a mistake, to be condemned to have a fortune in his hands, and have nothing more than a meager wage; he is treated with indifference, as if he does not feel, as if he does not have the right to enjoy himself like everyone else. And he studied for this, and his mother suffered so many hardships in order for him to be where he is today. (85)

Besides being a "counting machine," voiceless, and suffering inequality, Capetillo's protagonist, Ricardo, also underlines how capitalism is the cause and root of the destruction of "family values" and fidelity.

> It was torture to be born and grow up hearing cries and seeing miseries, to depend on others for an education, and finally to live among gold all day without aspiring for more happiness than to marry, to leave the wife always alone. Should she want to go to the theater or some other place, to entrust her with a friend, so that later—as happened to the cashier from another bank—while he was working, his wife would go and spend time in the country with another man who ended up being her lover! "No, no way! I have the right to live and to be happy. I won't leave my Matilde always alone, no!" he tells himself. The man that marries should take his wife with him or stay with her. Those marriages in which the woman, bored from being alone gives herself to the first friend, is desperate; they are not to blame. We are the ones who expose her to that. It would be one thing if they do it because of love, but no, woman has a terrible struggle to stay faithful. (86)

Deciding that he cannot tolerate the situation and capitalist system any longer, he devises a plan to rob a million dollars from the bank and escape with his wife, Matilde, by sailing off to St. Petersburg, an obvious utopia in the anarchist imaginary at the turn of the twentieth century. It is also a site familiar to Capetillo's own imaginary from reading famous nineteenth-century Russian literature (Ramos 47). Ricardo is, of course, successful and after touring through Europe's cultural and intellectual centers in St. Petersburg, Italy, and Paris, the couple settles in Granada in order to make a home for their soon-to-be-born first child, safe and assured from becoming once again embroiled in the institutionalized slavery inherent in the bourgeois and capitalist system.

In the fictional piece, "Loves," Capetillo weaves another tale of orphaned youth, but this time with a soon-to-be-absent-present protagonist. It begins with the sad, unnecessary and undeserving death of a young, beautiful widow who dies of hunger with her small baby still in her arms. The remainder of the story is about her orphaned son within the over-arching theme of love. Capetillo criticizes social constraints and repression of the bourgeois class in a "star-crossed lovers," Romeo and Juliet trope. Jacinto, the orphaned son of the once lovely and adored theater diva, Gizelda, grows up never knowing who his parents were. Later he meets and falls in love with Alina, daughter of the wealthy and well-known Count and Countess del Prado. But although Jacinto has become a model citizen and perfect gentleman, Alina's parents refuse their union because the young man has no social title or knowledge of his lineage. While Jacinto is searching for information on his parents and lineage, Capetillo takes the opportunity to highlight the repressive social structures that squelch and dismiss female desire, subjectivity, and autonomy. An argument between Alina and her father demonstrates this point.

> "He will come bringing his social ranking or his fortune."
> Alina replied, "I don't want either of them, I love him."
> "Even if he is a nobody?"
> [. . .]
> "What do you mean, a nobody! Perhaps a cultured, educated, intelligent young man with a secure future, is a nobody?"
> "But, daughter, you are a child to be talking like that."
> "At sixteen years of age I am not a child, father."
> "Well, if he doesn't bring name or fortune, I can't make a decision, because I don't want to be at the mercy of criticism and gossip."
> "You will kill me."
> "Don't ask me for the impossible."
> "I want my happiness. No one has the right to question or to tell what sort of happiness I should desire."
> "You are much too young to know how to look for happiness. You do not have any experience."
> "Happiness and love are children, not old folks." (103)

Again, happiness is not predicated on economic or social wealth, but rather desire. Capetillo's own life story as a working-class woman in love with the son of a wealthy and socially powerful family also seems to be used a fodder in her fiction and plays.

The last section, which includes five short plays with female protagonists, explores Capetillo's ideology and propaganda against the oppressive capitalist and patriarchal social systems. As short pieces without many characters or explicit stage designs (except for the highly detailed "After her Death"), they seem to lend themselves well to union meetings or *juntas*. As both Kanellos and Dworkin y Méndez have shown, U.S. Hispanic working-class theater in Tampa was an important and thriving cultural tradition and expression. This assumption is based on research and recovery work done by both scholars regarding Hispanic theater in the United States, especially in Tampa/Ybor City, Florida.[25] This area became the home to the cigar-manufacturing industry and an enclave of Hispanic cultural production before the turn of the twentieth century. In addition, the historical and biographical research of Valle Ferrer on Capetillo discusses the probability of these works being presented in front of working-class audiences, most likely in the union halls in Tampa. She states:

> We do not know if these works were staged in any theater during the moment of their creation; but, we cannot doubt that they were probably performed during a dramatic evening sponsored by the Free Federation of Workers or the Federation of Tobacco Rollers, during strikes or union activities. (38; my translation)

Capetillo's plays were therefore presented to inspire and educate audiences already politicized, at least to a certain degree, in syndicalist ideology and social oppression.

Through her dramas, Capetillo created utopian and radicalized visions of female and working-class subjectivity. Implicitly, in her theatrical projects she exposed the inherent "constructed-ness" of all political systems, social communities, historical narratives, as well as social and cultural identities. These ideologies were heavily steeped in anarchism and contributed greatly to her feminist consciousness and practice. Definitions of anarchism always include the concept of domination, which in all of its forms is the source of all social problems. Whether exercised by governments, religious institutions, or through economic relations, domination is unacceptable. Although anarchism shares with many socialist traditions a radical critique of economic domination and an insistence on the need for a fundamental economic restructuring of society on a more egalitarian basis, it goes beyond Marxist socialism in developing an independent critique of the state, of hierarchy, and of authority relations in general. Where socialists have traced the roots of all domination to the division of labor in the economy, anarchists have insisted that power has its own logic and will not be abolished through attention to economic relations alone.[26] Capetillo's writing highlights this anarchist ideology and notion that any abuse of power is unjustified and is the root of all oppression.

In her plays, Capetillo articulates connections between politics, culture and gender that anticipated Stuart Hall's conceptualization of a "politics of representation" as well as the designs and desires for cultural resistance proposed by contemporary cultural critics, such as bell hooks, Cornel West, Henry Giroux, and Gloria Anzaldúa. Capetillo rejects the limits imposed on women by the roles assigned to them from patriarchal society and insists that these roles are not part of women's "natural" life. Instead, she reveals how they are merely social constructs that impose on their inherent freedoms.

By predicating revolutionary victory, Capetillo's dramas could renew the audience's commitment to struggle. The success of the social protest cause was shown to be distinct, specific and attainable. Capetillo's plays also presented empowering images of working-class people and gave workers a medium for disseminating the lessons of organized labor. These counter-hegemonic social protest performances interrogated and repositioned the power of theatrical representation and manipulated power as a creative force. The goal was to unite the audience and characters/performers in imagining a radicalized vision of gender and class equality that would motivate them to anarcho-syndicalist organizing.

The first section of plays is placed together under the title, "The Corruption of the Rich and of the Poor or How a Rich Woman and Poor Woman are Prostituted." They explain and illustrate Capetillo's concept of free love unions and female desire and criticize class division and gender inequality. In the first piece a young, bourgeois woman is forced by her father to marry a man she doesn't love in order to save her family from financial ruin. She is saved from this legal form of prostitution due to her own consciousness and strength of will. Together with her true love, a working-class young man who helps convince her that traditional norms do not serve either her or society, she is able to run off with him (and her inheritance) the night before the wedding.

Marina, an eighteen-year-old young woman, is forced to marry Don Filiberto, the Marquis de Azuria, a man she does not love so that her family can acquire the rank of nobility. Her real love, the youthful Roberto, sees her situation clearly and asks, "Because he is your father? And because of that he has the right to sell you, but you don't understand? It is the selling of your body for a title? . . ." (168). This question, placed in the mouth of a male protagonist, provides the example of not only women envisioning a liberation from patriarchy, but men as well. It dismantles the acceptance of marriages based on monetary convenience and women as exchanged commodities. It also reiterates Capetillo's precept of female sexual liberation as one of woman's natural rights.

In true Capetillo form Marina acts for herself, against the wishes and demands of her father, and goes off with Roberto. The drama ends with a meta-theatrical social commentary of two characters in a café. This didactic coda, like a Greek chorus, concludes the play:

> ONE. (*Arriving.*) Do you know about last night's play? Well, simply put, a banker wants to marry off his daughter to the ruined Marquis. The daughter accepts the proposition but loves another. The night of the wedding, when everything is prepared, she gathers her inheritance and flees with her lover, leaving everyone waiting.
>
> OTHER. Excellent for valiant women!
>
> ONE. This is why parents should not make business deals using their daughters; getting married without loving one another is a corruption. (133)

Once again Capetillo sets up a melodrama with all the usual conventions, only to turn it on its head, making it appear as if it has finally turned right-side up. She subverts cultural, societal traditions and conventions of arranged marriages of convenience to create a new social harmony and sense of poetic justice. Raymond Williams has said of theater that it presents the "dramatic possibility of what might be done within what is known to have been done" (11). Capetillo's plays also perform the function as explained by Baz Kershaw. He states that "the efficacious social protest performance challenges the spectators' ideological community, but at the same time, dialectically, it comforts the spectators and confirms their social purpose" (33). Capetillo's subversion, always based on the collectivity of the working class, challenges the gender status quo within her class community while at the same

time confronts that status quo in the dominant classes as well. Capetillo offers an alternate reality to her audience, a different mode of
empowerment and happiness only found through the freedom from gender and class oppression.

The second piece, entitled "Marriage Without Love, Consequence,
Adultery," is also about a young, bourgeois woman, but in this play she
is already married. Even though the characters' names are different, one
could read the plot as if the protagonist from the previous play hadn't
been a "valiant woman" and had married the man her father had chosen
for her. It is as if we catch up with her now, in an unhappy marriage,
prostituted. As with all these short plays, Capetillo demonstrates her
genius and quick, concise storytelling. All the important themes are
there in this "social drama," as she calls it. The title alone plays an
important role in the significance and message. Perhaps at first to her
audience (and readers) the title explains what necessarily occurs in a
loveless marriage—that the unhappy spouse will look elsewhere, outside the marriage bond to find happiness, resulting in adultery. But by
the end of the play the title clearly has another meaning, a meaning that
is directly aligned with Capetillo's concept of free love and the evils of
oppressive social norms. At the end the receptor is made aware that a
marriage or union based on love is not a marriage at all, therefore the
marriage, although it is legal and licit for the courts, according to the
concepts of free love, is adultery. This is yet another way in which, in
this case, a "rich" woman is prostituted.

The very brief, one-act, one-scene play, "The Prostitution of Poor
Women," is a dialogue between a prostitute and a young man. Once
again it is Capetillo's genius at subversion that unravels the play's message. When the prostitute is questioned about her so-called "career
choice," she responds by describing the miserable factory scene with a
lewd foreman. In this way the social dilemma is presented and conven-
tional thought is skewed: problems associated with prostitution are now
the acute problems of the factory worker. In the end it is this "back-
ward" society that has corrupted the poor and forced women into prostitution, which can be found in various exchanges of bodies and production and is comparable to being "sold" into legal marriage. What
these three plays do is express succinctly the concept of free love, the
social ills that oppress humankind, especially women and, most impor-
tantly, demonstrate a solution to these problems. By way of these short
plays, Capetillo attempts to explain women's situation and the unequal
distribution of privilege and power using gender, coupled with class, as

elements in her analysis. Patriarchy crosses all class boundaries and affects all women.

The play that follows, the two scene drama "In the Country, Free Love," demonstrates the idyllic possibilities for a couple that can escape the artificiality of modern life, an influence of Bakunin and Kropotkin's ideas of anarchism. Both Bakunin and Kropotkin "disapproved morally of the complacent, dull, and repressive bourgeoisie, and also of the results of industrial life; the anti-industrialization was part of the major concern with oppression, and a return to the Middle Ages that represented, at least to Bakunin and Kropotkin, a return to collectivization, not a nostalgia for the past" (Zavala 111). In the play the protagonists, Victor and Aurora, represent a freer human life working in conjunction with Mother Nature. They both work the land and after acknowledging their mutual attraction they unite in free love and make a home together in the country where they are free to enjoy and become one with Mother Nature. All their hopes and dreams seem possible and they plan to have many happy children together. Liberty is the overarching theme, whether referring to women's agency and gender equality or the social collectivity. When Victor asks Aurora if he can guide her through life's "torturous path" she replies "that woman should walk alone, that is to say united, yes, but that there be mutual protection" (149). To which Victor clarifies his response by stating:

> It hasn't been my intention to try to impose my will. I offered you my help in order for us to love each other mutually but it didn't occur to me that you could imagine that I was trying to inhibit your natural activities and your personal initiatives. In that I do not meddle. You are completely free to do whatever you please. (149)

By abolishing gender inequities they are able to create a social utopian vision that includes free property, free work in a wage-less social structure of agricultural exchange and they become the parents of children in this free society. The play ends as they vow to "go after our dream" and to make love in order to "sow seeds of freedom" (151).

The last play, which takes place in the tropics, in a "city in the Antilles," entitled "After her Death: A Play from Real Life in Verse and Prose," offers a different female protagonist, one who is already dead. In this sense it is the absent-present protagonist who speaks posthumously through her poetry, who is finally able to articulate the social inequalities forced upon women. The play underlines the senselessness of men's (socially acceptable) sexual ownership of women and the fatal and irrecoverable consequences of such actions.

Influencias de las ideas modernas ends with a short poem composed in Ybor City entitled "Your Blonde Hair" with the nostalgic emotion of human touch and affection. Because Capetillo left her children in her mother's care while she was in the United States, the poem could be read as a moment of reflection, thinking of her daughter and missing those sweet moments a mother can have exemplified in the braiding of her daughter's hair.

Capetillo's descriptor, "soy una equivocada" or "I'm a woman out of place, a woman misunderstood," seems to be something that Capetillo never stopped struggling with or negotiating, no matter where her artistic and activist migrations took her. This out-of-place space that she found herself in, misunderstood and subversive for not adhering to gendered social spaces, was also a creative place and a vantage point. Contemporary theorist and critic, bell hooks, describes this marginal space as a "space of radical openness" that depicts marginality as opposition to deprivation, as "the site of radical possibility" (149). Once understood in this manner, the marginalized can reclaim the space as a "position and place of resistance that is crucial for oppressed, exploited, colonized people" (150). Perhaps in the context of this analysis, "la equivocada" is she who understands her precarious position among established social structures and, therefore, resourcefully and strategically takes advantage of it to interpret and subvert power on her own terms to create social change, to enact revolution. She is neither categorized nor contained. For Capetillo, she crosses spatial boundaries and borders in order to blur, disrupt, and resist them. In doing so, she crafts other spaces and interstices or finds access to spaces that attempt to deny her and all women in general. Thus, woman is the catalyst to create a utopian society of equality and progress in which, "woman will always be a woman" (*Absolute Equality* 67), an instigator of social change, radical possibility, and revolution.

NOTES

[1] I would like to thank Dr. Nicolás Kanellos for the experience of "discovering" Luisa Capetillo and her work during my graduate study at the University of Houston, and for allowing me the incredible opportunity to translate her final published text, *Influencias de las ideas modernas* (1916) and introduce this bilingual edition. I am also grateful for his constant support and patience. I would also like to thank the Recovering the U.S. Hispanic Literary Heritage Project and Arte Público Press, as well as Dr. Gabriela Baeza Ventura, executive editor. I must also thank those who offered their support and

insight during this project. Many thanks go out to Viviana Tapia, Heather Bigley, Therese Tardio, and Catherine Nock.

[2] For example, Bernardo Vega's, *Memorias de Bernardo Vega*; Jesús Colón's, *A Puerto Rican in New York*; Arthur Alfonso Scholmburg's, *A Puerto Rican Quest for his Black Heritage*.

[3] Lisa Sánchez-González discusses the work of Vega, Colón, Schomburg, and Luisa Capetillo in her book, *Boricua Literature: A Literary History of the Puerto Rican Diaspora*.

[4] The Recovering the U.S. Hispanic Literary Heritage Project, founded and housed at the University of Houston under the direction of Dr. Nicolás Kanellos, has taken on this overwhelming and important task to recover and archive all the writing by Latinos in the United States prior to 1960.

[5] The ethnic label "Latina" or "Latino" is a broad term that includes diverse ethnic groups of Latin American descent and therefore also elides difference and variance among individual groups (see Suzanne Oboler's *Ethnic Labels, Latino Lives* for a discussion on ethnic labels and terms). I use the term here with no intention to disregard difference but rather to utilize its unifying connotation in regards to literary and cultural production by Latinas/os of varying backgrounds, ethnicities, races, classes, etc. in the United States. Also insightful and useful is Nicolás Kanellos' "Introducción: Panorama de la literatura hispana de los Estados Unidos" to *En otra voz: Antología de la literatura hispana de los Estados Unidos* in which he unites the writing by Latinos in the United States under the rubric of native, immigrant, or exile writing.

[6] I am specifically looking at working-class women writers and activists of Hispanic descent whose work in the United States was based on anarchist, anarcho-syndicalist, and anarcho-feminist principles and advocated for women and minorities' rights, along with the need for social revolutionary change. Examples are Lucy González Parsons (African-Mexican-Native American), Luisa Moreno (emigrated from Guatemala), Emma Tenayuca (Tejana-Chicana), and Josefina Fierro (Chicana).

[7] It is important to note the literary and cultural production (and even presence) of Latinos in the geographical area of what is now the United States during the past centuries and not just since the 1960s social movements. For excellent discussions on U.S. Latino production and presence prior to the 1960s, see Nicolás Kanellos, Juan Bruce-Novoa, Luis Leal, Genaro Padilla, Rosaura Sánchez, Walter Benn Michaels, Kirsten Silva Gruesz, among others.

[8] The selections from Capetillo's *Influencias de las ideas modernas* included in this book are: "Por qué decir;" "Visiones;" "Yo;" and "La opinión de muchos hombres y la mía."

[9] Ramos includes the following selections from Capetillo's *Influencias de las ideas modernas* in his text: an autobiographical essay that describes Capetillo's intellectual upbringing *Formación intelectual de Capetillo*; *El cajero*; *A un amigo bárbaro*; *Influencias de las ideas modernas*; *Los relojes*; a contemplation while looking at a cityscape with a church dome *Arquitectura y pobreza*; a selection denouncing child exploitation *Explotación infantil*; a selection pondering nature and ecology *Paisaje y ecología*; a selection about the survival of all living organisms *Sobrevivencia de un gusano*; a selection reflecting on the relationship between intellectual work and daily life *Trabajo intelectual y vida diaria*; *Exageraciones*; *Fragmentos de una carta*; a reference to George Sand and historians of women *Jorge Sand y los historiadores de la mujer*; a story of free love, *Amor libre: un relato*; and two short plays, *La corrupción de los ricos y la de los pobres o Cómo se prostituye una rica y una pobre*.

[10]It is important to note that in 2004 the Recovering the U.S. Hispanic Literary Heritage Project and Arte Público Press published a bilingual edition of Capetillo's complete 1911 text, *Mi opinión sobre las libertades, derechos y deberes de la mujer*, under the title, *A Nation of Women: An Early Feminist Speaks Out*, with an introduction by schol-

ar Félix V. Matos Rodríguez and an English translation by Alan West-Durán. Also, selections from Capetillo's other books—*Ensayos libertarios* (1907), *La humanidad en el futuro* (1910), and *Mi opinión sobre las libertades, derechos y deberes de la mujer como compañera, madre y ser independiente* (1911)—have been republished in Valle Ferrer's biographies (Spanish and English), Ramos' edition of *Amor y anarquía*, and most recently Gloria da Cuhna's, *Pensadoras de la nación*, which only includes a selection of texts from Capetillo's *La humanidad en el futuro* (1910) and *Mi opinión* (1911).

[11]Both Julio Ramos and Frances R. Aparicio refer to the importance of the *lectores* in the tobacco factories to the intellectual and political development of these men.

[12]A. Quintero Rivera in his article, "Socialista y tabaquero: la proletarización de los artesanos," explicates the impact of the readers, and the material being read, had on the workers and their working-class formation, intellect, and even revolution.

[13]Darwin's theory of evolution was published in the same period as Kardec's *The Spirits' Book* (Fernández Olmos 172).

[14]Tolstoy and his anarchist writings were of continual inspiration for Capetillo, especially in her play, "Influences of Modern Ideas."

[15]Virginia Sánchez Korrol explains the different forms of migration between Puerto Rico and the United States during the early twentieth century. She points out that although earlier documentation cites overpopulation of the island as a reason for voluntary emigration, "recent scholarship in Puerto Rico and the United States challenges the overpopulation thesis, rejecting the notion that migrants exercised free choice motivated by a desire to better their condition" (285).

[16]Lisa Sánchez González uses the term "genre-defying" to describe Capetillo's fiction ("Luisa Capetillo" 158).

[17]This concept is also reminiscent of Mary Louise Pratt's term, "contact zones," as defined in her 1992 text, *Imperial Eyes: Travel Writing and Transculturation*.

[18]I am employing the term performance here as proposed by contemporary theorists and critics such as Judith Butler and Marjorie Garber.

[19]Ana M. Echevarría analyzes this connection that Capetillo poses between women's use of clothing and fashion as artistic expression and its concomitant relationship with commodity exchange and the capitalist system in her dissertation, "Performing Subversion: A Comparative Study of Caribbean Women Playwrights."

[20]Perhaps Capetillo's most famous image is her photo—also reproduced on the cover of this book—that was taken in 1915 while she was in Havana, Cuba, in a man's suit, tie, and Panama hat. This photo was Julio Ramos' point of departure for his critical introduction of *Amor y anarquía: Los escritos de Luisa Capetillo*. The photo is also analyzed in conjunction with Capetillo's essay "I" in my unpublished article, "Sexing the Space of Resistance: Luisa Capetillo (1879-1922)."

[21]Darío referring to French suffragists writes, "Tengo a la vista unas cuantas fotografías de esas políticas. Como lo podréis adivinar, todas son feas; y la mayor parte más que jamonas. . . . estos marivarones —suavicemos la palabra— que se hallan propias para las farsas públicas en que los hombres se distinguen y que, como la Durand, se adelantan a tomar papel en el sainete electoral, merecen el escarmiento." ("¡Estas mujeres!" 549- 50)

[22]Pérez posits that "[in Chicano history] women are conceptualized as merely a backdrop to men's social and political activities, when they are in fact intervening interstitially while sexing the colonial imaginary" (7).

[23]Ramos notes that Capetillo is also criticizing the paternalism as a patriarchal construct relegated to the orphaned youth, citing Juan Gelpi's study, *Literatura y paternalismo en Puerto Rico*.

[24]According to Sánchez-González, "'The Cashier,' revises the usual 19th century romantic realism of authors such as Dickens, Charlotte Brönte and Zola, by appropriating the trope of the orphaned youth [. . . .] But unlike Jane Eyre, for example, who uses her mysteriously granted fortune to establish a bourgeois paradise, Ricardo is disgusted with his middle-class lifestyle . . . ." (162).

[25]According to Kanellos, "Unlike Los Angeles, San Antonio, and New York, there was very little truly commercial theatrical activity in the Tampa-Ybor City communities. [. . .] For the most part, the audiences were made up of tobacco workers and their families. The tobacco workers prided themselves on their literary and artistic tastes; they were considered an intellectual or elite labor class that had gained an informal education from the professional *lectores*, or readers, they hired to read aloud to them from literary masterpieces, newspapers, and other matter while they rolled cigars" (258).

[26]For an excellent description and study of anarchism in relationship to women, see Martha A. Ackelsberg's *Free Women of Spain: Anarchism and the Struggle for the Emancipation of Women.*

WORKS CITED

Ackelsberg, Martha A. *Free Women of Spain: Anarchism and the Struggle for the Emancipation of Women.* Bloomington: Indiana UP, 1991.

Butler, Judith. *Gender Trouble: Feminism and the Subversion of Identity.* New York/London: Routledge, 1990.

Capetillo, Luisa. *Ensayos libertarios.* Arecibo, PR: Imprenta Unión Obrera, 1907.

___. *Influencias de las ideas modernas.* San Juan, PR.: Tipografía Negrón Flores, 1916.

___. *La humanidad en el futuro.* San Juan: Tipografía Real Hermanos, 1910.

___. *Mi opinión sobre las libertades, derechos y deberes de la mujer como compañera, madre y ser independiente.* San Juan, PR.: The Times Publishing Co., 1911.

Chadwick, Whitney. *Women, Art, and Society.* London: Thames and Hudson, 1991.

Colón, Jesús. *A Puerto Rican in New York and Other Sketches.* New York: International Publishers, 1982 [1961].

Cunha, Gloria da. *Pensadoras de la nación.* Madrid: Iberoamericana, 2006.

Darío, Rubén. "¡Estas mujeres!" *Obras completas.* Vol. 2. Madrid: Afrodisio Aguado, 1950. 549-52.

Dávila Santiago, Rubén. *Teatro obrero en Puerto Rico (1900-1920): Antología.* Río Piedras: Editorial Edil, 1985.

Dworkin y Méndez, Kenya. "The Tradition of Hispanic Theater and WPA Fedral Theatre Project in Tampa-Ybor City, Florida." In *Recovering the U.S. Hispanic Literary Heritage, Vol. II*. Eds. Erlinda González-Berry and Chuck Tatum. Houston: Arte Público Press, 1996. 279-294.

Echevarría, Ana M. "Performing Subversion: A Comparative Study of Caribbean Women Playwrights." Diss. Cornell U, 2000.

Fernández Olmos, Margarite, and Lizabeth Paravisini-Gerbert. *Creole Religions of the Caribbean: An Introduction from Vodou and Santería to Obeah and Espiritismo*. New York & London: New York UP, 2003.

Garber, Marjorie. *Vested Interests: Cross-Dressing and Cultural Anxiety*. New York: Routledge, 1992.

Hall, Stuart

Herzig Shannon, Nancy. *El Iris de Paz: El espiritismo y la mujer en Puerto Rico, 1900-1905*. Río Piedras: Ediciones Huracán, 2001.

Hewitt, Nancy A. *Southern Discomfort: Women's Activism in Tampa, Florida, 1880s-1920s*. Chicago: U Illinois P, 2001.

hooks, bell. *Yearning: Race, Gender, and Cultural Politics*. Toronto: Between the Lines, 1990.

Horowitz

Kanellos, Nicolás. "Brief History of Hispanic Theater in the United States." In *Handbook of Hispanic Cultures in the United States: Literature and Art*. Ed. Francisco Lomelí. Houston: Arte Público Press and Instituto de Cooperación Iberoamericana, 1993. 248-267.

Kershaw, Baz. *The Politics of Performance: Radical Theatre as Cultural Invention*. London/New York: Routledge, 1992.

Lavrín, Asunción. *Las mujeres latinoamericanas. Perspectivas históricas*. México: Fondo de Cultura Económica, 1994.

Matos-Rodríguez, Félix. "Introduction." *A Nation of Women: An Early Feminist Speaks Out*. Luisa Capetillo. Houston: Arte Público P, 2004. vii-li.

Pérez, Emma. *The Decolonial Imaginary: Writing Chicanas into History*. Bloomington: Indiana UP, 1999.

Poyo, Gerald E. and Mariano Díaz-Miranda. "Cubans in the United States. In *Handbook of Hispanic Cultures in the United States: History*. Ed. Alfredo Jiménez. Houston: Arte Público Press and Instituto de Cooperación Iberoamericana, 1994. 302-319.

Pozzetta, George E. *The Immigrant World of Ybor City: Italians and their Latin Neighbors in Tampa, 1885-1985.* Gainesville: UP Florida, 1998.

Quintero Rivera, Ángel. *Workers' Struggle in Puerto Rico: A Documentary History.* New York: Monthly Review P, 1976.

Ramos, Julio. Ed. *Amor y anarquía. Los escritos de Luisa Capetillo.* Río Piedras, PR.: Ediciones Huracán, 1992.

Sánchez González, Lisa. *Boricua Literature: A Literary History of the Puerto Rican Diaspora.* New York/London: New York UP, 2001.

___. "Luisa Capetillo: An Anarcho-Feminist Pionera in the Mainland Puerto Rican Narrative/Political Tradition." In *Recovering the U.S. Hispanic Literary Heritage*, Vol. II. Eds. Erlinda González-Berry and Chuck Tatum. Houston: Arte Público Press, 1996. 148-67.

Sánchez Korrol, Virginia. "In Their Own Right: A History of Puerto Ricans in the U.S.A." In *Handbook of Hispanic Cultures in the United States: History.* Ed. Alfredo Jiménez. Houston: Arte Público Press and Instituto de Cooperación Iberoamericana, 1994. 281-301.

Suárez-Findlay, Eileen. *Imposing Decency: The Politics of Sexuality and Race in Puerto Rico, 1870-1920.* Durham: Duke UP, 1999.

Valle Ferrer, Norma. *Luisa Capetillo. Historia de una mujer proscrita.* San Juan: Editorial cultural, 1990.

___. *Luisa Capetillo, Pioneer Puerto Rican Feminist.* New York: Peter Lang, 2006.

Vega, Bernardo. *Memorias de Bernardo Vega.* 4th ed. Ed. César Andreu Iglesias. Río Piedras, P.R.: Ediciones Huracán, 1988.

Williams, Raymond. *Drama in a Dramatised Society: An Inaugural Lecture.* Cambridge: Cambridge UP, 1975.

Zavala, Iris M. *Colonialism and Culture: Hispanic Modernisms and the Social Imaginary.* Bloomington & Indianapolis: Indiana UP, 1992.

ABSOLUTE EQUALITY
AN EARLY FEMINIST PERSPECTIVE

Sir and friend:

I have the honor to present to you this book, for the sake of human liberty, with whose product and with that of future works which I will publish I will found my desired

"Agricultural Farm School"

in Cuba, Puerto Rico or Santo Domingo.
Trusting in your generosity and benevolence, I dedicate this copy to you.

The Author.

PROLOGUE

This book, a compilation of my various writings of life in all its diversity. It has been written for the sole purpose of continuing my propaganda that favors women's liberty in all of life's manifestations.

It is hoped that with the product of this book and those that will appear in future times, the proceeds will help me to accomplish my projected "Agricultural Farm School" idea: I desire to put this idea into practice to demonstrate the benefit that it would bring to the community. My propaganda, based on justice, truth, and liberty is comprised of anarchist ideas in conjunction with the ideals of universal fraternal brotherhood. It is one of the necessary manifestations of progress.

The Author.

Influences Of Modern Ideas

(THREE-ACT PLAY)

CHARACTERS

ANGELINA (daughter of a rich business man)
DON JUAN DE RAMÍREZ (Angelina's father)
RAMÓN (house servant)
DON BALTASAR (foreman at Don Juan's factory)
ERNESTINA and MARIETA (two friends of Angelina)
MARIANA (widow of a former Ramírez employee who has died)
CARLOS SANTANA (Mariana's son and strike leader who, along with
   Simplicio Hernández, form the strike committee)
ROSALINDA (Ramón's fiancée)
DON JAIME LÓPEZ
DON ANTONIO RIGAUD
DON ROBERT HARTMAN

Written in Arecibo in November 1907.

ACT ONE

SCENE ONE

(An elegant parlor furnished in a modern style. When the curtain goes up, ANGELINA *is seated on the sofa dressed in an elegant morning bathrobe.* SHE *is concentrating on reading Tolstoy's* "The Slavery of Our Times" *and does not notice* RAMÓN *come in.)*

RAMÓN: *(Entering with a tray holding some cards.* HE *approaches the young woman.)* Miss, do you not remember that today is your birthday?

ANGELINA: Actually, I didn't remember. I've been concentrating these past few days on reading Tolstoy's *The Slavery of Our Times*, which has convinced me that the slavery of our times is the inflexible wage law. (SHE *takes the cards, looks at them, and leaves them on the table.)*

RAMÓN: *(Winks an eye to obtain the young woman's opinion.)* And how could we live without receiving a wage?

ANGELINA: By educating the poor that no one has the right to place a value on one's work, nor should fixed working hours be established; work should be free and spontaneous, and there should be equal consumption. Each individual should work according to their potential and consume according to their needs.

RAMÓN: That is an anarchist maxim, but how do we put it into practice . . . through violence?

ANGELINA: No, through instruction and education; the majority of injustices and crimes are committed because of ignorance. The capitalist class, for their own sake, should have tried to suppress the crimes and diseases created by the misery born of exploitation.

If fraternity existed, there wouldn't be this discord, which is caused by the competition that originates with the wage law.

A widow with four children who lives near here, lacks everything. The oldest child was learning a trade and was not being paid, as if he didn't have to clothe and feed himself.

His mother hires herself out as a seamstress, but it doesn't cover the expenses. She is the widow of an employee who was in my father's factory for many years. After working so much, and with his family in these conditions, one would have to surmise that he had been exploited.

RAMÓN: Naturally, because his salary wasn't sufficient to cover their needs, let alone could he save anything. Savings are only possible after all necessities are covered.

ANGELINA: Any other way is suicide. (RAMÓN *departs.*)

SCENE TWO

DON JUAN: (*Entering.*) Good day, my daughter. (*Kissing her on the forehead.*) How are you today?

ANGELINA: (*Gets up.*) Very well, Father, thank you.

DON JUAN: (*Presenting her a jewel box with a magnificent bracelet.*) Here, accept this piece of jewelry for your birthday. It is of flawless artistic taste.

ANGELINA: (*Opening the jewel box.*) It is really beautiful, (*Contemplating it and placing the jewel box on the table.*) but if you would have consulted me we could have spent that money on something more useful. (DON JUAN *makes an expression of astonishment.* SHE *continues.*) That is money wasted. Listen, Father, the widow of that employee who for so many years was at your service, lives on the next street in a modest room. She is poor and abandoned. She supports herself with the piecework she takes on. Last night she was here to see if I would help her, being that she owes two months' rent and her eldest son goes to the factory with worn-out shoes. We live surrounded by comforts in this twenty-room house, and they are five and live in just one room.

DON JUAN: (*Astonished.*) That may be true. I had already forgotten about that woman and I don't understand why I would have to forgo giving you this gift in order to help her.

ANGELINA: (*With vivacity and cheer.*) Are you willing to truly help her?

DON JUAN: (*Indifferent.*) Yes, as always I am willing to please you . . . (HE *moves from one side to the other.*)

ANGELINA: (*Gleefully, but without getting* DON JUAN *to smile.*) So tell me, (*Approaching him and smoothing his moustache.*) are you going to send her money? . . . How much? (*Interested.*)

DON JUAN: (*Releasing himself from her, paces around.*) I will take her five dollars.

ANGELINA: (*With a disgusted expression.*) That is a paltry sum! With that you can't pay your bills or buy what you need. (*Sitting down in the chair.*)

DON JUAN: (*Approaching her and looking at the audience;* HE *always ends up doing what* SHE *wants.*) Alright, how much do you want me to give to that woman?

ANGELINA: (*Getting up.*) How much did you spend on the gift?

DON JUAN: That jewel box, you will notice, has a diamond, a sapphire, and a ruby. I paid $500.00 for it.

ANGELINA: (*With a disdainful expression, pointing to the jewel box.*) Buying that doesn't remedy any human need. You didn't hesitate to spend that large amount. I remind you, with clear and precise details, of the conditions those victims of yours are living, and you offer $5.00 dollars. Thank you. (*Sitting down uncomfortably.*)

DON JUAN: "Victims of mine," you say! You are mad. I cannot avoid the consequences of the inevitable.

ANGELINA: "Of the inevitable," you say? So poverty is inevitable? (*Energetically.*)

DON JUAN: Inevitable. (*Pacing around with his cane.*)

ANGELINA: My father, you are very wrong. Poverty is the product of exploitation. (DON JUAN *pauses to listen to his daughter with his mouth open.*) And is due to the injustices and selfishness of men throughout the ages.

DON JUAN: (*While* SHE *is speaking* HE *says.*) How could this girl have been made aware of that? (*Aside.*) Am I a selfish exploiter?

ANGELINA: Unconsciously you are, because of your indifference to another's pain that is also ours.

DON JUAN: That seems to me to be simply an exaggeration.

ANGELINA: Yes, ours, because as long as there exists on earth even one man who suffers, the rest cannot be happy.

DON JUAN: I repeat, it is an exaggeration.

ANGELINA: You cannot be happy, as I am not happy, because we cause a lot of pain with our indifference. We are all brothers and sisters, and we will suffer thousands of obstacles as long as we do not help to destroy the cause of so much pain. Humanity is a chain in which we are the links, and when one moves, all move.

DON JUAN: (*Impatiently.*) Fine, daughter. It seems to me that that woman must be impatient, please allow me to take some money to

her. How much do you want me to give her? Do you agree with
$25.00 dollars? (*Approaching his daughter and taking her hand.*)

ANGELINA: As you wish, Father. I do not want to bother you any
longer. I too will give her something. Tell me, is this mine? May I
do with it what I please?

DON JUAN: Yes, daughter, wear it or put it away, it is yours; I will see
you later. I am going to carry out your wish. (HE *kisses her on the
forehead.*)

ANGELINA: See you later, Father. (SHE *walks her father to the door,
then goes back, sits down, and picks up the jewel box.* SHE *looks at
it and gets up.*) What a useless thing! And to think that there are
women who are capable of allowing their husbands to go to jail for
a trinket such as this. Many women surrender, feigning a love that
they don't feel, for an object of luxury. Ignorance! Ignorance! How
many victims you create. But I will not wear it. I will give it to the
widow Mariana—she will sell it. (*Pensive.*)

   (*The bell rings loud enough for the audience to hear.* ANGELI-
NA *lifts up her head.*) Who would it be? I think I hear two women's
voices. (SHE *gets up.*) Could it be Ernestina and Marieta?

SCENE THREE

ERNESTINA and MARIETA: (*Entering cheerfully, determined to greet*
ANGELINA.) We wish you a happy day, dear Angelina.

ANGELINA: I appreciate it.

ERNESTINA: We came to invite you for your birthday to go for a ride
in an automobile that Father received yesterday. We will come to
pick you up this afternoon.

ANGELINA: A thousand thanks, my friends, but it is impossible for me
to accept your invitation. If you wish to return, you may do so but
I will not go for a ride.

ERNESTINA and MARIETA: (*After a moment.*) Why, Angelina? Are
you ill?

ANGELINA: My health is fine, but I have been very sad and preoccupied, meditating about social injustice and poverty, so I'm not in the
mood to be entertained.

ERNESTINA: Fine job you've taken up, thinking about social injustice? Do you think you can solve the problem?

ANGELINA: I will do what I can for the workers. Don't either of you
read Malato or Kropotkin or Zola?

MARIETA: Angelina, you forget Mother is very religious and we cannot read anything but religious books. We prefer that to tormenting ourselves like you, by wanting to solve such problems.

You're very sensitive, Angelina, and if I were your age and in your position, I wouldn't torment myself that way.

ANGELINA: It is not a torment to concern myself with those that suffer from a lack of basic necessities. When I was a child they took me to church too, but I haven't gone back.

ERNESTINA: Mother has told us that if we're not religious we'll go to hell.

ANGELINA: For me, hell is a conscience full of regret, and heaven is fulfilling our duty to our fellow beings.

ERNESTINA: Your way of thinking will not alleviate the situation of the poor.

ANGELINA: But the consequence of thinking like that will lead me to the practice of justice. At least I will attempt to do something for them. You see this bracelet? Well, I will give it to a poor woman. (*Showing the jewel box to her girlfriends.*)

ERNESTINA and MARIETA: What a magnificent bracelet!

ANGELINA: My father gave it to me today.

MARIETA: But how foolish you are to give away a jewel of this value. Who is it for?

ANGELINA: For a widow of an employee of my father. For me, helping her has more value.

ERNESTINA: We can't stop you, but I believe that you can help that woman without giving it away.

ANGELINA: I don't need that jewel, I don't like adornments. (*With a disdainful expression.*) Listen, "Do not buy finery or jewels, because books are worth more than they are. Adorn your understanding with their precious ideas, because there is no luxury that dazzles like the luxury of science."

ERNESTINA and MARIETA: Fine, Angelina. We regret your whims, but we'll see you later. We'll be back in the afternoon. (THEY *leave.* ANGELINA *accompanies them to the door.*)

ANGELINA: Have a good time. (SHE *returns and says.*) What uselessness of women, and they could someday be the mothers of families. And the majority of women are in the same condition. (SHE *sits down to read.*)

SCENE FOUR

DON JUAN: (*Entering,* HE *says to his daughter.*) Angelina, I have carried out your wish.

ANGELINA: (*Reaching out her hands to her father.*) Thank you, you have restored part of what belongs to her.

DON JUAN: (*Very serious.*) I have only placated you. (*Taking a newspaper* HE *reads aloud.*) "Workers strike in Italy, they ask for wage increase." "Public meeting, socialists and anarchists will speak all day and night." "Uprising feared." "Latest news, strikers triumph, led by anarchists." (ANGELINA *had placed herself behind her father and says to him.*) What are anarchists, Father? (*With a mischievous smile.*)

DON JUAN: They're men with progressive ideas who wish to emancipate the workers from economic slavery.

ANGELINA: What methods do they employ? (*With interest.*)

DON JUAN: They inform the workers. They stir them up in public meetings so that they rebel against exploitation, and they better their conditions by abolishing the wage law.

ANGELINA: How will they abolish the wage law?

DON JUAN: Through a revolution, converting private property into common property, because that way there wouldn't be poverty or crime.

ANGELINA: Good! Good! Bravo. It gladdens me to know that you're informed about those issues. But tell me, how will they transfer the property?

DON JUAN: With a general strike of all tradesmen. They can do it if they are prepared to hold out. They won't accomplish it with petitions, because the bourgeoisie, as they call us, only concern themselves with amassing wealth.

ANGELINA: Do you agree with those ideas? Would you dare break from tradition?

DON JUAN: I wouldn't be able to do it alone. It wouldn't solve the problem.

ANGELINA: Why, Father? What are you afraid of?

DON JUAN: I'm not afraid of anything but without the other capitalists, the matter wouldn't be resolved, because only some would benefit.

ANGELINA: Do it so that the others follow your example.

DON JUAN: They won't follow it, my daughter. They would start criticizing us, hating us, and they would even pay an ignoramus to set my factory on fire, and they would mock us saying: "Here you go, common property!"

ANGELINA: Are you sure of that?

DON JUAN: Yes, my daughter, the time has not yet come. The working class will have to gain their freedom themselves. (*The bell rings loudly.*)

SCENE FIVE

RAMÓN: (*Entering.*) Don Juan, the foreman would like to see you.

DON JUAN: Tell him to come in.

ALBERTO: (*The foreman enters very nervously with his hat in his hands.*) Don Juan, there is a huge disturbance in the factory, come at once.

DON JUAN: What's happening? Why the rush? Are they going to burn the factory? Surely they're the disrupters.

ALBERTO: I don't know I don't meddle in affairs that don't concern me. To me, the unorganized ones are more agreeable.

DON JUAN: What you call "agreeable" is subservience, and because of that you find the others arrogant, since they understand their rights.

ALBERTO: Come, Don Juan, come.

DON JUAN: When you're in that much of a hurry, you must have done something.

ALBERTO: I was only distributing poor-quality material when all of a sudden, there was an uproar.

ANGELINA: Now they'll think that it was my father who gave the order.

ALBERTO: He didn't order it, but he has consented to it other times.

DON JUAN: Be quiet, don't talk too much, idiot. (HE *pushes him.*)

ALBERTO: That's it, now I'll pay.

ANGELINA: (*Turning to her father.*) If what this man says is true, it is an abuse that you authorize and permit.

DON JUAN: Let's go see what you've done. See you later, my daughter. (THEY *both leave.*)

ANGELINA: I will go out on the balcony so I can watch them leave. (SHE *goes out the door in the back.*)

Curtain.

ACT TWO

SCENE ONE

A garden, a sofa, a pedestal table; on the table a book, card file, and a bell.

ANGELINA: (*Entering from the right,* SHE *goes toward the table and looks over the cards.*) The strike was convenient for me. It was a good excuse to avoid going out for a ride yesterday.

I wonder how it's going for them? I haven't seen Ramón, he hasn't told me anything. (SHE *walks around and looks toward the trees.*) Now I see him. (SHE *presses the bell.*)

RAMÓN: What do you want, Miss?

ANGELINA: Do you know anything about the strike?

RAMÓN: I only know that tomorrow a commission will come to speak with Don Juan.

ANGELINA: Very well, sorry to bother you. (RAMÓN *departs.*)

SCENE TWO

DON JUAN: (*Entering.*) Were you worried? Well, there's no reason to be. They complained about the material and they offered to send a commission tomorrow.

ANGELINA: Did they ask for a wage increase?

DON JUAN: I still don't know what they want. Tomorrow I will know, and you will hear it.

ANGELINA: You knew that the commission was coming.

DON JUAN: It's the norm in order for them to get what they want.

ANGELINA: Father, you know that yesterday Marieta and Ernestina came to take me out for a ride.

DON JUAN: Did you go with them?

ANGELINA: No I was sad, and I stayed in here reading.

DON JUAN: Good decision. What are you reading?

ANGELINA: *Fecundity* by Zola. I already read *Truth*.

16

DON JUAN: Does that reading please you?

ANGELINA: I like it very much because of the truths that the author states.

DON JUAN: Fine. Tell me, does the bracelet fit?

ANGELINA: I still haven't worn it I don't need it.

DON JUAN: Don't be foolish. What are you going to do with it?

ANGELINA: Give it to Mariana. She can sell it.

DON JUAN: It'll be a shame, because when she sells it they'll offer her a lower price.

ANGELINA: It is stupid and shameful that there are human beings lacking the basic needs. If you would have consulted with me, we could have helped some poor families in a practical manner.

DON JUAN: We would have to invest whatever we have in aid.

ANGELINA: Come on! With a thousand dollars we could have helped several families with their most important needs.

DON JUAN: I have given you things on other occasions and it hasn't bothered you . . .

ANGELINA: But not like this.

DON JUAN: Because now I can do more. I'm in a better financial position.

ANGELINA: You must have exploited more, buying the tobacco at a lower price. Instead of accumulating so much money you should remember that the field hands are, with respect to civilization and progress, two centuries behind. Since working the land ages them, we should afford them the means to make progress; since their type of work does not allow them any other advantages, we should provide them with the means.

DON JUAN: Competition that forces me to employ those business practices.

ANGELINA: The same competition that destroys fraternal brotherhood and transforms individuals into wild beasts. You shouldn't follow that custom. What good is recognizing workers' rights if you don't practice them?

DON JUAN: I would love to follow your ideas but . . . what business could I undertake that wouldn't involve exploitation? What kind of work would I do?

ANGELINA: The same business. Now that they're on strike, you should take the opportunity to concede to their demands, and free your slaves.

DON JUAN: (*Laughing.*) My slaves? I don't force them to work. They show up voluntarily. What am I to do? Dismiss them when they come to work voluntarily?

ANGELINA: You don't enslave them intentionally, but you take advantage of their poverty and ignorance in order to exploit them.

DON JUAN: If I don't do it, someone else will, and under worse conditions.

ANGELINA: Do not follow the practice; impose a new one, pay them a higher wage. Why do you want to increase your capital even more? Listen, there's something else that I'm going to propose to you. This house is very large for us . . .

DON JUAN: Do you want to move?

ANGELINA: What I want is for you to build us one that is less extravagant, and give this one to your employee's widow . . . don't you think that she has the right to have a house of her own?

DON JUAN: (*Gets up and paces around.*) Can't you think of anything else? Truly you are too much, where will we stop?

ANGELINA: At liberty, it is the best idea that has occurred to me. Are you going to please me? . . . (*Getting up and caressing her father.*)

DON JUAN: (*Grabbing his hat in order to leave.*) Since your mother died I do nothing else but please you; I don't know where your madness will take me. (HE *leaves.*)

ANGELINA: (*Accompanying him to the door.*) Thank you, Father, see you later. (*Alone.*) Finally a great weight has been lifted from me. Will I see my dreams come true . . . without going to church, without rendering tribute to traditional formulas, or attending socials, where only cutting criticism and insults are heard?

SCENE THREE

RAMÓN: Miss Mariana wishes to see you . . .

ANGELINA: How timely that she has arrived. Tell her to come in. And what are you doing with that broom?

RAMÓN: Well, sweeping. (*Aside:* "She must plan to reform the world.")

ANGELINA: Well fine, I will buy a sweeper machine and that way you won't have to breathe the dust.

MARIANA: (*Entering.*) Good day, Angelina. How is your health?

ANGELINA: Good day to you too, Mariana. How are you?

MARIANA: So so. Since you saved me from my predicament, I'm doing better. (*Sitting down.*)

ANGELINA: What are you talking about? The paltry sum that I sent you? Is it not significant?

MARIANA: Not for you, but for me with four children, it has been so important. I bought shoes and clothes for my children. Imagine how happy and grateful I am . . .

ANGELINA: Well, to show you that it didn't mean anything at all, I was waiting to give you an object that will be of great use to you.

MARIANA: By no means can I allow you to make such a sacrifice.

ANGELINA: It is not a sacrifice, my lady. It is a gift that I have been given that you will be able to make use of, and I don't need.

MARIANA: I cannot agree to you giving up a gift that surely you can use.

ANGELINA: (*Presenting the open jewel box.*) You see now? I don't need this in the least. I am giving it to you. It is yours.

MARIANA: I cannot accept this gift. I don't wear jewels.

ANGELINA: Well then, sell it. To me it is a useless piece of junk.

MARIANA: Don't say that, Angelina. It is a piece of art and in any case it is valuable and you should keep it.

ANGELINA: It's useless to me. I don't want it and before I break it into pieces, you should make use of it, sell it.

MARIANA: Pleasing you is very important to me, but I can't. What would your father say? That I take advantage of your generosity to exploit you?

ANGELINA: My father knows you and furthermore, knows that I want to give it to you, so don't fear. He already knows.

MARIANA: To whom would I sell this piece of jewelry? (*Contemplating it.*)

ANGELINA: To any rich lady or to a jeweler.

MARIANA: Angelina, you place me in a dilemma.

ANGELINA: It was I who was in a dilemma, and I will continue in it while this remains in my possession.

MARIANA: Then I'll take it, since it bothers you so much.

ANGELINA: While there are needs to be satisfied, I believe it a crime to wear them.

MARIANA: What can be done so there aren't such needs?

ANGELINA: By destroying exploitation, which is the origin of all misery. "Capital is the product of work that isn't paid for. It is underhanded and legalized robbery."

I have quoted a socialist maxim.

MARIANA: Are you in favor of socialism?

ANGELINA: It is what will rule in the future that is to say, very soon.

MARIANA: My husband was a socialist, but he did not reveal this. He was a coward.

ANGELINA: Don't blame him. He has not been the only one. There are others who hide them, fearless of losing employment.

MARIANA: I still keep some socialist and anarchist works.

ANGELINA: Which ones?

MARIANA: "Anarchy" and "The General Strike," and various others that I don't remember because I haven't read them.

ANGELINA: Lend them to me. Don't forget.

MARIANA: Fine, Angelina. I'm leaving now, because I have to prepare lunch for my children. Good-bye. (*Shaking her hand.*)

ANGELINA: See you later, Mariana. If I may be of any help, please don't hesitate to let me know. Good-bye.

SCENE FOUR

RAMÓN: (*Entering somewhat hurriedly.*) Angelina, if your father finds out that you sent resources to the strikers. He'll be upset.

ANGELINA: Let him find out, he will still be upset because he knows that I speak clearly and I tell the truth. In all fairness, this is where the workers should be receiving their resources.

RAMÓN: He'll be upset because they have declared the strike against him.

ANGELINA: Don't worry. He's the one who has exploited them and he owes his wealth to them.

RAMÓN: What has happened? What has stirred these feeling in you?

ANGELINA: Well, sociology books. Am I right? Am I proceeding fairly?

RAMÓN: In a manner superior to what I would have thought.

ANGELINA: I think they are calling.

RAMÓN: (*Goes out and returns.*) Miss, the commission.

ANGELINA: Come in! Have them come in, Ramón.

(CARLOS SANTANA *and* SIMPLICIO HERNÁNDEZ, *the strike committee, enters.*)

CARLOS: (*Steps forward.*) Miss, at your service. (*Bowing*, SIMPLICIO *also greets her.*)

ANGELINA: It is a great honor for me to meet you and serve you. With whom do I have the pleasure of speaking?

CARLOS: We come as the commission. My name is Carlos Santana, I am Mariana's son, and this young man is Simplicio Hernández.

(*Both greet her, and* ANGELINA *says as an aside while they look over the papers.*) Heavens, Mariana's son! Justice, the son demands what his father didn't know or didn't dare demand!

ANGELINA: Please take a seat.

CARLOS: Your father is not here?

ANGELINA: He won't be long.

CARLOS: Will we be a bother waiting for him?

ANGELINA: Not at all. You have just arrived and besides, you are welcome here anytime.

CARLOS: Thank you very much. (*Aside*: She is very beautiful and nice.)

RAMÓN: (*Leaving.*) How quickly they liked each other. Miss, Don Juan is arriving. (HE *exits.*)

DON JUAN: (*Entering and upon seeing the young men* HE *turns toward them and speaks with kindness.*) To what do I owe the honor of this visit?

CARLOS: (*Steps forward.*) We are the strike commission and we have come to convey some propositions to you.

DON JUAN: Let's see what you want.

(CARLOS *presents the document to* DON JUAN.)

DON JUAN: Please read it to me.

CARLOS: (*Reading the paper.*)

FREE FEDERATION OF ARECIBO

Strike commission under the leadership of C. Santana and S. Hernández.

COMMUNIQUÉ:

Sir:

Considering: that up until now the working class has suffered and continues to suffer countless injustices, due to the enormous exploitation it is subjected to:

Considering: that only a strike can bring about a wage increase and other agreements that benefit the workers, the perennial victims of abuse.

The extraordinary General Board, which is in session has declared a general strike, with these petitions:

We have hereby decided:

1. That the daily minimum wage for the field hand and day laborer be $3.00 daily, and for the workers from the city, $5.00.

2. That the owner of the factory or the field provide each worker and his family with a house with modern conveniences and sanitary facilities.

3. That the owner should provide each worker that labors in dangerous, swampy terrains, with a special pair of rubber-soled shoes, and designate 20 percent of the earnings for a reserve fund, in case of illness.

4. In the tobacco workshops, seats should be separated approximately one meter from one steamer to another, and the windows should be open, keeping the tobacco in wet cotton so that the leaves do not dry because this would impede the manufacturing process. The seats should also be separated by plants that will purify the air.

Respectfully,

The Commission.

DON JUAN: I believe that you do not expect to receive concessions.

CARLOS: We don't need them; if they are denied, we will continue the strike. We have work to do on our cultivated lands, and we have money.

DON JUAN: I'm happy to know that. Don't think that I oppose your petitions. I fear other factory owners will hurt me through treacherous means.

CARLOS: Are you willing to concede to what we ask?

DON JUAN: Yes. You are demanding your rights, but my fellow partners are going to kill me.

CARLOS: We will defend you as one of our own. If you consent to our demands, it will be encouraging, and it will serve as a lovely example for the rest of them. You can count on our support.

DON JUAN: (*Determined.*) I will wait for you in my office tomorrow.

CARLOS: Well then, we will leave now that you are willing to support our requests.

ANGELINA: (*Gets up after sitting in silence.*) I congratulate you both on your successful negotiation.

CARLOS: Oh, Miss! One still doesn't know how this day will end. (*Saying good-bye.*) At your service. (*To* DON JUAN.) See you tomorrow in your office.

DON JUAN: See you tomorrow. (*The young men leave and* DON JUAN *walks around.*) As soon as the other factory owners find out, there'll be a big fuss, and I will be exposed to anything and everything. But even if I hadn't given in, the workers would have continued the strike. They have land and cooperatives.

ANGELINA: All of this is very opportune. It will bring about a new way of life, and there will be more good health and happiness.

DON JUAN: It would be opportune if all the workers made identical requests.

ANGELINA: The other workers will now declare themselves on strike, you'll see.

DON JUAN: It would be convenient if those who were not organized would organize themselves. The cooperatives would grow, and they wouldn't be exploited so much.

ANGELINA: It'll be a small revolution.

RAMÓN: (*Entering with a card.*) Don Juan, three gentlemen wait at the door; here are their cards.

DON JUAN: (*Reads the cards.*) Jaime López, Robert Hartman and Antonio Rigaud. (*Turning around to* RAMÓN *who is still waiting.*) Have them come in. (RAMÓN *leaves.*)

(*The three gentlemen enter. They graciously greet* ANGELINA *and turning themselves to* DON JUAN. THEY *shake his hand.*)

SCENE FIVE

DON JUAN: What brings you all here? Have a seat.

DON ROBERT: (*German accent.*) Ramírez, I haf come here to know vat you haf conceded to your factory vorkers. I haf a stake in all zis, my good sir, so tell to me vat you haf arranged. I to come here lightly to know vat you are doing; I to be sure about ze strike.

DON JUAN: Well, you have come very quickly because the commission just left.

DON JAIME: Can you tell us the conditions they presented?

DON JUAN: They have left me a copy of the petition. Here it is. (DON ANTONIO, DON JAIME *and* DON ROBERT approach him.)

DON JAIME: (HE *reads it and then says.*) That is scandalous. Where are we headed? We'll be ruined. Have you already agreed to it? What did you do? Tell us.

DON ANTONIO: Do you agree with these conditions?

DON JUAN: My friends, I think differently. I have studied something of socialism, and I don't have a problem with granting rights to my workers.

DON JAIME: But those petitions are exaggerated. You all will be left in ruins. (*The others speak quietly to* ANGELINA.)

DON JUAN: Their doctrines do not permit them to cause damage, instead they permit them to defend themselves. You're surprised because you don't understand the uselessness of money locked up

in a safe and you think that when I don't have it I'll lack the basic
necessities.

DON ANTONIO: Think it over well. Don't do anything crazy.

ANGELINA: Father has thought it over well, and furthermore this fortune is not his alone.

DON JAIME: Who else does it belong to, Miss?

ANGELINA: Those who have labored for it, the workers.

DON ANTONIO: We see that you also agree with them.

DON JAIME: Provided they don't kill us and rob us.

DON ANTONIO: I think it is madness.

ANGELINA: Madness? To concede to the workers that which is theirs?
No, sir.

DON JUAN: I don't think that this will harm anyone. I'm thinking of
going to Europe. I will leave the factory to them so that they can run
it and I will also turn over this estate to them.

DON JAIME: To the workers?

ANGELINA: The mansion goes to the widow of a house servant.

DON ANTONIO: Do you all think that leaving the factory in inexperienced hands will yield results?

DON JUAN: Inexperienced! Have you looked closely at the document?
Are you saying we're experts?

DON JAIME: Do you think that they are educated and worthy to be
owners of the factory? That is why we are the stockholders.

DON JUAN: And they, with their ignorance, can produce for us?

DON JAIME: I see you are very interested, and I will not be the one to
make you desist.

DON JUAN: It would be useless. It is a matter of conscience.

DON ANTONIO: Fine, we'll say good-bye. (DON JAIME *and* DON
ROBERT *take their hats, say good-bye and depart.*)

ANGELINA: How selfish they are, Father, how they resist to being rea-
sonable.

DON JUAN: Well, now the conflict is over for me. That kind of resistance is ignorance. I'm going to the post office. So long. (DON
JUAN *leaves.*)

RAMÓN: (*Entering.*) How did it go, Miss? What did they work out?

ANGELINA: My father has made up his mind. Those gentlemen were
surprised by my father's decision. I don't know what they'll decide,
since they didn't agree with him.

RAMÓN: What other recourse will be left for them other than to
accept?

ANGELINA: What we really need, Ramón, is knowledge; knowledge is the foundation of people's happiness and the mother of liberty.

RAMÓN: If all women concerned themselves with education, the future generations would reform the world. (RAMÓN *goes out the door to the balcony, and yells.*) Angelina, come up! Come up here! (*Faraway voices and shouts are heard.*)

ANGELINA: What is happening? (SHE *goes in* RAMÓN's *direction.*)

RAMÓN: Do you see the tobacco factory workers cheering Don Juan? They are all around him!

ANGELINA: He looks bewildered! He's already approaching, wiping his brow.

DON JUAN: *Ay, Ay!,* my daughter . . . (HE *falls into the chair.* ANGELINA *hurries to wipe his brow.*) What's wrong, Father?

DON JUAN: They weren't going to let me pass. Upon leaving the post office, a loud mouth said, "There goes Don Juan," and another said, "Which Don Juan?," and when others said, "Where is he?," I found myself surrounded in such a manner that I thought they wouldn't let me go.

ANGELINA: Why, foolish man, didn't you realize that they were saluting you? You're very upset. You should take something or you'll get sick. (SHE *rings the bell and* RAMÓN *enters.*) Make me a drink with some drops of brandy. (RAMÓN *leaves.*)

DON JUAN: This will end with a conflict; I'm going to Europe. Those capitalists will hate me, but I will leave the young man from the commission, Santana, who seems very nice to me, in charge of everything.

RAMÓN: (*With a tray with the cup of punch, says in aside.*) He also likes you.

ANGELINA: (*Approaches her father and says to him.*) Don't worry. Drink this, it'll do you good. And rest.

DON JUAN: (*Drinking the punch.*) Do you think we should leave it to that young man? Doesn't he seem to be the brightest?

ANGELINA: (*Impressed.*) The one who spoke with you?

DON JUAN: Yes, he told me his name and I don't remember.

ANGELINA: His name is Carlos Santana.

DON JUAN: Santana? . . . that was the name of your protégée's husband, my old employee.

ANGELINA: Yes, he's Mariana's son. He is very well mannered. I like him very much.

DON JUAN: You like him very much, you say? Well, we will leave it to him. He seems capable of handling it, and besides, he will reap what his father didn't know how to take advantage of.

ANGELINA: His father had the same ideas.

DON JUAN: It didn't seem like it. His son is more intelligent.

ANGELINA: He was also intelligent, but his son is more courageous, and the world belongs to the bold.

DON JUAN: Is that a phrase from some philosopher?

ANGELINA: No, it's mine, but I feel bold, so I said it to you. If it were possible, I would change the world.

DON JUAN: Go ahead and begin, because bold people don't think things over for long.

ANGELINA: I'm already doing it. Perhaps you have forgotten that I have been leading you to the objective that I proposed?

DON JUAN: Yes, now I see that you have won me over.

ANGELINA: Like Carlos wins over his father. It is the new century and the wish for progress that are pushing us.

DON JUAN: I congratulate you! Forgive me for leaving you; I am exhausted and I'm going to sleep. Good night. (HE *kisses her on the forehead.*)

ANGELINA: Finally I will see my wishes fulfilled. (*Exits toward her room.*)

Curtain.

ACT THREE

SCENE ONE

RAMÓN, ANGELINA, DON JUAN.
(The set from Act One.)

RAMÓN: (*Cleaning, talking to himself.*) All the factories are on strike, the federation is full, and at the eleventh hour the anti-unionists came when they saw that their demands had lost, and they understood that we were winning the strike.

ANGELINA: Good day, Ramón. Are you talking to yourself? (*Looking over some press reports on the table.*)

RAMÓN: It said that all the factories were on strike.

ANGELINA: Are you sure? I am very happy.

RAMÓN: The truth is that the issue is very complicated. If you saw the throng at the federation that I have seen this morning it looks like a revolution.

ANGELINA: How lovely it will be to hear those men advocate for their rights and propose a new way of life.

RAMÓN: But aren't you afraid? (*With astonishment.*)

ANGELINA: Not at all. It's as if it gives me new energy. Long live the revolution! (*Very animated.*)

RAMÓN: Long live . . . a . . . ahem . . . .

DON JUAN: (*Fixing his tie.*) What is going on? (*Looking at himself in the mirror.*) What was that shouting?

RAMÓN: I was telling the young lady that I go out for a walk very early in the morning . . .

DON JUAN: It seemed to me that I heard "Long live," and I thought I understood it as "long live the region."

RAMÓN: It was me telling the young lady a very curious detail. (RAMÓN *and* ANGELINA *make gestures of silence to each other.*)

DON JUAN: Fine, continue with your stories. I'm going to the office. See you later. (*Says good-bye and leaves.*)

RAMÓN: (*Goes out on the balcony and comes back in and says.*)
Angelina, the demonstration, come out here. Do you see the ban-
ners there at the end of the street?

ANGELINA: So many red flags! What an immense crowd!

RAMÓN: There are twelve thousand workers! Let the bourgeoisie take
us on, now let them come! They're singing the workers' hymn.

ANGELINA: Where are they headed? It seems like they are coming
here.

RAMÓN: It is possible and very logical. Yes, the young man from the
commission must be coming to our house. He is already approaching. (RAMÓN *leaves and* ANGELINA *prepares herself to receive
him.*)

SCENE TWO

CARLOS: Good day, Miss. How are you?

ANGELINA: Very well, and you? How is it going with the strike?

CARLOS: It's going fine. In fact, I have come to find out if you will
allow the approaching demonstration to stop here and sing the
workers' hymn.

ANGELINA: Yes, they can. I will take great pleasure in hearing the
hymn that I'm not familiar with.

CARLOS: (HE *rings the bell.*) Well then, I will send word that they stop
here.

RAMÓN: How may I be of service?

CARLOS: Please go to the commission and tell them that they can stop
here. (RAMÓN *leaves.*) You are an angel, allow me to kiss your
hand.

ANGELINA: (*Gives him her hand.*) What have I done that you express
yourself in such a manner? They are my ideas; for me, there is nothing special about that.

CARLOS: Your ideas? And which ideas are those?

ANGELINA: Anarchist socialism.

CARLOS: Oh, mysterious designs of nature! They unite us in this great
moment of social emancipation and allow me to recognize in you
the ideal of my dreams. (*Slowly* HE *takes her hand and kneels
down. At the same time the workers' hymn is clearly heard. They listen peacefully and sing along.*)

ANGELINA: So then, my friend, don't be surprised by my actions. I have read Malato, Malatesta, Tolstoy, Zola. So I understand many things that I couldn't understand before.

CARLOS: Oh blessed knowledge that fills my soul with cheer to find in you, the ideal woman!

ANGELINA: And that amazes you?

CARLOS: Yes, because I didn't think that you would share my ideas.

ANGELINA: I will explain to you how I started. I was studying Spiritism on my own. I felt a desire to know something about the afterlife, since my mother died when I was very a young girl. And furthermore, I wanted to understand the diversity of inhabited worlds and to fully accept diverse existences. This made me a revolutionary, because it explained to me that all men are brothers, that no one has the right to hurt others or to impose their ideas on them or to enslave them, and I also realized that luxury was a crime as long as there was misery.

So, more than understanding the grandeur of the universe, it made me a humanitarian; something perhaps no one could have accomplished.

CARLOS: (*Who had been absorbed in the conversation.*) Go on, I will keep listening tirelessly to you, a woman liberated from religious dogmas.

ANGELINA: Some believe that Spiritism is a religion. The word "religion" has been confused. The least religious have been the priests; they appeared to be so, but they are the ones that worry the least about following the teachings of Jesus. They live according to their own personal convenience. So those who try to follow the doctrines of Jesus are the truly religious ones, because a religious person is the one who keeps a relic and follows the doctrinal precepts to the letter.

Because the study of psychology is a science, it isn't obligated to follow definite dogmas, because it doesn't have any. One analyzes, scrutinizes, researches, and studies by observing the cases and experiments of that science.

CARLOS: Very well, I accept it all in the way that you explain it.

ANGELINA: Now to instill anarchist socialism, everyone must feel a sense of fraternal brotherhood and not feel hatred or rancor, because in pure anarchy, those with cruel instincts will continue as such, and anarchy will not transform them when it transforms the system.

CARLOS: Do you believe that all anarchists have read the maxims of human love that were preached six thousand years ago in Asia by Krishna, a messiah like Jesus, and later Yao, the emperor of China; also Confucius, during the same era, and later Fhilon, and afterwards others, until Jesus? The emperor Yao said: "If anyone suffers hunger I am to blame; if someone commits a crime, I am its author." And that man left his throne and dedicated himself to preaching.

ANGELINA: I don't believe that all anarchists know those details. Many are anarchists out of desperation, because they don't enjoy the essential comforts. They call themselves anarchists in order to take power, after which they are as tyrannical or even more so than the rest. They don't love humanity, nor do they concern themselves with helping the libertarian propaganda.

CARLOS: You are quite right. The majority of those who call themselves anarchists do not love humanity. They willingly criticize their fellow human beings without doing anything to instruct them.

ANGELINA: I think that true anarchists will find the history of the Bible* doubtful and will reject institutions with selfish objectives. But all of those that you quoted earlier are true anarchists—that is if you apply the real meaning of the phrase, that is to say "humane" in every sense of the word. It also means just, sincere, tolerant —anything that doesn't constitute harm toward others.

CARLOS: I am of the same opinion.

ANGELINA: Furthermore, I think that it is necessary to avoid misery by all possible means, to be able to adequately prepare people's minds to take in and understand redemptive ideas, and to defend them.

CARLOS: Very well. While hunger and its diseases exist, it is impossible for the poor to have sufficient energy to obtain rights to the product of their labors.

ANGELINA: I agree. Only then would one be able to think of contemplating the immensity of space, and dream of other inhabited worlds.

CARLOS: Exactly. While there is one person that dies of hunger or from lack of everything needed to sustain life, we cannot think of other issues. That doesn't prohibit those who individually concern themselves with such research from continuing it.

ANGELINA: Agreed, even though I don't understand why they cannot study both.

---

*In the Bible there are written sublime truths, let us practice them.

CARLOS: Yes, they can dedicate themselves to that, those who wish to do so. Now forgive me, but I must go. I would stay and listen to you more—your easy attractive speech enchants me. Before I go, allow me to tell you that you are the only woman who has impressed my soul in such a wondrous way. Angelina . . . I love you . . .

ANGELINA: (*With joy.*) Really? . . . I wasn't alone in my feelings? . . . I am so happy!

CARLOS: What! You have thought about me? You love me? . . . but is this a dream? . . . (*Takes a step toward her.*)

ANGELINA: (*Approaches him and takes his hand.*) Yes, a dream that is coming true. I had a premonition about you. I waited for you, as the flowers wait for the dew and the little birds have a sense that spring is coming.

CARLOS: What happiness! So unexpected and so lovely! . . . (*Kissing her hands.*)

SCENE THREE

DON JUAN: (*Entering.*) What a big surprise!

(CARLOS *has suddenly separated himself from* ANGELINA, *and* HE *very sheepishly greets* DON JUAN.)

ANGELINA: Forgive me, Father.

DON JUAN: (*Takes some papers and puts them in his pockets.*) Why? Hadn't you already told me about him?

CARLOS: (*With interest.*) What did she tell you?

DON JUAN: There's no rush to talk about that. Right now you need to find out about another more urgent matter. I thought that you would be involved with the strike and I find you here.

CARLOS: I have come to ask permission for the protest to stop here and sing the workers' hymn.

DON JUAN: Alright, well listen, you are about to find out that we are headed off to Europe, and you . . .

CARLOS: (*Interrupting.*) Good-bye, my golden dream! . . .

DON JUAN: Don't be alarmed, for now your wishes will be fulfilled. You and your family will come to live in this mansion.

CARLOS: I can't allow it, not at all. Everyone will think that I have made some sort of deal . . .

DON JUAN: Don't interrupt me, for these are decisions Angelina made before she met you.

CARLOS: I'm listening . . .

DON JUAN: After you all get settled in here, you will take over the management of the factory, and hire the same foreman. All petitions with regard to improved conditions will be honored. You will set up workshops for shoemaking, carpentry, and blacksmithing on the first floor. The rest is up to you.

CARLOS: Is that your decision?

DON JUAN: Furthermore, when I return you will marry my daughter.

CARLOS: Are you mocking me? I cannot believe what you are telling me.

DON JUAN: As you heard, tomorrow I am leaving the city.

ANGELINA: So soon, and we have barely met . . .

DON JUAN: And so? There's no harm in that.

CARLOS: Then, I'm going to see my mother and later I will come to see you in your office.

DON JUAN: Until this evening.

ANGELINA: (*Accompanies* CARLOS *to the door.*) I won't rest while I'm far away from you. (*They take each other's hand.*)

DON JUAN: Enough conversation, you're going to get me very teary-eyed. . . .

(CARLOS *blows a kiss to the young woman and departs.*)

SCENE FOUR

DON JUAN: Come now, you can't complain. Everything is going according to your wishes.

ANGELINA: (*Feeling sad.*) Now you don't want me be sad, leaving that boy here alone in such a dangerous situation. And if they kill him?

DON JUAN: Don't be foolish. I have advised the Chief of Police of my decision and I have told him that the young man's life is in his hands. Don't fear, he will advise his officers, and besides, we will return soon.

ANGELINA: That's a relief. How has the strike turned out?

DON JUAN: It continues, but they are getting organized. Do not fear, solidarity will be established, and the cooperatives will grow.

ANGELINA: It shouldn't take long because they have propagandists in the fields everywhere.

DON JUAN: I hope so. Now pack your suitcases and whatever you'll need. I'm going to my study to get the paperwork necessary to transfer the property rights.

(ANGELINA *leaves from the center and* DON JUAN *from the right.*)

RAMÓN: (*Enters with two suitcases.*) Now I am worried. I have never had to serve anyone else. I don't know what the new owners will be like.

ANGELINA: (*Entering with another suitcase.*) Here, Ramón, take all of them to the station.

RAMÓN: When will you return?

ANGELINA: Soon, don't worry. When I return, I will marry Carlos.

RAMÓN: Congratulations! So, I have the right to do the same.

ANGELINA: You have a fiancée?

RAMÓN: A union worker.

ANGELINA: You should speak with Father so he can give orders to provide you with what you need.

RAMÓN: I'll wait until he returns.

ANGELINA: You should do it now, because if the propagandists don't know that you are without a job they won't say anything to you. Take the keys to the chests so when Mariana arrives you can explain it to her. Tell me your fiancée's name, if it's not a secret.

RAMÓN: With pleasure! Her name is Rosalina. She is olive-skinned with black eyes.

ANGELINA: Congratulations. I'll say good-bye now. I'm going to my father's office, I won't be back here, so I'll see you when I return. (THEY *shake hands.*) You will be at the station until we board; the ship will leave tonight at 12:00.

SCENE FIVE

RAMÓN: (*Alone.*) Because our society is so full of hypocrisy, it will be a scandal that this girl has turned the system on its ear. (*Exaltedly.*) Some people explain anarchism as a doctrine of crime and violence; however, millions of human beings have been burned in the name of Christ; thousands were guillotined in France in 1893 in the name of liberty. Anarchy did not commit those crimes; that some fanatic has erased a Carnot, a Canovas, a Humbert, a McKinley from the scene, these are isolated cases and furthermore, they are not taught in any institution; they are pardonable. Anarchists like Ravachols, Pallas, and Angiolillos are few, but the Torquemadas and the Louis IXs multiply with an astounding ease.

MARIANA: (*Entering.*) Who are you taking to, Ramón?

RAMÓN: I'm rehearsing, Madam. Allow me to give you the keys.

MARIANA: Wait a moment, my son is coming. Here he is now.

CARLOS: What do you do want, Mother?

MARIANA: Ramón wishes to give you the keys.

CARLOS: They are the keys to the house. Show me which cabinets they belong to.

RAMÓN: (*Points to the cabinets and says good-bye.*) Before I go, I need you to give me a job in the factory.

CARLOS: You don't need to say a word. You'll go with me later.

MARIANA: Listen, son, how is the strike going?

CARLOS: We're doing well. Now we just need the rest of the factories to hand over their fees. We have five hundred homes under construction, two thousand workers employed, and each home with its own spacious garden and all modern conveniences.

MARIANA: When do the textile machines arrive?

CARLOS: Soon. They are now preparing the building for the factory. Being that they only work six-hour shifts, it is necessary to employ more people.

MARIANA: And agriculture?

CARLOS: They have bought more land, and all of it is being cultivated and planted with fruits and grains. In the coming year, we will have a large ranch. We're waiting for catalogues for the machines.

MARIANA: Tell me, where is Ramón going? Isn't he going to stay and live here?

CARLOS: I don't believe so, because he has asked my permission to go to the factory. Since he is getting married, he wishes to have a small house of his own.

MARIANA: What ideas that man has? When I came in he was talking to himself, and I was surprised to hear such odd things.

CARLOS: It must be because he believes that there is an exact analogy between anarchism and primitive Christianity; there was common wealth and there weren't any managers, or masters, or privileged people. But today after thousands of different leaders they have adopted the name of psychology, Christian science, spiritism, and theosophy, and each one wants to be the sole purveyor of the truth.

MARIANA: And which one out of all of them is the one that someone should follow?

CARLOS: No one possesses absolute truth. All are based in psychological science, in the mental strength of individuals of both sexes, in the willpower that each person, male or female, possesses.

MARIANA: And does Don Juan share those ideas?

CARLOS: Yes, because he is a spiritist, and therefore he accepts all those different names for the same one thing.

MARIANA: But does he accept your ideas of equality?

CARLOS: Yes, they are the foundation of his doctrine.

MARIANA: And Angelina also believes that doctrine?

CARLOS: She is a fervent admirer of Christ and a defender of reincarnation and of different inhabited worlds. She believes that the spirit will live again and that we have to pass through different phases of life in order to progress. She is a believer.

MARIANA: But does Don Juan know that you aren't in favor of civil or religious marriage?

CARLOS: He figures as much, since he knows our propaganda well. He pretends now because the moment to accept it hasn't arrived. But he is well aware of the infamies of the current social structure and of the abuses that are committed.

MARIANA: So then nothing will oppose the fulfillment of your propositions?

CARLOS: I fear nothing. Angelina is a libertarian that, according to her, has lived in the Christian era and isn't afraid of my revolutionary concepts.

SCENE SIX

RAMÓN: (*Entering with* ROSALINA.) We are here so you know when we take possession of our house.

CARLOS: I'm very happy to meet your partner, even though you haven't introduced her to me.

RAMÓN: Forgive me, Carlos, it was an oversight.

CARLOS: Anyway, you are going to start your household in a new way, and you must know you are the first; we have to applaud this young woman for her courage.

ROSALINA: I am sure that Ramón loves me and therefore have no fear of failure.

CARLOS: Very well, you are sure of his love and fear nothing.

MARIANA: If only all women could say the same.

ROSALINA: They don't say it, Madam, because they are ignorant. The majority of them do not have willpower. They yield to the circumstances and don't want to confront them. But if they were brave and willing to defend their rights, I assure you that no man would take advantage of our supposed weakness and they would be careful about thinking of us as simply as objects of pleasure.

CARLOS: (*Applauding.*) Bravo! That's the way to talk. Don't you applaud her too, Ramón?

RAMÓN: She knows that I admire her and that I applaud all her bravery.

MARIANA: It's a shame that not all women are as learned as you are.

ROSALINA: Some day complete emancipation will arrive.

CARLOS: Fine, here is my authorization to occupy the most pleasant site, the nicest house. Until we are all united, all these requirements are needed.

RAMÓN: It is necessary, and it doesn't bother me. May I go then?

CARLOS: Yes, give that document to the one in charge, that's all.

ROSALINA: What do you all think? If past generations had ever heard of a marriage without God, without master, without king and without priest, they would have been amazed.

CARLOS: In the first stages of the human race, there weren't any rites —they married freely. After Christianity, marriage became institutionalized.

ROSALINA: Naturally, that is how it should have continued. A man and a woman have the most perfect right to freely unite if they mutually love each other, without deception.

CARLOS: Deception doesn't belong where there is liberty, because if they have made a mistake with regard to character, they can freely separate.

ROSALINA: I understand, but wish to say that they should love each other, that it not be simply desire that unites them.

CARLOS: Desire is a natural thing, you can't deny it. If two people like each other, naturally they are attracted to one another, and if afterwards they get along well, they will continue living together. But that desire should not transform into habit, rather they should always feel love and passion for each other. So that if that man sees another woman, he doesn't desire her, and if that woman sees another man, she doesn't desire him. But if he doesn't feel attracted to his woman, necessarily he has to notice the other one. So that both of them are enough for each other.

ROSALINA: I understand. Now if you'll excuse me, it's late. We shall retire. See you later, Carlos. Good-bye, Madam.

CARLOS: Take care.

MARIANA: (*Accompanying them to the door.*) Good-bye, child.

CARLOS: Now I have to work on the proposals to the other manufacturers.

MARIANA: I think someone is at the door. (SIMPLICIO *and* JUAN HERNÁNDEZ.)

SCENE SEVEN

SIMPLICIO: (*To* CARLOS *who greets both of them.*) We need to send the propagandists into the fields. I found out that the manufacturers have sent agents for the workers to the fields.

CARLOS: I agree, we should name two for the different neighborhoods.

SIMPLICIO: Let them name them tonight in the Junta.

CARLOS: Any of the boys from the proposal committee can be sent.

JUAN: Well, if there are no other problems, we'll leave.

CARLOS: See you later. (*They leave.*)

SCENE EIGHT

MARIANA: What will they do, my son, after the rest agree?

CARLOS: Well, assure the workers' rights, then no one will stand in the way of their happiness.

MARIANA: Will everyone be prepared for that?

CARLOS: Why do we have the teaching centers? So that they educate those that don't know their rights; even though they don't know about them, they are entitled to the profits from their work.

MARIANA: Someone's at the door. (SHE *looks.*)

CARLOS: Come in!

POSTMAN: (*Hands a letter.*) For Mr. Carlos Santana.

CARLOS: At your service, is there anything else?

POSTMAN : No, that's all.

CARLOS: Thank you, good afternoon. (*Opening the letter.*) It is from Don Juan. (HE *reads.*)
"Grand Hotel Spain"

Barcelona, May 17, 191[?].

Mr. Don Carlos Santana.
Arecibo, Puerto Rico.

Esteemed friend:

I will arrive at home next week. Angelina and I are well; we have traveled around some important places, such as museums, parks, and theaters. I believe that is enough for now.

A hug from Angelina,

With affection from your faithful servant,
Juan de Ramírez.

MARIANA: After two months, it isn't much. Will they come and stay
     here?

CARLOS: I will make them welcome, and I will not allow them to go
     anywhere else.

MARIANA: Angelina must be very beautiful. She must have had a very
     good time.

CARLOS: Not really, she didn't go for pleasure. (*Aside*: Someone's at
     the door again. What is happening?) Come in! (*A young man hands
     over a letter and leaves.*)

MARIANA: We should prepare the room for Angelina.

CARLOS: (*Reads.*) My dear Sir:

     We have decided to agree to the strikers' demands, as it is in our
     best interest. I am notifying you so that you may inform your work-
     ers' organization.

Affectionately,
Kolber & Rigaud.

CARLOS: Magnificent! They've been fooling around for six months; it
     was enough. Congratulation. Now that this conflict is ending, I
     need to send the details of the settlement and our benefits to all the
     companies. (HE *sits down to write.*)

The curtain falls.

EPILOGUE

*An elegant reception hall, mirrors, sofas, other pieces of luxurious
furniture.*

(CARLOS *is pacing around, preoccupied.*)

DON JUAN: (*Enters.*) What are you thinking about?

ANGELINA: Carlos! . . .

CARLOS: Finally I see you again! (*Kissing her on the forehead.*) Now
     I am calm. (ANGELINA *goes to her room to change her clothes.*)

DON JUAN: (*Embracing him.*) How are you doing? How's your health?

CARLOS: My health, fine.

DON JUAN: How are your business affairs coming along?

CARLOS: My affairs? Now they are yours again.

DON JUAN: I have said "your affairs" because I'm not planning to take
     them up again. You're the director, inspector, everything.

CARLOS: So you are leaving me the whole business and you won't help me with anything?

DON JUAN: Yes, I will help you, but I'm nothing more than an employee. You will pay me for my inspection work or whatever it may be.

CARLOS: If you insist, I will indulge you.

DON JUAN: Fine. Tell me, how is everything going?

CARLOS: Marvelously. There haven't been any conflicts, our neighborhoods don't need judges or police, there's no drunkenness, every month there is a party or an excursion. We have night and day schools, musicals, theaters, recreational games, and gymnastics.

DON JUAN: There aren't any people who are ill?

CARLOS: Yes, they receive special treatment in the countryside. They do what they most enjoy: look over the plantations or take a walk. There are covered terraces adorned with climbing vines and rocking chairs.

DON JUAN: And what have the manufacturers done?

CARLOS: Well, the first few weeks they held out. Later they came to see the factories. We showed them all the departments, the general laundry, the common kitchen where each month there is a different cook. Everything is powered by electricity. They saw the doors that open automatically, the cleaning system, the farming.

Manufacturers said that it would not last very long. Visitors, amazed, said that we would be ruined. But they haven't been able to halt our progress.

DON JUAN: And how do you handle those with different religious ideas? Catholics, Protestants, and all the rest of the sects?

CARLOS: We don't have any churches. He who wishes to carry on with his errors, let him do it in his own house. We have an ample library hall, grand large posters hung on the wall that explain the different Asian doctrines of humanity. A small observatory for astronomy and psychological experiments, which may be used without charge. There are public lecture halls for philosophy, arts, sciences, agriculture, sociology, theosophy, and psychology. We have teachers of music, painting, sculpture, mechanics, natural healing, hygiene, archeology, navigation, and engineering. Each individual has the right to follow their inclinations.

DON JUAN: I am amazed by the tranquility that reigns here. And the teachers, do they live here?

CARLOS: They are very satisfied. They have their work schedule and when they are not working they are free to spend their time as they wish.

DON JUAN: What is their salary?

CARLOS: They don't have salaries, we don't have money in circulation. Those with families take what they need from the large storehouses; couples do the same. Almost everyone is married here, that is to say, they have freely united. If two people are attracted to each other, they tell their parents so that they know why they are leaving home and then they go live together.

DON JUAN: Magnificent! Well, Carlos, we are going to end here today so that those who most deserve it have time to enjoy their happiness. And Mariana?

CARLOS: Mother has gone out to order some small things for Angelina's dresser.

(*Various friends enter, members of the committee.*)

FINAL SCENE

(*Everyone greets* DON JUAN, *especially* SIMPLICIO *who shakes his hand.*)

SIMPLICIO: How are you and the young lady Angelina?

DON JUAN: We're all fine. She'll be right out, she's changing her clothes.

ANGELINA: (*Enters dressed in white, simple and elegant.*) Good afternoon, gentlemen. How do I look, Carlos?

CARLOS: Most elegant!

FRIENDS: Long live free women! Praises to women who knew how to spurn privilege and traditional norms, and help us to be free!

ANGELINA: Oh, I don't deserve such praise. It is all thanks to a mysterious fairy and her teachings.

SIMPLICIO: As well as modesty. You embody the most desired attributes in human beings.

CARLOS: We'd better end this, as it will soon make us late.

DON JUAN: Will you remain here or will you go to the country?

CARLOS: We will go to the country.

SIMPLICIO: In that case, I will accompany you, if you don't mind.

ANGELINA: The absence of Ramón and his wife is very noticeable. We can't suddenly destroy old habits that we formed with an individual. Ramón has been with us since I was a girl; not having him here today would indicate a great oversight on my part; we must send word to him.

CARLOS: They will come soon. Do you think that he doesn't already know that you have arrived?

ANGELINA: All right, and your mother, where is she?

CARLOS: It won't be long until she arrives. Look! There she is!

MARIANA: (*Enters.*) My daughter! How beautiful you are! (*They embrace.*)

ANGELINA: Mother! . . .

CARLOS: Here are Rosalina and Ramón.

ANGELINA: (*Runs to give her hand to* RAMÓN *and* SHE *embraces* ROSALINA.) We haven't seen each other in so long! How are you? Are you happy?

ROSALINA: Yes, very! (*With an air of satisfaction.*) (*The Marseillaise [the French National Anthem] is heard.*)

CARLOS: (*Takes* ANGELINA *by the hand.*) Starting today, we unite our existence, as long as destiny wishes; the day that you don't love me, that you are tired of me, you have the right to go off to wherever you please. (ANGELINA *throws herself into his arms.*)

ANGELINA: I will be happy as long as you love me. When I see in you indifference or aversion I will leave, but remain your friend.

DON JUAN: (*Who observes and listens.*) I represent the past, rendering tribute to the present that embodies the future.

RAMÓN: (*To* ROSALINA.) Come into my arms. You complement my soul and my aspirations. We are two more people that live the life of love without evasiveness or obligations.

SIMPLICIO: Now let's have some fun in the theater, in the country, wherever each one is most happy.

MARIANA: I'm staying here. I will care for the house and will keep Don Juan company.

ANGELINA: You'll accompany Father, but tonight you'll go to the theater with us.

MARIANA: My daughter, it's been twelve years since I've gone out at night.

ANGELINA: I marry you two, you and Father. (*Everyone laughs and celebrates the proposition.*)

SIMPLICIO: Let them marry. They are still young. They can give a pair of little doves to the revolution.

DON JUAN: Don't pay any attention, my daughter is joking . . . I am too old for Mariana, and furthermore I have made a decision . . .

(Glances furtively at MARIANA *and finds her looking at him, smiling.)*

CARLOS: The refusal seems ridiculous, dear mother . . .

MARIANA: Son! I had sworn . . .

CARLOS: You two had made promises that you didn't know if you could keep. Let's go all together . . .

ANGELINA: *(Taking both their hands and joining them, the two older ones look at each other, smile and embrace. The young ones that surround them shout.)* Long live free union! Down with exploitation! Down with the wage law! *(They all leave with great liveliness.)*

Before the lowering of the curtain.

ANGELINA: Beautiful girls who have listened, if you wish to be free and to be mothers of conscious generations, do not get married in civil courts or in churches, because that is like selling yourself, and selling is prostitution. Love must be free, like the air that you breathe, like the flowers that open their petals to receive the fecund pollen and offer their perfume to the air, and as such you should offer your love and prepare yourselves to have children through love.

Curtain.

Philosophical, Naturalist, Psychological, and Moralist Notes, Annotations, Thoughts, Concepts, Definitions, Maxims, and Reflections

STARTED IN YBOR CITY, JULY 24, 1913

(*Newssheets*; *Gazette* from *Gazzetta,* which is what newspapers that only cost a coin were called at the beginning of the seventeenth century.)

I was writing about mental strength and its power, detailing the benevolent influence of those who knew how to live a truly natural life, free from evil desires and useless pettiness. I lingered on the fifth page . . . while writing my mind reflected and compared the details of individual and collective manifestations. I paused in my narration and said to myself: This opinion is not right. If it happens, it must be necessary. One does not live out an existence without gathering something good. By chance, do I know who they have been in their previous lives? A criminal—according to the majority's opinion—a deviant as a result of spontaneous impulse, does not comprehend the extension, nor the intensity of his actions. He proceeds like a lion or tiger that devours a lamb without compassion for its victim; for these as for those others, it is a satisfaction, a necessity. In the same manner, they accommodate the ignorant by tormenting or mocking others, without it occurring to them that a calumny, an exaggeration, a mockery, could inflict a wound similar to that of a dagger.

I concluded my description by understanding that each person tends to achieve their aspirations or necessities in accordance with their temperament, modifying the impulses of their internal self at each stage of their terrestrial and ultra-terrestrial life.

August 1, 1913

One morning, upon unwrapping a piece of cheese that I was saving to eat by the slice, I discovered in one of its small cavities a white worm with a black snout, like a beak, then another and another. I observed that they moved about the cheese and I carefully closed it up and placed in the same spot again. The next day I observed it again and once again I left the worms alone. I did not feel repugnance or repulsion or the desire to destroy them. I have felt compassion for animals, as if their vulgar appearance holds a semiconscious soul.

The other day while reading *From My Life* by Zamacois, I found a description of worms. I said to myself, "I was right not to destroy them." But why? Perhaps I had anticipated a kind of revenge with them, because they will invade my body. I contemplate with great interest all living beings great and small; it does not please me to interrupt them in their task. To the contrary, I provide the means to feed themselves or evolve as they please and as I can. It does not please me to kill hairy spiders or centipedes for pleasure without there being a justified motive.

If one bites me, surely another person will kill it, not me. I have had the opportunity to see them up close and didn't fear them. One time (1) some boys were chasing a "hairy spider" and I stopped them from killing it. The keen spider crouched itself up against the wall and within a moment, when the boys made a noise, it ran and inserted itself into a hole that seemed made for just that. It was a hole drilled in the wall in the very door of the house. August 1, 1913.

This observation was made in Cuba, in Cárdenas, and I write about it now as I copy it from the original written in my notebook in Tampa, adding this to complement my proceedings.

In other eras public clocks would be in the palaces of kings and then in the churches. For centuries, it was the church that exhibited and showed us the time. Later, when people changed customs and privileges for other things because of revolutions, the clock marked the time in the union halls. Now in the factories, which have the appearance of palaces with their elegant towers that raise up to represent the dignity of labor, but it is where man is humiliated, where they exploit him, where he gets sick and from there goes to the hospital or to beg for alms.

Palaces, churches, city halls, and factories: kings, clergy, the representation of the people and the bourgeoisie.

Meanwhile twelve o'clock slowly sounds on a clock in one of the factories of Ybor City.

The mother who loves her children does not whip them; she guides them by depriving them from going out for walks or diversions.

Wrath is the mother of crime, daughter of ignorance. There are many crimes that are the children of calculation and this engenders misery.

There are well-dressed thieves that they call gentlemen and thieves dressed in rags that they call beggars. Some rob from the stock exchange and others from businesses; others pickpocket in the streets, plazas, or houses due to poverty or vagrancy, which the present social system engenders, while others speculate because of selfish ambition. The second ones mentioned are more admissible than the first.

To slander, envy, distrust, insult, bite, scratch one way or another, is that living? Hampering others, provoking, scheming in order to cause pain, lying to injure others or someone in particular, is that living?—No.

Being a man or a woman does not authorize someone to be vulgar, brutal; it is not to impose oneself or deceive. That is to be ignorant and cowardly.

Politics isn't for making laws that benefit the rich; it isn't for wasting public funds for private uses.

If politics is the art of governing the people, then to do the aforementioned actions is not the art of governing, it is simply an abuse, a way of living off public finances. To be a politician means not to be greedy or ambitious, just as being a Christian is not to hate one another, or offer Mass and charge for it, or baptize and do the same. These are simply rites invented in order to speculate in the name of Christianity.

Similarly when politicians and others see things done badly they say, that is the policy!

No! It is laziness, greed, ignorance, and speculation in the name of politics.

True politics would do the best thing in favor of the best, purest, and most honorable men and it would reform laws in order that a few men do not exploit the rest, which is the same as creating happiness for the people.

The same mistake exists in regards to anarchy. If someone throws a bomb, they are called anarchist; if there's an individual attack, it is an anarchist; if there is a robbery or an assault in the fields or streets, also anarchists. They do not say that it is poverty, that it is exploitation that causes it.

It is kind of them not to call bank and business embezzlers anarchists.

We are in advantageous times, like to be exposed or confused with the bandits of the political barricade, with the speculators of the stock exchange, the bank embezzlers and the street robbers, even though the latter are products of the others. Because we preach free love, within a short time any woman that goes off with a man will be an anarchist and any man going off with a girl, an anarchist. They are going to categorize us together with the depraved, the egotists, the money lenders, etc., etc.

A true anarchist would not utilize perverse means to cover his needs nor would he slander or insult another in order to usurp his well-being or to filch others' accomplishments, nor does he envy them.

If he sees a happily married couple, even if he is in love with the woman, he does not provoke a breakup in order to take advantage of it and satisfy a whim.

If they seem unhappy to him because only one is in love with the other or the husband mistreats the wife, then he must separate them without getting involved. For that reason anarchists do not like to use formulas. The ignorant believe that a simple formula binds individuals together; generally the woman, is more ignorant than the man, due to the fact that she does not have a concept of her freedom and her rights, and because of her education, which is a consequence of man's egotism, she believes that he should support her while she does not work. That is the way man has made laws and women do nothing more than uphold them, taking advantage of the salary of their slavery.

We progress and yet there are thousands of parents who believe they have the right to punish their children and impose their tastes and whims, and order them to obey without inquiring about their desires. They force their children to marry someone who pleases them, the parents, with no mind to the freedom of the individual. They allege that they worked a lot in order to raise them and educate them, but they should not do it to enslave their children, but rather they should guide them to work for their own sustenance without attempting to control their actions.

It is in the home where free men and women are created, starting with the parents reproving their own imperfections.

In order to create beautiful and good children, parents must be good and just because "beauty is a form of truth." If the parents are good, that is to say patient and tempered, then necessarily the children will be beautiful and good.

The day that borders are abolished, which is a form of egotism, when there is no other religion other than "Love one another:" when it becomes useless to say, "Love your enemies, bless those that curse you, and pray for them that despitefully use you and persecute you," because we will all be brothers and sisters. At that time, we will have perfected the way to securely close the distances between us. Then humans should remember the Master and where he was born and preached, and build a temple there unlike no other on the earth that can be an observatory and pulpit that searches heaven and earth, a museum of the arts and sciences in the memory of the just. His figure, painted in magnificent colors, should cause us to remember him with exactness. Let there be a gallery for those who preached and helped to illuminate the truth. In that way, we will pay homage to justice, which, as Renan says "No other person knew in his life how to submit his own love's pettiness to the interest of humanity" adding: "The idea of Jesus was the most revolutionary idea that the human mind ever could conceive."

Those who affirm that living again on this planet is not possible because they do not remember anything from their previous existence have a **case study in the following**:

"Philosophical Works," Diderot, p. 72

"Schulenburg, at 16 years old, had a violent concussion from a fall and had no memory for six weeks. He forgot all that he knew, returning to an infant-like state. They taught him how to read and write and even walk. Later he became a skillful artist and has made a mark in natural history."

Some would say that his case is not the same but it is. He that has died has slowly lost the capacities of perception and memory, and he with his fall destroyed it all of a sudden with odds in favor of a reincarnation. He who dies leaves his body, and he who received the blow did not leave his body. He has motives to remember that which he had learned and done, because he who sees himself obliged to change into another body, does not find another the same and this man found the same one upon awakening and must have thought: which of the two of them has more reason to remember? Do not argue with me that the spirit is the one that learns and because of that upon changing bodies it should not forget. He who suffered the fall without changing bodies forgot, but it was also the spirit that learned. Why did it forget?

The majority of men do not have character or intelligence; they are cruel, perverse, vain and indiscreet. I have had the occasion in an infinite number of cases to hear them in cafés and meetings questioning and criticizing, especially after the women who have been in the meeting have left. One time a woman forgot a letter and a very **obsessed** man took it, opened it, and read it. It was a love letter.

Later I had the opportunity to return to find the same young man in the street and together we walked to the post office. I mailed a letter and he requested one. They searched for his name and found the same name, only it lacked one syllable. The address was different and the writing was not familiar to him, but in doubt, he opened it.

He realized that it was for someone else, and he laughed very imprudently. It bothered me to see such weakness of character.

I could have lied and I didn't. I could have exploited the labor of others. I had the opportunity to habitually use jewels and luxury, and I was modest. I have had the opportunity and motives to avenge wrongs and slanders, to provoke envy and receive ovations, and I scorned some and forgave the others.

I have had and do have ways and motives to despise those who society judges inferior and I did not act on them. I never find sufficient motives to accuse or avenge insults—to me they all seem a result of ignorance.

Curiosity is what dominates the most in the world. Curious people are very annoying, imprudent and inopportune. All that curiosity is the result of ignorance and laziness.

There is scientific curiosity that ennobles and elevates and that leads to wisdom. There is another curiosity that only occupies itself finding out that which it shouldn't in order to criticize and lower the reputation of others. The first transforms into methodic and persistent observation and takes on the name of Science.

The second is transformed into gossip and degenerates into **slander or insult**.

Criticism is admissible and even interesting when it is employed to regenerate humanity, whether in private or public acts.

There are many who believe that meddling in issues that harm others who are weaker or younger, is occupying oneself with things that are of no importance.

One day a door-to-door milk wagon stopped in front of the Vegetarian Restaurant* where I was sitting out on the balcony. A child got out, opened the small door at the back of the wagon and tried to grab a large jug of milk. The jug was too heavy for him and upon grabbing it, he spilled a bit of milk on himself. The jug slipped to the ground with a consequent din but without spilling. Upon hearing the noise, the man in charge of the wagon leaned back and lifted his whip. He was going to let the boy have it. I yelled. "Why are you going to hit him if he can't carry the jug?" The man restrained himself but in less than three minutes he protested, mixing the language: "These are my **businesses!**" which is the same as saying "**It is none of your business.**" He repeated it two more times while looking at me. Meanwhile the boy entered the house where I was, barely holding onto the jug.

No one protested that event. Most people believe that it is very natural and even just and well done that a parent exploits their children and, furthermore, mistreats them. No one worries about warning the strong as to their duty with the weak. There is an animal protection society but what about the children, the elderly, the sick? They are mistreated,

---

*This happened in Tampa.

exploited and beaten, but no one says anything nor do they remember to protect them.

An interesting detail about equality between men and women is published in "Philosophical Works" by Diderot—when Miss L'Espinase says to Dr. Borden, that an extravagant idea has come to her as thinks that man is none other than the "monster of woman," or vice versa. Dr. Borden answers her: "This idea would have occurred to you earlier if you would have recalled that a woman has all the parts of man, except for an invaginated pouch; that a female fetus is almost confused for a male fetus; that the part causing the error begins to disappear in the female fetus as the interior pouch enlarges; that that part is always preserved in its first small form, being susceptible to the same voluptuous movements that its gland, its foreskin has and, in its extreme, there is an orifice to a urinary canal that has been closed."

This analysis is very interesting. Man developed his arrogance so much that he believed and still believes that all beings were created for his amusement and domination. He does not believe in progressive and intelligent continuation of creation, but rather thinks he is master and lord of it all, without laboring for his own progression and increasing even more his pride **"God extracted woman from one of his ribs,"** to affirm that woman even in the beginning was one of his parts, private property that he could enslave.

And the female gender of animals, from where was she extracted? Each female is the rib of the male of that species?

In accordance with the concept that man is an animal, that nature does not take more care of him, nor distinguishes him or separates him from the rest. In its seismic evolutions the lion has as much of a right to eat man as man does to kill the lion. In the same vein, then a horse is loaded down in order to carry man to eat, as man can load himself in order to feed the horse.

Both should be free.

The most revolutionary man and lover of liberty was he who invented motorized power to move himself and objects long distances, proclaiming freedom from the animals, the right to live without enslaving them.

TO AN UNCIVILIZED FRIEND

You have told me that those who write do not produce, that only those who plow the earth are producers. This is an erroneous understanding of the phrase. He who tills the soil, plants, and later, harvests. The only thing he does is cultivate. He is a helper; his special labor is to watch over the fruit in order that the crops are not lost. The artistic merit of an architectural work, for example, isn't found in he who builds it, but rather in he who conceives it. His usefulness is that he invented it, not that he made it.

He who builds a house makes something useful, but he does not create it, he builds it. Mother Nature creates and produces, and man uses her products. Here you will see the superiority of creative intelligence. This does not mean that the intellectual has more of a right to life or commodities, nor to being superior as a human being.

A tree gives forth fruit: it is a natural product of the tree, cultivated or not. A man or woman writes a book and it is the product of their intelligence. You don't want to call it a product? Then we will call it luminous details, radiations of light condensed in principles of wisdom, defined concepts of an idea, science, analysis, research, invention, discovery, observation, in its different forms and varieties. Is it not a product that defines a concept from a visible form of nature, divides it, classifies it and selects it? Yet it is more: it will be an inventor and he who invents, produces, he who plants has not invented the way to do it, nature has already done that, he did nothing more than imitate nature. I believe that the first person who produced and invented a book did not imitate it because he had not found any book, like a product from a tree on the earth. This neither denies nor refutes that nature is an open book for him who knows how to read it; and nature contributes to the formation of all the raw materials which are cotton, resin, and colored liquids from trees and plants. Paper and ink are not products of the farmer. They cultivate the raw material but do not **create** it, neither have they combined it to **create** paper and ink. These are products of intelligence.

It is not brute force that controls intelligence, however: intelligence is strength and light.

Poetry that provokes in you delight, loving ecstasy, mental abstraction is a product of a man or a woman. A book, through its critical details, philosophical concepts, scientific arguments, historic narration, or social descriptions causes you to meditate, acquaint, conceive, reflect and protest. Isn't it the product of study, observation and assimilation of life and the things that man or woman has done?

Then, you don't look at things as they are or for what they are worth, but rather for what they look like.

In that case, friend, you will be exposed to many mistakes, while beholding the very appropriate saying of Jesus: "In truth I tell you those who have eyes and do not see, those who have ears and do not hear."

You also said that you do not comprehend an anarchist-spiritualist, which I already wrote about in my previous book, **"My Opinion."**

In view of the eternity of the centuries, what is human suffering? Nothing . . . Faced with the immensity of the infinite and its everlasting eternity, what is human struggle? Smoke, dust, nothing . . . In view of the interminable succession of planetary systems in continuous and interminable splendid transformation through centuries and centuries, what are civilizations and the continuous invention of our race?

An insignificance . . . but grains of sand form the ocean beds and the dikes that kiss its waves or, in other words, beaches. . . .

October 22, 1914, Havana

It was a deformed tree that grew on the banks of the sea, from the root to the middle of the twisted trunk and from there to the treetop that wanted to be upright to receive direct solar caresses, lifting itself up in spite of its deformity.

Surely that tree suffered by not being able to display its elegance or corpulence with natural ease. Children would climb it and hang from it; lovers would sit to sweetly chat against its old trunk.

Every once in a while some little bird would rest on it, but all lamented the misery of the poor tree that with barely any branches and without leaves didn't offer shade or a cool breeze. Poor and sad tree, without branches, without leaves nor fruits to offer; what a most desolate condition, most ruinous in that splendid site in front of the sea and across from the line of cars where the travelers could contemplate the loneliness and orphanhood of the poor tree, deformed by human roughness.

Who would have been the first to rest his foot and mutilate its arrogance, obliging it to lose its litheness, bending it over the ground to convert it into a sterile skeleton?

The murmuring waves kissed and nourished its roots, but without being able to give back its gallantry, since its sap was not circulating through its vegetable tissues and core, it languished and the sun could not revive what the cruel hand of man had damaged and mutilated. Have mercy! Mercy for all living things of creation!

Tampa, 1913

It seems to me that I wouldn't be a complete woman if I weren't a mother. A complete woman should be a mother.

A perfect mother who breastfeeds her children and endures with patience without becoming upset at the **nonsense** of children without punishing them, mistreating them, or avenging on them the annoyances that their childish age provides. I say **nonsense** because that is what some ignorant people of both sexes have called children's protests. But they are not nonsense; they are natural expressions common to that age and one should allow the child to protest as such and to study their inclinations to recommend good ideas and noble practices to them, even though the best way to create good children is by the parents being good and experiencing the kindness that should be innate in them so that the children will inherit it. If the mother gets upset, it irritates her nervous system and the nervous system of her children. The mother and father should be moderate in all and be of good habits so that their children are the same.

I love the hymns of all countries. They are like a feeling produced or inspired by Mother Nature in each region of the globe. That is how I admire the landscapes of all climates and how I respect the customs of all people. I honor the memories of all ages, and I bless the relics of all families because all of these different details are felt and lived by the great human family and contribute to the sublime and inimitable universal harmony.

Ybor City, 1913

Two human beings see one another; they look each other up and down and whisper in their internal self, "Behold, my complement." They like each other, they unite, they fuse into one, without fears, without obstacles or evasiveness of any kind. Like waves they become confused, as a volcano that overflows and unleashes the abyss from which it spouts.

That is how I conceive of two united as one with the beautiful reproduction that perpetuates the memory of that unleashing of natural powers within an individual.

Could there be greater wealth, quality, honors, or glory lovelier than the satisfaction of two souls that fuse into one, of two that freely search for each other and complete each other? There isn't greater happiness than that of loving and being loved; or greater martyrdom, or hell more terrible than not to attain the love dreamed of, the love searched for.

No doctrine can be against two souls that attract each other, two bodies that search for each other because they desire one another in the freest form of love's manifestation, until they tire of one another or become confused without fear of time or old age, or anything, since nothing will perturb the spontaneous union of race and beautiful truth that comes from free love.

In nature, nothing is orphaned, or alone, or abandoned, or in perpetual wandering. The atoms and molecules unite due to an affinity to form bodies, sound unites to form sublime harmony, light forms itself in indefinite lines, water agglomerates in millions of distinct particles that condense into clouds. "Love, like life, is eternal without possible end!"

Love! . . .

Irradiations of light that illuminate consciences; vibrations of universal life that encompass all forms; undulations of breeze that distributes the aroma of flowers, perfuming the surroundings and carrying the fertile pollen of plant reproduction into the jungle and the forests, the fields and the gardens.

The law of action that governs individuals and bodies, that impulses intelligence and matter, the constant and perpetual selection of all the beings of creation to indefinite perfection. Life in its diverse and various manifestations governed by love . . .

Tampa, June 26, 1913

FRAGMENTS OF A LETTER

Now, with respect to what you are telling me, that you only want to be my friend . . . I will tell you, you write that now, but the first time that you had an opportunity to talk to me in Palmetto, your intention, which I do not censure, I understood that it was the same as how we feel when we find a nice flower and we want to smell its fragrance even though we will never know its name or ever find it again. There is nothing strange in that. It was a very natural desire and I would have given in to it if it were not for the diverse circumstances that surround me. My aspirations were also influencing my feelings to impede that I detoured from my intention, which is to not waste my mental energies or perturb my astral tranquillity that is found precisely in the self-control of the material body. In other words: sexual reserve to assay mental strength.

One cannot possess mental fortitude or make it powerful if the material body is like a weathervane that sways according to which way the wind blows.

Do I explain myself? Your friend? Have I stopped being that perhaps? Has my affectionate and expansive temperament and my sweet and patient character, in spite of my activity and energy, caused some to dream of some material delights? I don't doubt it, nor does it surprise me because those individuals, even though they remain mistaken, believe that one cannot be affectionate outside of carnal possession.

But I do not have the right to judge those individuals, only to be careful not to be caught unawares by them, since I am on a superior plane.

In spite of my vigilance and in one of those naiveties, they catch me unawares and recognize my indifference after the shock. It is natural and demonstrates my good faith. If I abstain, it is not because of egotism or to cause pain, or to create it unnecessarily, but when it is done very purposefully to others, and I see myself backed into a corner, I have given up my weapons without rancor or arrogance. But I avoid provoking those wars in order not to leave dying on the battlefield my mental reasons and energies. What do you wish? What do you propose? That I be your friend? With sincerity I am.

P.S. I reread your letter, and you say that you are an admirer of my theories, but they are also practiced! What happens is that it is not possible to please the whole world, nor has everyone found themselves in the situation I described, but do you believe, perhaps, that I am only going to think about pleasing those that do not understand me? And, furthermore, not admitting it, because it would become a business to be bought and sold and there are enough of them on the market. To descend the risky mountain that I am on would be to confuse me without a justifiable motive of merchandise. Do you believe that I should descend? When I am at the inaccessible summit of the idea? And very close to undertaking the journey, to enter the path of wisdom!

Let me go to it. Help me if you can and want, in order that the journey not trip my feet with the thistles of the path . . . .

Meanwhile, know that I am your dedicated friend and defender of
truth and justice.

June 26, 1913, Ybor City

How beautiful Spain must be! . . . and how I desire to see it!

This exclamation leaped from my soul, and my lips pronounced it
with such slowness upon repeating it again, is to taste the desire to see
it and to sleep under the shade of the orange trees that would perfume
the delicious breeze. E. Sá del Rey in his quick description of Córdova,

> You have made me dream
> of that lovely Spain
> that one cannot forget.
>
> Of which in our veins
> runs Hagarian blood.
>
> May her triumphs and glories
> stay in our memories.

July 8, 1913, Ybor City

Have you observed a flower as it slowly closes its petals, carefully
guarding its fecund pollen in order to transform itself into delicious
fruit? Oh magical nature!

What enormous effort I must make in order not to cry! . . .

Each time that tears come to my eyes, I impose my will like a
supreme command to my emotion to detain them I must not remember!
Heart, you should not beat! Thoughts, stop your activity! Feelings flee,
drown yourself in the emptiness! My soul, soar to other regions and do
not worry about the miseries of this earth!

Soar! Soar! And soaring, where will you go? There, where the fruits
of my lost love are!

There in that region surrounded by water, where one hears the continual surf of the Atlantic Ocean, in the tranquil rocky prominence of the

palm trees where the soft and fragranced breeze from the boriquen jungle kisses my children's faces and the ardent, and beautiful tropical sun bronzes their skin.

Swarm and stir thought, search for a way out, drown my tears that struggle to gush out. Soar even farther, traverse the air, the heavy atmosphere, rise even more, reach the sidereal spaces, search for an ideal world, imagine it formed from thousands of thoughts that those thoughts have colors, sounds, light, millions of lights, mixed with different colors and diverse sound. What delightful harmony one would hear!

The wound of my soul is more powerful than you. Return again, nostalgia of love! It takes control of me, saddens me, shakes me, squeezes my heart, suffocates me, smothers me! . . .

Duty forces me to subdue my pain, to fight, to smile, to work . . .

One day my concentration was thinking of a monologue that I had written and wanted to recite for the benefit of a friend, that I took the pen to button my **polacas** (as they are called in Cuba) and when I realized it, I laughed marveling that my concentration could carry me to what could be called a distraction.

July 11, 1913, Ybor City

That white ghost watched over the northern city. The silver dome of the small tower of the Jesuit fathers' church, in spite of the night shadows, stood out from the rest of the homes with its fantastic aspect of nocturnal vigilance, mute, with an eloquent silence, and its cross atop the cupola challenging, with its twenty centuries, the inclemency of time and the incredulousness of new generations.

Christ! Christ! Who could forget thee after having lived among millions of generations during twenty centuries! Who could be indifferent to whom thy maxims, thy sufferings, and death would not have moved with emotion! We do not need them to occupy themselves perpetuating thy memory; thy figure is in our minds and in our hearts thy examples. Per chance are those churches necessary?

They are useless. They continue empty in those great cities in which thousands of unfortunate ones sleep in doorways, public benches on the riverbanks, in the ships or freight cars detained at the docks . . .

Meanwhile the dome stands defiant, shining its white and elegant figure, reflecting its silver finish in the pale light of the electric bulbs that scarcely illuminate due to their height above the houses.

THE TWO CAGES

We fear freedom. We run from it as if it were a disease, even though we desire it. This caused me to contemplate an American movie—remembering human affairs and whims—that detailed with eloquent silence the life of a princess, the only daughter of a king who wanted to marry her off as he pleased, according to tradition. One day he enters her room to tell her that the next day her wedding will be announced and that she needed to present herself to the court in order that they could greet her. She receives the order disgusted and sad, because she does not know who her future husband is, she does not know him, she then presents herself in the throne room so that her father can introduce her and announce the wedding.

She returns to her rooms and goes to greet her small bird: she compares herself to the poor encaged bird. She and her lady-in-waiting go out for a drive in her car. They travel through a nearby open field. Upon passing by a cultivated terrain, she sees a man stooped over working the earth. She feels attracted to that figure and continues watching until the car drives away from that place, and she sees other landscapes. She meets a married couple who come out of the village church; they are peasants with their usual clothing. The automobile pauses and the retinue approaches the princess who entertained the couple and gave a gold coin to the newlywed bride.

They return, and alone in her room she greets her small bird and decides to dress herself like a villager and compare herself and the little bird to two prisoners that should free themselves. She grabs the little bird and throws it into the air and out the window. She goes off to the open field with the idea of meeting the field hand.

She leaves, meets a poor man whom she helps, and continues along until she pauses in front of the fence where the man was working. She called out, and the young man dropped his labor tools and approached the fence where the young woman was resting. They talk and her expression shows she is hearing affectionate phrases. The young woman does not answer; she remains with her head down. The provocative, seductive field hand suddenly embraces the young woman and kisses her lips. The girl, scared, resists, struggles, loosens herself from the arms that bind her, and flees.

She travels across the open field alone and returns to the palace in whose garden she pauses. Looking on all sides and walking slowly, she finds the poor little bird on the grass. She looks up and sees that it couldn't fly and remained in the same spot where it had fallen. As she returns to her prison, she picks up the tiny bird, kisses it and silently goes up into the regal castle and places the small bird in its cage. Her chambermaid approaches to disrobe her from her villager clothing. Meanwhile the promised prince arrives at the palace, enters the throne room with his retinue, greets the king, and waits. A lady leaves the throne room and approaches the princess and announces that the prince and her father are waiting for her. The princess puts on her royal cloak and prepares herself to leave. She walks through the covered balcony that separates her from the throne room, appears coming down the stairs, and then climbs the steps to the throne. She bows her head in front of her father and waits. The young man approaches and places himself in front of her in an identical stance. The king unites their hands and blesses them while the court applauds, thus ending the ceremony.

She leaves for her room and says to her little bird: "Both of us have returned to the cage, as freedom bothers us."

The kiss that she received freely in the open field scared her. The little bird accustomed to finding its food in the cage felt too weak to look for it, became scared upon seeing the immense open field, and remained in the spot where it fell. She was in search of freedom, and the kiss, without preambles or formulas, scared her and she returned to obtain it through rites and social fulfillment. She was in search of love and liberty, and the clash between that and slavery was cruel. Habit, the elder daughter of slavery, triumphed.

After daily and detailed observations, it was affirmed that earthly beings modify themselves and change their appearance according to their nourishment, climate, and lifestyle.

Out in the countrysides of America in West Tampa, I observed plants and animals. As if one lone mold could have been the origin of all things. Without a doubt I firmly believe that the human race does not have the right to imprison other living beings of creation that they suppose are under their dominion.

March 22, 1914, Havana

I speak with perfect understanding of that which I say, with a profound intuition that guides me. I have not been able to study anything according to the policies of schools, universities, or halls of higher learning because my parents never sent me to them. My father had the saintly patience to teach me to read, to write, and to know the four rules of arithmetic. Later, I arrived at a school directed by an island professor, Dr. María Sierra de Soler I was awarded various diplomas after she examined me on the subjects of grammar, sacred history, geography, reading, etc. Now I have introduced myself as a propagandist, journalist, and writer, without any authorization other than my own vocation and initiative, without any recommendation other than my own, or any help other than my own effort. I care little about the criticism from those who have been able to procure a formal education that allows them to present their better written observations, protests, or literary narrations. I gladly welcome them and savor their exact expression and I excuse them when they are ordinary.

Literature is irresistibly attractive to me, for my writing is the most enjoyable occupation. It is what most entertains me: it is what most adapts to my temperament, so then I feel obliged to cultivate this art and perfect myself at it, not to covet praise or recognition, or to become rich or establish distinctions. My only intention, the only motive that has propelled me to write, apart from the delight that it affords me, has been to speak the truth, to point out the uselessness of certain customs deeply rooted in religious teaching that have been converted into a traditional imposition; to remember that natural laws should be obeyed in preference to all other legislation and, as a consequence, reform the mistaken concepts that exist about morals, human rights, and equality, trying to make humanity happy and providing the easy means for its quick and certain fulfillment.

Why call George Sand **indecent** in the publicity for her books? I protest such a qualifier. It is incorrect to adjudicate such a cultured and intelligent woman. It is unworthy of educated people.

How can women who are on higher moral ground than men be called "prostitutes" and "depraved"?

I see queens, empresses, intelligent women who ask for vindication because their conduct and behavior have been exaggerated in an abusive manner. Why accuse a free woman like Ann Boleyn of being a prostitute and others whose names I will not mention because they still have relatives living?

Historians have had no other motive for exaggerating the conduct of women from other eras except for the preponderance of men who have been the legislators, historians, and cultivators of all the sciences, arts, literature.

They are accustomed to exaggerated flatteries among themselves in order to exalt and elevate their reputations, yet with indifference toward cultured, free, educated women, believing that these women are inferior and incapable of producing any sort of original intellectual work.

I refuse to accept as depraved or perverse any woman conceptualized as such by any historian who erroneously believes that women do not have the right to use their complete freedom without being perceived as depraved, frivolous, etc., while men have been able to do and attain whatever they want, to concoct the most absurd and ridiculous whims without being judged negatively, scorned, or prohibited from entering any place they choose without fear of not being attended to, respected or sought after. We will put an end to the unfairly applied law to secure tranquillity for the just and to pay tribute to the truth and justice that our sex deserves.

March 22, 1914

VISIONS

I suddenly heard a noise, like an immense roar of an agitated crowd far off in the distance. . . .

In reality, there was not any sort of disturbance where I was that could justify such a perception, but I heard it clearly and distinctly, and in that moment the memories of the French Revolution came to my mind; as if I could see the convulsive multitudes pass by in a formidable roar, crossing Rivoli Street on their way to the Bastille . . . Ah! How lovely was that moment! . . . but how painful for me when I remembered in successive visions the crying of that poor child, mistreated by Simon . . . Poor Simon, how that must weigh on his soul now! What fault did that poor child, that weak creature have? . . . even his parents were innocent. His only fault, the grave error of tradition! . . . Oh, people! Multitudes become agitated, demanding justice that they have yet to know! . . . Demand it! Demand your rights, impose them if you want, but respect the weak, the innocent, who are only guilty of having received a misguided education. Try to destroy power, but not people. You have no right to suppress lives that you have not created. Violence can never be the mother of freedom, only its stepmother.

Education is the mother of liberty; science, her eldest daughter, and her sisters, tolerance and prudence with rights and responsibilities.

August 26, 1912, New York

I saw a great lion that was running quickly through the green and lovely field, adorned by a limpid atmosphere irradiated by the sun's rays. The lion wore a crown dyed in blood and blackened by the flame of the bonfire. Because of its heaviness, the crown tilted and slipped from the beast's lovely head and into a steep precipice. The crown tumbled down into the unfathomable abyss, precipitated by a movement that made the lion stagger.

The lion, surprised to find himself without the heavy, massive circle, shook his long mane and inhaled strongly, making the mountains and the plain tremble with his roar. He climbed onto a rock. He displayed himself majestically and arrogantly, challenged the sun king with his mane, and licked his round and shiny haunches. The lion had broken the tradition that obliged him to wear the crown and . . .

I saw an eagle that, while soaring up into flight, crossed the sky displaying very proudly the imperial crown. A cloud appears, formed by a whirlwind of bullets from a city. It stuns the eagle who becomes enveloped in it and falls wounded by the bullet. Upon falling, the crown tumbles off and smacks and breaks and is soiled, and the dying eagle is taken to a palace.

This eagle's wound heals, but she will leave without her crown. It is the imperial eagle of Germany.

I saw a beautiful eagle standing on a rock contemplating the precious panorama of the city of Moscow. The eagle descends, is imprisoned, and taken to a cell by armed henchmen.

An immense cloud covers the city. The bullets cross and the eagle dies.

It is the Russian imperial eagle.

Another popular emblem emerges, and the land is partitioned or divided.

I have never used carriages of state or displayed diamonds, or lived in palaces, or worn silks and tinsels, or dazzled the poor with the insulting luxury of jewels and excess. I despised honors, rejected privileges, did not pay attention to flatteries nor accepted supplications. This in plain abundance, and, without having studied the social issue, I believed that everyone in the whole world had the right to be clean, to have shoes and I did not understand why they did not. I figured that they all knew how to read and write, and it astonished me when I became aware of the contrary. Ignorance, mistress and madam of the world, imprisons people's souls and their conscience. Unfathomable abyss whose door was the Church that has marked with its seal the generation of twenty centuries! I protested that reviled mark, because I was not a slave. I did not carry my children to the infected baptismal font. I protested, I screamed, I went hoarse asking for justice for the poor when I understood their pains, through the streets and plazas, roads and villages, cities and towns. I proceeded according to the innate ideas in my soul, which were visible in my character. I was impartially generous, I forgot the affronts, I forgave the calumnies, I gave more than I could when there was not enough even for me. I dried the tears, comforted afflictions, I spoke of joy among the sadness. I gave in abundance my soul, my body, my thoughts, my ideals, my attentions, my knowledge. I was persevering in struggle and calm in misfortune. Never did I hate or speak badly of my neighbor, nor speak slanders of my adversaries, nor have I exploited anyone for personal gain. My soul is diaphanous and my consciousness shines. Never have I wallowed in vices, I was always tempered in my protests.

A stoic woman in life. Neither does pleasure drive me mad, nor pain kills me. Even so I believe that I am very imperfect, but, as a result, others more imperfect criticize me.

I have observed contempt, I have seen mockery, I have listened to slander, I have tasted calumnies, I have received betrayals, and even these I have helped and forgiven. I have felt the kiss of Judas on my face. The only thing is that I have not paid tribute to the social formulas that have always seemed ridiculous and hypocritical to me; and in fact they are.

Now then, after having been slandered, insulted, mocked, scorned, and betrayed, they want to put obstacles in my ascending path, placing in my way a stone, a lie, not knowing that the eagle would be bothered by the reptile. But what I did not know was that the reptile, instead of crawling, flew: the only way such boldness is understood. But it is useless insistence. With the movement of the eagle crossing the heavens, he lets loose a stone and crushes the reptile that coils between the destroyed thicket, without name and without funeral. Meanwhile the eagle travels across the sky to settle on another rock and is able to look at the sun face to face.

It rains, and the poor reptile rolls with the impulses of the stream descending from the mountain and piece by piece it falls into the abyss at the foot of the mountain and tumbles to the bottom. But it does not disappear. Soon a strange, sinister flower emerges, surrounded by sharp thorns. Envy was its mother, she is hatred and engenders betrayal. But the eagle will not go there: other reptiles will poison and wound themselves with thorns. He who sows evil, reaps evil.

Because ignorance is the origin of all evil.

We should, then, contribute so that all are enlightened and that no one becomes a victim of their ignorance.

So now after long years of absence, I ask, what damage did I do? What have I done in order that they harass me with such cruelty? Show me the wounds that I have inflicted, tell me the insults that I have pronounced, repeat to me the slanders that I have hurled, point out to me the misery that I have engendered; accuse me of the pains that I have produced; pronounce the lies that I have uttered and predicated. Tally the victims that I have caused. Where? When?

What then do you want? That another Christ ascend to Calvary and die between two wretched men? To redeem who? Humanity? It is useless because there is not a redeemer nor redeemed? In that manner, there is only one victim and the tears from an ignorant people. And you do not need redeemers, you yourselves can be them, without a victim that sheds its blood in order that it fall on your generations. Search for the truth, do not worship anyone, explore Mother Nature, study her effects, and you will see the cause. We are Gods and sinners. Let us endeavor to be gods and the sinners will disappear.

Do you understand this? Let us be gods and not accept superiority of any kind. In this way sinners will disappear along with the weak and cowardly; only studious and valiant individuals will remain.

When you no longer feel the nostalgia for borders and only long for infinity, when you never utter a lie, when the fear of the unknown does not intimidate you, when you scorn the calumnies, when you consecrate yourself to study and to good, you will resemble terrestrial gods, but we will ascend to heavenly gods. It is a question of time and patience. So then, yes, I have had the courage to show my weakness, and later, through patience and study to make myself free. What do you have to reproach me? Are you my judges? There is no other judge than the conscience: it is uncompromising and honest. If I have done any evil, it has been to myself, through generosity. And generosity is not a crime, unless humanity has invented new laws. With what right? It could be with the right of perfection, the superiority acquired by perfection. And perfection is everything, heaven and earth, abyss and mountains, wisdom and love. Do you know why? Because wisdom began its journey in the atom and it is in the abysses as on the mountain peaks, it trembles the waves of the ocean as it shines in the sun's rays, it stirs in the aurora borealis as it lives in the shadows of the night, it bustles in the calyx of the flowers and crosses the sky on the wings of the breeze. It is perfume and it is poison. It is in fire and in snow. He who has passed through all these stages necessarily must be wise, just, and powerful.

Who in mankind finds themselves in those conditions in which to judge me? Who is perfect in order that he judge me? Who is superior here that he might humble me?

Space is infinite, it is superior, I have studied it. The storm is powerful and I have defied it. The abyss is dark, and I have not feared it. The sea is dangerous, and I have crossed it.

If the strength of the unknown will, dazzling with power, did not fear to give me a spark of its intelligence, without daring to judge me outside of myself, then who are you who pretends to penetrate the interior of my conscience filled with justice? Do you not see that you can blind yourself if you penetrate into the sacred confines where the fire of my ideals is fueled? Do you not understand that the owls do not need light, that they cannot go in front of the sun. And the sun is beauty and beauty, truth. Do not examine other souls, study your own, do not try to correct others before having corrected yourselves, and afterward you will not need to correct, only teach.

Why waste time in useless things that will not benefit us? You are foolish. Leave others alone and correct yourselves, that if you do as such, there will not be as many ignorant persons in the world.

August 13, 1912, New York

I . . .

(To the artist Manual García, San Juan.)

I am a misunderstood woman.

I believe I have the right to enjoy all that is created by Mother Nature, all that is invented by man in art, industry, mechanics, astronomy, etc. and to observe all that has been discovered by scientists.

But I only use that which is necessary and almost always scorn that which is superfluous. Selfless to a fault. Indifferent before vanity, the spectacle of extravagance and riches.

Sometimes, in order that they do not forget that I possess an artist's soul, like most women, I dress up, but without ostentation. And if I were not such an anarchist, that is to say, such a "Christian," I would dress splendidly, with true art, and with exquisite taste; but, the unfortunate who lack all necessities? The hungry and the naked? . . . What cruelty! What sarcasm! We are all brothers, although some die of hunger and others foolishly squander their excess, and each day some new extravagance is invented. Meanwhile what is useful, what is necessary rots in the depots and warehouses of foodstuffs, clothing, and shoes, while so many go hungry, naked and barefoot!

I am helpless to remedy so much misery!

Oh! The problem of extreme poverty is my great concern.

Meanwhile, this madwoman proclaims equal rights for all, human brotherhood, the abolition of laws and governments.

Difficult things!

Instead of prisons, let's have schools, art, and vocational colleges; free trade, free love, the abolition of marriage, the substitution of private property for public property.

An endless amount of **nonsense** is imposed! And the next era is demanding it, and it is soon approaching.

In spite of all this frankness, I have not been understood, but instead, slandered, and misinterpreted . . .

THE OPINION OF MANY MEN AND MY OPINION

Women should be women! Women's work is in the home! They shouldn't be macho! Mend stockings and underwear! Doze by the heartwarming fire knitting socks! Who asks for their opinion, or to become involved in politics, or to aspire to be an elected candidate? This cannot be tolerated! Haven't we already permitted them to enter the lecture halls to become lawyers and doctors? But they are not satisfied: now they want to be judges, mayors, chiefs of police, legislators. Is that why we have allowed them to study, so they can cast us aside, aspiring to monopolize our positions and desiring to surpass us? I do not know how these women forget their weakness and their indiscretion; one cannot trust them at all or teach them anything because immediately they want to take over. But how can a woman imitate a man? She can't, she's inferior! Even Mother Nature condemns her to seclusion during childbirth and breast-feeding!

The majority of men express themselves in this way, and this is what they think women deserve. The men forget about their wives, their mothers, and their daughters.

But do not fear that all is lost or that these discussions will disturb the placidity of the home. A woman does not stop being a woman because she engages in politics or expresses her opinion, or because she becomes a legislator or detective. A woman will always be a woman, whether she is a good or bad mother, whether she has a husband or a lover. She is a woman, and being a woman is not only being powdered and covered in ribbons and lace. Just as he who belongs to the male sex does not stop being a man upon learning to cook, mend, sweep, and sew. Many men do that!

Women do not pretend to be superior to men, at least that is not their intention nor the objective of their aspirations. They will, however, surpass men by their conduct and through the fulfillment of their duties.

The immense majority of women does not smoke or get drunk. And this is one of the conditions that will make them superior in all branches of human knowledge. So it is not the intention of women to imitate men, especially not in their faults, but perhaps in their strengths and good habits. A few days ago I read of a young woman who solicited the job of a stoker in a steamboat, and later the boss said, "She does a better job and furthermore, she doesn't drink whiskey." This makes one suppose that in the future, women will be preferred and men will have to abandon their vices in order to obtain employment. And this will benefit the human race. Women are preferred for nursing, inasmuch as men are not able nor are they of use for that. Women will be preferred as medical doctors because of their values and good faith, since they will heal through love and because they cannot bear to see suffering. Women will be preferred as lawyers because of their strength of understanding and persuasion. They will be preferred as legislators because their laws will correct the abuses against the unfortunate workers and the disinherited. Women will be preferred in politics because they will not sell themselves and will fulfill their promises. All this in general terms, with few exceptions. Women will not invade the gambling halls, nor will drunkenness cause them to mistreat their husbands and children. Women do not want to invade men's terrain to acquire his vices and abuses; a woman will always be a mother even if she has no children.

She will strive to correct all that might harm future generations.

Women will not be warriors, even though they know how to die like any brave soldier. If instead of it being men who have enjoyed all the advantages up until now, it would have been women. Genius warriors like Napoleon and Alexander would still have emerged, even though they would be named Lucrecia, Cleopatra, or Semiramis. But our era was decadent: now it begins. From a few centuries ago up until now, the social system has not changed, but it is probable that we may see it. Even in spite of our slavery we had Joan of Arc, Augustine of Aragon and many others.

In science we have Madame Curie and Hypatia. In law, Conception Arenal and others. In medicine many are beginning. In the legal profession we have an infinite number and several other in literature. In all of the branches of human knowledge we have women. And in architecture we should not forget who ordered the construction of the magnificent chalets and the famous floating gardens of Babylonia; it was Semiramis, empress of Egypt that completely changed the style of that era. The same in France with Diane of Poiters, Madame Du Barry, and others, as it happened in music and in poetry.

In painting we should not forget that man is inspired by Venus, and women do not have that resource: they do not like to be inspired by themselves, first, because she would draw a woman badly, perhaps out of a spirit of rivalry. Just as there haven't been male Saint Teresas or Mary Magdalenes. Female imitators of Jesus exist. In chemical combinations there are many female fans. What women should procure is to surpass men in their conduct, in their procedures. To be master of themselves, beginning by acknowledging their faults and weaknesses in order to correct them, and in that way to better the human race. By not stopping being a mother, and to be a mother is to breast-feed her children and care for them until they can walk. If there were a procedure that improved upon physical lactation (and it is certain that it will be attained), only then would we not recommend maternal breast-feeding. But we will accomplish it. This is not at odds with that.

TO VARGAS VILA

Oh Poet writer!:

You write: "This lover of the night who dreams of the fortunate ruins of his heart. He no longer feels the need for caresses and he is dead to the shameful beggary of kisses." Solitude, the only dispensary of caresses without baseness has put him to sleep with hers, and her lips **without lust**—I should say without desire—killed in his lips the torpid thirst of another's kisses and divested of love, the solitaire freely enters into the world of flight, leaving life behind, like a chrysalis in pieces, "free, like the stars and the winds."

"In the shadows too far away from Life, memories sing the song of triumphed pains—all of this, how much she must have suffered, and how much she loved your strong and sincere soul! And when returning to mention Amiel, you write, "Was it that he was never moved, before the luminous and ecstatic clay that is the body of a woman?"

Have you wished to say **aesthetic** or **ecstatic**? The first is beauty and the second is frigidity, impassiveness, imbecility. Whichever way you want to say it, you say it correctly—everyone has their way of saying things, the essential thing is to understand it—since there are very imbecilic women, others who are cold or perverse.

You have delighted your soul in the contemplation of some feminine beauty. You did not find yours, your soul's twin. Ah! and how you must have suffered if you found someone and she did not understand you.

When you refer to Nietzsche, you write, "and he did not display a mistress as an appendix and he did not desire the women of others, scorning to seduce them: they will tell you that he didn't love love, or woman and they will tell you worse things too" and in all you portray your soul, your temperament and character.

Oh! I am struggling to enter into that solitude that you adore. I am in continuous rebellion with my burning and passionate temperament for the man that I love. I understand absolute love, and they do not understand me! . . . I desire to live in all and for all for the person whom I love and that he live for me; they call that selfishness in a woman but not in a man. Life's injustices; how my soul cries savoring the paragraphs of "Voluptuous Sadness," and how I delight in this distance from the world and its things, rereading your beautiful poetic prose: having a premonition that someday I will say, like you in "my memoirs." "Leave me in the topaz of the afternoon to undo my rosary of memories, and revive the pensive roses that adorned my gardens in another time"; "it is beautiful, in the serene twilight, tremendous of that of the Past, to rise like a mountain in the Silence."

I, like you, desire to quench the thirst of my lips; you must have already calmed, tamed yours; but not yet I. I am in the agony of love. If

I do not manage to make my dream tangible, I will seal my soul to love. I will silence my eyes and my lips to the voluptuousness of love, and the passion will not return to roar like a tempest in my bosom. The silence and the forgetfulness will take custody of a living sepulcher, dragging a soul in pain that sinned because of having loved so much . . . and I will wander like a specter through the solitary places of my soul, behind the footprint of a memory, to light a candle to Cupid as they do for the dead. While you travel over that desert of sad things already dead, tears will pour out of my eyes, the last one like a crystalline shroud with which one covers the dead; and my living ghost, like a soul in pain that revives warm memories; its bitterness will slip away between the murmur of the kisses that echo fleetingly in the garden of remembrance, and the patient gardener woman, who cultivated those lilies with such care and meticulousness, will gather them up, wilted from the coldness of forgetfulness, and plant them in her bosom, as vestiges of days and sweet hours of torment of the one who, loving so much, so much, is only left with the memory. Ah! gone, brief hours of joy never forgotten; lilies of my loves, wilted by insipidity; my sad and happy songs, smothered by my regrets; now I cannot even cry, I can't even sing; I need to be insensitive to the pains of my love.

I am always opposed and opposing in the desires that my poetic mind conceived and longs to realize, for the satisfaction of its internal romantic esthetic.

Now I understand the love of Saint Teresa for Jesus, and how could she not feel it if it was great, beautiful, good, just, and holy? If she looked for it on earth, it was possible that it wouldn't be found; it was so great and so good that instead of being offended by the love of Magdalene, Jesus gave it to her. He gave her the mysterious innocence of his soul and of his body . . . I want to imagine how he would embrace that "sinner," that virginal, tranquil, and revered body in which the tempestuous waves of passion had not splashed upon the impeccable face of the just one, and where he would, with holy innocence, give in to the fervent caresses of his loving lover and faithful disciple.

Virtues 32, Havana

An automobile passes by. The driver observes a woman walking down the street. He pauses and asks her, "Where are you going?"

"To 25th Street and 14th Avenue," she says.

They are friends who know each other.

"Would you like me to take you to where you are going?"

"Fine, take me."

The woman gets in and the automobile disappears. They arrive.

"Thank you, see you later."

"Don't go so soon. You know if it were up to me, I would keep you by my side and I would have taken you . . ."

"Where?"

"To my house."

"For what?"

"To have you very close," he says.

"And later?"

"Well, later, as always, I would be devoted at your feet."

"I mean, when, after I go to your house?"

"Well, stay however long you wish. I live alone. If you'd like stay a month, until you get tired . . . if you want less, well then less."

"When do you want me to go?"

"Whenever you want? When can you go?"

"Tomorrow . . ." she says indecisive.

"Well then tomorrow. At what time?"

"In the morning."

"As you wish. I'll escape from the office, I'll come to get you, and I'll take you, just as if you were in your house. You can have what you need."

"At 9:00, in front of the Cuban Club."

"Very well. Listen, explain that to me again."

"Yes, that it not be out of habit, but desire. When that ends, then . . . the attraction goes away."

"You mean while we like each other?"

"Of course, when you don't like me anymore, you leave."

"And if I like you more than you like me?"

"I doubt it, but we'll try it. In any case, we'll have our friendship, and we'll resort to that when we see love in danger . . . do you agree?"

"Yes, but what will friendship do?"

"Well, it will establish the courtesy, the consideration, so that we won't fight if we don't like each other . . ."

"Now I understand. Very well, very clever, so until tomorrow—good-bye."

The young man leaves in his automobile, and the young woman enters her house.

The Next Day

Two busybodies.

"What is Elena doing on that corner?" asks one.

"Is she waiting for someone?" responds the other.

"Let's wait."

An automobile arrives, the chauffeur greets her, and Elena approaches him.

"Are you ready?"

"Yes."

"Well, get in."

He opens the small door, and they drive off.

"Didn't I tell you we should wait?"

"I figured that she was waiting for someone, but why should we care?"

"Well, to know what kind of women he deals with . . ."

"And why worry about that?"

"Well, to know what she does, so that they don't come pretending they are something they're not."

"What can she pretend?"

"That she's never known a man."

"And is it a bad thing to know a man?"

"Yes, because they deny it. Why do they do that?"

"They deny it because we would like to demand that they don't meet. But is it a crime that that young woman goes for a ride with her friend?"

"They're not going for a ride."

"And what are they going to do?"

"To be alone, some place . . . "

"And is that a crime? What wrong is there in that? Do they like each other? Well, they meet and withdraw from sight to prevent others from envying their joy. What is more natural and lovely than two people expressing and showing that they like each other?"

"And afterward, that young woman will seek another man to make her his wife?"

"But we can do whatever pleases us and women cannot?"

"That's because we are responsible for our actions."

"And they are not? Valiant argument! That is to say that a woman cannot go where she pleases and be responsible for what she does?"

"And later she will want to be another man's woman?"

"But do they make any objection because we have been with not only one, but rather many women?"

"Not them, because they don't risk anything."

"And what do we risk?"

"Our money."

"Man, what a remark! But those two that have lived together, are they in danger of losing something?"

"Not them, but what about me? If I had wanted that woman, after she had been with another man?"

"And we can go with whomever and wherever and they cannot?"

"We don't lose money or even honor."

"And the woman loses with whomever she goes?"

"No, because she doesn't belong to anyone."

"But what about us? Even after having a woman, do we not do the same? What do we lose?"

"Nothing, because we are the ones that pay and work."

"Well, in the same way, the woman will proceed. She will work."

"Well then, she will not marry."

"Why not?"

"How! And who will take care of her?"

"Her job. Or is it that you figure that what she earns is yours also, as a right that weighed over the slaves in times past?"

"And the children, who takes responsibility for them?"

"Those that made them. Is it not both of them? They belong to them both, except during the time of lactation."

"Fine, but I don't agree. I want a woman for only me."

"Yes, while you like her and she likes you and you alone."

"But I don't want her to have been with other men before me."

"But if she were to demand the same of you, that you have not been with other women before?"

"She cannot demand that, because it is a need . . ."

"Well, precisely because it is a need. She too has the right to satisfy it."

"But I lose nothing."

"Nor does she. She fulfills a natural law. What bad can there be with two people that like each other and express it alone between them?"

"I am not willing to have woman deceive me."

"But we are the ones who deceive ourselves."

"But we are the ones that work . . ."

"They work, too. Do you have no other argument with which to defend yourself?"

"Yes, they should be content that the man works for them."

"But they're not. They want to be free and equal, before nature, friend. I'm leaving. I see that you represent tyranny against women. Until another day, good-bye, liberator."

While those two were arguing, Elena and Andrés arrived at a lovely villa, simple but comfortable, surrounded by a small forest of pine trees and climbing vines. There were flowers and birds. Elena stepped out and Andrés said to her, holding her hand, "Until 5:00. I will come and spend the afternoon with you. You're free to be here. If you desire something that is not in the house, ask the man and he will fetch it for you."

"Fine," said Elena, "see you later. Andrés, would you give me a kiss?"

They kissed, and the murmur of lips freely united echoed in the jungle, and the breeze blew by and carried it even further, and the birds imitated the strange sound, and the flowers opened their petals upon contact with the breeze that brought them the fecund pollen of love with the harmony of kisses.

Afternoon arrived, the twilight announced the approaching of night. Andrés strolled with Elena among the bushes, and they hid themselves between a shadow of plants to sing the song of love, free from tyrannical impositions, in the middle of the jungle, to the poetic and soft light of the afternoon that sent hidden Febo on a cloud, saying good-bye to that American region. The birds in their nests were witness to the chaste union.

They say some time passed, and Elena did not return alone to the city; she returned with a precious child to see her family, who had wanted to recriminate her, but she said to them, I am free and I am happy. If you wish that I not see you again, I will not return, but I desire nothing other than love.

Some years later the two busybodies had the occasion to go hunting, and they surprised Elena who was nursing a child and two others played by her side, a girl and a boy. Love had made miracles: it had converted two into five. The miracle of the bread and the fishes. They had multiplied following the counsel of the author of miracles.

Reproduction is the loveliest and most enchanting mystery of the creation: sow a seed of corn and you will have thousands; give a kiss and two will produce a sound and the echo will return another to you. Unite yourselves and the two of you will become three, four . . .

July 2, 1913

*   *   *

"Upon listening to a theologian exaggerate the act of a man, who God made into a rouge, upon lying down with his female companion, who God made complacent and lovely, anyone would say that a cataclysm has occurred in the universe. Reader, listen to Marc Aurelio and you will see that you do not offend your God by the voluptuous rubbing of two intestines."

"Philosophical Works," Diderot

EXAGGERATIONS

On different occasions, when referring to the Chinese, I have heard comments judging them as a backwards people, the opposite of modern civilization, and there was no other cause other than their straight hair and not understanding their language. But they have not paid attention to their industriousness, their perseverance to overcome difficulties, their personal hygiene, and their various virtues.

An infinite number of people believe that to be civilized is to wear patent leather shoes, a new collared shirt, and tie even though the undergarments stink of sweat, and one doesn't bathe, not even once a week, and furthermore they overeat like cannibals, and they lose control like satyrs. They have no control whatsoever: they overindulge in everything, in eating, drinking, sleeping, dancing. They do not comprehend that all excess dulls the body: that we do not live to grossly eat or amuse ourselves; that life has higher objectives than excessive eating or constant enjoyment; that the first achievement of a man who comprehends the objective of life and wants to progress, in order not to be a beast, is to know oneself, as Socrates has already said. One temple in Greece also bears the inscription: "Know thyself." Know your strengths and increase your faculties; moderate your violent tendencies in all areas of life.

And those individuals, so full of imperfections, call themselves civilized because they wear their hat to the side without washing their hair before leaving for work; they change the exterior suit while the interior is dirty; they wear a different tie each day and do not change their socks; they perfume themselves and do not bathe. You get close to one of these persons and they have a strange smell, despite their tie and high collar. The mixture of barbershop powders with sweat and the special smell of the factory combines into a type of "perfume" that makes one sick.

One gets close to a Chinese man that has worked all day, and he does not have that disagreeable smell. Oh! and the mouth, a center for infection together with the mixture of food with tobacco, it is another "exquisite perfume" that causes one to faint. They do not wash their mouths nor do they brush, nor does it occur to them to go to the dentist so that he can examine their teeth and tell them the way to keep them clean. What most attracts their attention are the ties and shoes in the store window.

And the girls concern themselves more with ribbons and lace than doing a little exercise and bathing and changing undergarments frequently. These girls also (with the valid exceptions of those of the opposite sex; they are notable) perfume themselves without changing their shirt or pants, and they adorn themselves without washing their hair or ears or their neck and without having bathed themselves. And so in order to call oneself or believe oneself to be civilized, one must be clean.

Civilization, modern progress rests upon hygiene.

Therefore in order to keep up with progress and call oneself civilized, it is necessary to do a little exercise, bathe daily, and furthermore, before going to bed, to again wash those parts exposed to the open air. In order to eat, it is obligatory to wash and disinfect your hands. One should not eat too much because that affects stomach hygiene. When the stomach doesn't digest the food that would nourish the body, it ferments in the stomach and produces digestion that degenerates into dyspepsia and produces stomach disorders that will cause great distress.

Some friends have found it strange that during the day I will eat some fruit and some crackers, or two or three slices of bread, almost always alone, very few times with cheese or cream cheese, until 6:00 in the evening when I go to Mr. Argüelles' Vegetarian Restaurant. In the morning I always get up early: when I go to bed late, around 1:00 or 2:00, I stay asleep. Never have I been found in bed at 9:00 in the morning. (I like to get up early because the morning is very beautiful, and as a great admirer of nature, I like to contemplate it and breathe in the morning breeze. I also enjoy the early hours of the evening when I observe the immense illuminated space. But in order not to get up late, I do not do this often. If I had an astronomy observatory. I would dedicate some hours observing the sidereal regions). Forgive my digression.

Afterward I do a little exercise or Swiss gymnastics that consists of lifting and lowering my arms several times, tilting my body while supporting myself on only one leg, arms lifted and uniting my hands up high and going back and forth from one side to the other. Then, place my body straight and lower my arms until I touch the tips of my toes with the tips of my fingers, keeping my legs together until I am able to do it with ease. I do this for a few minutes each time until I reach twenty minutes. This exercise is very good, even for nasal colds, because when you lower your head, the blood rushes down while you maintain this position.

After various exercises of this kind, alternated with those previous mentioned, I go to the bathroom. There were some years that I bathed my head before anything else. Now I wet my feet first and, with a wet, soapy towel, I rub myself and then I pour water over me. If the bathtub is scrupulously clean, very white and shiny so that it doesn't have black lines that are receptacles of dirt and can be contagious, I lie under the water many times without wetting my head. Then I rub my body with my hands and without drying myself off, I put on a bathrobe or kimono, without much more clothing than some long pants. I stand or sit at the side of my window (I do not have a dining room available) to breathe the air. I always eat some fruit, with delight, be it oranges, mangos, apricots, apples, melon, or pineapple. When there are oranges, I always eat oranges, and then I eat some "Uneda" milk biscuits and a small glass of milk until 12:00 when I eat a few crackers and another small glass of milk, half of a five-cent jar. When there are no oranges, I eat a pear and an apple, other times mangos and apricots. If there are no apples, then I eat whatever there is. Sometimes there are grapes, so I eat grapes, or a pear, or two apricots. If they are very big, only one; then I eat three slices of bread with or without cream cheese. If I feel a pang in my stomach or emptiness, I eat another piece of fruit and two slices of bread. As of last month, I no longer drink milk because it did not seem clean to me. I make do with fruit and bread or crackers. One of my favorite dishes is julienne potatoes fried in oil like my mother used to make.* They are potatoes cut very thin and placed in boiling oil so that they do not go soft. I like to eat them right away. They are fried with olives and a small piece of sweet red pepper. This dish, with a nice piece of bread and some flan or a little sweet guayaba skin, is sufficient food for me until the next morning when I eat fruit and bread. Then I begin to answer the correspondence that I receive and to revise my papers or produce new ones.

After writing for many hours I fall asleep at the table. I nap for five or ten minutes depending on my tiredness. I attempt to distract myself by reading in order to begin again. Later I go out.

For me, bread constitutes my primary nourishment, when I cannot or do not have the means of finding prepared vegetarian food.

---

*My mother is French.

"HUMAN EQUALITY"

I spoke to the rock and the rock answered me . . .

I observed the atoms and the atoms showed me their continual evolutions. From mineral, to vegetable and animal.

Like atoms that detach themselves in mutual solidarity in a continuous and inimitable manner. From the trees, the breeze transported them imperceptibly to animals and to humans.

In continued mutual aid that was never interrupted, they shared nourishment without selfishness, impartiality without superiority. So the atoms in perfect and continuous evolution fulfilled their triumphant and persevering labor in a calm and orderly manner, contributing to the formation of the worlds, from the beginning until the end. The invisible particle, at a simple glance, detached from a lion did not refuse to join with another from a monkey and to unite with one from a dog or to nourish the retina of a girl or an old man.

The nitrogen particles detached from a tree and the oxygenated iodized ones that launch the waves in their continual ebb and flow, never repelled. In unison, they continued their lovely destination to fortify the weak lungs of a person infected with tuberculosis. They did not refuse to be breathed by that diseased body on the verge of death, where one must go to become part of the world of atoms and molecules.

What beauty and harmony in their continuous laboring of life and for life!

I contemplated the waters, and they sang to me in the sweetest melodies, sometimes in muffled murmurs, others in arrogant and fearful threats, various others, the lovely song of life came through diverse manifestations, feeding millions and millions of tiny fish in its immense breast, without distinction of color, shape, or habits. All were equal, according to their strengths and according to their needs without violence or restriction.

Incessantly kissing the rocks, penetrating through its thousand little holes and fissures, giving life to innumerable snails, insects, and an infinity of tiny sea animals in which they dwell without preferring the playful "little crab," or the tender little snail, the waters bathed all equally.

I penetrated the forests and **heard,** among its luxurious and corpulent trees, an infinity of precious little birds jumping from one tree to the next, from one branch to another, cheerfully trilling, some calling their lovers, others bidding good-bye, others carrying fragile little twigs to build their nests. No tree refused to receive them or pointed out differences, nor were there any among them—all had equal rights.

They would divide into numerous flocks with the approach of winter from one country to another, without direction, without passport, without fear or suspicion, and they established their lives in other climates.

They quickly crossed the sea and returned at the end of the season, cheery and mischievous to form new nests with new loves . . . No priests! . . . or judges! . . . or governors! . . . or police! . . . or exploiters! . . . or usurers! . . . or hunger! . . . or misery! . . . or tuberculosis!

I ascended the mountains and **saw** in the valleys diverse species of trees and plants, big and small, corpulent and rickety, fertile and sterile; none of them reproached one another. All nourished themselves from Mother Earth, without envy or pride. The corpulent one at the top did not threaten the weak little coffee tree. The luxurious mango tree did not insult the humble mallow tree. There on the mountain I inhaled the oxygenated breeze, fragrant from the flowers of the valleys and the perfume of the jungles. I **saw** that they used the subtle air equally, the delicate butterfly like the swift swallow, the sad seagull and the caudal eagle. I climbed up another steep summit, and I **saw** off to one side another one like a cracked plain that supported the eagle's nest . . . with two hungry eaglets! I was lying down over the peak, and I observed as the good mother lightly brushed her enormous beak over her little ones, moved her large wings, and flew across above my head, perhaps without seeing me. I saw her descend onto a plain very close by. I got up to follow her descent, but I did not have time, since she returned with a small calf in her claws. Not making a move I waited for her to descend, and then I went back to the previous site. There was the little animal agonizing, torn between the three hooked beaks of the eaglets and the eagle . . . Poor calf! . . . When it had satiated the hunger of the three of them, the mother lifted up into flight and rested her arrogant and lovely figure on top of the summit close to where I was. I sat up, placing myself on the ledge of the high peak. The eagle observed me: I looked at her, and we remained with our eyes locked on each other. Then seeing that the queen of the birds did not cease to look at me, as if asking me . . . What were you doing? . . . I decided to ask her: Are you happy? She fixed her gaze on me, and I heard her say, "I am happy. I have fulfilled the law of conservation. Do you do the same?" "No. Among my fellow beings, the law of conservation is not enough. What governs them is the law of ambition. After satisfying all basic needs, pleasures, whims, vanities, and superfluous trinkets, they accumulate gold and more gold in the vault, provisions in the storehouses, and people die of hunger. Shoes and clothes in the stores, while the naked and barefoot shiver; an infinity of fellow beings of both sexes, children and elderly, exposed to a thousand illnesses and thousands of afflictions and bloody sorrows . . ."

The eagle's eyes sparkled, and she said, "And that is created by your own fellow beings, and you don't remedy it?"

"Through what pacific means? Through education. But in the meantime the unfortunate working class dies of hunger, of poverty."

"Fight and you will overcome! It is never too late," she told me and looking toward her children, she arose and lost herself in the faraway horizon to search for new prey . . .

I went down to the valley, and I saw doves, peacocks, ducks, guinea hens. In the small lake, I noticed various swans, very majestic and happy. They swam back and forth across the lake from one end to the other.

I stopped to contemplate the entire lovely scene and continued into the jungle . . .

I entered the jungle, and I saw a beautiful sleeping snake; I continued, and the alligators and lizards ran in all directions. I heard another snake hissing, and I caught sight of some rabbits.

And I told myself: harmony, fraternal brotherhood, the satisfaction of being alive reigns everywhere. And I continued believing all were happy. . . .

I returned to the shores of the sea. I changed my clothes and submerged myself in the salty waters that seemed not to have any waves, its immense surface was so calm.

My daring hand penetrated down to the bottom where I grabbed what I saw through the crystalline liquid. It was a lovely snail. I looked at it, and it showed its velvet paws and eyes. It told me, "Put me back where I was and continue searching because in the place where you found me there is a square piece of marble. Lift it up, and you will go down a small staircase that you will see."

I did so. I came to the staircase, and I went down. Before me I saw a door also carved of marble, very white. I pressed on a spring that I **saw**, and it opened. I saw another staircase, but even more beautiful. I went down and entered into a spacious oriental-styled vestibule with extravagant ceilings and very beautiful adornments. The arches were made of carved marble also. A table sat at an angle in each column adorned with Corinthian spires that supported artistic and elegant urns filled with the loveliest flowers that perfumed the large room.

I came across a cabinet covered in tapestries and flowerpots.

I went out into a very beautiful garden where some artistic fountains spouted water in thousands of playful forms to thousands of plants that perfumed the entire palace. The delicious trickling sound of the water mixed with the softest whisper of the breeze which played with the enchanting roses, jasmines, tuberoses, violets, carnations, honeysuckles, etc., etc., that surrounded the fountains. To the side, under the magnificent fruit and between the most special shadows, one could see benches made of stone. Everything was so spacious that it felt like being in a forest or in a large jungle, such was the diversity of plants, trees, and fruits preciously mixed together.

I went down a pretty road of symmetrically aligned trees. I returned to the pavilion contiguous to the garden and rested a few minutes.

I went into a spacious and luxuriously perfumed hall. I reclined on a cushioned sofa and gathering up all the mental power I could I said, "Muse of my ideal that I have dreamed of for so long, appear before me!"

When I finished my evocation I remained engrossed, observing how the hall would light up with a soft white glow, a subtle wind like a little breeze, like a light breath caressed me and perfumed the entire surroundings. Before me was a radiant, splendid, magnificent figure wrapped in a white transparent tunic with a diadem on it that in sparkling letters read: **"Anarchy."** Her perfectly oval-shaped face with light, beautiful eyes of a delicate blue, a divine mouth; that face reflected the most complete harmony, the most admirable sweetness. What grandeur of demeanor! What appearance most delicate!

She looked at me with a calmness that moved me.

She remained standing—proud, imperious, magnificent. Her look was an interrogation. "I have called you because my sadness is infinite, my anxiety for human welfare consumes me. I desire to transform human suffering . . . have mercy! . . . tell me, when will another Christ redeemer come to this humanity to make them happy?" She lifted her arm and pointed with her index finger to the front. And on a window of the wide, main door was written: "The present suffering is a consequence of past errors. But soon this golden kingdom will end. Work will be the norm of future societies. He who cannot offer the fruit of a few hours of daily labor of whatever purpose to the community will not be esteemed by his equals." I accept that explanation and that maxim. But tell me, when and how will that change begin since there still are no signs? I turned to look at the window and it read: "In the eternity of time, centuries are minutes, generations will pass, and upon passing they will change their ways."

THE CASHIER

By one of those coincidences of life, Ricardo had found a patron who had paid for his studies in accounting. Born into the greatest poverty, his mother had raised him by working thousands of jobs. She was anemic, a skeleton, thin without life, extinguishing herself like a lamp without oil, making superhuman efforts to be sure that her son was neat and clean before he left for school. The only hope that was left for her, when she thought about the helplessness of the boy, was a benefactor, a man of a certain age: austere, sober, who had made some money with an austere business, widowed, and without children. How she would have gladdened if Don Castro remembered her son! He was rich; he could take care of him. The day that Ricardo turned twelve years of age, she hoped the benefactor would arrive with the accustomed gift. She told him:

"Don Castro, this boy is now a young man who should be sent away to study."

"What do you wish to make of him, woman?"

"That is up to you. What do I know?"

"Fine. I will see and I'll let you know."

"Don Castro, God will protect you," and Ramona, kissing her son and watching as Don Castro walked away with a slow pace that rocked his body like a pendulum.

After a few days Don Castro returned and told Ramona to prepare her son for Thursday. "Take this," and he gave her some money, "make him some undergarments and send him to get fitted for a suit. Then send him to me so he can take the train to to New York."

"Are you going with him?"

"No, I will send a friend with him who is going to that city, and I'll put him in charge of placing him in a school."

"Thank you, Don Castro," said Ramona. "When my son comes I will notify him about it."

"Good," said Don Castro, "see you some other day."

"May God keep you well, Don Castro," uttered Ramona.

Don Castro went away satisfied. He believed he had fulfilled a duty.

In the afternoon when Ricardo arrived, Ramona said to him: "My son, Thursday of next week you will go away to study." And taking the boy's head between her hands, she kissed his head and said: "My poor son! How happy it makes me that you will be able to work when I'm no longer able," and she wiped away some tears.

Ricardo said to her, "Don't worry. In a few years my work will be sufficient for both of us."

"Amen, my son, you'll help your mother who will soon be very old."

"I hope it will be so, my mother," and kissing her on the forehead, he sat down to read one of his books.

On Thursday Ricardo was waiting for his mother to pack his suitcase and accompany him to Don Castro's house. It was one o'clock in the afternoon when Ramona left with her son to take him to the benefactor's house.

Don Castro dozed off while reading a newspaper. Upon arriving, Ramona said, "Don Castro, here is Ricardo."

Don Castro got up and told them to sit down. Ramona entered and sat down and Ricardo did the same.

Don Castro addressing the boy, "And what do you think of the trip?"

"I go with pleasure. It pains me to leave my mother all alone, but I want to help her and lighten her work."

Don Castro prepared a cigar.

At two o'clock, Don Valentín García, a businessman who was going shopping in New York arrived. He greeted all of them and asked Don Castro, "Is this the boy?"

"Yes, he is the godson, I recommend him well. Take five hundred duros in order to pay for the school and whatever the boy needs."

"Very well," said Don Valentín, taking the bills and storing them in his wallet. "Now we can go, since the 2:30 train that goes to New York will be here."

"Yes, you can go now," said Don Castro.

Ricardo and Ramona got up and said good-bye to Don Castro, who took the boy's head and kissed him on his forehead. "Study, my son, be studious."

The three walked toward the station. The 2:30 train was at the station: "Twenty minutes," shouted the conductor.

Ramona hugged her son and kissed him. Ricardo boarded the train and Don Valentín followed with his suitcase.

Ramona waited for the train to leave, waving good-bye to Ricardo for the last time. The train whistle blew, and the conductor gave the warning before boarding.

The train began to breathe as it prepared to leave, and Ricardo leaned out the window and waved good-bye to his mother. The train left and Ramona continued waving her handkerchief.

Finally she lost sight of the train traveling on the serpentine rails of steel. It would pass among the pines, palms, and the rough foliage that showed the dry, arid ground in which it grew, from extensive desert and the gentle sea, which was ready to receive all kinds of vessels.

When Ramona lost sight of the smoke from the locomotive, she returned home and cried a great deal. When would she see her son again? Then she sat down to pray, believing that prayers would help her son.

Eight months passed, and Don Castro decided to take some money to Ramona. He remembered what Ricardo had said about wanting to help his mother. The miserly, selfish old man didn't recall a similar kindness in his life, except for his deceased wife. Upon recalling this, Don Castro felt it would do him well to take something to Ramona, even if it was barely enough to pay her rent. But his good intentions were late in arriving. She was worn out from working. Life was quickly fleeing her, as she had worked day and night all her life. In the past, when she found herself without recourse she resorted to shopping at Don Castro's store where she could charge the expense, knowing how difficult it would be to pay back. When her son was very young, she had to care for him—so much anguish and desperation! She had to sew from evening until one or two o'clock in the morning to finish the promised piecework without stopping. She had destroyed her youth and was losing her vision. Now she wore glasses, and it took so much work to thread the needle. She was in the prime of her life at thirty-five years of age, and yet her strength had drained, and now Don Castro came to help her, when so many times, with tears in her eyes, she had gone to tell him that she could not repay him, and he never dissolved her debt. Could humankind be so blind? Selfishness caused people to lose the most natural of feelings. Her son wrote of the progress he was making, and she dreamed of seeing her son become a well-to-do man.

One day she could not sew due to the pain she felt; she had to lie down to rest. She spent a week in bed with a fever and a headache while a neighbor lady cared for her. When Don Castro found out, he sent for the doctor. The doctor told Don Castro that it was a waste of time, that she had tuberculosis, and that there was no cure. She spent a month in that condition. Don Castro informed Ricardo that his mother was sick but without alarm; he didn't want to hamper the boy. One day Ramona told the neighbor lady to tell Don Castro that she wanted to see her son. Don Castro sent him a telegram telling him to take the train and to come see his mother.

The boy became alarmed and said: "Such a rush? How strange."

He arrived within three days, and his mother received him into her arms. "My son! My final good-bye. Be good and studious."

"Mother of mine, do not leave me all alone!" exclaimed Ricardo with a painful expression; he did not observe the sick woman's face, nor did he realize that Ramona was no longer breathing. When he saw that she was immobile, he cried out, "Dead! What a disgrace!" And he fell to his knees crying.

Some years have passed: now Ricardo is a cashier in a large business building in a large U.S. city. He is making an average salary, but he is a slave and at times feels frustrated with life. The people that come to make business transactions do not remember nor do they concern themselves with the young cashier.

The owner, in the sort of boredom that is afforded by the security of a good position, doesn't concern himself with the cashier either. Ricardo is like the usher in the theater; he has the baton in hand and passes by unnoticed. The smallest distraction in his job could cause serious complications, and there you see him bent over his high desk in his rotating chair. He is allowed time to eat his lunch and at five o'clock, he leaves for the day without another break or other benefits. Ricardo says, "What a life!" He passes money from one side to the other, millions of dollars without being able to make use of one cent. He is corralled, muzzled, made into a counting machine with no aspirations other than to be careful not to make a mistake, to be condemned to have a fortune in his hands and have nothing more than a meager wage; he is treated with indifference, as if he does not feel, as if he does not have the right to enjoy himself like everyone else.

And he studied for this, and his mother suffered so many hardships in order for him to be where he is today. Worthless life! It was torture to be born and grow up hearing cries and seeing miseries, to depend on others for an education, and finally to live among gold all day without aspiring for more happiness other than to marry, only to leave your wife always alone. Should she want to go to the theater or some other place, to entrust her with a friend, so that later—as happened to the cashier from another bank—while he was working, his wife would go and spend time in the country with another man who ended up being her lover! "No, no way! I have the right to be happy. I won't leave my Matilde always alone, no!" he tells himself. The man that marries should take his wife with him or stay with her. Those marriages in which the woman, bored with being alone gives herself to her first friend, is desperate; they are not to blame. We are the ones who expose her to that. It would be one thing if they do it because of love, but no, woman has a terrible struggle to stay faithful.

"But I am not accomplishing anything here by just thinking. Something must be done to get out of this situation."

When he returns home, he says that the following day, on Sunday, he will go to the harbor and inspect the ships that will take sail. But no, its better to go to New York and embark from there to the desired destination, he thinks. "I will let Matilde know so she can prepare herself."

The next day he goes to see Matilde and tells her: "We must go silently, you know. Prepare yourself for Saturday, and tell your aunt that it would be advisable for her to keep quiet, that you will give her five hundred pesos in case she goes out to live in the country."

Matilde says to him, "What is it that worries you? Is there any danger?"

"No, but I need to take these precautions in order to avoid problems."

"I will do as you tell me."

The next Saturday night, Ricardo speaks with Matilde's aunt and explains to her. "You will not give information regarding your niece to anyone. You will say that she went to New York to find work, and you will leave for the country with the money I give you."

"I will be careful in order not to endanger you."

"Yes, but tell me that you do not oppose my involvement with Matilde."

"No, she loves you."

"Then I am at peace."

"Say good-bye. Matilde and I will take the train." Ricardo has disguised himself with a moustache and sideburns and a different name; holding Matilde's arm he looks like a foreigner.

They arrive at the station ten minutes before the train arrives. The train finally pulls up and they board. The train leaves. They arrive in

New York and because Ricardo knows the city he informs himself of the steamboats that are leaving. That same day one is leaving for St. Petersburg, and he takes it. Now there is no danger. When they realize that he is not at the office on Monday afternoon, it is already too late. Monday there is hardly any work and so they think he will come in on Tuesday.

Tuesday arrives, several of Ricardo's business colleagues are sent to ask for him. The neighbors say they have not seen him. The coworkers then ask for information from those they believe are his friends, and they also contact the police to see if they can find out about the travelers who left Saturday and Sunday. Nothing can be found. Meanwhile weeks and months pass by, and there is not even the slightest trace of Ricardo, nor does anyone know if he's taken Matilde, because the old woman has gone to the country, and no one knows for certain about their relationship. One day some friends go to the country to visit the aunt, and they ask her about Matilde. She says that she is in New York and will be returning soon.

"Aren't you aware of the news and daily happenings out here? Ha! As withdrawn as I live caring for my chickens and plants, I do not concern myself with other things."

"There was a big conflict at work, the cashier of the large business Jacob & Company left with a million dollars."

"Oh my!" says the old woman, "and who was it?"

"Ricardo."

"When my niece finds out she will be surprised, because if I am not mistaken that is the name of the young man who fell in love with her."

"He must be one and the same." And the old woman conceals the information well.

The friends leave saying: "She knows nothing and it would have been better not to have told her, because now she will tell her niece and if she loved him she will suffer."

But now it was all for nothing. They did not find out where the young man is.

Meanwhile, Matilde and Ricardo calmly stroll through the museums and leave St. Petersburg for Italy, they pass through Paris, and go to Granada where they purchase a small house that is ideal for preparing a nest for a baby, because Matilde will give birth in two months and she cannot continue traveling. There, in the beautiful city of Granada, Matilde gives birth to a girl whom they name Aurora.

When Ricardo is alone in the garden, he says: "Now let those egotists come to bother me, they used to deposit great amounts and did not give a cent to the poor. All were speculators, with the exception of a widow, but what does it matter. 'Every cloud has a silver lining.' I feel sorry for the poor who were there, but those haughty and vain ones, let them pay for their insolence now: they considered themselves honest and were very satisfied with their speculative business deals."

Later they question the old woman about Matilde. She says that she has married in New York and that she is doing fine. One day she receives a letter from Matilde and she is very happy to know that her niece is doing well and is happy.

May 20–25, 1913, Ybor City, Tampa

LOVES

"Help! Some aid for a poor widow with a newborn child!" she dared to say on a corner of one of the streets in Rome. Gizelda, a woman who had been admired in the theater for her beauty, had had many men fall in love with her, and some appeared to have been her lovers. One time she confided in one of them that she liked him, he told her that he loved her, and she went away with him. She sacrificed her glorious future, her brilliant profession, in order to love and completely consecrate herself to her lover. Some years passed, and no one knew anything about her. One day she appeared pale and older, with a child in her arms, asking for help. No one knew her and no one helped her.

Days and weeks passed by, and the woman languished. She was working as a servant, but her child? Flower of her love! She did not have anyone with whom to leave him to care for him. One time she crossed the plaza and fell while sitting down on a bench. She could not get up with the child in her arms. The child was scared from the jolt from the mother's fall, but it seems that she held him in such a way that in the great moment of supreme and unique anguish, the child did not fall out of her arms. He only cried uncontrollably, hitting his hands on his mother's face. He cried more and more, wanting to open the clothing that hid his nourishment, a dried up breast to console himself.

She was dead. Upon hearing the cries of the child, a cripple that passed by came near and tried to recognize the mother. He didn't recognize her, but he noticed a locket. He examined it and said, "Gizelda!" And he detached it and took it with him. Because he couldn't lift her, he went to the corner as quickly as his strength permitted and called out with a whistle to the corner policeman.

The policeman ran, accompanied by the cripple, went to the bench where Gizelda had fallen and picked up the child. The policeman asked the "Watchman," as they called the cripple, because generally he would let them know that something had happened, to watch over Gizelda in case she awoke and that he would fetch a doctor, and at the same time, would notify the ambulance. The policeman went to the telephone on the corner and since the ambulance was about two blocks away, it did not take long to arrive. The policeman ran to hear what they were saying to Gizelda. But upon lifting her up he understood that she was dead. The doctor said: "To the operating room, to do an autopsy." They all got in the ambulance, and it left for its destination. The Watchman, the cripple, continued watching as the car left, and taking a small bottle of sugar water mixed with gin, took a swig and said: "How beautiful she was, dazzling with her luxury and astonishing with her prodigalities and intoxicating with her amorous madness! She was so good!" He wiped two tears that lingered, welling up in his eyes, passing his right arm over his face. In the hospital, the Watchman found out that Gizelda had died of hunger and that the child had been sent to an orphanage for poor children. Every day the Watchman went to inquire about the child, who was healthy and lovely and grew in an exceptional manner. He was not able to ask the mother the name she had given the child; in the orphanage they named him Jacinto del Bosque. Now the child had a first and last name. Several years had gone by, and one day on his daily visit, the Watchman found out that they had taken Jacinto to a public state school to learn English, shorthand and bookkeeping. After ten years of being in school, Jacinto left with all the requirements to be able to make a living wage. He was beautiful like his mother had been, of slight stature, elegant stride. Everyone knew that he was Gizelda's son, but his eyes were not those of his mother nor was the tone of his confident and assertive voice. His face often contracted with a desperate gesture. When alone in a café, he did not have anyone with whom to exchange opinions. One day while daydreaming, the mayor called to him, saying that he knew who Jacinto was. The mayor, being among a group of young friends, introduced him to the group and invited Jacinto to sit with them. Jacinto sat down and continued conversing about various issues. A week had passed since Jacinto had left school, and he had secured a job in a business office. Every afternoon he went to the café and met with some of the young men whom the mayor had introduced to him.

Jacinto had always noticed there was a young woman who watched him when he left his office in the afternoons; he would look at her, greet her with his hat, and continue on to the café.

This scene repeated itself every day until one night they saw each other face to face at a dance that the mayor held for his wife's birthday. Someone introduced them and invited both of them to dance together. He asked her to dance a waltz and she, a polka. They danced the waltz, and Jacinto felt that he was happier at her side than at the side of any other girl—an irresistible affection attracted him to Alina del Prado.

When they danced the polka he said to her, "When will we speak again and be close once more?"

Alina answered: "It is possible that they will celebrate my birthday at my house."

"When?"

"May 25th, I will have them invite you or I will invite you."

"Thank you very much," replied Jacinto. "And will I dance with you?"

"Certainly," said Alina. "Why not?"

And they continued arm in arm through the room, which was splendidly lit and they went through one of the doors that connected the garden to the room into the trees and flowers of the garden. Some time passed, and they returned to the hall because the musical harmonies let them know that the dance had begun again.

The dance ended, and everyone said good-bye. The next day he took a bouquet of flowers for Alina. He wrapped them well without wilting them, and he tossed them onto the balcony, along with a small card with these words:

Miss Alina:

I feel a great affection toward you. You attract me in an irresistible way. I tremble before you like a fragile leaf shakes in the wind. Should I keep quiet or manifest it without evasiveness? If I have been imprudent or hasty, do not answer me.

S.S.Q.B.S.P.
[Your servant who kisses your feet]
Jacinto del BOSQUE

Alina woke up late that day because of the dance the day before. But her first impulse, even while still in her nightgown, was to go to the balcony. She leaned out and saw the package that was on the ground. She grabbed it and opened it. They were roses, white lilies, and violets. She placed them in a small vase. Carrying them to her dresser, she opened the card, and a cheerfulness, a great satisfaction, was reflected in her eyes, in her entire face.

Immediately she sat down to answer the card:

My love! What a joy your card has brought me. Why keep quiet? If you didn't do it today, I would have done it soon enough. Since I saw you, you attached yourself to my soul, and you live in my mind. I adore you.

Alina.

She then sealed the card and sent it in the mail. They loved each other without knowing who they were, having seen each other was sufficient. He was a poor, intelligent, and studious young man. She was nice, beautiful, had the title of countess by inheritance, even though her parents were still alive. He saw in her the woman that he dreamed of, his ideal. She saw in his confident demeanor and in his imperative, beautiful expression, her dreamed desire, the kind of man that her artistic mind imagined; he presented himself as real and tangible, loving her and longing for her more than she had ever hoped for. Would her fate, which provided her with her beloved, be so benevolent that it would not interrupt her happiness? That we shall see. Alina del Prado, the only daughter of the Counts of Torreón, was still a girl, and her parents must concern themselves with her liberty; their will still ruled all in the house. But she did not imagine that in choosing her beloved she would have to counsel with her parents.

Jacinto received the letter in the afternoon, and the satisfaction that he felt was demonstrated on his face. He left his office, went to the café, saw Alina on the balcony, and greeted her with his hat and a smile that illuminated his love for her. Upon seeing such a gallant figure enter the café, anyone would have figured that he was a great gentleman. He had a demeanor so distinguished that if his mother had seen him, she would have been left ecstatic.

In the café, he met with some of his friends; they greeted one another, and he kept himself quietly reserved at another table, as if avoiding joining their group. He wanted to be alone to savor the unmatched pleasure of loving and being loved.

Upon seeing that Jacinto did not join their group they murmured among themselves. The mayor's son who was there said, "He is prideful. He shouldn't forget that my father recommended him and sent him to school." Another, the son of the Marquis de la Villa, said, "And who are his parents? Because if he doesn't hold a title, he shouldn't have any pride at all." "His parents? I do not know. I heard it said to my father that his mother had been a great artist and that she had had some romantic affairs." "Bah!" said a prostitute, "it is not even worth mentioning." Another added, "None of this matters if he is a good, upstanding gentleman." This boy was the heir of another title, the nephew of the Barons del Río, a nice boy and very amicable with the entire world. So those three concerned themselves with him and entertained themselves by playing with insults. Jacinto read and reread Alina's letter; he was not concerned nor had he ever been concerned with the lives of others nor did he worry about investigating who his family was or their social rank.

The three young men agreed to go and left without saying good-bye to Jacinto since he was absorbed in the contemplation of the letter. He didn't know who those young men were. They had introduced themselves, but he did not know that they had concerns and prejudices.

On the morning of May 25th, upon leaving for his office, he did not see Alina. He knew that it was her birthday, and he had a precious gift for her. He sent it and a card with a house servant. The gift was a lovely gold and mother of pearl pen, a precious little gift, with a charm that contained a small portrait of himself.

Jacinto left the office early. His intelligence had won the mercantile interest of the owner, whose kind nature had obliged him to promote Jacinto to a higher position and increase his salary. Jacinto hurried home to prepare himself for the evening dance. When he arrived at his house and opened his room with the key, a man dressed in a service uniform entered hastily and handed him an announcement card.

Jacinto greeted the man, opened the envelope, and read the invitation.

At 10 o'clock in the evening, the splendidly illuminated ballroom of the Counts of Torreón barely offered enough room to the gathering that was the most select of nobility and the most notable of the bank. Among thousands of diverse sounds and noises, groups formed, others strolled around, and that multitude entertained themselves in a way unlike any other. Jacinto did not know that he would rub shoulders with the oldest of nobility, and at the same time, with the principal usurers. They were those who, with a thousand assaults and stunts, had made millions to raise their status and walk very puffed up among the titled heirs. There were schemers and moneylenders made wealthy improvisationally, led there for a game of chance which in one night rendered thousands of dollars to a socially ranked friend who took it and showed off his winnings.

Jacinto was the purest of all those gentlemen and merchants. He walked around—a stranger to everyone—with Alina on his arm; the music now had joined them with its delicious harmonies.

Jacinto did not notice that he caught the attention of the women with his lovely, confident demeanor. They figured he was some foreign prince, invited by some ambassador. The gentlemen looked at him and did not recognize him. The women asked their husbands, who was that young man? No one knew him; he passed by like a beautiful acquisition of Alina, making a twosome that would very soon be invited and enjoyed by everyone at the latest gatherings.

The dance ended, and they went into the sitting room where there was champagne, distinct liquors, and sweets—true objects of modern confectionary art. Alina said to Jacinto, "My parents have watched you a great deal. Let me introduce you to them. This is against all the rules, but indispensable." They stood in front of Alina's parents, she spoke first and introduced her parents; Jacinto greeted them respectfully and said his name: "Jacinto del Bosque." Alina's father looked at Jacinto's entire face, trying to remember and repeated, "del Bosque? del Bosque?" and added with utmost etiquette, "What? Count? Baron? What?"

The young man simply answered: "Jacinto del Bosque," and saying good-bye stepped away.

The father said to his wife: "Who has introduced this young man here? And to my daughter?"

"I don't know," she replied, "you know that these days one cannot demand many requisites because we are all mixed together."

"It is true, but they should have introduced him to me." The count remained pensive, remembering those eyes and that expression.

"Let's go to the table. Don't worry," said the countess. And they mingled with the rest of the people.

Alina's father's questions seemed strange to her because she had already seen other people there who wanted to be like Jacinto, so elegant and so lovely. And she told Jacinto not to worry about what her father said. They went to a table and sat down to drink some cream, a little bit of Chartreuse. All had come to an end. Jacinto had mingled among these people like something shiny, like a storybook Cinderella, without having satisfied their curiosity. Finding out who he was would be an object of conversation—in the car, in the bedroom, and in the stores.

Alina received thousands of cards from girlfriends who asked her the address of the young man, in order to invite him to the next party. The next day, Alina waited out on the balcony for Jacinto to pass by, and he paused in order to gaze at her longer. The street was not very busy. The main balcony of Alina's house corresponded with the other street. This was on purpose; and they could speak if only the balcony weren't up so high. He blew her a kiss and continued on. Jacinto was very studious. He wanted to graduate as an engineer, and he worked on his studies at home, with the goal of soon taking the examinations.

Many months have passed. The romantic idyll continued. Alina would go for a ride in her car and see Jacinto. She would get out and read in a garden with plants and flowers, and a little later he would arrive. One day Jacinto said to her, "Your father must be made aware of our love, so he doesn't think that I come to take advantage of your little girl innocence. Would you like that?"

Alina took his hands and said to him, "Yes, when are you going to go?"

"Tonight, if you like. It's Thursday and it's visiting day, according to what you have told me. Therefore, I shall go tonight." At 6 o'clock, they both got in their car and left the garden.

By 8 o'clock, Jacinto was ready. At 9 o'clock he was in the parlor awaiting Alina's father. They exchanged greetings and courteous phrases. "Sir," said Jacinto, "I come to ask for your daughter's hand. I am an engineer and qualified accountant."

"Gentleman," said the count, "I need to know the origin of your family and also your social position . . ."

"Sir, I am not a millionaire, nor very rich, but I am in a condition to marry."

"You know," said the count, "I would have liked it if you held a title like she does."

"Sir, I have not concerned myself with knowing if I had one or not," replied Jacinto. "I do not need them, nor do I want them. We are in love. I am sure she doesn't worry about that detail either nor did she concern herself with knowing who I am nor did I investigate or search for appearances. It has been a year. We love each other and that's enough."

The count exclaimed, "A year! And where did you two meet?"

"Quite easily. Upon leaving my office each day, we would see each other. Then we spoke at the mayor's dance. Sir, I need to know your decision."

The count told him: "I cannot answer you yet, as my daughter is very young, but I will let you know."

Jacinto got up and with a gracious salutation said: "Sir, don't forget that we love each other, and love is greater than these obstacles. Tell me, may I visit your daughter?"

"No, not yet. Later, you'll know."

They both said good-bye and departed.

In his house, Jacinto paced back and forth in his bedroom and said, "But how was I not made aware of that detail. She didn't have to tell me. Why? For what? I have never sought them. Oh, delightful girl, what innocence! Tomorrow I will see you," and he sat down to read.

Meanwhile, the count informed his wife about the motive of the visit. "That young man has come to ask for our daughter."

"Do they love each other?"

"So it seems."

"She is unselfish and loyal."

"Are you in accordance with that relationship?"

"Why not?"

"He is not rich nor does he hold social titles."

"Why does it matter?"

"It seems, Margarita, there must be some objection."

"I do not see it."

"We shall see."

"Call the girl, so that she knows that the young man was here for her."

"Yes, we'll let her know." The count rang a bell and a servant appeared. The count said, "Advise Miss Alina that she is to come to the parlor where her parents are."

The servant returned and said that the bedroom was closed and dark, so he supposed she was sleeping.

"Leave that to me for tomorrow," said the countess.

The next day after breakfast, the countess called her daughter and had her sit down at her side. She said to her: "Why hadn't you told me, my Alina, that you were in love? Do I not deserve your trust?"

"It seemed as though it was not an obligation to tell you, mama."

"Very well, then what did you expect?"

"My mother," said Alina, embracing her mother, "forgive me I was expecting him to do it."

"He already did it last night, and your father told him that he needed to know his lineage, and then he would let him know."

"My poor love, how sad he must be."

"Don't worry. There will be a solution. Please excuse me because I need to see about fixing the garden door." And kissing her on both cheeks, she left leaving Alina pensive.

That afternoon Alina and Jacinto strolled among the foliage, and they promised to love each other in spite of all the obstacles and they said good-bye.

Jacinto was preoccupied. How could he find out who his parents were? He himself didn't know, but surely someone must have known them. Suddenly he paused and said, "What an idea! The mayor should know. I will go to see him." And at 8 o'clock he was at the mayor's house waiting for him to arrive.

"What a pleasure for me to see you," said the mayor entering. "How may I be of service?"

"My friend," said Jacinto. "I come to ask you as a friend to tell me who my parents were."

"Who wants to know, my son? I suppose that it would not be you who is concerned about it. You know that your mother's name was Gizelda, 'The Diva.' I don't know her surname."

"But my father?"

"I don't know, son, but I can find out through the police."

"Through the police, Sir? And what facts could they be able to give us about them? Were either my father or mother arrested?"

"I don't believe so, son." The mayor was indecisive about telling or not telling what he knew.

"Tell me, my friend, you seem to become silent. Tell me with frankness what you know."

"Well, fine," replied the mayor. "I will tell you what I know now that you demand it. One day I was notified that there was a child whose mother had been found dead . . .

"Where!"

"Listen, do not become impatient. She carried you in her arms, she suffered some pain . . . and she fell. You were crying. A poor cripple passed there by who notified the police in order for them to pick her up . . ."

"And where is he? Why didn't they take my mother to her house?"

"Why? I don't know. Wait, my son, I will ask the police to search for the cripple so that he can better detail what he described to the doctor."

"And the doctor, where is he?"

"He knows nothing—only what I have told you."

"He should know why she died."

The mayor thought a moment and said, "Of hunger . . . "

"Mother of mine!" cried Jacinto, covering his mouth with his handkerchief and resting his forehead in his open hands with the handkerchief, "what cruelty!"

The mayor got up and grabbing him by the arm, said to him, "Let's go to the garden so that I can send for the cripple." The mayor sent the police to search for the cripple that we know as the "Watchman" and took Jacinto for a walk in the garden to distract him. "My son," he told him, "don't despair because she died poor."

"Sir, not poor, hungry! And why did she die like that?"

"We will know soon enough. Be productive for yourself and honor where you have been born with your intelligence and integrity."

"*¡Ay!* But happiness will taste bitter to me, thinking that my mother died of hunger! It is horrible!"

"Yes, but tell me, Jacinto, where does this interest to know your lineage come from? What has happened?"

"I am in love," said Jacinto, "We have been together for a year from when I first spoke to her."

"Who is she?"

"Alina del Prado."

"Oh my! Well you have aimed high, boy."

"No, sir, I did not know. The first time that I spoke to her was here, at the dance to which you invited me. After that we used to look at each other from the balcony while I was on my way to my office. We would see each other on the boulevard."

"Alone? Strange that they would let her go out alone."

"She used to go out alone to a friend's house, and at times she went alone in the car until we tired of talking by hand gestures and letters. She then decided to invite me on her walks, and I would wait here for her among the beautiful branches. I decided to make her father aware of our relationship, and here you have me with my misfortune."

"And what did her father say to you?"

"That he wanted to know my family and my position. I told him who I was, and I came here to find out about my family.

They notified the mayor that they were looking for him.

"Wait, Jacinto. It must be the 'Watchman,' the cripple."

He went out and found a servant who told him: "Watchman is sick and in the hospital. Also there is an old man who has been looking for you for various weeks, but we thought it was some sort of whim, and we did not want to bother you. But yesterday and today he has persisted in such a way saying that he has something for you."

"Fine, we will go to see him."

Don Eliseo returned to the garden to look for Jacinto and found him pensive. Don Eliseo said, "Let's go, Jacinto" and taking him by the arm, he pulled him as they crossed through the garden and the veranda.

"Where are we going?" whispered Jacinto.

"We are going to the hospital," said Don Eliseo, "to meet with the 'Watchman.'"

They got in the car that was waiting for the mayor and they drove off.

At the hospital they asked to see the Watchman. Jacinto was taken by an employee to the Watchman who was sitting in a chair. He was pale, about forty-two years old

"Good day," said Jacinto.

"Good day," said the cripple.

"Tell me," asked Jacinto, "would you be able to tell me who Gizelda was, and who her husband was?"

"Are you family of hers?" said the Watchman.

"Do not concern yourself with that. Please answer my question. Who was she and what did she do for a living?"

"I don't know if I am wrong to do this, but here I go. I was a young man, sixteen years old, when the train destroyed my legs. I thought I died, but I was saved. I was always around the theater. During that time, a very famous, very beautiful artist arrived. I was desperate to go see her enter and at times to help her in some way. When I was able to go out, my first trip was to the theater. I sat on the marble staircase, and there I waited in the dark and later under the trees out front. One day I saw a young, divine woman get out. She was the most beautiful woman I had ever seen, and I had seen a lot. What eyes! What a mouth! I tell you, Sir, I was stunned. And from that day on, I have followed her everywhere like a fool. And she had a group of friends from the upper crust of society, they called out the finest compliments, they fought to offer her a hand while she was getting in her car, despite the fact that each one of them offered his car. 'The Diva,' as we called her, did not accept and got in her modest little car. One day they made such noise, trying to give her a hand, that she said, and I heard her because she was on the other side of her car. 'If you do not behave, I will call that cripple who appears as a sentinel. You can always see him here; ready to give me a hand.'"

"'With great pleasure,' I replied and ran toward her with a smile. She looked at me and stretched out her hand with a coin. 'You are not able to help me, but thank you.' She said it to me with such sweetness. If you would have met her, you would have admired her gentility, her sweet and happy character, a gladness that seemed to emanate perfumes of jasmine and roses. When she went shopping, what luxury! What an abundance of grace! Good heavens! There hasn't been another like her."

Jacinto was moved: he didn't breathe but said that Watchman should drink some water, "And whose daughter was she? Was she alone?"

"Always alone with an old woman who cared for her theater costumes."

"Whose daughter was she?"

"I heard that she belonged to the foreign upper class and that because of conflicts with her family she had dedicated herself to the theater that she loved. She spoke perfect French and Italian, but I don't know if she was from either country. The language she used most frequently was French. Later it was said that the Marquis de la Villa courted her; he accompanied her in her car. But it seems that this gentleman did so without the intention of marrying her. She did not allow him to get in her car again. This happened at the gate one day when he was getting in. She told him, 'Please, Marquis, forgive me, but I cannot allow it any more. You did not want to be my friend, but rather my lover, and in order to be my lover you must dedicate yourself to me, and you have a fiancée.'

"'I don't have a fiancée, Gizelda. My family has imposed that relationship on me.'

"'Very well, and if you do not have the courage to put your foot down, you need to rethink this and end it.'

"'I can't, I love you.'

"'Well, show me.'

"'I am the only son, my inheritance is not much, and I have two sisters. How am I going to get married now, if I am in school?'

"'Well, friend, then there is nothing more. We will end this because it causes me grief.'

"She got in her car, and the man stayed at the gate with his hat in his hand, pale. I pretended to be asleep upon seeing the pain of that man, and he left. One day I found out from the others that she loved the Count of Torreón, or at least she esteemed him, he was the most self-reliant. He had a brother but he was still young and in school. The mother was old, the father had died. He was the only one who could have pleased her because he was handsome with those eyes and a gesture and a presence unequaled. This gentleman had arrived from Paris, where he had gone to arrange the affairs of his inheritance. They fell in love as soon as they saw each other. Gizelda told me one day, 'Tonight will be the last night that I will sing.'

"'Why?' I asked her. 'Because I am going to the country with my lover, and I am not coming back to the theater for now.' This she told me upon getting out of her car, and before she entered the theater. The news disconcerted me because I adored that woman like a goddess. That night when the show ended the young count waited for her in his elegant carriage. I waited for her because each night she gave me a coin. That night she gave me an *escudo* and told me, 'If you need something, you'll let me know by way of my servant, Rogelia. Do you know her?'

"'Yes, madam.'

"'Good-bye, eh? And take care.'

"The car drove off and much time passed without seeing her again. Madam Rogelia would bring me money. In the cafés where she had squandered her money and sang, they spoke badly of her. Women envied her, men desired and hated her. In the theater, the owner was another wretch. The only one who defended her was the marquis, whom she had not accepted. He later married, and today he has a son, a big gambler. I found out later that the mother of the Count of Torreón had died and the son, Gizelda's lover, was the one who would mostly be in charge of his brother's education. He took his brother to Paris and took Gizelda as a stowaway. Rogelia told me this.'"

"Where is Rogelia?"

"She has died. She was very old by then. I found out through letters that Gizelda had written to Rogelia from Paris in which she asked about me. She said the count behaved well, he would take her to the theater, and that they were very happy because Gizelda was pregnant and they dreamed of naming the child the same as his father: Alberto. I was very content with the path these lovers had taken, because she deserved it. One day Rogelia came crying to tell me that she had received a letter from Gizelda in which she said that the count had died. He had been in an incident in a café, provoked by a drunk. Gizelda said that the person who shot the count was in love with her, and he believed that killing the count would free her. The letter was filled with profound grief, and it said that she would return home. Within a month I received news that she had given birth to a very beautiful boy and that she was penniless, that she was returning to Rogelia. Rogelia became sick during those days and didn't go out again. I searched for her and did not find her. Months passed, and one day as I crossed the plaza in front of the theater I heard the screams of a child. I looked, and it was a woman who had fallen. I hurried as much as I could to get to her and the child. I focused in on the woman, and it seemed that I knew her. I saw a locket that hung from her neck, and I opened it. I looked at it, and it was her; it couldn't be anyone else. I detached the locket and called the police so they could take her to the hospital. Later I found out that she had died . . . from hunger . . ." He wiped some tears that fell onto his beard.

Jacinto as if awakening said, "And that locket and the letters?"

"I have the locket. I only have two of the letters because Rogelia was the one who received them."

"That day I cried because I had known her and because of how she died in front of the theater that had glorified her as an artist and as a woman of beauty. Later, I found out that she had traveled through the streets, begging in the cafés and plazas, and they gave her nothing for her son because I am sure that she would not have asked for herself. No one lent her a hand nor was I able to help her."

"How did she get to that state in such little time?"

"I don't know. I suppose that staying there without resources she went about selling her belongings and then came here as fast as she could. She lived with Rogelia, but Rogelia died, and they threw Gizelda in the streets, because no one knew where she lived."

"Listen, Watchman," said Jacinto. "I can pay you whatever you ask for your revelations and for the locket and the letters. I am Gizelda's son."

The Watchman looked him up and down and with such an expression of astonishment said to him, "You're Gizelda's son? You're that little one in school? How you have changed! Jacinto smiled and told him, "Don't you recognize me?"

"No, I would go to ask about you at the orphanage every day. And if you are her son, I will give you the locket and the letters." And taking out a small box that he had his pocket, he gave it to him.

"What do you want for that?"

"Sir, I will not sell it. I will give it to you in her name. That was for you. Upon seeing you come in, I figured that you were related to the count, because you look a lot like him."

"I am his son."

"I know now, but I didn't know that then."

"Well, Watchman, I am off. Thank you and if you need me let the mayor know that you are a friend of mine."

"Thank you very much." They shook hands and said good-bye. The mayor's car was waiting for him. When he arrived home, he entered hastily, and opened the small box. The locket and its chain were magnificent works of art and made of good quality gold. It had some diamonds and rubies. He opened it and watched the contents spill out on the table. It was then that he saw the portrait of his mother and on the other side, a young man: it must be his father! He cleaned the locket well, and after kissing both portraits repeatedly, he placed it in his pocket and went to the office.

Meanwhile, at the mayor and count's table, they commented about Jacinto's resolution to find out who his parents were. "I was not here at that time. I know nothing, but from the boy's looks and instinctive nature, he must be from good parents," said the mayor to his family.

In the count's dining room, he said, "He will come bringing his social title or his fortune."

Alina replied, "I do not want either of them. I love him."

"Even if he is a nobody?"

"What do you mean, a nobody! Per chance a cultured, educated, intelligent young man with a secure future, is a nobody?"

"Are you well-informed about his life?"

"Yes and no. I see him leave his office every day, every day I suppose that he doesn't gamble or drink. He works, then goes home to study. Could you wish for an example that would give greater prestige to my children."

"But, daughter, you are but a child to be talking like that."

"At sixteen years of age I am not a child, father."

"Well, if he does not bring name or fortune, I can't make a decision, because I don't want to be at the mercy of criticism and gossip."

"You will kill me."

"Don't ask me for the impossible."

"I want my happiness. No one has the right to question or to tell me what sort of happiness I should desire."

"You are much too young to know how to search for happiness. You do not have any experience."

"Happiness and love are children, not old folks."

"You will think twice about that later."

"I have my mind made up."

"Very well, calm yourself," said her mother.

They finished eating, and Alina kissed her parents and retired to her room. Passing by a garden door, she glanced to see if the car was waiting for her and returned to her bedroom to finish getting ready. She put on a hat in the style of Charlotte Corday and went down to the garden. She went out and stepped into her car. When she arrived at the customary place, Jacinto was already walking among the rows of trees. Alina sat down to read. Jacinto saw her and approached, "My love, I come peacefully and courageously to tell you my impressions, because my soul is not afraid to meet with yours and because worldly formulas and vanities cannot separate us. Doesn't that prove I trust in your love?"

Jacinto had taken Alina's hands and she, asked him to sit at her side as she told him, "I am proud of you and happy to know that you understand me and know me. Now tell me what has happened to you?"

Jacinto said, "I went to see your father and he told me that I must bring name or fortune. What I have is not enough for him. He desires someone with a social title for you. You are del Prado, I am del Bosque. Your father believes that a Bosque is inferior to a Prado. I believe that he is wrong. Now tell me what you are thinking."

Alina, looking with kindness at her beloved, said to him, "Those foolish details of old-fashioned people do not concern me. Don't speak to me of those things."

"I tell you these things so that you are aware of the details that could interrupt our relationship."

"Fine, but I had thought to appeal to the laws. I'm free. I'm not a slave, and no one has the right to obligate me or to oppose my desires."

"Had you thought of something that would resolve our situation in case of an objection?"

"Yes."

"Then tomorrow you will tell me how you will settle it."

"It is already settled. My father opposes, so I will test his resistance. If he persists then I will avail my rights."

"How courageous you are! Allow me to kiss you without evasiveness, and embrace you in my arms," and Jacinto, hugging her tightly, kissed her.

Alina told him, "I am leaving I hope that they have not decided to send someone to look for me."

"Until tomorrow!"

"Until tomorrow, my Alina."

They separated and Jacinto slipped away on the other side while she stepped into her car. Jacinto arrived home and began to contemplate the portraits in the locket. He rolled it around in his hands and decided to open it, loosening the portraits from the frame to observe if they had something written on the back. He started with his mother's. He detached it and there was written: *For my love, Alberto, from your Gizelda. December, year and month.* Then his father's, which said: *To my love, the only woman whom I have loved and will make my wife. Alberto del Prado.*

Jacinto upon seeing the signature became astonished. He exclaimed: "Good heavens! What does this mean? That is also Alina's name. But I can't be her brother because her father is alive. How do I decipher this? Who can I ask for help?" He placed the portraits as they were and decided to go to his patron, the mayor. It was 9 o'clock and Don Eliseo was on his way out when Jacinto appeared.

"Hello, my dear young man," said Don Eliseo. "What results did you obtain from the Watchman?"

"Well, it was interesting. He gave me this locket," said Jacinto.

Don Eliseo took the locket that Jacinto held out to him and said, "Magnificent piece. Your mother's?"

"Yes, Sir, but the piece is not the only valuable thing. There are two portraits of my father and my mother," and he opened it to show Don Eliseo.

"Oh my!" he exclaimed, "what a beautiful woman and the man, how handsome, what a distinguishing appearance."

"Now," said Jacinto, "you should read what is written on the other side," and he detached the portraits allowing Don Eliseo to read.

After he read he said, "Very well. This serves as proof for you, but is this the Prado family of your fiancée?"

"I don't know," said Jacinto, "that is why I have come for you to settle it or help me."

"Fine," said Don Eliseo, "leave me the locket. I will go to a friend tomorrow and find out."

"Thank you, Don Eliseo," said Jacinto, "until tomorrow."

Jacinto went home to sleep off the many impressions of the day. He was in need of rest.

The next day after leaving his office, he went home. He changed his suit and went to eat. He later walked to the boulevard to meet his valiant Alina. He walked around for a while and later sat on a bench to wait, but he waited in vain. Alina did not arrive. Six o'clock came and went. Alina did not come. He returned home and didn't know what to do to find out what happened. He decided to wait until tomorrow, and he sat down to read.

Meanwhile, what had happened to Miss Alina?

Alina had quickly closed herself in her room that afternoon, and it made her mother fearful of something. A few minutes later, the countess called for her daughter but when Alina did not answer, the countess entered her room and found it empty. She then looked in the garden and asked about if they had seen her but no one had seen Alina leave. The countess rang a bell, and a servant appeared. She said to him, "Ask the doorman if Alina has gone out."

The servant left and within ten minutes he returned, saying: "No, madam. I did not seen her go out through the main door."

"Go look for the chauffeur."

The servant left, and the pensive countess was pale.

The servant returned and said, "Madam countess, the chauffeur is not there."

"Then go to the house of the Baroness de Río and see if the car is parked out in front."

He left, and the countess said, "And why wouldn't she have gone out through the main door? It's very odd."

The servant came back when Alina was returning through the garden.

"Madam, the car wasn't out front, it is in front of the garden. Alina stepped out of it and entered the garden."

"Very well, you can go."

The countess went to Alina's room and said to her, "My daughter, I searched for you, and you had me worried not knowing where you were."

"I went out for a walk to distract me," said Alina, kissing her mother. "Did you need me?"

"No, but why didn't leave through the front door?"

"I much prefer going through the garden, mother."

"You shouldn't go out alone anymore. You are exposed to all kinds of accidents, and it really scares me, you know? Don't do it again. I won't have it."

"But, mother, I returned immediately."

"I don't like it, daughter."

Alina kissed her mother again and was walking away when her mother stopped her. "Don't go. Read something to me so that I might be entertained."

Alina picked up a book that was on the table and began to read aloud, but by 9 o'clock the countess had fallen asleep.

When the count arrived, he saw his wife sleeping, and taking his daughter by the hand, he kissed her forehead and said to her, "Until tomorrow."

Then he called his wife and, helping her up he said to her, "Let's go to our room if you are sleepy."

The countess got up and said, "Let's go to the balcony for awhile because I want to talk to you." When she reached the balcony, the countess said, "Listen, our daughter is all grown up. She mustn't go out alone."

"Why?"

"It seems that she is accustomed to go out alone every day, because yesterday I went to her room and I didn't find her. I searched for her throughout the entire house and finally she appeared in the garden."

"Alone?"

"Yes, alone."

"Do you know if she had a meeting with someone?"

"I don't know."

"Well, we must find out." He called the chauffeur and asked him.

"Are we going to make this chauffeur spy on our daughter?"

"Somehow it must be known."

"Fine, but find another way."

"There isn't another way more certain than to follow her. But it doesn't feel right to me."

"What are you going to do?"

"Going with her would be better," said the count, "and that is for you to do."

"But that way she won't go where she usually goes," the countess exclaimed

"It doesn't matter. That way no suspicions are established."

"Fine."

They left the balcony and retired to their rooms.

The next day Alina, not knowing what they had plotted, did not warn Jacinto. In the afternoon at the end of the dinner hour, the countess said to her,

"If you are going out, let me know. I want to go with you."

Alina replied a bit surprised, but restrained. "I don't go out every day. Tomorrow I'll go, mother."

The countess looked at her, observing if she was upsetting her but Alina remained mute and seemingly very satisfied: she went out on the balcony. Then, taking a walk on the balcony, she remembered about the chauffeur who was waiting for her. What should she do? Then silently she passed through the corridor, entered her room, and went down to the garden. She told the chauffeur, "I'm not going out this afternoon, but tomorrow I will."

The chauffeur went away and she continued walking through the garden, saying to herself. "What will Jacinto think? My darling, he is such a good man."

She decided to go up to her room to write him and tell him to stop by the garden.

We shall see what Jacinto thought, because he waited for a letter from his beloved. He couldn't imagine what had happened.

He hoped that Alina would settle the matter, and he desired to know what had happened since she had not come to the meeting.

He was writing in his office when the postman arrived. The assistant handed him a letter. It was from his Alina. He opened it hastily and read:

My love,

Come this afternoon to the garden so I can talk to you. I desire to see you. Yesterday I could not go out for a stroll.

I adore you, Alina.

We leave Jacinto savoring the letter and we shall see what Don Eliseo has done.

The next day as he had told Jacinto, Don Eliseo went to see his friend, the Marquis de la Villa. He found him smoking and reading the morning paper in his visiting room.

Upon seeing the mayor, he got up and said, "Hello, my friend! To what do I owe this pleasant surprise?"

Don Eliseo made himself comfortable in his armchair and began, "Dear Marquis, approximately eighteen years ago I was notified that they had found a dead woman with a child in her arms in the plaza in front of the theater: they didn't know what to do with the child. When they presented him to me, I saw the most precious child that I had ever seen. I sent him to the orphanage and later recommended him to a school. Today he is a model young man, studious, judicious, and very educated. But since complete happiness doesn't exist, the boy has fallen in love with the daughter of the Count of Torreón and since he has no social title, it turns out he didn't know what to do."

"But first tell me," interrupted the marquis, "What is his name?"

"We named him Jacinto del Bosque. But it is not a surname that would be recognized as nobility through a genealogy search, nor is he rich. But it occurred to the young man to ask me, and I told him what I knew. I recommended that he go to the cripple who was in the hospital. He followed my advice and came back with this locket that he says was his mother's." And Don Eliseo showed the locket to his friend and told him: "Open it so you can tell me if you know those gentle people."

The marquis opened the locket and exclaimed: "Gizelda! And Alberto."

"Did you know them?" said the mayor.

"Yes! Very well. I fell in love with this woman and would have married her, but I was in an inheritance dispute and didn't think I should marry. She liked the count very much, and he took her to a villa. After his mother died, they went to Paris. We were intimate friends but we grew apart a bit during her absence, since he knew that I was in love with her. Afterward I did not hear about them until his brother returned from his studies, mourning Alberto who had died from a gunshot in a café—they did not know who did it. Afterward I didn't hear from her, I and did not go out much. Then I got married and that is it, until now. You said that she died of hunger. I didn't know that, because I would have helped her."

"In the greatest poverty."

"It is odd. I would have done so much for her, having known her in the past! Why didn't you bring her son to me so I could have seen him?"

"Because I didn't know if you knew his parents and I thought it would be unsuitable."

"Well, bring him when you wish."

"So you will help his situation?"

"Certainly, it will be a gift to the memory of that woman. Listen, Eliseo, she had a heart of gold, so beautiful and unassuming that they called her 'The Diva.'"

"But have you forgotten that I told you that Jacinto has fallen in love with Alina del Prado? Perhaps you didn't understand."

"Oh my! I didn't understand what you said. Well then, they are cousins and her father can't refuse."

"You think so?"

"Yes, I will go to speak personally with Alina's father."

"Well then, Rafael, I am off. I will return soon to hear what he decided."

"Very well, Eliseo, as you wish."

"Until later!"

Don Eliseo was pleasantly impressed to know that his friend would help his protégé and that he would be able to please him.

Meanwhile, we shall see if Jacinto went to the garden meeting. We find him passing in front of the gate, he decides to push it and enter. He sits down on the first bench he finds. And we see Alina hurriedly coming down the staircase to greet him.

Jacinto got up and received his Alina with open arms.

They both sat down and Alina said to him: "Did you go out for a stroll yesterday?"

"Yes, I did and I returned very sad because I didn't see you."

"I couldn't go. Mother needed me. Yesterday, when she realized I wasn't home, she was very upset. So late yesterday, before leaving the house, she told me, 'If you are going out, let me know so that I can go with you.' I told her that I wasn't planning on going out today, and then I wrote to you so that you would come over."

"Nothing else?"

"Nothing else."

"Well I have managed to get the mayor to concern himself with my situation. He is going to investigate."

"Jacinto, remember my father. Please tell him everything you told me."

Jacinto was making drawings with his cane when the count walked over to him.

"Good afternoon, young people," said the count, "Are you having visits in the garden?"

"Sir, I was passing by and I saw your daughter so I stopped to greet her. If it is imprudent, I will go.

"Father," said Alina, "this is very natural."

A servant interrupted the conversation saying: "Sir count, here come Sir Marquis de la Villa and Sir Mayor."

"But here, in the garden?"

"Yes, sir, they did not want to wait."

The servant escorted them in, and as they approached, the marquis said, "Forgive us for interrupting such a lovely meeting."

Meanwhile the mayor, after greeting everyone approached Jacinto and told him, "We have come to discuss your situation."

"Do you know each other?" asked the count.

"Yes, Sir," replied the mayor, "he is my protégé." And addressing the marquis: "Sir, allow me to introduce you to Jacinto del Bosque."

"It is a great pleasure, sir," said Jacinto stretching out his hand to the marquis.

"Well," said the mayor, "we need the count, if you'll excuse us, we'll leave you both alone."

"Let's go, I'll be happy to help."

"Excuse us," said the marquis, tipping his hat.

The three of them went up to the hall and Jacinto, accompanied by Alina, walked through the garden.

After everyone had assembled, they all sat down and the mayor said: "Sir count, we have come here to clear up a situation. The young man that we left down there is under my tutelage, and he has related to me the problem you have with respect to your daughter. I desire to know your motives."

"My friend, I only told him that I wanted to know his lineage, because I did not recognize his surname, and in what conditions he was to marry."

"Well, he can marry. As for a social title," replied the mayor, "he has it."

"Also," said the marquis, "I knew his mother and his father, and you know his father also. His mother was a great artist. When you were in school, his father took her away just before the death of his mother. His name is Alberto del Prado."

"My brother!"

"Exactly, and later they went to Paris. If they married there I don't know the date, but I can show you their portraits." And addressing the mayor, he said, "Show him the locket."

The mayor held out the locket, and after the count examined it, he shouted an exclamation of astonishment: "My brother, and a woman!"

"A distinguished woman of high social rank who dedicated herself to the theater against the desires of her family," said the marquis.

"Now," said Don Eliseo, "you should check the reverse side of the two portraits." The count took them out of the locket and read what was written.

"Sir," said Don Eliseo, "that young man's name is Alberto del Prado and for that reason I ask for her hand in marriage on his behalf."

"What right do you have to give him that name?"

"Count," said the marquis, "you can't deny that he is your brother's son."

"I don't doubt it, but my brother didn't make a will. For that reason I can't respond to you at this time."

"What are you afraid of?" said the marquis.

"Be certain that if you did not demand this, he would not be concerned about it. He did not know that your daughter had special titles or that she was rich," said the mayor.

"So he is very selfless."

"He is a model gentleman," said Don Eliseo.

"I wish to be the best man at the wedding," said the marquis.

"I appreciate the request you are making but let's go down to the garden, and there we will decide."

"You are right. Have someone sent to call them and we will do it here or in the parlor."

"Very well," replied the count ringing a bell. A servant appeared and he was told to notify Alina and the young man in the garden to come in.

Five minutes passed. When they entered the parlor, the marquis got up and said, "Ladies and gentlemen, allow me to introduce the gentleman Alberto del Prado." He took Jacinto by the hand, but Jacinto could not believe what he heard. Alina was astonished and said, "My cousin!"

"Nephew!" said the countess, accepting the hand that Alberto extended to her.

Alina asked, "What have you decided?"

"Well, Miss," responded the mayor, "we have decided that you should marry, because you both deserve it."

"Thank you," uttered Alberto. "I didn't expect that decision."

"Well, my children," said the count, "both of you go out to the garden so you can make arrangements and decide when you will marry."

They both went out smiling and the four remaining people continued to talk, enjoying the drinks that were served. The count invited everyone to stay for dinner. "I will stay," said the marquis, "but allow me to advise my wife not to wait for me," and he went out to make a phone call.

When it was time to sit down at the table, they called Alina and Alberto. "What have you decided?" the count asked the young people.

"That we should unite this month."

"I agree," the countess replied, "but that is very rushed and you aren't taking into consideration the friendship and marriage bans."

"Fine, and when can we do it?" asked Alberto.

"Wait until next month."

"It has already been close to two years that we have been in love and I believe it would be prudent to end this situation."

"We understand," said the count, "but don't forget that we have some requests. You can shorten the time if you wish, but do not stray from the social requisites so quickly."

"I accept and in this case I will leave the matter in your hands." The marquis said, "Sir count has the authority to do it and he will do it well."

They finished eating, and the marquis and Don Eliseo said good-bye. Alina and Alberto went out to the garden as soon as the count and countess went to the balcony. The countess wanted to know how it was that they were relatives. "Very simple," said the count, "my brother had romantic relations with a beautiful artist, and there you have the son."

"So when are you making the invitations?"

"Tomorrow," answered the count.

Throughout the community, in the meetings, assemblies, and parties, the commentaries about Alina's wedding were innumerable. Where had that fiancé come from, and why the hastiness for the wedding? This went against everything correct and traditional. A young man arrives and doesn't know who he is, a girl parades around on his arms, and within a few days, marriage? "What imprudence!" said some envious women, and other commented, "How selfish. She let him come to our parties when we asked her for his address in order to invite him, she told us that she didn't know it."

Meanwhile, Alina prepared for her wedding and did not worry about the criticism from her friends. The night of the wedding arrived, and the ballroom, the garden, and the dining room were illuminated. There were so many flowers that the air one breathed was delightful.

All the guests waited to see the bride and groom. Finally, the servant announced them, and they entered the reception hall. They had improvised a small courtroom, where the justice of peace, the witnesses, the Marquis de la Villa, the mayor, and other guests waited. Alina and Alberto walked into the hall to greet their admirers. Now they were united, and they announced that they were off to Switzerland and then on to Paris.

Everyone moved into the dining hall, and after dinner, they said good-bye. Alberto and Alina remained until the end with their parents and the witnesses until one o'clock in the morning as these people were their most intimate friends. The next day, Alina and Alberto left for Switzerland.

Alina's mother and father decided to take a trip to Venice and Milan.

EPILOGUE

One year later, the count received news that the young folks had a daughter who they had named Gizelda. Five years later, the Count of Torreón died, leaving his children heirs to everything. The countess went to live with her children and two grandchildren, Gizelda and Alberto, named in memory of those lovers they never knew.

Alberto came to gather that which by law was due him, and without using vulgar methods, he became the owner of an extensive wealth. He was happy man.

The Watchman died in the hospital while Alberto and Alina were in Paris.

The Marquis de la Villa was now old and widowed, and his son had married. The mayor spent his days with his grandchildren everyday in the forest . . .

Interesting Letters from a Panamanian Anarchist

My dearest sister Luisa Capetillo:

After keeping silent for more than a year, today I send you a letter to inquire about you. My objective is to not be too inappropriate since I believe that we gain nothing with diatribes.

Tell me, did you receive the portrait of Ferrer that I sent you in the month of May? I sent it by certified mail under the name Juan Chiet.

On the 28th of this month, the Most Excellent Señora Doña Emilia Serrano Baronesa de Wilson gave a presentation in the grand theater of Panama. It was a failure because wealthy gentlemen do not like philosophy.

I am sending the newspaper clipping.

Answer me, you hear? Answer me.

Dear Luisa,

Your letter is in my possession today (what good fortune of mine and I answer it without losing a moment). Don't be surprised by my forced silence. When I was fighting in the Zone for the propaganda of our ideas, I didn't think that the working class would plunge me into dishonor, but it was so. To argue with Perez, never again. I recognize his right to attack me, but I cannot take into account the reasoning of a scoundrel.

I earn my livelihood with my business. When they criticized me I stopped being exploited, and I made myself a businessman. I should have put this into practice much earlier, but I suffered for propagandizing in the field of the workers. Am I the scoundrel, the one who sacrificed my tranquillity for that of my brothers?

Let's leave that, and let's discuss your life, my dear sister. I know you suffer much and that you go through bad times. I do not have a fortune, but if you come to Colón and with what I earn, you will eat and clothe yourself as if you were my mother. I only have one life, and I love it a great deal. You know that I esteem you and I love you as if you were my sister. I don't pass up work. I am strong and I can earn for the two of us. I won't tell you again.

Listen, I am sending *Romeo and Juliet.* I am a bit romantic with you.

A hug, and take my advice.

Dear sister Luisa Capetillo,

If you decide not to come here and you have many pamphlets, send me six of each, and I will sell them if I can. If not I will send you their value within a month, counting from the day they arrive.

I wish that you would come, because if you don't have other means for a better life than the one you have, count on my job which will provide for both of us.

You don't know me, but I am a friend who keeps his promises.

Don't stop searching for the newspapers that I entrust to you. They are of great importance to me.

Dear sister Luisa,

On the 20th of this month, I received two newspapers from the Tampa Union with two valiant articles of yours. Since I am familiar with your labor in the field of struggle, I do not doubt that you have great opposers who disapprove of your work in favor of the emancipation of oppressed women. The men of today do not love women: they love the flesh of Lupanar or of exploitation for their unbridled appetites of lust.

Humanity cannot enjoy freedom while women are not free. A woman who gives her body over to the spasms of an enslaved pleasure will never bring forth healthy, strong children. Maternal bosoms that dilate in the pleasure of coitus, under the pressure of pain and fear that reign in today's marriages will not produce the fruit with all its liberty, because the muscles of life don't take pleasure in its dominion and recreation of maternal functions.

If a man of fine features stands before a mirror when he is possessed by fear, his facial muscles will be contracted in such a manner that it would be difficult to recognize him. This happens with the woman in her maternal function.

Fight with valor in the field of women's liberty. Woman is the one who gives humanity its life and direction. Without free women, man cannot be free.

That is all for today. I am your most affectionate brother. I love you . . . .

Dear sister Luisa Capetillo,

Your letter from the 9th is in my possession. Thank you for your punctuality. I lament that my previous letter is not in your hands. I sent it on the 15th and it was certified with the no. 2911. It contains a post-card a bit more romantic, since in its contents I am very affectionate toward you.

Your struggle sustained in the defense of women is great, and it brings you a great number of enemies that will give you your sorrows. If in Tampa you had set up a tavern with many **Beautiful Women,** the bourgeoisie would have been your friends and the lewd scoundrels would have greeted you with love. Great souls do not search for applause from the mob. When a drunken bourgeois woman applauds a fighter, it is to prostitute the sanctity of his work. The fighter is misunderstood. When humanity does not understand Christ, they spit on him, they crown him with thorns, they dress him as a buffoon, and they crucify him. Each applause from the mob has a drop of hemlock for the Socrates of the struggle. They are the root of all evil works that spread the titles of Very Great, Very Noble Sir.

When the world adopted Christ's doctrine, it was so prostituted that instead of the Drama of Golgotha, it is the comedy of mockery. Flee from the masses with your greatness and you will be great. In complete sorrow is the glory of love and struggle—struggle redeems great souls.

"What amount of martyrdom do you suffer with your sorrow?" a king asked Diogenes: "Lord, said the wise man, my patched clothes and my barrel are sources of hope for my kingdom." When you cannot take on more pain in your heart, search for the mantle of your wisdom, and you will be queen among your executioners.

Struggle and love, the struggle is life, love is the essence of struggle. Without struggle and without love, life would be sorrowful. And when your executioners are most enjoying their triumph you give their women freedom through your propaganda, and you will have the comfort of glorifying the most holy of creations: woman redeemed from the exploitation of the prostituted man.

Your brother that loves you.

Listen, send me some of your pamphlets if you can. I am inclined to know of your present work.

My dear sister Luisa Capetillo,

How I esteem your letter dated April 27th. I received it in the days of loneliness and abandonment that I spent in my bed with a fever. Only you and my mother have remembered me. Thank you, dear sister.

Your letter dated April 9th arrived the 15th of the same month and I had already fallen ill. I was hoping, and I hope, that the fever leaves me so I can fight in the press, condemning the brutalities of your gratuitous enemies. If things don't go well in Tampa, I would suggest that you come to Colón. With what I earn at my job you can eat and be clothed until luck changes. I respect you and suppose that you don't deserve to suffer the contempt of the bourgeoisie and the scoundrel abandonment of the prostituted Gleva.

Each day I have more hatred and contempt for the mass of ruffians. They are always the same throughout history: crucifying Christ, giving Socrates hemlock, burning Galileo, scorning Diogenes, and cutting off the heads of all those who stand out from the heap of flesh without eyes that composes prostituted people.

The law of human progress is so dreadful for the propagators that a lone suicidal spirit or a personal vision of the glory can take noble souls and exquisite spirits to spread freedom. When the world wins in its moral and material perfection, the propagator loses his reasoning and his mind, and the law of compensation is lamentable, because the one who gives his soul and his life in human struggle, after losing all his attributes and faculties, dies burdened with pain and with disappointment in the corner of public contempt.

The flames of the great ideals of justice and redemption burn the wings of the condors of thought, and when they cannot travel across the sky with their impetuous flight they fall in the social swamp where toads destroy the fibers of their luminous soul so avenge themselves of the difference that Mother Nature languishes on her dearest daughters.

Dear sister, excuse me for I can't write any more, or any better. My head is very ill and my pulse very weak. When I get better I will begin my letters with largess. When you are not able to fight in Tampa, know that you can count on your brother in Colón, who offers you half of what he earns with his work.

Dear sister Luisa Capetillo,

Since my last letter, I have the ghost of remorse in my soul. I listen to the conscience that shouts to me: Wretch! He who cannot give joy, do not take away someone else's! When a man loves solitude and silence, he does not look at the world outside of himself, because the world is inside everyone, and only in the interior world can you not be betrayed, nor can one betray oneself. Why divulge the pain in a society of cowards? Life without its sorrow is not life and he who can't withstand its sorrow can go now with a firm pace toward death. It is the supreme hour in which man is greater than God.

When a man persists in searching for happiness, he has to cry like a child who studies in the womb of his dolls their mechanical organism of movements. Ay! Each doll is constructed for a specific function, and each desire in search of happiness is printed by a mechanism and this mechanism holds the mechanic's reasoning.

When I remember the pain of my amorous disillusionment, I am very unhappy. Why? I loved God above all things, and the day that I found out that God is me, it gave me much sorrow; as much sorrow as the slave of Elos who stopped eating rats in order to not stop being a slave. Then, I so loved men and found them slaves to their passions, and I fought for the freedom of the oppressed. Ay! Sorrow, I am betrayed by my brothers and I understood that each one of the exploited wanted to exploit my good faith and so much cowardice scared me. And I loved woman. Inside woman's heart there isn't love: the woman loves the one that enslaves her and despises the lover. I searched for the female as male, and it only gave forth the fruit of reproduction. With so much bitterness and so much sorrow in my soul I was broken down by the disappointments, and I loved solitude.

What is solitude? The greatest representation of human liberty, because in solitude you can't be betrayed nor can you be a traitor. You will tell me that in order to love solitude, one is uncommunicative. No, in solitude if one doesn't know how to be in it, it scares them, like he who enters a palace for the first time. He admires it contemplatively, but if there is a scream, he is scared of the echo of his own voice. When I entered solitude I cried out many painful cries, and I wasn't scared of the echo of my voice. With all the bitterness of a child and the experience of a loner, I searched for communication for my sorrow. I searched for you, who is alone on the cusp of bitterness, heavy with the sorrow of your soul and struggling with human disillusionment.

You, through these letters, perhaps can understand that I am a failure. No, failure is not knowing how to live in solitude. He who searches in his soul a throne, and in his understanding an art, in his heart a shield, in his life a positive freedom, and in his pain a book, he isn't unsuccessful. It is he, he who made all the Gods, all the prejudices, all the false ideals, all the religions, and all the false loves, to enter by his own will into the kingdom of solitude and of meditation.

The failure is in searching for the communication with one's soul. And my soul isn't—it can't be communicative.

Tell me, are you bothered by my last letter? I don't understand your silence; I am so fond of your letters. Soon I will send you some postcards and some maps of the Canal.

Dear sister Luisa Capetillo,

Without any letter to which I can refer, I am sending you this letter. If I were to ask myself why I write to you, I would be able to answer my question with complete satisfaction. But what if I tell you that I have a premonition in my soul and it brings me great sorrow? I understand that I never should have sent you my confidential letter, because neither you nor I are responsible for the fact that my soul isn't wrought for my material body. I have a soul that because of its greatness, doesn't fit in the body of a sad, solitary man burdened with traitorous disillusions. And since my soul and I are far apart, my sorrows have to search for a place to expand their pain. It was in that supreme moment that I sent you my letter, because the pressure of my sorrow had 95 degrees of atmospheric pressure, and I felt that my head weakened and that moral madness reigned in me. What did I tell you in my letter? . . . Of a great love that was betrayed by an illusion. An illusion that dies in the soul when the soul is already dead from sorrow. A sorrow that doesn't fit in my chest. It bursts into myriads of atoms and tarnishes with its emanations the interior world of my dear sister. That is my letter, a letter of sorrow, where the dead illusions are the reality of a life that loves and will love, until the pain kills the flesh and feelings and thoughts.

Ah! Those who love and are loved! In life only sorrow is positive, and love is a madness in itself. With what I shared in confidence I would have put an end to my bitterness. Today I will be tranquil but . . . Ah! I continue in a place of torment, and you have taken part in my sorrow in order to embitter your soul, without which you could offer comfort to my bitterness!

Answer me. Tell me that you are not upset with me, that you do not hate me, and that you trust in the affection of your brother who loves you.

Sister of my soul,

I have a great bitterness in my heart. My last letter, the letter that I sent and that afterward hurt me, because now I comprehend my lack of prudence. That **mysterious** and briefly meditated letter only gave me counterproductive results, because your soul and your sentiment as a woman and a mother are inundated with a materialist disease that upsets my understanding. What can you do in my favor to distract my suffering? My wretched love makes me so disorientated that now I am not even a shadow of myself. My entire soul, so pure and so naïve like that of a child, is so destroyed and so exhausted that only with my strength of will can I console life. Never could I suppose that a love would be so strong that it could cause a deep sorrow capable of causing death.

How to understand that love, the source of all human life was to be the source of death? All of my life I had great prudence for love. I understood that to love a woman in the present society would bring me great troubles. A man who loves freedom and art in the most grandiose manifestation of life, without pretenses or cowardice, will never encounter a companion who gives the love of her bosom with the natural frankness of her altruistic feelings. It is for the business of love and the flesh that woman is educated, not for the love and beauty of love and life.

With this deduction and this understanding of my soul and the human soul in general, I went on dreaming a life of platonic love and since this love did not have a way to reveal itself, a melancholy so profound invaded my soul that I had moments when I dreamed I renounced my being. At that time (1910) I communicated to you these sorrows of my soul, and understanding you to be of highly artistic taste and of unusual education and of a superior soul, I put in your hands my education and my soul in order that as an artist and as an educated woman, you would mold my childlike soul and my spirit as a dreamer.

I remember that in a letter you told me with all your naivety that I would love a woman who searched for a companion. Ay! To love a woman is easy, to search for a companion is impossible. In love, the woman is the flesh and the companion in life, the wife of the **Song of**

songs. With all the strength of my goodwill, I tried to harmonize these two human and divine tendencies, and I searched the books. I loved life and searched for woman. Your letter had the solution to my great problem. You wrote: "When yours arrived I was leaving the factory with a wounded heart, and my soul was destroyed by all the great sorrows of my life of bitterness. The doctor took me to a café and treated me to bonbons and lemonade."

The mystery of my sad and solitary life was exiled completely from my soul, because the portrait of poetry that you painted me in this letter was the key to a mystery of all that is mysterious. And I loved with all my soul because my soul was sick from a thirst of love. But how do I harmonize these tendencies that are so diametrically opposite? By a supreme effort of my auto-vision, which killed in me all the pure and poetic aspects of my superhuman love, helped me find a woman who I searched with the purest light of all my illusions, she was so perfect, as perfect as was my love. Those mysterious mirages were taken from your life. I said to myself: My sister suffers, and in her suffering, she searches for the balm of life in life itself. She does not love, but life is a dream and it dreams with love—**an illusion of the soul**—and with the dream of life in dialogue with suffering and with philosophy it enjoys the purest essence of love—Suffering . . .

It was in this manner that I loved. I loved with all the passion of my soul: I killed the suffering of the legitimate son of my passionate soul and handed over my heart a priori with all the frankness of my candid soul.

Because of this I suffer, because of this I cry. I do not doubt that I am loved, but the traitor's shadow put itself in my path and killed the glory of my love.

Forgive me for these letters of so little pleasure.

Dear sister Luisa,

Your letter from the 18th of August is in my possession and you do not know how much I appreciate you for taking so much longing in my suffering. The woman who I love so much is in Colón. I have had a romantic relationship with her for a year now. Upon first meeting her I feared her, given her temperament and upbringing. She limited me to only be her friend and to frequent her house on a visit. During these frequent and gracious visits, I searched her soul and I always confirmed my pessimistic, substantial, and defined opinion: that my beloved was so corrupted by the educationalist principles of this country that my love was one degree away from madness.

I understood inside my heart of hearts that I loved her, but I put my strength of will before my love and struggled against my own feeling. This is the epilogue to a drama so violent that it could have had dreadful consequences.

In the month of June 1912, I was sick in bed with a fever. I live alone in my room and I am very distant from her house. My acquaintances asked about me and found out about my illness. They came to my house very frequently, and sent me medicines, and cared for me.

I became very fond of the family, and then I began to love with a passion. What is love without gratitude? In this manner a year passed by. I don't deny that in that year of love I had moments of intimate happiness and all of the coldness of my soul toward my lover left me transforming into a fire that consumed my existence. This fire was on many occasions the cause of great upsets in my body, since I had a very great need to love in my soul, and given the impetus of my love, I searched in my beloved for the source of comfort to mitigate my thirst.

The woman, dominated by the love of money and willing to sell her love and her favors, never attended to a supplication of mine, and she proposed the matrimonial ecclesiastic contract as a definitive condition. Since I loved her with all my soul, I met her halfway and promised her a civil marriage. Never—she told me with a boldness typical of a hardhearted woman, and this was the cause of my estrangement. What can I expect from a companion who, upon giving me her love, transfigures herself into a Delilah? A love that offers itself covered in so many exigencies and so well-thought-out like, that of my beloved cannot be love. Love cannot depend on a mathematical calculation like the business cashbook. My rebellious soul cannot yield to women who are so methodical that they give a kiss of love (pretending) in order to propose a social contract stipulated in a vicarage with the foolscap. This is the reason for my misfortune.

How much time did I take in discovering the betrayal? Why didn't I investigate this woman before loving her? When we began the relationship, I doubted, but today she tells me a family misfortune, tomorrow a disease that undermines her body, then a bitterness that destroys her soul: another day I catch her with tears in her eyes, later she swears love on her sister's grave, and with all these manifestations of a supposed or pretended sorrow, I went so far as to place all my love in her love just as if I were to have placed it in my own mother. So much was my love for this woman that if I didn't discover her betrayal today I would have placed my beliefs at her feet, because I was willing to be married canonically.

Don't criticize me, my sister. A man that doesn't have the heart to suffer with another's sorrow is lost to the cause of liberty, and I have inside my soul a very pure place, where all my sorrows are kept, sister. If a man tells me his life story, a life full of bitterness and sorrow, I listen to him as a courtesy. But if a woman tells me her sufferings with eyes full of tears and her arm around my neck and her chest resting on mine, I don't have the heart to defend myself. Rather I offer her all that I am and all that I am worth. I have a Mother!

What isn't mine doesn't hurt me: I don't love the material. What hurts me is that today, after giving all my love and my tranquillity, this woman takes joy in my pain and sorrow.

Dear sister Luisa,

Your letter of August 25th is in my possession. You know I lament in my soul that you took my last letter so far out of context. I can't deny that you have misunderstood my letter.

When I sent that letter I had a very great sorrow. My childlike soul was so bitter that the gloomiest visions stained with blood and gall engendered themselves. With this sort of thinking and behaving, I don't doubt that my letter contained expressions that were very little thought through. But at the core of my letter, far from looking for an argument that I can't sustain, I searched for your sane and prudent counsel. I understand that I don't have the right to share my sorrows and my pains, but a man who loves much suffers much, and I love so much and suffer so much that I have moments in which I lack the strength and valor to fight. I found myself in this dilemma when I sent you the letter that has upset you so much.

I like sorrow. I love sorrow: sorrow is so necessary—like the light of day. But I am a man; I have weaknesses and short-comings. In other words, when the blow is very hard I can't bear it. This weakness of mine put me in the situation of entrusting you with my sorrows, without method or calculation, without neither great or **pure** preparations, which were felt in my soul. I understand that in pain and in sorrow one proves the greatness of their soul and the strength of their character; but I have moments of supreme bitterness that prove that the strength of resistance reaches its maximum. This is the situation you found me in when I wrote to you.

After all, you are within your right to protest my letter, because the tranquillity and joy of everyone is their exclusive birthright, and if one can't increase the birthright or the joy of others, he has not the right to diminish it. What right do I have to sour your soul with my sorrow or bitterness? In the struggle for life, everyone has the right to secure their own tranquillity and welfare. And I understand that love is a disease that Phinon includes in his biology. Within struggle, we endeavor to practice the principle of the fittest with all regularity because of that the farmer prunes the sterile branches by hand; through the laws of conservation, we kill noxious insects that we find afterwards; and with very good resolution, we scorn those that do not concur with us or are spent due to their sorrows. I repeat that this is logical and natural. We can say whatever we wish, but we always practice those principles.

How can I refuse the love of a woman? I know the history of Delilah, of Juliet, of the Lady of the Camellias, of Mary, of Dora, and of my Mother, which overcomes all the romanticisms of ancient and modern history. But that is not an obstacle to having my soul destroyed by a woman whom I love more than my life. She loves me and we cannot be together. This is nothing more than the sorrow that kills our souls, and this is the point of discussion that we can search for in my last letter. Revisit my letter; look at my ideas, they are uttered from a different, clearer perspective, and you will understand that my letter is the faithful reflection of a soul that only sees its sorrow, without studying the cause or its remedy. I repeat that I do not have the right to perturb your tranquillity, but from this to my letter being subjected to a calculated or meditated exposition, there is a world of contradiction. I told you my sorrows and my bitterness because I supposed that I had the right to your consolation—which I do—even though you deny me it. Because, have you not implicitly given me this right with your affectionate motherly advice?

Each day I have more control over myself. The sorrow of my soul should be subjected to a profound study. Each day I love it (sorrow) more because I take from its depths a spring of profound knowledge that by other means would have been impossible for me to acquire. I used to think it was a world of bitterness; a possible suicide has become a source of pleasure and of philosophy. Now is the greatest venture of my soul; but this does not mean that I am searching for the female who would not be a Mother. I do not deny the law of reproduction. What I tell you is just, my letter was not dictated with judgment, it came out without order or harmony, like ideas coming out of a feverish forehead.

If you doubt it, search within your soul, the place of sorrow, and recall the most unfortunate day of your life, in your notes or memories, and tell me, perhaps preserved with clarity: Did you act in judgment? Did you have control over yourself? Didn't you deny the source of all reason? Didn't you doubt life? Didn't you scorn humanity? Didn't you hate the world? . . . My sister, in order to know our hearts more science is needed than to know the heart of others. To forgive an offense, more courage is needed than to commit a crime; it is darker and more laborious to comprehend our own soul than the soul of our brothers.

Dear sister Luisa,

I already find myself much better from my head cold. I have more strength and I rest more peacefully. Since last month around the 10th I have been in bed, and today I am counting on a little more valor and health.

When I feel more tranquil I will answer some of your letters. I have in my hand a letter from last month that I should have sent you and it remained on the table because no one could take it to the post office. On the night of the 1st or 2nd we had a great earthquake: the tremors were very intense and lasted a long time. Soon I will give you complete details.

Your brother.

Dear sister Luisa,

Your portrait is in my possession, I realize that I committed a lack of prudence for not remembering your arrival, but my life and my soul were so upset that I did not have the desire for anything. I only had the strength of my sorrow as a dark and bloody vision. Today the meridian light of reason has taken transmittable power and with its luminous strength I can exile the gloominess of my soul.

In the portrait you look very well, but I find in you a look, something that I do not comprehend. I don't know if you search for uncertain earthly limits, or if you search the sky, or if you explore the field of a new philosophy that is in your mind in the gestational state. Is your look so harsh? Tell me, with the mass of rocks and the serf crashing on them, what are you searching for? Those Goya etchings, I don't understand.

All the rest I understand, but I do not have great imaginative strength to understand all that art expresses like in one of your paintings.

When a soul dreams and awakens, all the conjectures or hypotheses are null in their emission. I can't express and I don't express my opinion on a painting that I can't comprehend.

When I meet your soul and I have room to think with more command, I will give you my definitive opinion of the painting that I have in my possession. Today I only tell you that I give you a million thanks for your gift and in my heart I have a great affection for you.

Since my letter consists of many pages I do not want to take up any more of your time. I only beseech a special pardon for me for not having much dignity in not being able to control my sorrow which gave you the displeasure of all my misfortunes. I trust in your benevolence and believe that in your soul you will not hold a grudge against me for this stupid frankness and for this savage love that almost cut the thread of my life.

.My dear sister,

When I left the post office after mailing two letters to you, one from a past date and another from today, they gave me your wished for letter from the 26th of last September.

These days, and to my regret, I have not been able to send letters or anything. I suffered a strong head cold, and in this climate a head cold is worse than malaria.

I have now recovered from all my sufferings (physical and moral). I feel like fighting, and I have strength for the struggle because in my past life I did not hold onto the memory of unhappy and cruel times. It seems that all the misfortunes came on the same day as if I did not have any purpose of justice or any right of reason to defend or to fight for in the field of life.

When an illness or misfortune takes possession of nature, great vital strength and carelessness disappear in the individual and the diffidence and mistrust that take over the body are the most secure conductors of a defeat in the struggles for life. I have observed that the triumph of the things we gain in a rough and constant struggle are not in the more or less resistance that the things themselves offer, but rather in the faith that one has inside to secure his control over what he desires for his convenience or recreation. All things are in the category of the possible: the impossible is within our cowardice.

Four months ago to the date, I had a series of failures that make me disconcerted in such a manner that I do not take a step without sure footing. Each day I draw new conclusions and definite calculations, and each day I have new failures and new contradictions. This state is so pitiful and so contrary that it made me think about my situation and I realized that total victory or total failure is found within me and that each disillusion of my soul is the current product of a great cowardice, owner and master of a small soul.

This is a very strange riddle. The foolish and the cowardly search for justification of their own cowardice. I have a different reflection for my inner analyses. I can't comprehend and I do not comprehend that if I trip on a stone in the street and I fall and break a leg, these things are subject to the strength of one's own natural resistance, and in its evolutionary march toward the posthumous finality, all that is placed in your path is defeated if it is weaker. And if it is stronger, it is defeated to the contrary (the fight for life), and when this principle is put properly in its place and exact in its form, I understand that all my defeats are within me and that I am the one in whom I don't have faith nor strength to fight in my own defense.

With such a strange life and so pitiful a state, I have to fight so that they disappear. Otherwise, through the law of evolution, I will cease to exist. I wouldn't like that because it seems to me of little practicality.

The Corruption of the Rich and of the Poor
or
How a Rich Woman and a Poor Woman Are Prostituted

A ONE-ACT AND FOUR-SCENE SOCIAL DRAMA

To the illustrious, lettered and distinguished friend,
Don Herminio Díaz Navarro.

CHARACTERS

MARINA, young woman 18 years old.
ROBERTO, Marina's boyfriend
DON PASCUAL, (banker)
DON FILIBERTO, Marquis de Azuria.

ACT ONE

SCENE ONE

Elegant sitting room, a small table with a flower vase.

MARINA: (*Entering with two jewelry boxes in her hand that* SHE *sets on the table,* SHE *sits down.*)

    At last tonight the sacrifice will be consummated I will be Marchioness de Azuria, and I will enrage the daughters of the Duchess who always try to insult me with their titles.

    I don't love that man, but my father has dazzled me with thousands of offers and finally I will make a decision.

    I was indecisive about Roberto, but he will become accustomed to it. Poor Roberto! How upset he will be with my decision.

ROBERTO: (HE *leans out and seeing the young woman alone,* HE *decides to enter.*) My darling! At last I see you again!

MARINA: How did you get in here? Didn't they see you? (*Taking each others' hands.*)

ROBERTO: Don't worry. Your father will be furious, but then he will calm down. But talk to me. Tell me, have you thought about me?

MARINA: Truthfully you have been absent for some time. What were you doing?

ROBERTO: Business deals, buying in Paris, in Germany, in Barcelona, I have not had time to enjoy myself one day.

MARINA: I suppose that my father would have communicated the news to you?

ROBERTO: About what?

MARINA: About my wedding. Tonight I'm getting married.

ROBERTO: Marina! . . . wretch! That is why he sent me abroad, and you also, you consented to this farce? You are a coward and a hypocrite . . . yes, you pressured me to leave so that you would not see me and be able to push yourself into that abyss of selfishness, and I would not defend you, to mock me, and you tolerate all of it for a vile title . . . .

MARINA: Quiet! You are offending me! And furthermore he is my father, and I should obey.

ROBERTO: What do you mean, quiet? Because he is your father? And because of that he has the right to sell you, but don't you understand? It is the selling of your body for a title, and that is vileness, infamy. They make a mockery of me with that man. Scoundrels! . . .

MARINA: Silence! They will hear you and even if I believe you, the rest of them will not do the same. I love you and I would be yours, but the circumstances that surround me have forced me to proceed in this manner.

ROBERTO: And for that you have told me so many times in the garden that you loved me, there under the blossomed orange trees that perfumed the surroundings with their citrus blossoms between which the moonbeams glided across the sky, causing me to dream of an ideal world, of never interrupted happiness. Ah! Sarcasm of destiny, what a fool I am for believing you. No, I should forget you! Cruel perjury. I'll go away and I'll curse you. You have destroyed my dreams, between that old man and you; I won't ever see you again.

MARINA: (SHE *detains him.*) No, if you go denying my love, I will poison myself and my death will be a very sad and painful memory for you. (SHE *pulls him until* HE *sits down on the sofa with her.*) Come here, my love I am yours, my soul and my thoughts are yours. (SHE *caresses him, stroking his hair, passing her hand over his forehead with a triumphant smile.*)

ROBERTO: I can't resist your words. You captivate me. (*Getting up.*) This woman will drive me mad! I should in no way consent to this dreadful play. If you do not love that man, why are you going to marry him? No! Either him or me . . .

MARINA: Now the master who orders appeared. I'll get married and I'll love you. You are my soul, my life . . .

ROBERTO: Don't toy with me that way! Marina! Do not abuse my kindness. My patience will explode, or it will end badly for all! I will denounce you and your father!

MARINA: No, you won't do that. You love me, isn't that true?

ROBERTO: But you don't understand that you torment me, that you irk me, that if you ask me again to demonstrate it to you, I will be capable of killing your father, the marquis, and of choking you in my arms . . .

MARINA: Silence! . . . I heard a noise out on the veranda. Leave and then return. I will wait for you at twelve o'clock.

ROBERTO: You have told me to leave. I don't care if someone comes.
If it was your father, I would cast his behavior, his baseness, in his
face, and you tell me to return? For what?

MARINA: I'll tell you. I'll wait for you in the garden.

ROBERTO: I will return, yes, but tonight you make your decision and
my destiny, until tonight.

SCENE TWO

D. PASCUAL: Good afternoon, my daughter, here you have my wedding gift (*Handing her a document.*), a lovely estate that belonged
to your mother.

MARINA: Thank you.

FILIBERTO: At your feet, Miss. I am infinitely happy to meet both of
you.

MARINA: I kiss your hand and I invite you to see the wedding gifts.
Come.

FILIBERTO: With much pleasure.

MARINA: Come, my father.

D. PASCUAL: Let's go, my daughter.

SCENE THREE

*A garden that opens to the street, front steps that connect with the
garden and* MARINA'*s house.*

ROBERTO: (*Wrapped in his cape,* HE *opens the gate and sits down,*
MARINA *appears, covered with a veil, coming down the stairs.*)

ROBERTO: (*Taking her hand.*) Here I am. What did you want me for?

MARINA: Did you suppose that I would get married? No, because it
was all a farce.

ROBERTO: So what are you going to do? What are your plans?

MARINA: Flee with you with my inheritance. Last night, I went to my
lawyer, whom my mother recommended me to before she died, and
I gave him my proposal. He handed over my inheritance, and furthermore, I have the paperwork for an estate of my mother's that my
father gave me yesterday. So if you agree we'll get going.

ROBERTO: The automobile awaits, because in case you resisted, my
intention was, to carry you away in my arms . . . . (*They embrace
and leave.*) I wasn't willing to wait any longer.

SCENE FOUR

Commentaries in a café. Various people seated in front of the tables of a café.

ONE: (*Arriving.*) Do you know about last night's play? Well, simply put, a banker wants to marry off his daughter to the bankrupt Marquis. The daughter accepts the proposal but loves another. Then the night of the wedding, when everything is prepared, she gathers her inheritance and flees with her lover, leaving everyone waiting.

ANOTHER: Excellent for valiant women!

ONE: This is why parents should not make business deals using their daughters; getting married without loving one another is a corruption.

Curtain.

Marriage Without Love, Consequence, Adultery

CHARACTERS

ESMERALDA
RICARDO
EDUARDO
A SERVANT

ACT ONE

PROLOGUE

ESMERALDA: (*A young woman married to a rich businessman.* SHE *appears seated calmly, embroidering*).

I don't know what's happening with me, but something is going on. It has been a year since I got married. I possess all that an artistic imagination such as mine could imagine: an idealistic temperament. I don't have children, perhaps that is what I lack, but I have more than sufficient of everything else: servants, automobile, money, amusement, and travel. It has been a month since I arrived from Barcelona; I was in Paris; I visited London, its somber streets made me sad, and we quickly left there. We passed through Italy, enchanting country; I dreamed of the lakes of Venice, I admired Milan, and I observed Geneva and Naples.

Nothing! I have a sick soul, I lack love, I don't think I know what love is, since I married in order to rescue my father from a serious debt. And here you have me, sad, but I need to amuse myself so I'll go out shopping, and I'll look at the latest fashions from Paris.

SCENE TWO

EDUARDO: (*Handsome young man who passes in front of* ESMERALDA *while leaving, the young man greets her properly, they simultaneously turn to look at each other.*) Lovely woman. Are you married or single? Tomorrow I shall find out.

ESMERALDA: (SHE *wears an elegant outfit while shopping.*) What a handsome young man and how courteous, how fine. He appears to be single. I shall find out.
(*A car horn sounds.*)

Interior Curtain.

ESMERALDA: (SHE *returns from the stores with some packages, the horn sounds again,* SHE *drops one of the packages.*)

136

EDUARDO: (*From the corner, runs and picks up the small package. They look at each other and greet one another.* SHE *enters her house.*) I have asked the chauffeur, and he has told me that she is married, but that she doesn't have any children. That woman will be mine.

Curtain.

ESMERALDA: (*In her house.*) Who would that young man be? How he looks at me, his stare goes straight to my heart. How cultured and delicate.

RICARDO: (*Her husband.*) What is wrong? Are you sad? Do you want to come with me? Tonight I will leave for New York. I'll return before the end of the month. Are you going to accompany me? (*Caressing her hands and kissing them.*)

ESMERALDA: No, I believe that I lack a child. I'm not going to accompany you, I am too tired for traveling. I would need a powerful attraction to make a trip. If you can offer me that, I'll accompany you.

RICARDO: What can I offer you? I know of nothing that could stimulate your nerves and excite your temperament. If the desire to know other cultures is not sufficient, I don't know what to tell you. You tell me.

ESMERALDA: Nothing, only that I'm not going. I would be bored all alone while you tend to your business.

RICARDO: Then, see you when I return. (HE *kisses her.*)

ESMERALDA: Have fun and return soon. (*To herself.*) I almost said too much and said something rude to him. When he told me that he didn't know what could excite my temperament, which seems to be dormant, I felt a desire to tell him. There is something very powerful, and you can't offer it to me. What greater stimulus than love could make my body quiver? He doesn't even ask, he only guesses.

But doesn't he understand that I need to feel that natural and spontaneous feeling that makes you feel delirious, that makes you lapse into complete madness? Do men believe that we don't have feelings?

It doesn't occur to them that we feel our desire nor do they imagine that we can tire of putting up an act in which we have only put forth a small effort to save the family from a perilous situation. They marry a woman without having the complete certainty of being in love, which seems to them of little importance. As if we didn't feel or think, as if we were a piece of furniture that is bought without asking if the owner likes this one or the other. Well, in the same manner, they do it with a woman. If they like her, they persist in possessing her even though they know that the man is not loved, nor do they dedicate themselves to seducing her, it is nothing more than possessing her.

Fine, I am going to amuse myself at the dressmaker's shop. (SHE *leaves.*)

Interior curtain.

SCENE THREE

In the street.

ESMERALDA: (SHE *returns from the dressmaker's shop, accompanied by* EDUARDO, *a car horn honks and drives away.*) Thank you for your courtesy: you have been very timely. I am enchanted by your attention. I want you to be my friend. My husband is not here now. You can come tomorrow, Thursday. You shall accompany me on my daily stroll. You don't have any objections, do you?

EDUARDO: In my life I won't have greater pleasure or satisfaction than to place myself at your service. (HE *gives her a card.*) Tomorrow, I'll be here. At what time?

ESMERALDA: From seven to eight o'clock in the evening, we'll meet; from five to six o'clock, we'll stroll through the Castellana.

EDUARDO: Very well, Madam, with the deepest respect I am your faithful admirer. Until tomorrow. (HE *leaves.*)

ESMERALDA: What a coincidence! When I stepped out of the automobile I dropped my pocketbook. One more moment and the wheel would have smashed it. I don't know how that young man was able to pick it up. How I like him, how attentive, how delicate, how prudent. Later he didn't want to accompany me. (*Sighs.*) Now to sleep, I'll read a little from the observer of women, Octavio Picón. (SHE *retires.*)

Curtain.

SCENE FOUR

Esmeralda at home.

ESMERALDA: What a long day! I have tried to distract myself but in no way have I been able to avoid thinking of that young man. He pursues my thoughts, and I look again at the clock and it doesn't tick any faster. It seems that it delays its minute hand in order to torment me. How long today seems to me. I don't know what to do in order not to be glued to the clock. The hour is already nearing; it's a quarter past four o'clock. Determinedly it seems to me that today something new will occur in my life. I don't know, my heart beats quickly. (SHE *gets up and looks at herself in the mirror.*) I look fine, elegant. (*The horn sounds.*) He is already here. Courage! I think even my eyes will show the emotion I am experiencing.

EDUARDO: (*Making an elegant greeting.*) Madam, my most enthusiastic congratulations. You are enchanting. I pay a fervent homage of admiration to the lady as artist and as woman . . . forgive me, Madam. (*A bow.*) I am very frank in displaying my affections.

ESMERALDA: I didn't know that you noticed the details of the art of dressing in a woman. Thank you for your praises.

EDUARDO: I have spoken the truth. Anyone of good taste knows how to appreciate feminine refinement.

ESMERALDA: Shall we go?

EDUARDO: You are in charge, Madam, I obey. We shall go. (*They leave and the car horn sounds.*)

Interior curtain.

ESMERALDA: I am desperate, but I have to decide tonight, or he will leave me . . . I shouldn't allow happiness to pass by my side without offering it asylum, without offering it the opportunity to entertain me. I'll leave everything, nothing will keep me here. The consideration for my husband . . . but what consideration did he have for me, making me his without consulting with my heart, without asking my consent, only for a business deal? Nothing, I will go far from here to form a new love nest. I am fed up with sadness and sacrifices. Have someone else sacrifice themselves I can't do it any more.

EDUARDO: Allow me to greet you, Madam . . .

ESMERALDA: Come in, my friend. I was waiting for you. My loneliness demands a pleasant company, and my feelings ask for one who is cultured and sincere.

EDUARDO: Do I have those qualities to satisfy such a most gracious lady?

ESMERALDA: Surely, my heart doesn't know how to deceive me. You should know that I have made a decision.

EDUARDO: Please, Madam! Don't make me dream. Have pity on me. If you aren't happy, if you live sadly, vexed in your affections, in your aspirations, besides you have stolen my soul, and if I am not mistaken, you also love me, why torment ourselves in this manner?

ESMERALDA: But how impatient you are. You haven't allowed me to explain. I was going to let you know my decision, and you anticipate it and give me a lecture.

EDUARDO: Forgive me. I thought that you were telling me bad news.

ESMERALDA: Well, I am going to tell you. Are you willing to leave tonight?

EDUARDO: Right now? But is it true? I just saw you and heard you last night and thought it would be so difficult to convince you, that I thought I would be headed off to London tonight right after your refusal today. It was a matter of life or death for me.

ESMERALDA: Well then, we shall go together.

EDUARDO: Allow me to leave to gather my money and make some arrangements. Now you will place your hand in mine. (*Taking her hand and kissing it.*) Until later.

ESMERALDA: When will you return?

EDUARDO: In one hour I'll be here, and I'll accompany you to dinner, that is to say in order not to provoke attention from the servants, we'll go to a restaurant. Would you like to?

ESMERALDA: It is something new for me. Let's go. (EDUARDO *leaves.*) (*To herself.*) At last the critical moment of my life has arrived. I'm going to go after my dreams without knowing the world and its conditions. I'm going to try a new way of living in accordance with my feelings and my desires. How will I fare in the adventure? I don't know, but man doesn't ask, he goes after it and fights, and woman stops herself. She resorts to doubts, questions, and guarantees that do not assure her if her happiness is going to be eternal or not. I believe that it shouldn't be so. She too should take the risk—whatever happens, happens. She should fight, she should invent, she should defend herself with solid arguments.

EDUARDO: (*The horn of an arriving automobile is heard.*) What are you thinking? Don't worry. Are you ready now?

ESMERALDA: I'm not thinking, and I'm determined.

EDUARDO: Let's go. (*They leave.*) (*The automobile bades farewell with its horn.*)

SERVANT: (*Arranging the sitting room and gathering up some papers. The horn is heard again.* SERVANT *leaves.*)

RICARDO: I return and the missis is out for a stroll. (*To* SERVANT.) And the missis?

SERVANT: She has gone out.

RICARDO: Didn't she receive my telegram?

SERVANT: I gave it to her in the garden this morning.

RICARDO: Very well. (HE *sits down and reads a newspaper.* SERVANT *leaves and returns with a letter, then leaves.*)

RICARDO: What! She has gone? I thought that I had conquered her heart. Well, to Paris, to forget the mistake. (HE *calls* SERVANT *and says to him.*) Prepare my baggage again, I'm leaving, I'll wait for you at the station. To Paris!

Curtain.

How Poor Women Are Prostituted

ACT ONE

SCENE ONE

Modest living room.

WOMAN: (SHE *comes onto the scene in a housecoat, followed by a well-dressed man who gives her a coin.*)

YOUNG MAN: Are you happy with this life?

WOMAN: No, but what choice do I have?

YOUNG MAN: To resort to the factory.

WOMAN: I have no trade, and besides, what would I earn?

YOUNG MAN: Enough to live on.

WOMAN: You're telling me to go and earn a miserable wage, to breathe impure air, and listen to the vulgarities of a loathsome foreman? That does not solve the problem! We women will always be sacrificed in this infinite holocaust to social hypocrisy and lies. It is all the same. Whether it be me or another woman, it is human flesh that is humiliated or despised, that is sold and that atrophies, that is outraged, that is used and trampled on in the name of Christian morality. (*Energetically.*) What can you tell me that another woman does not deserve to hear? It is all the same. Allow me the same as any another woman. We can only vindicate ourselves as a whole, or not at all. I am no better than any other woman.

YOUNG MAN: It is true that one alone is powerless. All women have the right to be happy and to be respected.

WOMAN: Social respect, in combination with stupid formulas, is a farce! Tell me, what is the point of a poor tubercular girl being respected, if they don't prevent her from getting sick? Would respect give her the means to live comfortably? Due to their virtue and decorum, the rich would give her an apology when her soul has been mangled and her body is in the factory. Why doesn't respect guarantee health and banish deprivation? Useless words!

YOUNG MAN: Ignorant lady, selfishness incarnate.

143

WOMAN: Why doesn't that virtue make the poor masses inaccessible to the grave? Why doesn't it remove the stench of fermentation in the ditch? If two girls of the same size and age are buried, one an immaculate virgin, the other surrounded by vices and misery, would the earth respect one more than the other? Would the earth free the virgin of worms?

YOUNG MAN: No, Mother Nature does not establish distinctions; for her the virgin is the same as the prostitute. She is equitable, the leveler par excellence.

WOMAN: So, my friend, what does it matter if she lives one way or the other? The same is given. The social hypocrisies do not disturb my soul nor perturb my mind.

YOUNG MAN: I understand, but if that doesn't matter to you, I should remind you that you are exposed to thousands of diseases and to the practice of vices in order to do business pleasuring the mob of degenerates who use you and then treat you with scorn.

WOMAN: All that being said is very splendid, but if you found yourself in my circumstances, surely you would accept willingly or by force. One day a drunk arrived and reason did not matter to him. It made me sick to go near him. He usually comes every Friday, so surely he will come tonight. What am I going to do about it?

YOUNG MAN: Well, I have to get going. Forgive me for my insistence, until another day. (HE *courteously tips his hat to her.*)

WOMAN: (*Alone.*) Excellent, young man, but it's already very late. What can I do? And besides, it's the same to do it with one as to do it with many. Are all not brothers according to the Bible and all religions? In any case, all of this useless rambling seems ridiculous and foolish to me. If everything is for sale, why do they worry so much. Because we charge a fee? If she who unites herself with a man, whether through civil marriage or through some religious formula, is she not also selling herself? Doesn't the husband have to attend to all the costs? There are very few women who go to the factories, but isn't that a kind of exchange? They don't want to call it that, but it is a business deal just like ours.

DRUNK MAN: Good evening!

WOMAN: Come in.

MAN: May I? Very well then, hurry up, I need to go. (*Staggering.*)

WOMAN: Well, enter, I am already on my way . . .

MAN: No, you go first. You want to leave, right? See, you're nothing but a thief, you don't listen not even when you're being paid. Let's go or I'll flog you! (*Pushing her.*)

WOMAN: I'm going, crude boor. I would be better off committing suicide.

MAN: For what you're worth, you may as well have already done it. (*They enter the adjoining bedroom,* HE *pushing her forward.*)

Curtain

In the Country, Free Love

CHARACTERS

AURORA, young peasant
VICTOR, young worker

ACT ONE

SCENE ONE

It is morning when the cool greenness of the fields shines artistic and poetic hues of springtime. A young woman, AURORA is wearing a linen hairnet with the ties hanging loose. SHE trims flowers in her orchard. VICTOR walks by with a jacket over his shoulder. HE pauses to look at the young woman.

VICTOR: Beautiful profession . . . (*Leaning against a tree.*)

AURORA: (*Lifts up her head.*) You are rising very early. That is very healthy.

VICTOR: In order to see you before going to work . . .

AURORA: Yea, yea, as if I would believe you . . .

VICTOR: Believe me, child, he who lives with nature does not lie. I come to see you because you attract me like a magnet to steel. I lean against this living tree, and I feel as though I am united with it, or at least that this vegetal brother is interested in me watching you. I look at you, and I do not want to look at anything else. I don't know, little girl, but you have me deeply worried because I don't know what to do about the situation.

AURORA: Well, the opposite is happening for me. When I see you . . . I close my eyes and I run away, until I don't see you.

VICTOR: Liar, go ahead, tell me what happens to you, what you feel, go ahead! Come over here and give me your hand!

AURORA: (*Approaching him slowly.*) Well, I'm going to tell you . . . but let me be free . . . I feel . . . I won't tell you! . . .

VICTOR: Begin, foolish girl, you are making me suffer!

AURORA: (*Leaving her hand in VICTOR's.*) Well listen, I saw you for the first time, and later I leaned out very quietly to see you pass by without you seeing me, and I watched you; I have seen other men but I like you more, and I was very impressed, and later I missed seeing you.

VICTOR: See how you like me too, and you were afraid to say it. Ay! What gladness, how happy you make me. Well, I hadn't stopped before in fear of bothering you and you, you also desired me.

AURORA: Get to work. It's late. Come back in the afternoon when the earth in these parts has left the sun behind, and the birds trill, and the breeze brings us perfumed aromas, when, having finished our task, already bathed and with clean clothes we are rested. Then we'll go together under the trees.

VICTOR: At six o'clock I'll be here. Give me a kiss.

Curtain

SCENE TWO

:VICTOR: (*Approaching* AURORA *walking in the field.*) The solemn hour of evening twilight recedes, wrapping us up in its tenuous and melancholic brightness, leaving us nostalgic for it, through its enchanting combinations of colors and its eloquent silence, as if it spoke to our souls the mysterious language of love. How lovely life is! . . . Aren't you satisfied with it?

AURORA: I understand that beauty gives us ecstasy, but I still haven't enjoyed it in all of its manifestations.

VICTOR: Will you allow me to guide you through that torturous path and prevent you from tripping?

AURORA: With great pleasure. But I believe that woman should walk alone, that is to say united, yes, but that there be mutual protection so it doesn't make woman appear under tutelage or direction which in the end results in hatred, which makes her appear always and in all occasions inferior. It doesn't allow her to acquire sufficient confidence in herself whatever the case of urgent necessity. Furthermore, it disables her because she doesn't have the opportunity to use her intelligence, and her physical and moral faculties atrophy.

VICTOR: Very well, but for that she needs to educate herself and prepare herself. It hasn't been my intention to try to impose my will. I offered you my help in order for us to love each another mutually but it did not occur to me that you could imagine that I was trying to inhibit your natural activities and your personal initiatives. In that I do not meddle. You are completely free to do whatever you please.

AURORA: I agree. Now tell me, have you thought of me?

VICTOR: Yes, all day, as if I had your portrait in front of me. I want you to tell me if you like the country life.

AURORA: Yes, caring for the flowers and fruits and the animals, looking at nature in all its splendor all the time.

VICTOR: And having children?

AURORA: Yes, is Mother Nature not fecund? Yes, to reproduce ourselves with our flesh and our bones, how beautiful is reproduction, lovely and healthy with the loveliness of health and good habits; as nature reproduces everything, to observe in our children nature made of flesh and conscious intelligence.

VICTOR: How many?

AURORA: I don't know, however many that come. There is sufficient land for all, isn't it so?

VICTOR: Then I won't return to the factory. I'll remain here with you. I'll till the earth, and I'll go sell my crops to the people.

AURORA: Will you look for someone to help you? Won't you get tired?

VICTOR: Soon I will have one or two men who will help me. I'll breathe pure air, and I'll be happy with the free land.

AURORA: When we have a son, we'll plant a small orchard for him with useful plants.

VICTOR: We won't obligate him. He'll do what he likes most.

AURORA: Yes, and neither will we teach him religious ideas. We'll make him understand that the soul is immortal and that we are all brothers and sisters.

VICTOR: And us, what will we do?

AURORA: Mutually please each other with complete freedom, go for a walk each afternoon at dusk. It will be a renewal of enthusiasm in our new life.

VICTOR: And in the mornings I'll go wake you from your slumber with many kisses, to renew the memory of the first morning.

AURORA: And when I look at our children, I'll see in them our reproduction made into flesh and spirit through the labor and grace of our love.

VICTOR: And we'll see our children's children.

AURORA: (*Laughing.*) Aren't we counting our chickens before they are hatched?

VICTOR: It doesn't matter. It's better to wish for them than to avoid them; of course having the surety that they'll be fine.

AURORA: There are many who don't want to have children because they can't support them.

VICTOR: There are also many who can support them and care for them well, and they prefer to leave them dirty and barefoot in order to dress in the latest fashion and make woman a slave.

AURORA: We'll be free helping ourselves. (*They embrace and go away, pointing to the moon that pokes out among the trees.*)

VICTOR: How beautiful the moon is. Let's go then, to enjoy our freedom in love being we can't enjoy other freedoms for now. But imagine if the earth was free and we were to choose a place of our liking and if work was free and we didn't use wages, we would work to exchange products. Each week the fruits from the vegetable garden would be gathered and at each harvest the trucks would go out loaded to the city. My fellow men would receive the fruits, and how proud and content I would be to receive in exchange all the necessary objects for my comfort.

AURORA: And how happy I would be, being the mother of free persons.

VICTOR: Let's go then, the path of freedom toward the throne of love.

AURORA: Lovely nature, and the moon shows its pale face. United we sing a hymn of peace.

VICTOR: We shall go after our dream, we will delight ourselves with our love and we'll sow seeds of freedom in Mother Nature's sacred bosom represented in you, before which I'll bow in the sign of homage and admiration. We'll multiply ourselves in the Augustan temple of love and free nature, having as its canopy the splendid stellar space illuminating our chaste bed of love, paying tribute to the great unknown strength that rules the universe. (*While talking they have seated themselves down on the soft grass and they embrace.*)

Curtain.

The duet from The Merry Widow.

After her Death

A PLAY FROM REAL LIFE IN VERSE AND PROSE

To my excellent friend, the intelligent, gallant, cultured gentleman,
and gentle poet, Dr. Manuel Martínez Rosselló

CHARACTERS

LELIA, 26-year-old young woman.
MAULY, 38-year-old gentleman.
FABIO, 34-year-old gentleman.

PLACE

The action takes place in the tropics in a city in the Antilles.

SCENERY

A splendid tropical jungle, a fence that simulates a garden, trees, garlands, colored lights, a grave with a marble headstone surrounded by flowers; a lamp suspended between the trees that hangs over the tomb.

The tomb will be placed on the right side of the stage near the curtain.

ACT ONE

SCENE ONE

LELIA: (*Enters the scene with a peaceful demeanor and seems meditative in an elegant white dress.* SHE *goes toward the tomb, picks up a flower that has fallen on the white headstone, and contemplates it.*)

It was a flower that offered its fragrance, it was a hidden pearl in the churned up human sea!

Who would have been able to find it and string it together like a diamond?

Poor withered flower
at the first rays of sun
humble hidden violet
among stems without scent
brilliant pearl that one day
shone without ostentation!

It was perfume that soared
in pursuit of another mansion,
it was a pearl that sparkled
without provoking attention;
as a flower it was divine,
as a pearl, matchless
as if it were a rose without thorn
that never wilted.

(*Speaking with pauses, with delight, as one who savors some delicious nectar in a gentle, delicate, expressive manner.*)

The flower with cruelty snapped
one morning without sun,
the pearl was loosened
from its crown of love.
As such the days passed by
painfully contemplating

154

that flower of joy
which withered from love.

(*Kissing the flower that defoliates in her hands.*)

You fled lovely psyche
to the mansion of light
go with your rich aromas
to perfume another blue.

MAULY: (*Properly dressed with tailcoat, gloves, cane and cape, opens the gate, the stage in semidarkness, lightning and thunder, as if it were thundering in the mountains. Upon opening the gate and entering on stage,* HE *shoots a look up into space, raises his eyebrows and exclaims.*) All is somber, just as I am, it looks as if nature wishes to accompany me in my sorrow, in my indescribable anguish . . . (*Putting his hand into an inside pocket of his tailcoat,* HE *takes out a wallet, opens it, and reads.*) Today is December 25th. (HE *writes on it, puts it back, and continues toward the tomb where* HE *finds* LELIA. *Confused with this encounter,* HE *gives her a gallant greeting and remains pensive.*)

LELIA: It was the furthest thing from my mind to think that you would come here today, Mauly . . .

MAULY: Today is a memorable date for me. I didn't think that I would find you here either . . .

LELIA: I live near and care for her flowers everyday. She asked me to do it . . .

MAULY: A day like today I saw her for the first time in her house, angelic divine! With a simple pink-violet flowered dress that made her so attractive; I was introduced at her house by a lawyer friend of ours, who has also died.

When I entered, it seemed to me that the doors of the unknown were opening for me, offering me a world of unexplainable delights!

Upon seeing me together with her, I trembled. That girl had taken control over me, tranquillity carried me away, and it deranged me.

LELIA: How long ago was that, Mauly?

MAULY: Eighteen years ago! Listen, when, in order to follow the customs, they offered me a beer, I couldn't contain myself and said to

her, I will get down on my knees at your feet if you do not drink
first . . . it moistened her divine lips . . . and I drained the contents
of that finest glass, as if I wanted to absorb her breath. I took one of
her hands, and I kissed it full of delight. That girl who began to live
had me unhinged; upon looking at me she imprisoned my soul with
her mysterious eyes . . .

LELIA: She doesn't exist any more. Why remember her now? All of that
you should have told her while she was alive. Now what's the use?

MAULY: Let me speak. Allow me to rest here in front of her tomb, that
I suffocate myself . . . within a few days, we promised to love each
other: every day she would write me interminable letters, very
affectionate: she would copy poems and send them to me, scrib-
bling her love in frenzy.

Some years passed. Her faithfulness was such and her perseverance was idolatry, I began not worry myself so much that between
trips and absences, two years passed by.

LELIA: But what were you doing insomuch that now you recognize
that you behaved badly? A bit too late.

MAULY: Ignorance, my friend. Listen, that patience and sweetness per-
sonified, that mad love that she felt, which filled me with satisfaction and pride and contributed to my not concerning myself with
my duty. That ignorance of life, it was awakened. The enslaved love
rebelled. Patience fled to punish my carelessness.

This loving enthusiasm she translated into writing daily poems
of celebrated authors and delirious letters calling out to me, would
come to an end and I would flee . . . I would flee from that fire
believing that it consumed itself on its own. (*Wiping his brow.*)

LELIA: But how? Were you indifferent to those manifestations? Were
you perhaps already insensitive? Why did you act in that manner?

MAULY: My friend, the previous excesses caused me to guard myself
to a certain measure that I couldn't explain to her nor would she
comprehend it. So, upon my return from my trip to Paris, I had
barely left to go see her, when certain enjoyed pleasures diverted
me from her house and led me to take advantage of them in the
brothels . . . .

LELIA: Vices and bad habits have more power than love! What have we
come to! What repugnance! And how shameful! For that social
morality . . .

MAULY: Don't interrupt me so much, my friend. Listen in silence, and
besides, and beyond that, I was ill . . . Within a few months some

news froze my blood and turned me red with shame. Upon thinking
about the mistake I had committed with her, carelessness that I paid
for with the loss of my dearest affections and illusions, another man
reminded her that I hadn't fulfilled my duty, that the luxury that surrounded her was not incentive for a soul in love . . . and she was in
love with me! . . . and that man was a friend . . . who represented
for me in that moment an apparition from hell! . . . He threw my
behavior in my face, my abandonment of that exceptional woman
whom I adored, in whom I had condensed all my first memories of
love, and for whom I saved for the future, for my sad and desolate
old age I wanted to preserve that embodied purity to delight myself
in it, and they awoke it in me . . .

LELIA: But, sir, how selfish you were. You wanted to deform her
nature, mold her to your whims. What cruelty!

MAULY: Let me finish and don't recriminate me. I have had enough
sorrow. So when that naive woman with unmatched frankness, con-
fessed to me her indifference, recounting to me the scene . . . how
guilty that man appeared to me! . . . if he had noticed something in
his medical opinion, he should have warned me, notified me, in
order to prevent my disgrace. Wasn't he my friend? . . . but ah! Disappointment, desperation took control over me upon hearing that
detailed confession, the heaven of my illusions darkened. My eyes
shed burning tears. (*Energetically.*) In that moment I would have
crushed that man! I would have smashed him, as one smashes a rail-
ing, as one who waits for the opportune moment to infiltrate his
poison to betrayal! What did he influence in that woman-child in
order to awaken her? Her loneliness, my carelessness? Not even
then, I don't blame her! No! A thousand times no! That man has
been a criminal. I said to myself, and in a vertigo of madness I challenged him, and in a wide open plaza, I would have slapped him in
the face if not for the friends that intervened, because that man for
a moment of pleasure destroyed my happiness and threw my love
from its cradle of dreams . . . Stupid! Senseless! And so many times
he used me as a friend! Despicable traitor! Traitor! Cynic! . . .

LELIA: You should not blame anyone of that carelessness. You have
received the just recompense for your behavior.

MAULY: But she told me for many years that she hadn't loved him, that
her thoughts and her soul were mine.

LELIA: And why didn't you forgive her, return to her?

MAULY: Because of social concerns that obliged me to demonstrate something that I didn't feel.

LELIA: What cowardice, and you have let her suffer knowing that she loved you. You do not have a heart, and she is like those children who are deprived of our caresses and direct protection.

MAULY: It's true. You are not mistaken. They have destroyed me. I have suffered much.

LELIA: You could have prevented it from happening. Why were you not at her side?

MAULY: Through ignorance of human passions, but let me implore her. (*Approaching the tomb.*) Forgive me, charming vision of my unrealized dreams! You soared to other regions while I vegetate in sorrow, sorrow for having made you suffer! Forgive me . . . (HE *remains silent with his head bowed.*)

LELIA: (SHE *watches him with a compassionate countenance. Neither of them see a cloaked man who is protected by the darkness. This man approaches the tomb and kneels down. Upon seeing him,* LELIA *says.*) A man! . . .

MAULY: (*Surprised,* HE *gets up.*) A man! What are you looking for here? (*Aiming with his revolver.*)

FABIO: To fulfill a promise! Who are you to ask me for explanations?

MAULY: (*Approaching the light from the lamp.*) Look!

FABIO: Heavens! What are you doing here?

MAULY: And I am asking you the same! What sarcasm! Here where I should be and am able to be, at the grave of the woman that I loved, as one cannot love again.

FABIO: You make me laugh. After her death, your love has awoken. When she was alive, you abandoned her. Have you come to take custody of her remains?

MAULY: It is none of your business if I abandoned her or not. Some audacity you have to present yourself at this hour and in this spot.

FABIO: Is this grave yours? Why do you cast me out from her? Or is it that the virility you didn't possess when she was alive has now awoken?

MAULY: Insolent! You don't even respect her grave. If you don't defend yourself I'll kill you as you deserve. (*Aiming at him with the revolver.*)

FABIO: Shoot, this is how brave men behave. (*Presenting his chest.*)

LELIA: (*Who had remained silent, runs and intervenes.*) What are you going to do friends? Is this how you honor her memory? After her death, what good do these arguments bring? Allow me to recite to you a composition of our friend's.

TO YOU

Who is it who invokes me
at my solitary grave,
and whispers a prayer
of sweet and mad phrases?
Who is that sad shadow
that silently meditates
and in the mysterious night
only thinks of me and speaks my name?

Listen in order that you understand;
He who is other to my destiny
in my painful path
crossed my way
and troubled my lovely life.
That bold man who wanted
to extinguish my happy star
and at such an early time
destroy my sweet nest.
The man who temerariously
profaned my soul
penetrating into the sanctuary
that was my total joy,
That man . . . I forgive him
and no one can judge him
as no one can give him
his punishment! . . . Except God!

MAULY: She forgives him! . . . . (*Because of the surprise,* HE *drops the revolver from his hands. It fires a shot that wounds* FABIO. HE *wobbles and falls.*)

LELIA: (*Who upon finishing the poem stepped away, upon the sound of the revolver* SHE *turns and sees* FABIO *on the ground.* SHE *asks* MAULY.) What have you done?

MAULY: It wasn't me. It went off when it fell. (*They both go to* FABIO's *side and try to lift him up.*)

LELIA: How can we stop the hemorrhaging?

FABIO: Take a bit of Bermuda grass, squeeze it tightly, and cover the wound with it . . .

LELIA: (SHE *does it, and between the two of them they try to lift* FABIO *to his feet.*)

FABIO: (*To* MAULY.) Are you happy? Do you forgive me now? I'm not the only guilty one. She wanted to avenge your indifference and estrangement! I knew that it was not love that she felt for me. I was persuaded because she was a tempting woman. I was so weak that I couldn't resist her curious influence, in that loneliness in which I always found her!

MAULY: She proposed it to you?

FABIO: It was not a premeditated situation. It was weakness on my part, excess of life in her, overwhelming loneliness that made her desperate and anxious for love's caresses . . . she threw herself into my arms . . . forgive me!

MAULY: Did you force yourself on her?

FABIO: Never that! I have always been a gentleman; you were guilty because of your abandonment . . .

MAULY: If you are such a proper gentleman, why didn't you advise me to fulfill my duty?

FABIO: In order to comply with her. Did I have to warn you? . . . (*With irony.*)

MAULY: I'm not happy. You have taken on liberties that don't belong to you; and that part about her wanting to avenge my estrangement. Did she manifest that to you?

FABIO: No, but I figured as much because that woman was crazy about you. She came to me immediately, asking if I had seen you, if I knew where you were.

MAULY: What did you tell her? Why didn't you let me know?

FABIO: I told her that I had seen you in the casino or in the café, and I did not let you know because thousands of circumstances impeded it.

MAULY: Nothing more? You didn't turn her against me?

FABIO: There was no motive. She had sufficient reasons to be upset . . .

MAULY: Well then in spite of it all I believe you to be guilty and I cannot be your friend. Your presence upsets me, you hurt me, you are impelling me to kill you!

FABIO: Kill me, end it once and for all, go ahead! (*Putting himself in front of* MAULY.)

MAULY: No, go away! . . . no one will find out about this unexpected encounter; since I was gone no one will know about it, I'll leave again and that will be it.

LELIA: (*To* FABIO.) Are you in pain?

FABIO: A little. Accompany me to the gate. (LELIA *takes him by the arm and guides him to the gate door.*) Thank you, I appreciate it. Good-bye!

MAULY: (HE *has stayed pensive while* FABIO *leaves.*)

LELIA: Good-bye. (SHE *returns to the scene, at* MAULY*'s side.*) What are you thinking?

MAULY: Of she who suffered so much and has forgiven, it won't be me who punishes him. Could you believe that I wounded him?

LELIA: A logical conclusion. You had threatened him first. Later I understood that it had been an accident.

MAULY: My friend, I am off, I will take advantage of the darkness to go away like a criminal. Now you see that the events require it, the circumstances obligate me. Good-bye and do not forget me. Pray for me and for her. Good-bye!

LELIA: Good-bye. Take a flower with you from her grave. (*Snaps off a flower and gives it to him.*) Good-bye. (SHE *remains somewhat sad and repeats.*)

> You fled lovely psyche
> to the mansion of light
> send your rich aromas
> to perfume this sadness.

Ybor City, Florida.

YOUR BLONDE HAIR

In long locks of hair floating down your back
extends your blonde hair unmatchless
as a perfumed and beautiful garland
that would shine pearls of rain in the sun.

The breeze plays with them
with disorderly ease
the sun delights in them
sending its light from above.

Why don't you let me unite them
in beautiful braids, your golden hair,
in order that the moonbeams kiss
that gentle head that I adore?

Allow me also to play with them
in the placidity of the breeze
to adorn your fair forehead
with golden threads of your hair.

June 15, 1913, Ybor City

INFLUENCIAS DE LAS IDEAS MODERNAS

Señor y amigo:

Tengo el honor de presentar a Vd. este libro, en pró de la libertad humana, con cuyo producto y con el de las futuras obras que publicaré he de fundar mi anhelada

"Granja Escuela Agrícola"

en Cuba, Puerto Rico o Santo Domingo. Confiando en su generosidad y benevolencia, dedica a Vd. este ejemplar

La Autora.

LUISA CAPETILLO

INFLUENCIAS
DE LAS IDEAS MODERNAS.

NOTAS Y APUNTES

ESCENAS DE LA VIDA

—TIPOGRAFIA NEGRON FLORES. SAN JUAN LUNA 37 —

—1916.—

PROLOGO

Esta obra, compuesta de varias partes y escenas de la vida en sus diversas manifestaciones, aparece con el fin de continuar mi propaganda en pró de la libertad de la mujer en todas las manifestaciones de la vida.

Ella es parte de mis aspiraciones; con el producto de ésta y las que aparecerán en tiempos futuros, me servirán para mi proyectada "Granja Escuela Agrícola" idea que deseo llevar á la práctica para exponer la ventaja que reportará á la comunidad. Mi propaganda, basada en la justicia, verdad y libertad que encierran las ideas ácratas, en obsequio á la fraternidad universal, es necesaria, es una de las manifestaciones del progreso.

La Autora.

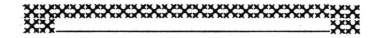

INFLUENCIAS DE LAS IDEAS MODERNAS.

(Drama en tres actos.)

PERSONÁJES.

Angelina (hija de un rico comerciante)............

Don Juan de Ramírez (padre de Angelina)... ...

Ramón (sirviente de la casa)............ ....

Don Baltasar (capataz de la fábrica de don Juan) ....

Ernestina y Marieta, (dos amigas de Angelina)

Mariana (viuda de un antiguo empleado de Ramírez, que ha muerto)............................

Carlos Santana, (hijo de Mariana, y director de la huelga que con Simplicio Hernández forman el comité de la huelga........................

Rosalina, (novia de Ramón)............... ....

Don Jaime López...................................

Don Antonio Rigaud..

Don Roberto Hartman...

Escrito en Arecibo en noviembre de 1907.

ESCENA PRIMERA

(Un elegante salón amueblado estilo moderno. Al levantarse el telón Angelina está sentada en el sofa en elegante traje de mañana leyendo muy abstraída **"Esclavitud Moderna"** de **Tolstoy**, y no siente a Ramón entrar.)

(Ramón entrando con una bandeja con algunas tarjetas se acerca a la joven y dice:

Señorita, no recuerda Vd. que hoy es su cumpleaños?

Angelina—En verdad, no lo recordaba, tan abstraída estoy hace días con la lectura de este libro de **Tolst'y**, **"La esclavitud Moderna"** que me ha convencido que la esclavitud moderna , es la férrea ley del salario. (tomando las tarjetas y mirándolas dejolas sobre la mesa).

Ramón—(guiñándo un ojo para sorprender la opinión de la joven) ¿Y de qué manera hariamos para no percibir salario?

Angelina—Ilustrando a los pobres, de que nadie tiene derecho de valorar el trabajo, ni de señalar horas de labor, el trabajo debe ser libre, expontáneo y el consumo igual.

Cada individuo debe trabajar según sus fuerzas y consumir según sus necesidades.

Ramón—Esa es una máxima anarquista, pero como ponerla en práctica?.......por la violencia?

Angelina—No por la instrucción y la educación, la mayor parte de las injusticias y crímenes se cometen por ignorancia. La clase capitalista, por conveniencia propia, debía de tratar de suprimir los crímenes y enfermedades que crea la miseria engendrada por la explotación.

Existiendo la fraternidad no habría esta discordia establecida por la competencia que origina la ley del salario.

Aquí, muy cerca vive una viuda que carece de todo, con cuatro hijos, el mayor estaba aprendiendo un oficio, y en tanto, no le pagaban, como si no tuviera que vestir y comer.

La madre se alquila a coser, pero no cubre sus gastos. Es viuda de un empleado, que estuvo muchos años en la fábrica de mi padre, después de tanto trabajar su familia esta en esas condiciones, he de suponer que ha sido explotado.

Ramón—Naturalmente , pues su sueldo no le alcanzaba para cubrir sus necesidades, menos podría economizar. El ahorro es aceptable después de cubiertas todas las necesidades.

Angelina—De otro modo es un suicidio. (Ramón se retira).

ESCENA SEGUNDA.

Don Juan (entrando), buen día hija mía (besándola en la frente) como estás hoy?

Angelina—(se levanta y dice) Muy bien, papá , gracias,

Don Juan—(presentándole un estuche con un magnífico brazalete) Toma acepta esta prenda por tu cumpleaños, es de un acabado gusto artístico.

Angelina—(abriendo el estuche, exclama) Bellísima en verdad (comtemplándola, y colocando el estuche sobre la mesa), si me hubieras consultado hubiéramos empleado ese dinero en algo más

útil. **Don Juan** hace un gesto de asombro) ella
continúa): ese dinero esta mal empleado, oye papá:
en la próxima calle vive en modesta habitación, la
viuda de aquel empleado que tantos años estuvo
a tu servicio, pobre y abandonada, sosteniéndose
con las costuras que le envían. Anoche estuvo aquí
a ver si la ayudaba, pues debe dos meses de casa,
y el hijo mayor va a la fábrica con el calzado roto,
en tanto nosotros vivimos rodeados de comodidades en este edificio que tiene 20 divisiones, ellos son
cinco y viven en una sola habitación.

Don Juan—(asombrado) será cierto todo eso,
pero ya no me acordaba de esa Sra. y además no
comprendo porque había de privarme de traerte este regalo para socorrerla a élla.

Angelina—(con vivacidad y alegría) ¿Estás dispuesto para ayudarla en buena forma?

Don Juan—(indiferente) Sí como siempre
dispuesto a complacerte...........(volviendo de un
lado a otro)

Angelina—(alegremente, pero no consigue
hacer reir a don Juan dice) Entonces dime, (acercándose a él y arreglándole el bigote) vás a enviarle
dinero?...........¿cuánto?..............(con interés).

Don Juan—(desaciéndose de élla, pasea) Iré
a llevarle cinco dollars.

Angelina(con un gesto de disgusto) ¡Eso es
una miseria! con eso no puede pagar sus deudas, ni
comprar lo que necesita. (sentándose en un sillón)

Don Juan—(Acercándose y mirando al público, siempre terminará por hacer lo que quiere)
Vamos, cuanto deseas que le regale a esa Sra.?

Angelina—¿cuánto has gastado en el regalo?
(levántándose).

Don Juan—Esa joya, te habrás fijado que
tiene un brillante un zafiro y un rubí, he pagado por
ella $500.00 dollars.

Angelina—(Con un gesto desdeñoso, señalando el estuche) Para comprar eso que no remedia ninguna necesidad humana, no vacilaste en gastar esa crecida cantidad. Te refiero con detalles claros y precisos, en que condición viven esas víctimas tuyas, y ofreces cinco dollars, Gracias, (sentándose incomodada).

Don Juan—¡Víctimas mías has dicho! estas loca yo no puedo evitar las consecuencias de lo inevitable!

Angelina—¿De lo inevitable has dicho? Acaso la miseria es inevitable? (con energía).

Don Juan—Inevitable. (paseándose moviendo su bastón).

Angelina—Padre mío, estas en un gran error, la miseria es el producto de la explotación. (don Juan se detiene, a oir a su hija con la boca abierta) debido a las injusticias y egoismos de los hombres de todas las épocas.

Don Juan—(mientras ella habla,) dice ¿cómo se habrá enterado está muchacha de eso? (aparte) Seré yo un egoista explotador.

Angelina—Lo eres inconcientemente, por tu indiferencia ante el dolor ajeno que es el nuestro.

Don Juan—Eso me parece simplemente una exageración.

Angelina—Sí, nuestro, pues mientras exista sobre la tierra un sólo hombre que sufra, los demás no pueden ser felices.

Don Juan—Repito que es una exageración.

Angelina—Tu no puedes ser feliz, como yo no lo soy porque causamos con nuestra infiferencia, muchos dolores. Todos los seres somos hermanos, y sufriremos miles entorpecimientos, en tanto no ayudemos a destruir la causa que ocasiona tantos dolores, pues la humanidad es una cadena, de la cual somos eslabones, y cuando mueven uno se mueven todos.

Don Juan—((Impaciente)Bien hija me parece que esa Sra. estará impaciente, dejame llevarle dinero, ¿cuanto deseas que le entregue? Estas conforme con $25.00 dollars? (acercándose a su hija y tomándole una mano).

Angelina—Como quieras papá, no quiero molestarte más. yo también le daré algo. Dime, esto es mío? ¿puedo hacer lo que me plazca con el?

Don Juan—Si, hija, usarlo ó guardalo, es tuyo; hasta luego voy a cumplir tu encargo. (besándola en la frente)

Angelina—Hasta la vista papá (acompañándo a su padre hasta la puerta) vuelve y sentándose y tomando el estuche lo observa y se levanta diciendo: ¡Qué cosa más inútil!, y pensar que hayan mujeres que por una joya para su adorno son capaces de permitir que sus maridos vayan a presidio, y muchas se rinden fingiendo amores que no sienten por un objeto de lujo, ¡ignorancia! ¡ignorancia!, cuantas víctimas creas. Pero yo no lo usaré, se lo regalaré a Mariana la viuda, ella lo venderá: (pensativa).

Suena el timbre, (que debe oirlo el público) Angelina levanta su cabeza y dice: ¿quién será? oigo como voces de dos mujeres, (se levanta, ¿serán Ernestina y Marieta?

ESCENA TERCERA.

Ernestina y **Marieta**—(entrando alegres decididas, a saludar a Angelina,) Día feliz te deseamos querida Angelina.

Angelina—Muy agradecida a vuestra atención,

Ernestina—Venimos a invitarte por tu cumpleaños á pasear en automovil que recibió ayer papá, para lo cual vendremos a buscarte a la tarde.

Angelina—Mil gracias amigas mías. pero me

·es imposible complaceros, si quereis volver, podeis hacerlo pero no iré a pasear.

Marieta y **Ernestina**—(a un tiempo). ¿Por qué Angelina? estas enferma?

Angelina—De salud estoy bien, pero he estado muy triste y preocupada, meditando sobre las injusticias sociales y la miseria que no me encuentro dispuesta para distraerme.

Ernestina—Buena ocupación has tomado, pensar en las injusticias sociales? Piensas resolver el problema?..............

Angelina—Haré lo que pueda, por los trabajadores. Ustedes no leen a Malato a Kropokline, a Zola?

Marieta—Olvidas Angelina que mamá es muy religiosa y de no ser libros religiosos no podemos leer otra cosa, pero preferimos eso a mortificarnos como tú en querer resolver tales problemas.

Eres muy sensible Angelina, y a tu edad y con la posición que ocupas no me mortificaría de ese modo.

Angelina—Para mi no es un tormento el ocuparme de los que sufren por carecer de lo necesario También me llevaron cuando niña a la iglesia, pero no he vuelto.

Ernestina—Mamá nos ha dicho que si no somos religiosas iremos al infierno.

Angelina—Para mi el infierno, es la conciencia llena de remordimientos, y el cielo, el deber cumplido con nuestro prójimo.

Ernestina—Tu modo de pensar no aliviará la situación de los pobres.

Angelina—Pero la consecuencia de pensar así me llevarán a la práctica de la justicia, por lo menos procuro hacer algo por ellos; ves este brazalete? pues lo regalaré a una pobre. (mostrando el estuche a sus amigas.)

Marieta y **Ernestina**—¡Qué magnífico brazalete!

Angelina—Me lo regaló mi padre hoy.

Marieta—Pero que tonta eres al regalar una
joya de este valor. ¿Para quién es?

Angelina—Para una viuda, de uno que fué
empleado de mi padre. Para mi tiene más valor
el ayudarla.

Ernest.na—No podemos contrariarte, pero
creo que tu puedes socorrer a esa Sra. sin regalarla.

Angelina—No necesito esa joya, no me gustan los adornos, (con un gesto desdeñoso) oid, "No
compres galas ni joyas que los libros valen más que
ellas, adorna tu entendimiento con sus preciadas
ideas que no hay lujo que deslumbre como el lujo
de la ciencia".

Marieta y **Ernestina**—Bien Angelina lamen-
tamos tus caprichos hasta luego. A la tarde volveremos. (Se marchan , Angelina las acompaña a la
puerta).

Angelina—Que se diviertan, (vuelve y dice)
que inutilidad de mujeres, y que esas jóvenes puedan ser algún día madres de familia. Y en esa condición están la mayoría de las mujeres. (sientase a
leer).

ESCENA CUARTA.

Don Juan—(Entrando le dice a su hija): Angelina he cumplido tu encargo.

Angelina—(Estrechando las manos a su padre). Gracias, has restituído parte de lo que le correspondía.

Don Juan—(Muy serio). Te he complaci-
do solamente. (tomando un periódico lee en alta voz): Huelga de braceros en Italia, piden aumento de salario.

Meeting público, por el día y por la noche, ha-
blarán socialistas y anarquistas. Se teme haya

motin. Última hora, triunfo de los huelguistas, guiados por los anarquistas. (Angelina se había colocado detrás de su padre y le¹ dice, ¿Qué son anarquistas, papá? (con picaresca sonrisa).

Don Juan—Son hombres de ideas avanzadas que desean emancipar a los trabajadores de la esclavitud económica.

Angelina—¿Que procedimientos emplean? (con interés).

Don Juan—Instruyendo a los obreros, los agitan en meetings públicos, para que se rebelen contra la explotación. y mejoren sus condiciones, aboliendo la ley del salario.

Angelina—¿Cómo abolirán la ley del salario? ·

Don Juan—Por la revolución, transformando la propiedad privada en común, pues de ese modo no habría miseria ni crímenes.

Angelina—¡Bien ¡Bien! bravo, alegrame saber que estes instruído sobre esas cuestiones. Pero dime ¿cómo transformarán la propiedad?

Don Juan—Con una huelga general de todos los oficios, pueden hacerlo si estuvieran preparados para resistirla. Con peticiones, no conseguirán hacerlo, pues los **burgueses** como ellos nos llaman, debido al medio actual solamente se ocupan de acumular dinero.

Angelina—¿Estas conforme con esas ideas? ¿té atreverías a romper con la tradición?

Don Juan—Yo solo no podría, no resolvería el problema.

Angelina—¿Por qué papá? ¿Qué temes?

Don Juan—Nada temo pero yo sin los otros capitalistas, no resolvería el asunto, pues serían beneficiados algunos solamente.

Angelina—Hazlo para que los demás sigan tu ejemplo.

Don Juan—No lo seguirán hija mía, empe-

żarían por criticarnos, odiarnos y hasta comprarían
a un ignorante para que incendiase mi fábrica, y se
burlarían diciendo : toma propiedad común!

Angelina—¿Estas seguro de eso?

Don Juan—Si hija mía, aún no ha llegado la
época. La libertad obrera ha de ser obra de ellos
mismos. (suena el timbre con fuerza).

ESCENA QUINTA.

Ramón—(Entrando dice), don Juan el capataz
lo procura.

Don Juan—Dile que pase.

Alberto—(El capataz entrando) con el sombrero en la mano muy agitado). D. Juan en la fábrica hay un alboroto fenomenal, venga seguida.

Don Juan—Que pasa para que esa prisa, van
a quemar la fábrica? Segúramente que son los no
organizados.

Alberto—No se, no me inmiscuyo en lo que no
me importa. Para mí los desorganizados son más
simpáticos.

Don Juan—Lo que llamas simpatía es servi-
lismo, y por eso encuentras a los otros arrogantes,
porque comprenden sus derechos.

Alberto—Venga don Juan, venga.

Don Juan—Cuando tienes tal prisa, algo habrás hecho.

Alberto—Solamente repartir material en mal
estado, y al momento fué un escándalo.

Angelina—Ahora creerán que ha sido mi papá
el que ha dado la orden.

Alberto—Hoy no la dió pero lo ha consentido
otras veces.

Don Juan—Calla, no hables demás, idiota,
(y lo empuja).

Alberto—Eso es ahora pagaré yó.

Angelina—(dirigiéndose a su padre) Lo que

dice este hombre, si es verdad, es un abuso, que autorizas y consientes.

Don Juan—Vamos a ver que has hecho, Hasta luego hija mía.

(Salen los dos)

Angelina—Me asomaré al balcón para ver cuando salen. (Sale por la puerta del fondo).

Telón.

ACTO SEGUNDO

ESCENA PRIMERA.

Un jardin, un sofa un velador, sobre el velador, un libro un tarjetero, y un timbre).

Angelina—Entrando por la derecha, se dirige a la mesa, revisa las tarjetas y dice: La huelga me convino, fué un buen pretexto para ayer no haber ido al paseo.

Como irán, no he visto aún a Ramón para que me cuente algo. (da un paseo y mirando hacia los árboles dice: ya lo veo, y oprime el timbre).

Ramón—¿Que desea Srta?

Angelina—¿Sabes algo de la huelga?

Ramón—Sólo se, que mañana, vendrá una comisión para hablar con don Juan.

Angelina—Muy bien perdona la molestia (Ramón se retira).

SEGUNDA ESCENA.

Don Juan—(entrando). Estabas inquieta? Pues no hay motivo, se quejaron del material, ofrecieron enviar mañana una comisión.

Angelina—¿Te pidieron aumento de jornal?

Don Juan—Aún no se lo que desean, mañana lo sabré, tu lo oiras.

Angelina—Tu sabías que venía la comisión.

Don Juan—Es lo corriente, para ellos obtener lo que desean.

Angelina—Sabes papá que ayer, vinieron a buscarme para dar un paseo, Marieta y Ernestina.

Don Juan—Fuiste con ellas?

Angelina—No, estaba triste, y me quedé leyendo.

Don Juan—Has hecho bien. ¿qué lees?

Angelina—"Fecundidad" de Zola. Ya leí "Verdad"

Don Juan—¿Te agrada esa lectura?

Angelina—Me gusta mucho por las verdades que dice ese escritor.

Don Juan—Bien, dime, ¿cómo te ha quedado la pulsera?

Angelina—Aún no me la he puesto, yo no necesito eso.

Don Juan—No seas tonta, ¿que vas a hacer con ella?

Angelina—Regalarla a Mariana, ella podrá venderla.

Don Juan—Será una lástima, pues al venderla le darán menos precio.

Angelina—Torpeza y lástima es que hayan seres humanos careciendo de lo necesario. Si me hubieras avisado, hubieramos consolado de un modo práctico algunas familias pobres.

Don Juan—Tendríamos que invertir lo que tenemos, en socorros.

Angelina—¡Que va! con mil dollars hubieramos ayudado a varias familias, en sus necesidades más importantes.

Don Juan—Como otras veces te habría obsequiado y no te había molestado............ ......

Angelina—Pero no de este modo.

Don Juan—Por que ahora puedo hacerlo mejor, estoy más desempeñado.

Angelina—Habrás explotado más, comprando el tabaco a más bajo precio. En vez de acumular tanto dinero debes recordar que los campesinos están en cuanto a civilización y progreso dos siglos atrás. Ya que ellos labrando la tierra se envejecen debemos proporcionarle medios de progresar, ya que su forma de trabajo no les permite más ventajas, debemos proporcionarle los medios.

Don Juan—Es la competencia la que me obliga, a emplear esos medios de especulación.

Angelina—Esa competencia es la que destruye la fraternidad, y convierte a los individuos en fieras humanas. Tu no debes seguir esa costumbre ¿dé que vale que reconozcas el derecho de los trabajadores si no lo prácticas?

Don Juan—Yo desearía seguir tus intenciones pero............que negocio emprender que no sea explotación? ¿a qué me dedico?

Angelina—El mismo negocio, lo que debes aprovechar ahora que están en huelga es conceder lo que pidan y libertar a tus esclavos.

Don Juan—(riendo) ¿Esclavos míos? Yo no los obligo ellos se someten voluntariamente. Que voy a hacer a despedirlo cuando vienen a trabajar voluntariamente?

Angelina—No los esclavizas intencionalmente pero te aprovechas de su miseria e ignorancia para explotarlos.

Don Juan—Si no lo hago yo, lo hará otro con peores condiciones.

Angelina—No sigas la costumbre, impón una nueva, pagale más jornal, para que quieres aumentar tu capital aún más? Oye, otra cosa que te voy a proponer, esta casa es muy grande para nosotros...

Don Juan—Deseas mudarte?

Angelina—Lo que deseo es que fabriques una sin gran lujo y esta la regales a la viuda de tu empleado............ ¿no crées que tiene derecho a tener una casa de su propiedad?

Don Juan—(se levanta y paseándose dice: ¿No se te ocurre otra cosa? En verdad que eres tremenda, a dónde iremos a parar?........ ....

Angelina—A la libertad, es lo mejor que se

me ha ocurrido, ¿vas a complacerme?.............
(levantándose y acariciando a su padre).

Don Juan—(cogiendo su sombrero, para salir)

Desde que murió tu madre no hago otra cosa que complacerte, no se á donde me conducirán tus locuras. (se va).

Ángelina—(Gracias papá hasta la vista, acom pañándolo hasta la puerta. (Sola). Por fin se me quita un gran peso de encima, ¿veré mis sueños rea lizados?...............sin concurrir a los templos, sin rendir tributo a las fórmulas tradicionales, ni a reu niones llamadas sociales, donde solamente se oyen críticas hirientes y calumnias.

TERCERA ESCENA.

Ramón—Srta. Maríana desea verla. ....
Ángelina—A propósito llega, dile que pase. Y tu que haces con esa escoba?

Ramón—Pues barriendo, (aparte, se habrá propuesto reformar el mundo).

Ángelina—Pues bien compraré una máquina de barrer y así no harás polvo que tu respiras.

Mariana—(entrando) Buen día Angelina, hay salud?

Ángelina—Bueno lo tenga Mariana, ¿cómo estás?

Mariana—Así, así, como Vd. me sacó de apuros, voy mejor, (sentándose).

Ángelina—De que Vd. habla, de la miseria que le envié? eso no tiene importancia.

Mariana—Para Vd. nó, pero para mí que tengo cuatro hijos, ha sido tan oportuno que compré calzado a mis hijos y ropa, figúrese como estaré de contenta y agradecida.. ....

Ángelina—Pues, para demostrarle que eso no tiene valor alguno, la estaba esperando precisamente, para regalarle un objeto que a Vd. le será de gran utilidad.

Mariana—Yo no debo permitir que Vd. se sacrifique, de ningún modo.

Angelina—Si no es sacrificio, señora mía, es un regalo que me han hecho, que podrás aprovechar y que no necesito.

Mariana—No puedo consentir que se prive Vd. de usar un regalo que seguramente Vd. puede usar.

Angelina—(presentando el estuche abierto). Ya ve Vd.?, para nada necesito yo esto, se la regalo, es de Vd.

Mariana—No puedo aceptar ese regalo, yo no uso joyas.

Angelina—Bien pues, la vende, para mi es un trasto inútil.

Mariana—No diga eso Angelina, es objeto de arte y de todos modos es de valor, y debe Vd. conservarla.

Angelina—Que para mi es inútil, no la quiero y antes que hacerlas pedazos, Vd. debe aprovecharla, véndala.

Mariana—Es superior a mis deseos el complacerla, no puedo, ¿qué diría su padre?, que yo aprovecho su generosidad para explotarla.

Angelina—Mi padre la conoce a Vd. y sabe además que se la regalaría a Vd. de modo que no tema, que mi padre ya lo sabe.

Mariana—¿A quién venderé yo esta prenda? (contemplándola).

Angelina—A cualquier dama rica, o a un joyero.

Mariana—Angelina Vd. me coloca en un conflicto.

Angelina—En el conflicto estaba yo, y seguiré mientras continúe en mi poder.

Mariana—Me decido a llevarla, ya que tanto la molesta.

Angelina—Mientras hayan necesidades por satisfar, creo un crimen usarlas.

Mariana—Cómo hacer para que no las hayan?

Angelina—Destruyendo la explotación, que es el origen de la miseria. "El capital es el producto del trabajo que no se paga, es el robo disimulado y legalizado."

He repetido una sentencia socialista.

Mariana—¿Es Vd. partidaria del socialismo?

Angelina—Si será lo que regirá en el futuro. Es decir dentro de poco.

Mariana—Mi esposo era socialista, pero ocultaba sus ideas , era cobarde.

Aügelina—No le culpe Vd. que el solo no ha sido, hay quien las oculta, sin temor a perder empleos.

Mariana—Aún conservo algunas obras socialistas y anarquistas.

Angelina—Que título tienen?

Mariana—"La Anarquía" y "La Gran Huelga" y varias que no recuerdo porque no las he leído.

Angelina—Me los prestarás, no lo olvides.

Mariana—Bien Angelina me retiro, porque tengo que preparar la comida a mis hijos, adiós. (dándole la mano).

Angelina—Hasta luego Mariana, en lo que pueda ser útil, no tema en avisarme sin rodeos. Adiós.

CUARTA ESCENA.

Ramón—(Entrando algo precipitado) Angelina, si su padre se entera de que Vd. envió recursos a los huelguistas se molestará.

Angelina—Que lo sepa, ya se guardará de molestarse porque sabe que hablo claro, y digo verdades. De aquí es de donde con justicia deben recibir los obreros recursos.

Ramón—No por el dinero. Si porque es a él que le han declarado la huelga.

Angelina—No te ocupes, el ha sido el que los ha explotado y su riqueza a ellos la debe.

Ramón—¿Qué ha sido, ó que ha motivado estos sentimientos en Vd?

Angelina—Pues libros de Sociología, ¿tengo razón, procedo con justicia?

Ramón—De un modo superior, a lo que yo hubiera pensado.

Angelina—Parece que llaman.

Ramón—(Sale y vuelve) Srta. la comisión.

Angelina—¡Adelante! que pasen Ramón.

Carlos Santana y Simplicio Hernández (Comisión de la huelga, entrando).

Carlos—(se adelanta y dice) Srta. a los pies de Ud. (inclinándose), Simplicio , también saluda.

Angelina—Gran honor para mi en conocerle y servirle. Con quién tengo el gusto de hablar?

Carlos—Venimos en Comisión, mi nombre Carlos Santana el hijo de Mariana, y este joven Simplicio Hernández, (ambos se saludan y Angelina dice aparte en tanto ellos observan sus papeles). ¡Cielos el hijo de Mariana! justicia, el hijo reclama lo que el padre no supo o no se atrevió a reclamar!

Angelina—Tomen asientos.

Carlos—Su papá está ausente?

Angelina—No tardará en volver.

Carlos—¿No importunaremos esperándolo?

Angelina—De ningún modo, Udes. acaban de llegar y además están en su casa.

Carlos—Muchas gracias, (aparte) que bella y que simpática és.

Ramón—(saliendo) que pronto se han gustado, Srta. don Juan llega, y (sale).

Don Juan—(entrando) al ver a los jóvenes

se dirige a ellos y dice con amabilidad: ¿A que debo el honor de ésta visita?

Carlos—(Se adelanta y dice: Somos la comisión de la huelga y venimos a comunicarle algunas proposiciones.

Don Juan—Veamos que desean Vdes.

Carlos presentando el pliego a don Ju an.

Don Juan—Hágame el favor de leerlo.

Carlos—(leyendo el pliego).

FEDERÁCIÓN LIBRE DE ARECIBO.

Comisión de la huelga a cargo de C. Santana y Simplicio Hernández.

COMUNICÁCIÓN:

Sr.. ....

Considerando;

que hasta ahora la clase trabajadora ha sufrido y esta sufriendo infinidad de injusticias, debido a la enorme explotación de que es objeto.

Considerando; que la huelga únicamente, es la que hace subir el jornal la mayor parte de las veces, y que conduce a un arreglo beneficioso a los trabajadores, siempre víctimas de todos los atropellos.

La Junta General extraordinaria en sesión ha declarado la huelga general. con estas peticiones:

Hemos resuelto y resuélvase: 1º.—Que el jornal mínimo para el campesino como para el bracero, sea de $3.00 diarios, y para los obreros de la ciudad, $5.00 diarios.

2º.—Que el dueño de la fábrica o ingenio tiene el deber de entregar a cada trabajador con familia una casa con las comodidades modernas y exigencias de la higiene.

3º.—Que debe facilitar a cada trabajador que labore en terrenos pantanosos, un par de calzado especial con suela de goma, y destinar el 20% de las ganancias para reserva en caso de enfermedad.

4° —En los talleres de tabaqueros, los asientos, deben estar separados, como un metro de vapor a vapor, y las ventanas abiertas teniendo el tabaco en aparatos de algodón húmedo, que no permita secar la hoja, e impida la correcta elaboración de la hoja. Los asientos separados con plantas que purifiquen el aire.

Respetuosamente,

LA COMISIÓN.

Don Juan—Yo creo que Vdes. no esperan recibir concesiones.

Carlos—No la necesitamos, si se niegan, continuaremos la huelga. Nosotros tenemos trabajo, en nuestros terrenos cultivados y dinero.

Don Juan—Alégrame mucho, no crean Vdes. que yo me opongo a sus peticiones, temo a los otros dueños de fábricas que me hieran a traición.

Carlos—¿Está Vd. dispuesto a conceder lo que pedimos?

Don Juan—Sí. Vdes. reclaman sus derechos pero mis compañeros me asesinarán.

Carlos—Nosotros lo defendemos como a uno de los nuestros, si accede Vd. será un estimulante, un hermoso ejemplo para los demás. y cuenta Vd. con nuestro apoyo.

Don Juan.—(decidido) Mañana. lo esperaré en mi oficina.

Carlos—Entonces. marchamos, ya que Vd. está dispuesto secundar nuestros deseos.

Angelina—(que había permanecido silenciosa se levanta y dice): Felicito a Vdes. por el triunfo obtenido.

Carlos—¡Oh Srta.!. aún no se sabe el final de esta jornada (despidiéndose) a los piés de Vd. (a don Juan) hasta mañana que iré a su oficina.

Don Juan—Hasta mañana,(los jóvenes salens y don Juan se pasea). y dice: En cuanto los otros

fabricantes lo sepan, será el gran alboroto, y estaré
expuesto a cualquier cosa.   Pero aunque yo no ce-
diera, ellos continuaban la huelga, pues tienen terrenos, y cooperativas.

Angelina—Es muy oportuno todo eso, trae-
rá una forma nueva de vida, y habrá más salud y felicidad.

Don Juan—Oportuno sería que todos los trabajadores hicieran idénticas peticiones.

Angelina—Ahora se declararán en huelga los
otros trabajadores, ya lo verás.

Don Juan—Sería conveniente los que no están organizados se organizaran, crecerán las coope-
raticas, y no serían tan explotados.

Angelina—Será una revolución en pequeño.

Ramón—(entrando con la tarjetera) don
Juan, tres señores esperan en la puerta, aquí están
sus tarjetas.

Don Juan—(lee las tarjetas: Jaime López,
Roberto Hartman y Antonio Rigaud, y volviéndose
a Ramón que aún espera le dice, que pasen, (Ramón
sale).

(Los tres señores entrando) saludan cortesmente a Angelina y dirigiéndose a don Juan le dan la
mano.

QUÍNTA ESCENA

Don Juan—Que los ha traído por aquí? tomen asiento.

Don Roberto—(alemán) Ramírez: Yo viene aquí, para saber que tu va a conceder a los obreros de tu fábrica, yo tiene una estaca a la puerta,
mi capataz, decirme a mi que tu arreglaba con ellos,
yo viene ligero aquí para saber lo que tu hace, yo
estar seguro de la huelga.

Don Juan—Púes muy pronto han venido Vdes-
porque la Comisión acaba de salir de aquí.

Don Jaime—¿Se puede saber las condiciones que presentan?

Don Juan—Me han dejado una copia de la petición, aquí esta: (se acercan don Antonio, y don Jaime y don Roberto).

Don Jaime lee, y cuando termina dice: eso es escandaloso ¿a dónde vamos? a la ruina.

¿Ya Vd. concedió eso? ¿qué hizo? cuéntenos.

Don Antonio—Vd. está conforme con esas condiciones?

Don Juan—Amigos míos, yo pienso de modo distinto, yo he estudiado algo de socialismo, y no tengo inconveniente en conceder a mis obreros sus derechos.

Don Jaime—Pero esas peticiones son exageradas, quedarán Vdes. en la ruina. (los otros hablan en voz baja con Angelina).

Don Juan—Sus doctrinas no le permiten hacer daño, lo que hacen es defenderse. Se asombran Vdes. porque no comprenden là inutilidad del dinero en caja, y se creen que cuando yo no lo tenga careceré de lo necesario.

Don Antonio—Medítelo bien no vaya Vd. a cometer una locura.

Angelina—Papá lo ha meditado bien, y además esta fortuna no es de él solo.

Don Jaime—De quién más Srta.?

Angelina—De los que la han trabajado, de sus obreros.

Don Antonio—Vemos que Vd. también se decide por ello.

Don Jaime—Con tal que no nos asesinen y nos roben.

Don Antonio—Creo que es una locura.

Angelina—¡Locura! conceder a los trabajadores lo que le corresponde? No señor.

Don Juan—Creo que eso no perjudicará a nadie, pienso marchar a Europa y dejaré la fábrica a ellos para que la dirijan, y también este palacio lo cederé.

Don Jaime—¿A los obreros?

Angelina—El palacio a la viuda de un empleado de la casa.

Don Antonio—¿Creen Vdes. que le dará resultado dejar la factoría en manos de gentes inexpertas?

Don Juan—¡Inexpertos!, pero se ha fijado en el pliego? acaso somos nosotros expertos?

Don Jaime—¿Vd. cree que todos son ilustrados?, y respectos a ser dueños de la factoría, para eso somos dueños del capital.

Don Juan—Y ellos pueden con su ignorancia producir para nosotros?

Don Jaime—Veóle muy interesado, y no seré yo quien le haga desistir.

Don Juan—Sería inútil, es cuestión de conciencia.

Don Antonio—Bien nos despedimos, (tomando el sombrero don Jaime y don Roberto, también saludan y se retiran).

Angelina—Que egoistas papá, como se resisten a ser razonables.

Don Juan—Pero ya terminó para mí el conflicto, esa resistencia es ignorancia: ahora voy al correo, hasta después. (don Juan sale).

Ramón—(entrando). Que tal Srta. como arreglaron?

Angelina—Mi padre lo ha resuelto, esos señores se asombraron de la resolución de papá, no se que determinarán , pues no estaban de acuerdo.

Ramón—Que recurso les quedará, aceptar.

Angelina—Lo que hace mucha falta Ramón es instruír, la instrucción es la base de la felicidad de los pueblos, y madre de la libertad.

Ramón—Si todas las mujeres se ocuparan de

estudiar las generaciones futuras reformarían el
mundo.

Ramón se asoma a la puerta que da al balcón,
y grita ¡Angelina asómese! asómese! (se oyen rumo-
res y gritos lejos.)

Angelina—¿Qué pasa? (y va en dirección
donde está Ramón).

Ramón—¿Vé Vd. los obreros de la fábrica
de tabacos vitoreando a don Juan?, y le rodean!

Angelina—¡Viene aturdido!, limpiándose el sudor, ya se acerca.

Don Juan—¡Ay, Ay! hija mía......(se deja
caer en el sillón) Angelina se apresura a limpiarle
el sudor y le pregunta: ¿que tienes papá?

Don Juan—No me iban a dejar pasar, un imprudente al yo salir del correo, dijo ahí va don Juan,
y otro dijo· ¿qué don Juan?, y cuando otros decían
¿dónde está? me ví rodeado de tal modo que creí
no me dejaban salir.

Angelina—¿Por qué, tonto; no comprendiste que te saludaban?, estás muy sofocado, debes tomar algo te vas a enfermar (toca el timbre
y entra Ramón), a quién le dice: prepárame un ponche con unas gotas de brandy, (Ramón sale).

Don Juan—Esto terminará con un conflicto;
yo me marcho para Europa, esos capitalistas me o-
diarán, Dejaré al joven Santana de la Comisión,
que me está muy simpático, encargado de todo.

Ramón—Con una bandeja con la taza de
ponche, (dice aparte también le gusta a él).

Angelina—Se acerca a su padre y le dice, no
te preocupes y toma esto que te hará bien, y descansa.

Don Juan—tomando el ponche, ¿tú crees
que debemos dejar a ese joven?, no parece el más
listo?

Angelina—(Impresionada), ¿el que habló contigo?

Don Juan—Sí, me dijo su nombre y no lo recuerdo.

Angelina—Se llama Carlos Santana.

Don Juan—¿Santana?.. ... ...ese era el nombre del marido de tu protegida, mi antiguo empleado.

Angelina—Si es hijo de Mariana, es muy educado, me gusta mucho.

Don Juan—¿Con qué te gusta mucho?, pues lo dejaremos a él, me parece apto para eso, y además recogerá él lo que el padre no supo aprovechar.

Angelina—El padre tenía las mismas ideas.

Don Juan—No lo parecía, el hijo es más inteligente.

Angelina—El también lo fué, pero el hijo es más audaz, y el mundo es de los audaces.

Don Juan—Esa sentencia es de algún filósofo?

Angelina—Nó, es mía, pero como me siento audaz, por eso te lo he dicho. Si me fuera posible transformaba el mundo.

Don Juan—Empieza, que los audaces no meditan mucho.

Angelina—Ya lo hago, acaso has olvidado que te he ido conduciendo al fin que me proponía?

Don Juan—Sí, ya veo que me ganas.

Angelina—Como Carlos gana a su padre, es el siglo, el progreso que nos empuja.

Don Juan—Te felicito, pero perdóname que te deje, estoy rendido voy a dormir, hasta mañana. (la besa en la frente).

Angelina—Por fin veré mis deseos satisfechos, (saliendo para su habitación), cae el telón.

Telón.

ACTO TERCERO

Ramón, Angelina, don Juan.
(El mismo decorado de el primer acto).

PRIMERA ESCENA.

Ramón—(Limpiando hablando sólo), Todas las fábricas en huelga, la federación llena, y a última hora se presentaron los desorganizados cuando vieron perdidos sus reclamos, y comprendieron que ganabamos la huelga.

Ángelina—Buen día Ramón, hablas solo? (revisando alguna prensa que encontrará sobre la mesa).

Ramón—Decía que todas las fábricas están en huelga.

Ángelina—¿Estás seguro?, cuánto me alegro.

Ramón—La verdad que esta muy complicado el asunto, si viera Vd. el gentío en la federación como lo ha visto yo esta mañana; parece una revolución.

Ángelina—Que hermoso estará eso, oir a esos hombres discutir sus derechos, y presentar una forma nueva de vida.

Ramón—¿Pero no se asusta Vd? (con asombro).

Ángelina—Que va, si parece que me brindan nuevas energías. ¡Viva la revolución! (muy animada)..

Ramón—Que viva......aa.a.....

Don Juan—(Arreglándose la corbata). Que pasa?, (mirándose al espejo) que gritos eran esos?

Ramón—Le decía a la Srta. que yo salgo muy de mañana a paseo................

Don Juan—Me pareció oir, vivas, y creí entender viva la región.

Ramón—Era yo refiriendo a la Srta. un detalle muy curioso.   (Ramón y Angelina se hacen señas de silencio).

Don Juan—Bien, sigue tus cuentos que yo marcho a la oficina, hasta luego. (saluda y sale).

Ramón—Que se asoma al balcón, vuelve y dice, Angelina, la manifestación, asómese. ¿Vé Vd. los estandartes allá al final de la calle?

Angelina—¡Qué muchas banderas rojas!. ¡Qué inmensa muchedumbre!

(Se oyen acordes de música lejana).

Ramón—Son doce mil obreros!, ahora que se metan los burgueses con nosotros¡qué vengan!, y vienen cantando el himno obrero.

Angelina—¿Hacia dónde van? Parece que vienen para acá.

Ramón—Es posible, y muy natural. Si, para esta casa debe venir el joven de la Comisión, ya se acerca. (Ramón sale y Angelina se prepara a recibir al que llega).

SEGUNDA ESCENA.

Carlos—Buen día Srta. ¿Cómo esta Vd?

Angelina—Muy bien; y Vd. como va con la huelga?

Carlos—Marchamos bien. Precisamente he venido para saber si permite Vd. que la manifestación que se acerca se detenga aquí y entonen el himno obrero.

Angelina—Si pueden tendré mucho gusto en oir el himno que no conozco..

Carlos—(toca el timbre). Entonces enviaré decir que se detengan.

Ramón—¿En qué puede ser útil?

Carlos—Hágame el obsequio de ir al grupo que forma la Comisión y dígales que pueden detenerse aquí. (Ramón sale).

Carlos—Es Vd. un ángel, permítame que bese su mano.

Angelina—(da su mano), y dice: que he hecho para que Vd. se exprese de ese modo? Son mis ideas, en esto no hay para mi nada de particular.

Carlos—¿Vuestras ideas? ¿Y cuáles son esas ideas?

Angelina—El socialismo, ácrata.

Carlos—Oh !designios misteriosos de la naturaleza¡, que nos une en este gran momento de emancipación social; para reconocer en Vd. el ideal de mis sueños. (lentamente le toma una mano y se arrodilla) (En el mismo momento se oye claro el himno obrero. (Ellos escuchan con placidez, y cantan).

Angelina—Así pues, amigo no extrañe Vd. mis procedimientos. He leído a Malato, Malatesta, Tolstoy, Zola. De modo que he comprendido muchas cosas que no podía comprender antes.

Carlos—¡Oh! bendita instrucción que llena mi alma de alegría, al encontrar en Vd. el ideal de la mujer soñada.

Angelina—Y se admira por eso?

Carlos—Sí, pues no creí encontrar a Vd. dentro de mis ideas.

Angelina—Muy natural; le explicaré a Vd. como empezé. Estaba estudiando Espiritismo, pues, (como Vd. comprenderá, sola, sin creer en la rutina, la cual mi padre no me prohibía), sentí deseos de conocer algo respecto de ultratumba, pues mi madre había muerto siendo yo muy niña. Y además de comprender la pluralidad de mundos habitados y aceptar las diversas existencias, me hizo revolucionaria, pues me explicaba que todos los

hombres eran hermanos, que nadie tenía derecho
de molestar a otros, ni de imponerle sus ideas, ni de
esclavizarlo, que el lujo era un crimen mientras hubiera miseria.

De modo que, además de comprender la gran-
diosidad del universo, me hizo humanitaria; lo que
quizás no lo hubiera conseguido nadie.

Carlos—(que había permanecido absorto dice):—Continúe, me quedaría oyéndola, sin cansar-
me, una mujer libertada de los dogmas religiosos.

Angelina—Algunos creen que el Espiritismo
es una religión. La palabra religión ha sido con-
fundida, los menos religiosos han sido los curas,
aparentaban serlos, pero los que menos se ocuparon
de seguir las máximas de Jesus, fueron ellos, siguieron sus conveniencias particulares. De modo que
el. ó los que procuraran seguir las doctrinas de Jesus son los religiosos verdaderos, por que religioso
es el que guarda una reliquia y cumple religiosa-
mente con los preceptos de un doctrina.

De modo que el estudio de la Psicología es ciencia, no obliga a seguir determinados dogmas, porque no los tiene. Analiza, escrudiña, investiga,
y estudia observando los casos y experimentos de
esa ciencia.

Carlos—Muy bien, acepto todo, del modo como Vd. lo explica.

Angelina—Ahora para implantar el socialismo anarquíco, es necesario que todos sientan la fraternidad que no sientan odios ni rencores; porque
en plena anarquía, las personas de instintos crueles lo seguirán siendo, y la anarquía no los transfor-
mará, al transformar el sistema.

Carlos—Cree Vd. que todos los anarquistas
hayan leído las máximas de amor humano las que
predicó hace seis mil años en Asia, Christna, fué
un mesías como Jesús, luego el Emperador de la
China Yao. Confucio, en la misma época, luego

Fhilon, y después otros hasta Jesús. El Emperador Yao, decía: "Si hay quien padezca hambre
yo tengo la culpa, si alguién comete un crimen, yo
soy el autor". Y ese hombre dejó el trono y se de-
dicó a predicar.

Angelina—No creo que todos los anarquistas,
conozcan esos detalles, muchos son anarquistas por
desesperación, por que no disfrutan de comodidades, y se llaman anarquistas para conquistar el poder, después de lo cual son tan o más tiranos que los
demás, esos no aman la humanidad, ni se ocupan
de ayudar a la propaganda libertaria.

Carlos—Tiene Vd. muchísima razón. La mayoría de esos que se llaman anarquistas, no aman
a la humanidad, solamente están dispuestos a cri-
ticarlos sin haber hecho por instruirlos.

Angelina—Pienso que los verdaderos anarquistas, encontrarán dudosas la historia de la biblia
(1) y rechazarán las instituciones de fines egoistas.
Pero todo los que Vd. citó anteriormente, son ver-
deros anarquistas, si es que se le aplica el verdadero sentido a esa frase, es decir humano, en toda la
extensión de la palabra, justo, sincero, tolerante en
todo aquello que no constituya perjuicio para los
demás.

Carlos—Soy de la misma opinión.

Angelina—Además yo pienso que es necesario evitar por todos los medios posibles, la miseria,
para poder preparar bien los cerebros para que puedan recibir y comprender las ideas redentoras y de
fenderlas.

Carlos—Muy bien. en tanto el hambre, las
enfermedades que esta origina existan, no es posible que hayan energías para obtener el derecho al
producto íntegro del trabajo.

---

[1] En la Biblia hay verdades escritas sublimes,
practiquémoslas.

Angelina—De acuerdo, solo entonces, podría pensarse en contemplar el espacio inmenso, y soñar con otros mundos habitados.

Carlos—Eso mismo, mientras haya quien se muera de hambre o por carecer de todo lo que constituye la vida, no podemos pensar en otros asuntos, eso no prohibe a los que individualmente se ocupen de esas investigaciones que las continuen.

Angelina—Conforme, aunque no comprendo, porque no se pueden estudiar juntas.

Carlos—Sí, pueden dedicarse, los que quieran. Ahora perdoneme, pero es necesario que me vaya; permanecería oyendola más tiempo, su fácil y sugestiva palabra me encanta, permítame antes de irme quiero decirla, que es Vd. la única mujer que ha impresioando mi alma de un modo extraño, Angelina............yo amo a Vd.............

Angelina—(con alegría). De veras?........no era yo sola?........ que feliz soy!

Carlos—¡Cómo!, ha pensado Vd. en mí? me ama Vd?........pero esto es un sueño?........(adelanta un paso hacia ella).

Angelina—(se acerca y le toma una mano). Un sueño, si, que se realiza, te presentía te esperaba, como esperan las flores el rocío y presienten las avecillas el despertar de la naturaleza.

Carlos—¡Qué felicidad!, tan inexperada y tan hermosa!........(besándola las manos).

ESCENA TERCERA.

Don Juan—(entrando)   De las mas grandes!

Carlos—(que se ha separado de Angelina de repente), saluda a Don Juan muy tímido.

Angelina—Perdoname, papá.

Don Juan—(que saca papeles y guarda en los bo sillos) dice: ¿dé qué?, no me lo habías dicho?

Carlos—(con interés) ¿Qué le dijo?

Don Juan—Mucha prisa en saberlo, es preciso que Vd. se entere de otro asunto más urgente;
yo creí que Vd. estaría en sus asuntos de huelga y
me lo encuentro aquí.

Carlos—He venido a pedir permiso para que la
manifestación se detuviera aquí y entonasen el himno obrero.

Don Juan—Bien, pues prestad atención, habeis de saber que marchamos a Europa y Vd. se......

Carlos—(interrumpiendo) ¡Adiós mi sueño
dorado! ....

Don Juan—No se alarme Vd. que ahora se
cumplirán sus deseos. Vd. y su familia pasaran
a vivir a este edificio.

Carlos—No debo permitir eso, de ningún modo, se figurarán que yo he hecho algún negocio........

Don Juan—No me interrumpa Vd. que son
decisiones de Angelina antes de conocerle a Vd.

Carlos— Escucho..........

Don Júan—Después que Vdes. se instalen
aquí, tomará la dirección de la fábrica, con el mismo capataz; accedidas todas las peticiones refor-
mada los talleres en condiciones higienicas, esta-
blecerás en la planta baja talleres de zapatería y de
carpintería y herrería. Lo demás Vd. lo hará.

Carlos—¿Esa es su decisión?

Don Juan—Además, cuando regrese se unirá
Vd. a mi hija.

Carlos—¿Pero se burla Vd. de mí?, no puedo
creer lo que me dice.

Don Juan—Como Vd. lo oye mañana saldré
de esta ciudad.

Angelina—Tan pronto y apenas nos hemos conocido..........

Don Juan—¿Y qué?, por eso no se morirán.

Carlos—Entonces, voy a ver a mi madre y luego iré a ver a Vd. en la oficina.

Don Juan—Hasta la noche.

Angelina—(acompaña hasta la puerta a Carlos) No podré estar tranquila lejos de tí, (se dan la mano).

Don Juan—Basta de coloquio, que me van a enternecer.....

Carlos—(Tira un beso a la joven y se marcha)

CUARTA ESCENA.

Angelina—(Sientase triste.)

Don Juan—Vamos, ahora no podrás quejarte todo está a la medida de tus deseos.

Angelina—Ahora no querrá Vd. que me entristezca, dejar ese muchacho solo aquí al frente de esta situación tan comprometida, y si lo asesinan?

Don Juan—No seas tonta, he avisado al jefe de Policía le he explicado mi resolución, y le he dicho que la vida de ese joven esta en sus manos, de modo que el avisará a sus policías, no hay temor, y además volveremos pronto.

Angelina—Menos mal, ¿cómo ha quedado la huelga?

Don Juan—Continúa, pero sí se organizan todos, no hay temor, pues se establecerá la solidaridad, y engrandecerán las cooperativas.

Angelina—Siendo así, no habrá mucho que esperar porque tienen propagandistas en los campos en todas partes.

Don Juan—Así lo espero, ahora arregla tus maletas y lo que necesites, voy a mi escritorio, para tomar todo lo que necesito para pasar el derecho de propiedad.

Angelina—(Sale por el medio) (Don Juan por la derecha).

Ramón—(Entra con dos maletas). Ahora si que yo estoy preocupado, nunca he tenido que servir a otras personas, no se como serán los nuevos dueños.

Angelina—(Entrando con otra maleta), toma Ramón, á la estación todas.

Ramón—¿Cuándo volverán Vdes?

Angelina—Pronto no te preocupes, cuándo vuelva me uniré á Carlos

Ramón—¡Albricias!, así tengo también derecho de hacer lo mismo.

Angelina—¿Tienes prometida?.

Ramón—Una obrera organizada.

Angelina—Debes hablar con papá para que te dé orden para proveerte de lo que necesites.

Ramón—Lo dejaré para cuando vuelva.

Angelina—Debes hacerlo ahora, pues si no saben que estás sin empleo nada te dirán.

Toma las llaves de los muebles para cuando llegue Mariana le expliques. Dime el nombre de tu novia, si no es un secreto.

Ramón—Con mil amores, la llaman Rosalina, es trigüeña de ojos negros.

Angelina—Te felicito, y me despido ahora me voy a la oficina de papá ya no vuelvo aquí, hasta que regrese. (se dan las manos), estarás en la estación hasta que embarquemos, el vapor saldrá esta noche a las doce.

QUINTA ESCENA.

Ramón—(sólo). Será un escándalo, para esta sociedad llena de fórmulas hipócritas, esta niña dará un fuerte golpe a éste sistema. (con exaltación). Unos explican la anarquía como una doctrina de crímenes y violencias, sinembargo en nombre de Cristo sus representantes quemaron millones de seres humanos; en nombre de la libertad, los libertadores del 93 en Francia, guillotinaron millares, la anarquía no ha cometido esos crímenes, que algún fanático haya suprimido de la escena a un Carnot, a un Canovas, a un Humberto, a un Mac

Kinley, son casos aislados, y además no se escu lun
en institución alguna, son perdonables, los Ravachol
Pallás, Caserio, y Angiolillos, son pocos, los Torquemadas, los Cánovas, y los Luis IX, se multiplican
con una facilidad asombrosa.

Mariana—(entrando). ¿Con quién hablas
Ramón?

Ramón—Ensayando Sra. permítame que le
entregue las llaves.....

Mariana—Espera un poco, que viene mi hijo.
Ya está aquí.

Carlos—¿Qué deseas mamá?

Mariana—Ramón desea entregarte las llaves.

Carlos—Son las llaves de la casa, enséñame a
que muebles pertenecen.

Ramón—(Indica señalando los muebles, y se
despide). Antes de irme necesito que Vd. me de
una orden para la fábrica.

Carlos—No lo necesitas, luego irás conmigo.

Mariana—Oye hijo, como va la huelga?

Carlos—Nosotros vamos bien, ahora faltan
las demás fábricas, que cedan sus derechos, nosotros tenemos en construcción 500 casas, tenemos
dos mil obreros ocupados, cada casa con su jardín
espacioso, y todo las comodidades modernas.

Mariana—¿Cuándo llegan las máquinas de
tejido?

Carlos—Pronto, ahora se prepara el edificio
para esa fábrica. Como se trabaja solamente seis
horas, es necesario emplear más gente.

Mariana—¿Y la agricultura?

Carlos—Se han comprado más terrenos, y todo se está cultivando, sembrando frutos y cereales,
el año entrante, tendremos hacienda, esperamos
catálogos para las máquinasl

Mariana—Dime y Ramón a dónde vá? ,no
se queda aquí a vivir?

Carlos—Creo que nó, porque me ha pedido,

derecho para ir a la fábrica, pues como se casa, desea tener una casita sola.

Mariana—¿Qué ideas tiene ese muchacho? cuando entré hablaba sólo. y me asombre de oir cosas tan distintas.

Carlos—Debe ser porque el creé que hay idéntica analogía entre el anarquismo y el primitivo cristianismo. en el cual todos los bienes fueron co munes. y no habían directores, ni amos. ni privilegiados. Pero hoy después de miles cambios de nombres se ha adoptado el de psicología. ciencia cristiana. espiritismo. teosofía y cada una quiere ser la única poseedora de la verdad.

Mariana—¿Y cuál de todas es la que debe seguirse?

Carlos—La verdad absoluta no la posee nadie. Todas están basadas en la ciencia psicologica, en la fuerza mental de los individuos de ambos sexos, en la fuerza de voluntad que cada una o uno posea.

Mariana—¿Y don Juan participa de esas ideas?

Carlos—Sí, porque el es un espiritista, y por tanto acepta todas esos diferentes nombres de una sola cosa.

Mariana—¿Pero él acepta tus ideas de igualdad?

Carlos—Sí, forman la base principal de su doctrina.

Mariana—¿Y Angelina, también es de esa doctrina?

Carlos—Ella es una ferviente admiradora de Cristo y una defensora de la reencarnación, y de los diferentes mundos habitados. Cree que el espíritu vuelve a vivir y que tenemos que pasar por distiintas fases de la vida, para progresar. Ella es una convencida.

Mariana—¿Pero don Juan sabe que tu no eres partidario de el matrimonio civil o religioso?

Carlos—Se lo figura, pues bien conoce nuestras propagandas, ahora disimula porque no ha llegado el momento de aceptarlo. Pero bien enterado esta de las infamias de la actual forma social, y de los abusos que se cometen.

Mariana—Entonces nada tendrás que se oponga en el futuro a la realización de tus propósitos.

Carlos—Nada temo; Angelina es una libertaria, que según ella, ha vivido en la época cristiana y no se espanta de mis conceptos revolucionarios.

SEXTA ESCENA.

Ramón—(entrando con Rosalina). Aquí estamos para que Vd. sepa cuando tomamos posesión de nuestra casa.

Carlos—Me alegro mucho de conocer a tu compañera, aunque no me la hayas presentado.

Ramón—Perdoneme Carlos, fué una distracción.

Carlos—De todos modos, vas a formar hogar de un modo nuevo y es necesario, que sepas eres el primero, tenemos que aplaudir a esta joven por lo valiente.

Rosalina—Estoy segura que Ramón me ama, y por tanto no hay temor de fracasos.

Carlos—Muy bien, está Vd. segura de su amor y nada teme.

Mariana—Si todas las mujeres pudieran decir otro tanto.

Rosalina—No lo dicen Sra. porque son ignorantes en su mayoría que no tienen voluntad, que se plegan a las circunstancias, y no quieren luchar con ellas. pero si fueran valientes dispuestas a defender sus derechos, yo le aseguro que ningún hombre abusaría. de nuestra supuesta debilidad, y se guardarían de tomarnos como objeto de placer simplemente.

Carlos—(aplaudiendo), ¡bravo!, así se habla. ¿No la aplaudes tu también, Ramón?

Ramón—Ella sabe que yo la admiro y que aplaudo todas sus valentias.

Mariana—Lástima que todas las mujeres no estén preparadas como Vd.

Rosalina—Algún día llegará la completa emancipación.

Carlos—Bien, aquí tienen Vd. mi autorización para ocupar el sitio más agradable la casa más poetiza. Mientras no estemos todos unidos se necesitan todos estos requisitos.

Ramón—Es necesario, y no me molesta. Entonces puedo irme?

Carlos—Sí, ese documento lo entregarás al encargado, nada más.

Rosalina—¿Qué le parecen a Vdes? si las generaciones pasadas pudiera enterarse de un matrimonio sin Dios sin amo sin rey y sin cura. asombrados quedarían.

Carlos—En las primeras etapas de la humana especie no usaban entre ellos ningún rito, se unían entre libremente, después del cristianismo quedó el matrimonio constituído.

Rosalina—Naturalmente así debió de continuar, un hombre y una mujer tienen perfectísimo derecho de unirse libremente si se aman mutuamente, sin engaños.

Carlos—No cabe el engaño donde hay libertad, pues si se han equivocado respecto a su carácter, libremente vuelven a separarse.

Rosalina—Comprendo, pero quiero decir, que se amen, que no sea simplemente el deseo que los una.

Carlos—El deseo es una cosa natural, no puede negarlo, si dos se gustan naturalmente se atraerán, y si después se llevan bien, seguirán viviendo. Pero que no se convierta el deseo en costumbre, si-

·no que siempre se sientan enamorados, apasionados uno del otro. Que si ese hombre ve a otra mujer no la desée, y si esa mujer ve a otro hombre,no
lo desee, pero si el no siente atracción por su mujer,
necesariamente tiene que fijarse en otra. De mo
-do que ellos dos, se basten solos.

Rosalina—Comprendo, Ahora permítame
que ya es tarde, nos retiramos. Hasta luego Carlos, adiós Sra.

Carlos—Que les vaya bien.

Mariana—Acompañándoles hasta la puerta).
adiós hija.

Carlos—Ahora tengo el trabajo de las proposiciones a los otros fabricantes.

Mariana—Parece que llaman. (Simplicio y
Juan Hernández).

SEPTIMA ESCENA.

Simplicio—(a Carlos saludándolo a los dos)
Es necesario enviar propagandistas a los campos,
he sabido que los fabricantes han enviado agentes
para ir por trJbajadores al campo.

Carlos—De acuerdo, que nombren dos, para
los barrios diferentes.

Simplicio—Esta noche en la Junta que los
nombren.

Carlos—Cualquiera de los muchachos de iniciativa quef ay pueden enviarlos.

Juan—Entonces, si no hay otra dificultad,
nos vamos.

Carlos—Hasta luego. (ellos salen).

OCTÁVA ESCENA.

Mariana—Como harán hijo mío después que
los demás accedan.

Carlos—Pues, asegurar el derecho de los tra

bajadores, entonces nadie se opondra a que sean felices.

Mariana—Todos estarán preparados para eso?

Carlos—¿Para que tenemos los centros de instrucción?, para que ilustren a los que no saben y además aunque no sepan tienen derecho al producto de su trabajo.

Mariana—Parece que llaman (se asoma).

Carlos—¡Adelante!...(el cartero).

El cartero (entregando una carta), para el señor Carlos Santana.

Carlos—Servidor de Vd. ¿nada más?

El cartero—No hay otra cosa.

Carlos—Gracias, buenas tardes, (abriendo la carta). Es de don Juan. (leyendo)

"Gran Hotel España".

Barcelona, mayo 17 191.

Sr. don Carlos Santana.

Arecibo, Puerto Rico.

Estimado amigo:

En la próxima semana estaré en esa. Angelina y este servidor estamos bien; hemos recorrido algunos sitios importantes, como museos, parques y teatros, creo que es bastante por ahora.

Un abrazo de Angelina,

Reciba el afecto de su S.S.

Juan de Ramírez.

Mariana—Dos meses, no es mucho, ¿vendrán a hospedarse aquí?

Carlos—Iré a recibirlos y no permitiré que vayan a otra parte.

Mariana—Angelina estará muy hermosa, se habrá divertido mucho.

Carlos—No lo creas, porque ella no fué por su

gusto (aparte): otra vez llaman. ¿Qué ocurre?
¡adelante! (un joven entrega una carta. y se va).
Mariana—Me parece oportuno ir arreglando
la habitación para Angelina.
Carlos—(Leyendo). Muy Sr. mío:
Hemos determinado acceder a las peticiones de
la huelga, por convenir a nuestros intereses.
Lo que participo a Vd. para conocimiento de su
gobierno interior.

Afectuosamente,

Kolber & Rigaud.

Carlos—¡Magnífico!, ya tenían seis meses de
broma; era bastante; enhorabuena. ahora que termina este conflicto, es necesario enviar detalles ato-
das las sociedades, de la solución y de las mejoras
que poseemos.
(Sientase a escribir).
Baja el telón.

EPILOGO.

Elegante salón de recepción, espejos sofas, o-
tros muebles de lujo.

Carlos—(paseándose preocupado).
Don Juan—(entrando) ¿En qué piensas?
Angelina—¡Carlos!...........
Carlos—Por fín te vuelvo a ver, (besándola en
la frente), ya estoy tranquilo. (Angelina va al
cuarto a cambiarse de ropa).
Don Juan—(abrazándole) ¿Cómo vas?,es-
tas en salud?
Carlos—De salud bien?
Don Juan—¿Cómo marchan tus asuntos?
Carlos—¿Mis asuntos? Ahora son de Vd.
otra vez.
Don Juan—He dicho tus asuntos porque yo

no pienso volver a ocuparme de ellos. Tu eres el director, inspector, todo.

Carlos—Que me deja Vd. a mi todos los negocios, y Vd. no me ayudará en algo?

Don Juan—Si te ayudaré, pero no soy otra cosa, me pagarás mi trabajo de inspección o de lo que sea.

Carlos—Si Vd. se empeña, lo complaceré.

Don Juan—Bien cuéntame, como van las cosas.

Carlos—Maravillosamente. No ha habido conflictos, nuestros barrios no necesitan jueces, ni policías, no hay embriaguez, todos los meses hay una fiesta o excursión. Tenemos escuelas nocturnas y diurnas, músicas, teatros, juegos recreativos gimnásticos.

Don Juan—¿No hay enfermos?

Carlos—Sí, están en el campo tratados especialmente. Hacen lo que más les guste, si quieren revisar las plantaciones, o pasear. Hay terrazas cubiertas adornadas con trepaderas, con balancines.

Don Juan—¿Y los fabricantes que han hecho?

Carlos—Pues las primeras semanas se resistieron, luego vinieron a ver las fábricas le mostramos todos los departamentos, de lavado general, la cocina general donde cada mes se cambia de cocinero; todo movido por fuerza eléctrica. El sistema de abrir las puertas automáticamente, el fregado la agricultura.

Los fabricantes decían que eso no duraría mucho; los visitantes, asombrados dijeron que nos a rrui naríamos. Pero no han podido interrumpir nuestres propósitos.

Don Juan—Y cómo se arreglan los de ideas diferentes?, los católicos, protestantes, y demás sectas?

Carlos—No tenemos templos, el que desee

continuar con sus errores, que lo haga en su casa. Tenemos un amplio salón-biblioteca, grandes cartelones, colgados de la pared explican las diferentes doctrinas de la humanidad, nacidas en el Asia. Un pequeño observatorio astrónomico y de experimentos psicológicos, cada cual concurre libremente. Hay salones de lecturas públicas, de filosofía artes, ciencias, agricultura, sociología teosofía, psicología. Tenemos profesores, de música, pintura, escultura, mecánica, naturología e higiene, y arqueología, náutica, e ingeniería. Cada individuo, tiene perfecto derecho de seguir sus inclinaciones.

Don Juan—Estoy asombrado de la tranquilidad que reina aquí, pero bien y los profesores, viven aquí?

Carlos—Muy satisfechos, tienen sus horas de trabajo y cuando están libres cada cual sigue su gusto.

Don Juan—¿Qué sueldo tienen?

Carlos—No tienen sueldos, no tenemos dinero en circulación, los que tienen familia, toman lo que necesitan en los grandes almacenes, los que aún están solos con su mujer, de igual modo. Casi todos se han casado aquí, es decir se han unido libremente, se han gustado dos y se lo dicen a sus padres, para que sepan porque salen del hogar, se van a vivir juntos.

Don Juan—¡Magnífico! Bien Carlos, vamos a terminar hoy para que sean felices los que más derechos tienen a serlos. ¿Y Mariana?

Carlos—Mamá ha salido a ordenar algunas cositas para el tocador de Angelina.

(Varios amigos entrando, los del Comité).

ESCENA FINAL.

Todos saludan a don Juan, especialmente Sim-

plicio le da la mano dice: Como está Vd. y la joven Angelina.

Don Juan—Todos bien, ahora saldrá, está
cambiandose el traje.

Angelina—(Entrando vestida de blanco sencilla y elegante).   Buenas tardes señores.   ¿Estoy bien así Carlos?

Carlos—¡Elegantísima!

Los amigos—¡Viva la mujer libre!   ¡Loor
a la mujer que supo despreciar los privilegios, fórmulas tradicionales y ayudarnos a ser libres!

Angelina—¡Oh!, no merezco tal elogio, es la
instrucción la hada misteriosa que lo ha hecho.

Simplicio—Además la modestía, reune Vd.
las condiciones más deseadas en los seres humanos.

Carlos—Bien procedamos a terminar esto,
pues se nos hará muy tarde luego.

Don Juan—Permanecerán Vdes. aquí o irán
al campo?

Carlos—Iremos al campo

Simplicio—En ese caso, te acompañaré, si no
molesto.

Angelina—Hace notable falta Ramón y su
mujer, pues de repente no podemos destrozar costumbres que se han formado con el individuo.   Ramón está con nosotros desde yo niña, no estar hoy
aquí indicaría de mi parte un gran olvido de modo
que es necesario enviarle aviso.

Carlos—Ya vendrán, ¿tu crees que ya no sepan que has llegado?

Angelina—Bien, y tu mamá, ¿dónde está?

Carlos—No tardará en llegar. ¡mirala! ahí esta!

Mariana—(entrando) ¡Hija mía! que hermosa estas, (se abrazan).

Angelina—¡Madre mía!.........

Carlos—Aquí están Rosalina y Ramón.

Angelina—(corre da su mano a Ramón y a-

braza a Rosalina). Tanto tiempo sin vernos! ¿Có
mo estas? ¿Eres feliz?

Rosalina—¡Sí, mucho! (con aire de satisfacción (Se oye la Marsellesa).

Carlos—Toma a Angelina de la mano). Desde hoy unimos nuestra existencia, hasta que el destino quiera; el día que no me ames, que estes hastiada de mi, tienes perfectísimo derecho de irte a
donde te plazca. (Angelina se arroja en sus brazos).

Angelina—Seré feliz mientras me ames, cuando vea en tí indiferencia o desvío me alejaré sin dejar de ser tu amiga.

Don Juan—(Que observa y escucha). Yo
represento el pasado rindiéndole tributo al presente
que encarna el porvenir.

Ramón—(á Rosalina) Ven a mis brazos,
complemento de mi alma y de mis aspiraciones,
somos dos más que viven la vida del amor sin rodeos ni imposiciones.

Simplicio—Ahora a divertirnos, al teatro, al
campo. cada cual dónde más le plazca.

Mariana—Yo permanezco aquí, cuidaré la
casa y acompañaré a don Juan.

Angelina—Vd. acompañará a papa, pero con
nosotros, al campo, esta noche al teatro.

Mariana—Hija mía. Si hacen doce años que
no salgo de noche.

Angelina—Yo os caso a los dos, a ti y a papá.
(todos se ríen y celebran la proposición).

Simplicio—Que se casen están aún jóvenes,
pueden dar un par de pichones para la revolución.

Don Juan—No hagais caso mi hija bromea.....
soy viejo para Mariana, y además yo había hecho
resolución...............(mira con disimulo a Mariana,
y se encuentra con los ojos de Mariana que lo mira
sonreida)

Carlos—Me parece ridícula la negativa madre mía.............

Mariana—Hijo mío!, yo había jurado........

Carlos—Los dos habeis hecho propósitos que no sabiais si lo cumplirían. Vamos de una vez........

Angelina—(Tomando las manos de los dos y las junta, los dos viejos se miran se ríen y se abrazan. Los jóvenes que los rodean gritan: ¡Viva la unión libre! ¡abajo la explotación!¡abajo la ley del salario!. (salen todos con gran animación).

Antes de bajar el telón.

Angelina—Bellas niñas que habeis escuchado, si quereis ser madres de generaciones concientes, y ser libres, no hagais contratos en el registro civil, ni en los templos, porque eso es una venta y la venta es la prostitución. El amor debe ser libre, como la brisa que respirais; como las flores que abren sus corolas para recibir el polen fecundante, y brindan al aire sus perfumes, así debeis brindar vuestro amor y prepararos hacer hijos por amor.

TELÓN.

— FIN —

NOTAS, APUNTES, PENSAMIENTOS, CONCEPTOS DEFINICIONES, SENTENCIAS Y REFLEXIONES FILÓSOFICAS, NATURISTAS, PSICOLÓGICAS, MORALISTAS.

Empezadas en Ibor City, julio 24 de 1913.

("**Gacetilla; Gaceta; de Gazzetta,** periódicos que valían una moneda llamada así, á principios del siglo XVII")

* *
*

Escribía sobre la fuerza mental y su poderío, detallaba la influencia benéfica y su extensión, de los que sabían vivir la verdadera vida natural, exenta, de malos deseos é inútiles pequeñeces; me detuve en la quinta cuartilla; durante escribía, mi mente reflexionaba y comparaba recordando detalles de las manifestaciones individuales y colectivas; detuve mi narración y me dije, no es justa ésta opinión si ésto sucede, és necesario. No se vive una existencia, sin recoger algo bueno: ¿acaso, sé yo quienes han sido estos en sus anteriores vidas? Un criminal,—según la opinión de la mayoría,—un perverso por impulso expontáneo, no comprende la extensión, ni la intensidad de sus actos, procede como el león ó tigre que devora á una oveja sin conmoverse por el dolor de su víctima, para estos como para aquel, es una satisfacción, una necesidad, de igual modo se complacen los ignorantes en mortificar, en burlarse de los demás, sin ocurrirsele que una calumnia, una exageración, una burla, pueda inferir una herida semejante á la de un puñal.

Suspendí mi descripción por entender que cada cual tiende á realizar sus aspiraciones ó necesidades de acuerdo con su temperamento modificándose en cada etapa de su vida terrena y ultra-terrena, los impulsos de su yo interno.

Agosto 1°., de 1913.

* *
*

Una mañana al desenvolver un pedazo de queso, que guardaba, para comer una tajadita, descubrí en una de sus pequeñas cavidades un gusano blanco, con una trompita negra, á modo de pico, luego otro y otro más; observé que se dispersaban al mover el queso y volví á colocarlo cuidadosamente en el mismo sitio; al siguiente día volví á observarlo y otra vez los dejé. No sentí asco, ni repulsión, ni deseo por destruirlo; he sentido por los animales compasión, como si guardasen un alma semiconciente, en una apariencia grosera.

Al otro día leyendo **"De mi Vida" de Zamacoiz"**, una descripción de los gusanos, me dije,—bien hice en no destruirlos,—? por qué?—acaso me hubiera anticipado en una especie de venganza con ellos, porque serán los que invadirán mi cuerpo. Contemplo, con gran interés, todos los seres vivientes grandes y chicos, no me agrada, interrumpirlos en su faena, al contrario les facilito medios para alimentarse ó para desenvolverse á su gusto y según pueda. No me agrada matar ni las arañas peludas, ni los **cienpiés** por gusto, sin que haya motivo justificado.

Si alguna me picase, seguramente que otro la mataría, yo nó. He tenido oportunidad de verlos muy cerca y no temerlos, y al ver una vez (1) unos muchachos que perseguían una "araña peluda" im-

pedí que la mataran, y la muy lista se acurrucó con--
tra la pared y al momento, á un ruido de los chicos,
corrió y se metió en un agujero que parecía hecho
para ella; era un agujero hecho con barrena en la
pared, en la puerta misma de la casa.——1°. de a-
gosto 1913.—(1) ésta observación fué hecha en Cuba, en Cárdenas, y la escribo ahora, al hacer la copia de los originales, escritos en la libreta, en Tampa, añado ésta por ser complemento de mi procedimiento.

* *
*

Los relojes públicos estarían en otras épocas
en los palacios de los reyes, luego en las iglesias, durante siglos, fué ella la que lo exhibió, y nos señaló
la hora, más tarde, cuando el pueblo hizo cambiar
las costumbres y los privilegios por otros, con revo-
luciones, el reloj marcaba el tiempo en los ayuntamientos, ahora los hay en las fábricas, que
tienen aspecto de palacios, con sus torres elegantes
que se elevan representando la dignificación del
trabajo, pero es donde el hombre se humilla, donde lo explotan, se enferma y de allí al hospital o a
pedir limosna.

Los palacios, las iglesias, los ayuntamientos,
y las fábricas: Los reyes el clero, la representación del pueblo y la burguesía.

Entanto suenan las doce lentamente en el reloj de una de las fábricas de Ibor City.

* *
*

La madre que ama á sus hijos, no los azota,
los dirige y les impone privaciones de paseos ó di-
versiones.

* *

La cólera es la madre del crimen, aquella hija

de la ignorancia. Hay muchos crímenes, hijos del cálculo, que engendra la miseria.

* *
*

Hay ladrones de levita que los llaman caballeros, y ladrones con harapos que los llaman pordioseros. Unos roban en la bolsa y en los negocios, los otros sustraen algo de los bolsillos en calles, plazas, ó casas, por miseria o vagancia, que engendra el sistema social actual, los otros especulan por ambición egoista. Los segundos son más admisibles que los primeros.

* *
*

Calumniarse, envidiarse, desconfiar, injuriar, morder, y arañarse de uno ú otro modo ?es vivir? Entorpecer á otro, provocarle, formar intrigas, para dañarle, mentir en perjuicio de los demás ó de uno sólo, ¿es vivir?—No.

* *
*

Ser hombre ó mujer, no autoriza para ser grosero, brutal: no es imponerse ni engañar. Eso es ser ignorante y cobarde.

La política, no es hacer leyes que beneficien á los ricos, no es malgastar los fondos públicos para usos particulares.

Si la política es el arte de gobernar los pueblos, el hacer lo anterior, no es arte para gobernar, es sencillamente un abuso, un modo de vivir especulando la hacienda pública. Ser político no es ser usurero ni ambicioso, como ser cristiano, no es odiar á otro, ni decir misa, ni cobrarla, ni bautizar estos son simples ritos inventados para especular en nombre del cristiano.

Igualmente hacen los políticos, y los demás al ver las cosas mal hechas, dicen, ¡esa es la política!

¡No! esa es la pereza, ambición, ignorancia, es-peculación, con el nombre de política.

La verdadera política sería hacer las mejores cosas en favor de los mejores hombres, de los más puros y honrados; reformar las leyes para que unos hombres no exploten á otros; lo que es lo mismo que hacer la felicidad de los pueblos

*
* *

Igual equivocación existe con la anarquía, si lanza alguien una bomba, se le llama anarquista, si hay un atentado individual, anarquista es; si un robo ó asalto en los campos ó caminos, anarquistas también. No dicen es la miseria, es la explotación que produce · eso.

Sensible és, que no llamen anarquistas á los desfalcadores de bancos y negocios.

Estamos en condiciones ventajosas, expuestos á que nos confundan con los salteadores de la ba-rrera política, con los especuladores de la bolsa y los desfalcadores de los bancos y salteadores de ca-mino aunque estos últimos son productos de los otros. Como predicamos el amor libre, dentro de poco tiempo cualquiera mujer que se vaya con un hombre será anarquista y cualquier hombre que se lleve una muchacha, anarquista. Nos van á co-locar en el concepto de viciosos, egoistas, usureros, etc. etc.

El verdadero anarquista no utilizará modos perversos para cubrir sus necesidades ni calumnia-rá, ni injuria á otro para usurparle su bienestar ni escamotea glorias ajenas, ni las envidia.

Si vé un matrimonio feliz, aunque esté ena-morado de la mujer no provoca un rompimiento para aprovecharse de el y satisfar un capricho ó su amor.

Si los ve desgraciados, porque uno solo ama,

y el marido maltrata á la mujer, entonces sin interés debe separarlos. Por eso, á los anarquistas no les agrada utilizar fórmulas; los ignorantes créen que la simple fórmula ata á los individuos; generalmente la mujer es más ignorante que el hombre, porque no tiene un concepto de su libertad y de sus derechos, por su educación consecuencia del egoismo del hombre, ella creé que éste debe mantenerla sin trabajar. Así han hecho las leyes los hombres y ellas no hacen nada más que utilizarlas aproveehándose de el salario de su esclavitud.

Progresamos y aún hay miles padres que se creen con derecho de castigar á sus hijos y de imponerles sus gustos, caprichos, ordenarlos á obedecer sin consultar con sus deseos. Los obligan á contraer matrimonio con quien les plazca á ellos, sin tener en cuenta la libertad, individual. Alegan que pasaron muchos trabajos para criarlos y educarlos, pero no deben hacerlo con el fin de esclavizar sus hijos, sino conducirlos al trabajo para su propio sostenimiento sin pretender fiscalizar sus actos.

En el hogar es que se forman hombres y mujeres libres, empezando por corregir los padres sus propios defectos.

Para hacer hijos bellos y buenos tienen los padres que ser buenos y justos, porque "la belleza es la forma de la verdad" si los padres son buenos, es decir pacientes y moderados, necesariamente los hijos serán bellos y buenos.

El día que están abolidas las fronteras, que es una forma del egoismo, que no haya otra religión que "Amaos unos á otros". Cuando sea inútil decir "Amad á vuestros enemigos, bendecid á los que os maldicen y os injurian y orad por los que os calumnian y persiguen", porque todos seremos hermanos; cuando hayamos perfeccionado el modo de acortar las distancias de un modo seguro, entonces humanos, acordaos del Maestro y allí donde nació y predicó, construid un templo único que no tenga otro igual en la tierra que sea observatorio y Cátedra que escudriñe el cielo y la tierra que sea museo de artes y ciencias en recuerdo del justo; que su figura en magníficos colores pintado nos lo recuerde con exactitud. Que haya una galeria en donde estén todos los que predicaron y ayudaron á esclarecer la verdad. Así rendiremos un homenaje de justicia al que como dice Renan "Nadie como él, supo en su vida someter las pequeñeces del amor propio al interés de la humanidad" añadiendo: "La idea de Jesus fué la idea más revolucionaria que jamás pudo concebir cerebro humano".

Los que afirman que volver á vivir, en este planeta, no es posible, porque no recuerdan algo de su última existencia, tienen un caso de **estudio en el siguiente:**

(Obras Filósoficas, Diderot, P.72)—

"Shullemberg á los 16 años recibió una conmoción violenta en una caída y quedó seis semanas sin conocimiento. Olvidó todo lo que sabía, volviendo á un estado parecido á la infancia. Se le enseñó á leer á escribir incluso andar. Más tarde llegó a ser un hábil artífice y ha dejado nombre en la historia natural"

Algunos dirán que no és idéntico el caso va-

ya si lo és, el que muere ha ido paulatinamente per-
diendo la facultad de percepción y la memoria y
éste con la caída la destruyó de un modo repentino
con la ventaja á favor de la reencarnación, que él
que muere, deja su materia, y el que recibió el golpe no la dejó, temiendo motivos para recordar lo
que había aprendido y había hecho; porque el que
se vé obligado á cambiar de materia, no encuentra
otra igual y éste encontró la misma al despertar y
debió recordar ¿cuál de los dos tiene más razón para acordarse? No se me alegue, que el espíritu es
el que aprende y por tanto al cambiar, de materia
no debe olvidar, él que sufrió la caída sin cambiar
de materia olvidó, fué el espíritu también el que
aprendió, ¿porqué olvidó?

La mayoría de los hombres, no tienen carácter
ni inteligencia, son crueles, perversos, vanidosos ,
indiscretos. ha tenido ocasión en infinidad de casos
de oirlos en Cafés, reuniones. sobre todo después
que se alejan las mujeres que habían en la reunión,
averiguando, criticando: una vez se le olvidó á una
mujer una carta y un muy **poseído** se apoderó de
ella. y abriendola la leyó. Era una carta amorosa,
Luego tuve oportunidad de volver á encontrar
en la calle al mismo jóven y juntos caminamos hasta
el correo, puse una carta y el pidió una: buscaron
su nombre y encontraron un nombre igual , pero
faltaba una síbala la dirección era diferente y la
letra no era conocida de él, pues, en la duda, la a-
brió
Entonces se convenció que era para otro y se
reía muy fresco. Sentíame molesta. al ver tal debilidad de carácter.

Pude mentir y no lo hice. Pude explotar el trabajo ajeno. Tuve ocasión de gastar joyas y lujo y fuí sencilla. He tenido oportunidad y motivos para de vengar injurias y calumnias, de provocar envidias y recibir ovaciones y desdeñé unas y perdoné las otras.

Tenía y, tengo modos y motivos para despreciar á los demás que la sociedad juzga inferiores y no los utilicé. Nunca encuentro suficientes motivos para acusar ni vengar agravios, todos me parecen resultado de la ignorancia.

———

La curiosidad es lo que más domina en el mundo, la gente curiosa es muy majadera, imprudente, ó inoportuna, toda esa curiosidad es origen de la ignorancia y la pereza.

Hay curiosidad científica que ennoblece y eleva que conduce á la sabiduría, hay otra curiosidad que solamente se ocupa de averiguar lo que no debe para criticarlo y rebajar el prestigio de los demás. La primera se convierte en observación metódica y persistente y toma el nombre de Ciencia.

La segunda se transforma en murmuración y degenera en **calumnia ó injuria.**

La crítica es admisible y hasta interesante cuando en regenerar la humanidad se emplea, sea sobre actos privados ó públicos.

Hay muchos, que creen que inmiscuirse en asuntos que perjudiquen á otros débiles ó menores de edad, es ocuparse de cosas que no importan.

Un día, se detuvo, frente al Restaurant Vegetariano (1) donde yo estaba sentada en el balcón, un carrito de leche á domicilio. Bajó un niño, abre la puertecita posterior del carro y hace esfuerzos

———

(1) Esto sucedió en Tampa.

por cojer un jarro grande de leche, era superior á
sus fuerzas y al cargarlo se derramó sobre el un poco de leche, resbaló el jarro hasta el suelo sin derrae
marse, con el consiguiente estrépito. El hombre
que dirigía el carro al oir el ruído, ladeó el cuerpo
hácia atrás y levantando el foete iba á descargar su
fuerza sobre el niño, grité ¡cómo va Vd. á pegarle
sino puede con el!.........el hombre se contuvo, pero no tardó tres minutos en protestar, diciendo,
mezclando el idioma: ¡esos son mis **bussiness!** que
es equivalente á decir **á Vd. no le importa**—y
lo repitió dos veces más mirándome y alejándose
en su carro, entanto el chico subía con el jarro sin
poder y entró en la casa donde yo estaba.

Nadie protestó de ese hecho, la mayor parte de
la gente cree muy natural y hasta justo y bien hecho que un padre explote á sus hijos y además los
maltrate. Nadie se preocupa de advertir á los
fuertes su deber para con los débiles. Hay sociedad protectora de animales, pero los niños, los
ancianos y los enfermos se maltratan se explotan y
apalean y nadie protesta, ni acuerdan protegerlos.

———————

Un detalle interesante sobre la igualdad entre
el hombre y la mujer, publicado en "Obras Filóso-
ficas" de Diderot—cuando la Srta. L'Espinase dice al Dr. Borden, que se le ocurre una idea extrava-
gante al pensar que el hombre no és más que el
monstruo de la mujer", o viceversa. el Dr. Borden le contesta—"Esta idea se os hubiera ocurrido
antes, si hubierais recordado que la mujer tiene todas las partes del hombre, con la diferencia de una
bolsa invaginada; que un feto hembra casi se con-
funde con un feto macho; que la parte que ocasiona
el error va desapareciendo en el feto hembra á medida que la bolsa interior se agranda, que aquella

parte conserva siempre en pequeño su primera forma, siendo suceptible de los mismos movimientos
voluptuosos, que tiene su glándula, su prepucio y
se nota en su extremidad un punto que parece el ori-
ficio de un canal urinario que se ha cerrado".

Muy interesante es éste análisis. El hombre
desarrolló tanto su soberbia que creyó y aún creé
que todos los seres de la creación fueron creados
para su distracción y dominio, no se ha creido con-
tinuación progresiva é inteligente de lo creado, sino
dueño y señor de ella, sin laborar por su progreso,
y para acrecentar más su orgullo **"estrajo Dios
á la hembra de una de sus costillas"**, para afirmar que la mujer hasta en su origen era parte
suya, propiedad privada que podía esclavizar.

? Y la hembra de los animales de dónde fué
extraída? ?cada hembra de una especie distinta
de la costilla del macho de su especie?

De acuerdo con que el hombre es un animal,
que la naturaleza, no se toma más cuidado por él,
ni lo distingue, ni separa de los demás, en sus evoluciones seísmicas, tanto derecho tiene el león de
comerse al hombre como éste de matar á aquel; de
igual modo se carga á un caballo para que lleve de
comer al hombre, como puede el hombre cargarse
para alimentar al caballo.

Ambos deben ser libres.

El hombre más revolucionario y amante de la
libertad fué el que inventó la fuerza motriz, para
trasladarse él y los objetos á largas distancias, pro-
clamando la libertad de los animales, el derecho á
vivir sin esclavizarlos.

A UN AMIGO BARBERO.

Me has dicho que los que escriben no producen,

que solamente los que aran la tierra son productores. Esto es un concepto equivocado de la frase. El que labra la tierra siembra, y cosecha luego, solamente lo que hace es cultivarla, quien produce es la tierra, el que la cultiva, es ayudante, su labor especial es vigilar los frutos para que las cosechas no se pierdan. El mérito artístico de una obra de arquitectura por ejemplo, no la tiene el que la hace, si el que la concibe. Su utilidad está en el que la inventó no en el que la hizo.

El que hace una casa, hace una cosa útil, pero no la crea, la construye. La naturaleza crea y produce el hombre utiliza sus productos. Aquí verás la superioridad de la inteligencia creadora, esto no quiere decir que tenga el intelectual, más derecho á la vida ni á las comodidades ni á ser superior como ser humano.

Un árbol dá un fruto, es el producto natural del árbol, cultívese ó nó; un hombre ó mujer, escribe un libro y es el producto de su inteligencia; ¿no quieres llamarle producto?, pues le llamaremos destellos luminosos, irradiaciones de luz, condensada en principios de sabiduría, conceptos, definidos de una idea, ciencia, investigación análisis, invención, descubrimiento, observación, en sus diferentes formas y variedades. ¿No es un producto el que define el concepto de una forma visible de la naturaleza, la divide, la clasifica y la selecciona? Pues será más, será inventor, y el que inventa, produce, el que siembra no ha inventado el modo de hacerlo, ya la naturaleza lo había hecho, no hizo más que imitarla. El primero que produjo é inventó el libro no imitó, creo, porque no se ha encontrado ningún libro como producto de un árbol ó de la tierra Esto no niega ni rechaza, que la naturaleza es un libro abierto para el que sepa leerla; y que ella contribuye á la formación de todo con la materia prima que es el algodón, la resina y líquidos colo-ran-tes de árboles y plantas.   El papel y la tinta no son productos del agricultor, ellos cultivan la materia prima pero no la **crean** ni la han combinado para **crear** el papel y la tinta, estos son productos de la inteligencia.

No es la fuerza bruta la que rige es la inteligencia, sinembargo, la inteligencia es fuerza y luz.

Una poesía que provoca en tí, deleite, extásis amoroso, abstracción mental es el producto de un hombre ó mujer.   Un libro, que por sus detalles críticos, conceptos filósoficos, argumentos científicos, narraciones h stóricas, descripciones sociales, te hace meditar, conocer, concebir, reflexionar y protestar? no és el producto del estudio, observación y asimilación de la vida y de las cosas que ese hombre ó mujer ha hecho?

Entonces no miras las cosas, como son y por lo que valen, sino por lo que parecen.

En este caso amigo estarás expuesto á muchas equivocaciones, por tanto he aquí el dicho muy apro pósito de Jesús: ''En verdad os digo, que tienen ojos y no ven, oidos y no oyen''.

También dijiste que no concebias un anarquistó—espíritista, sobre esto ya escribí en mi libro anterior **''Mi Opinión''.**

———————

Ante la eternidad de los siglos, que es el dolor humano? nada............¿Ante la inmensidad del infinito y su eternidad, imperecedora, que es la lucha humana?............humo, polvo, nada.......Ante la interminable sucesión de sistemas planetarios en contínua transformación espléndida, é interminable por los siglos de los siglos? ?qué son las civilizaciones y el contínuo inventar de nuestra especie?

Una insignificancia ......Pero de granos de arc-

na está formado el lecho de los oceanos y los diques
que besan sus olas ó sean las playas................
Octubre 22 de 1914, Habana.

Era un árbol diforme, que vegetaba en la ori-
lla del mar, desde la raíz hasta la mitad del tronco
doblado y desde éste á la copa quería ser recto, recibir las caricias solares directamente, irguiéndose
apesar de su deformidad.

Seguramente que aquel árbol sufría al no poder lucir su elegancia ó corpulencia con natural soltura. En el subían los chicos y hacían maromas
los enamorados sentabanse á platicar dulcemente
en su tronco añoso.

De vez en cuando se posaba alguna avecilla,
pero todos lamentaban la miseria del pobre árbol
que no daba sombra ni brindaba fresca brisa sin ramas apenas; sin hojas. Pobre y triste árbol, sin
ramas, sin hojas, ni frutos que brindar, que condición más desolada, más ruinosa en aquel sitio
espléndido frente al mar y enfrente de la línea de
carros donde los viajeros podían contemplar aquella soledad y horfandad del pobre árbol, deformado
por la rudeza humana.

Quien habría sido el primero que posó su pié
y mutiló su arrogancia obligándole á perder su es-
beltez doblandolo sobre la tierra para convertirlo
en un esqueleto estéril.

Las olas rumorosas besaban y nutrian sus raí-
ces, pero sin poder devolverle su gallardía, pues la
sávia no circulaba por sus tejidos y entrañas ve-
getales, langüidecía y el sol no podía revivir lo que
la mano cruel del hombre había dañado y mutila-
do ¡Sed piadosos!, piedad para todos los seres vivientes de la creación!.............
Tampa 1913.

Me parece que no sería una mujer completa
sino fuera porque soy madre.   Una mujer completa
debe ser madre.

Una madre perfecta que lacte á sus hijos y so-
porte con paciencia sin molestarse, las **majaderías**
de los niños, sin castigarlos, maltratarlos ni vengar
en ellos las molestias que su edad infantil propor
cione.   Digo **majaderías** porque así han llamado
algunos gnorantes de ambos sexos á las manifestaciones de los niños, pero no son majaderías, son
expansiones naturales propias de la edad y al niño
se debe permitir manifestarse tal cual es y estudiar
sus inclinaciones para sugerirle buenas ideas y prácticas nobles, aunque el mejor sistema para hacer
hijos buenos es que los padres lo sean y sientan esa
bondad, que sea ingenita en ellos y los hijos la here-
darán.   Si la madre se molesta, irrita su sistema
nervioso y el de sus hijos.   La madre y el padre deben ser moderados en todo y de buenas costumbres
para que los hijos lo sean.

*
* *

Yo amo los himnos de todos los paises, como
un sentimiento producido ó inspirado por Natura
en cada región del globo.   Así admiro los paisajes
de todos los climas, como respeto las costumbres de
todos los pueblos y venero los recuerdos de todas
las edades y bendigo las reliquias de todas las familias, porque todos estos detalles diferentes son sen-
tidos y vividos por la gran familia humana contribuyendo á la sublime é inimitable armonía universal.

Ibor City 1913.

Dos seres, que se miran, se contemplan de arriba a abajo y murmuran en su yo interno, "he aquí
mi complemento" se gustan, se unen, se funden en
uno solo, sin temores, sin obstáculos ni rodeos de

clase alguna, como se confunden las olas, cual vol-
cán que se desborda y arrastra el abismo del cual
brota: así concibo dos unidos en uno solo con la bella reproducción que perpetuase el recuerdo de a-
quel desencadenamiento de las fuerzas naturales,
aglomeradas en el individuo.

¿Habrá mayor riqueza, categoría, honores,
gloria más hermosa, que la satisfacción de dos almas
que se funden en una, de dos que se buscan y se
completan libremente? No hay mayor felicidad
que la de amar y ser amado; ni martirio mayor, ni
infierno más terrible que no realizar al amor soñado, el amor buscado.

Ninguna doctrina puede estar contra dos almas que se atraen, dos cuerpos que se buscan porque se desean, en la más libre forma de la manifestación del amor, hasta que se hastien o se confundan sin temor al tiempo ni á la vejez ni a cosa alguna, pues nada podrá perturbar el ayuntamiento
expontáneo en pró de la especie y la belleza-verdad
que resulte del amor libre.

En la naturaleza nada hay huérfano, ni solo
ni abandonado ni en perpétua erraticidad, los átomos y moléculas se unen por afinidad para formar
cuerpos, el sonido se une para formar la sublime
armonía, la luz se forma en líneas indefinidas, el
agua se aglomera en millones de partículas distintas que se condensan en nubes. "El amor, como
la vida, eterno sin fin posible!"

Amor!............

Irradiaciones de luz que ilumina las concien-
cias, vibraciones de la vida universal que abarca todas las formas, ondulaciones de la brisa que reparte
el aroma de las flores perfumando el ambiente y lle-
vando el polen fecundante de la reproducción vegetal en la selva y los bosques, los campos y jardines.

La ley de at acción que rige los individuos y

los cuerpos, que impulsa á la inteligencia y á la materia, la constante y perpetua selección de todos los seres de la creación, hácia la perfección indefinida. La vida en sus diversas y variadas manifestaciones regida por el amor.................

Tampa Junio 26 de 1913.

FRAGMENTOS DE UNA CARTA.

Ahora respecto á lo que me dices, de que solamente deseas ser mi amigo........ te diré, tu escribes así hoy, pero la primera vez que tuviste oportunidad de hablarme por un hecho casual en Palmetto, tu intención, que no censuro la entendí, que fué la misma que sentimos cuando encontramos una flor agradable y queremos aspirar su perfume aunque no conozcamos su nombre ni volvamos á encontrarla. No tiene eso nada extraño, fué un deseo muy natural y me hubiera prestado á ello, sino fuera por las diversas circunstancias, que me rodean, influyendo también mis aspiraciones en mis sentimientos para impedir me desvíe de mi propósito que és no perder mis energías mentales ni perturbar mi tranquilidad astral que reside precisamente en el dominio de la materia. O sea la reserva sexual para aquilatar la fuerza mental.

No se puede poseer fuerza mental, ni se consigue que ésta sea poderosa si tenemos la materia como una veleta, que se mueve según el viento que sople.

¿Me explico? ¿Tu amiga? porque no, ¿acaso he dejado de serlo? que mi temperamento cariñoso y expansivo y mi carácter dulce y paciente a pesar de mi actividad y energía, haya hecho soñar á alguno en deleites materiales? No lo dudo, ni

me asombra, porque esos seres aún permanecen e-
quivocados, créen que no se puede ser cariñosa fuera de la posesión carnal.

Pero, yo no tengo derecho de juzgar á esos individuos, si tener cuidado en no dejarme sorprender
por ellos , pues estoy en un plano superior.

Que apesar de mi vigilancia, por una de esas
ingenuidades, me sorprendan y conozca mi desvío
después de sorprendida, es natural y demuestra mi
buena fé y que si me abstengo, no es por egoismo
ni causar dolor, si por creerlo innecesario, pero
cuando se ha hecho muy necesario á otros y me he
visto colocada en un callejón sin salida, he rendido
mis armas sin rencor ni soberbia. Pero evito provocar esas guerras, por no dejar moribundos en el
campo de batalla mis propósitos y mis energías
mentales. ¿Qué desea, que se propone Vd? que
sea su amiga?, lo soy con sinceridad.

P. D. Releo su carta, dice q. es un admirador de
mis teorías, pero si, también son practicadas!, lo que
sucede, es, que, no es posible complacer á todo el
mundo, ni todos se han encontrado en los momentos oportunos de que he dado detalles, ¿pero crees
acaso que solamente voy a pensar en complacer á
todos los que no me comprenden? y más aún, no
admitiéndolo como una profesión porque se conver-
tiría en comercio y para comerciar, bastante hay en
el mercado, sería descender de la olímpica montaña
en que estoy asentada, para confundirme sin motivo justificable en mercancia, ¿crees que debo descender?, cuando estoy en la cumbre inaccesible de
la idea!, y muy próxima á emprender la jornada,
á penetrar en el sendero de la sabiduría!........

Dejame ir á ella, ayudame si puedes y quieres,
para que en el trayecto no tropiecen mis pies con
los abrojos del camino............

Entanto sabes que soy una adicta amiga y defensora de la verdad y la justicia.
Ibor City junio 26, 1913.

*
* *

¡Qué bella debe ser esa España!...........y cuánto deseo verla!
Brotó ésta exclamación de mi alma y la pronunciaron mis labios con tal lentitud al volver á repetirla como saboreando el deseo de verla y dormir bajo la sombra de los naranjos que perfumarán la brisa deliciosamente.   E. Sá del Rey en su rápida descripción de Córdova,

Me ha hecho soñar,
con esa bella España
que no se puede olvidar.

De la cual en nuestras venas,
corre sangre de agarenas.

Que sus triunfos y sus glorias
guardamos en las memorias.

Julio 8 de 1913.   Ibor City,

*
* *

¿Habeis observado alguna vez una flor, como va cerrando sus pétalos lentamente guardando cuidadosamente el polen fecundante para transformarse en deliciosa fruta?   ¡Oh! mágica naturaleza!

*
* *

Que esfuerzo enorme tengo que hacer para no llorar!................

Cada vez que asoman lágrimas á mis ojos, im-
pongo á mi voluntad, como un supremo mandato,
á mis sentimientos, á detenerlas, no debe recordar!
corazón no debes latir!, pensamiento deten tu actividad! sentimiento huye ahogate en el vacío! alma
mía vuela á otras regiones, no te preocupes de las
miserias de este suelo!

¡Vuela! ¡vuela! y volando ¿dónde irias? allá,
dó están los frutos de mi amor perdido!

Allá en aquella región rodeada de agua, donde
se oye el contínuo oleaje del Oceano Atlántico, en
el tranquilo peñón de palmeras, donde la brisa suave y perfumada de la selva borincana besara el rostro de mis hijos y tostara su piel el ardiente y hermoso sol de los trópicos.

Bulle y rebulle pensamiento, busca salida, ahoga mis lágrimas que pugnan por brotar. Vuela más
lejos aún, atraviesa el aire, la pesada atmósfera, elevate aún más, registra los espacios siderales, busca un mundo ideal, imagínatelo formado de miles de
pensamientos que esos pensamientos tengan colores, sonidos, luz, millones de luces, mezclados de
colores diferentes y diversos sonidos, que armonía
deliciosa escucharía!

La herida de mi alma, puede más que tu, vuelve otra vez, la nostalgia de amor! se apodera de mi,
me entristece, me sacude, estruja mi corazón, me
asfixia! me ahoga!...............!

El deber me impone domar mi dolor, á luchar,
á sonreir á trabajar...............

* * *

Un día era tal mi abstracción pensando en un
monólogo que había escrito y deseaba recitar, para
contribuir al beneficio de un amigo, que tomé la
pluma, para abrocharme las polacas, (así las llaman en Cuba) y cuando me fijé, me reí al sor-

prenderme hasta donde podía llevarme la abstracción, que podía llamarse distracción.

Julio 11 de 1913.. Ibor.

*
* *

Cual un fantasma blanco, vigilaba la ciudad al
norte, la plateada cúpula de la torrecilla de una i-
glesia de padres jesuítas, apesar de las sombras de
la noche, se destacaba entre las demás casas, con su
aspecto fantástico de vigilante nocturno, muda, con
una mudez, elocuente, con su cruz sobre la cúpula, desafiando con su edad de veinte siglos, la incle-
mencia de los tiempos y la incredulidad de las nuevas generaciones.

Cristo! ¡Cristo! quién te olvidará, después que
has vivido entre millones de generaciones durante
20 siglos! quién será el indiferente á quien tus máximas, tus sufrimientos y muerte, no haya conmo-
vido! no necesitamos que se ocupen de perpétuar
tu memoria, está en nuestras mentes tu figura y en
el corazón tus ejemplos. ¿Acaso esos templos son
necesarios?

Inútiles son, pues permanecen vacíos en esas
grandes ciudades entanto miles de infelices duer-
men en los puentes, bancos públicos, en las orillas
del río, en las embarcaciones ó las mercancias dete-
nidas en los muelles.........

Entanto la cúpula, continúa desafiadora, luciendo su blanca y elegante figura, reflejando su
plateado esmalte á la pálida luz de los focos eléc-
tricos, que la iluminaban escasamente debido á su
.altura sobre las demás casas.

LAS DOS JAULAS.

Tememos á la libertad, huímos de ella como de un contagio, apesar de que tanto la deseamos. Esto me lo hizo comprender una película americana,—recordando las cosas y caprichos humanos—que detallaba con mudez elocuente la vida de una princesa, hija única de un rey que deseaba casarla á su gusto y de acuerdo con la etiqueta. Un día entra en su habitación á comunicarle que al siguiente día se anunciará su matrimonio y que necesitaba presentarla á la corte para que la saludasen. Ella recibe la orden disgustada y triste, por no saber quien és su futuro, no lo conoce, se presenta, pues en el salón del trono y sube para que su padre la presente anunciando el matrimonio.

Vuelve á sus habitaciones y va á saludar á su pajarito y se compara con el pobre enjaulado. Salen ella y su dama de honor, á dar un paseo en automóvil y recorren una campiña cercana al pasar por un terreno cultivado, ve un hombre encorvado, labrando la tierra y sientase atraída hácia aquella figura y sigue mirando, hasta que el auto se alejaba del sitio y vió otros paisajes, se encuentra con un matrimonio que sale de la iglesia de aquella aldea, eran campesinos con sus trajes de costumbres, se detiene el auto y la comitiva se acerca á la princesa que agasajaba á los conyugues y les regala una moneda de oro á la desposada.

Regresan, y en su habitación sola saluda á su pajarillo y se decide á vestirse de aldeana y comparándose ella y la avecilla con dos presos, que deben libertarse, coje el pajarillo y lo lanza al espacio por la ventana y ella se marcha á la campiña con la idea de encontrarse con el labrador.

Se aleja y se encuentra con un pobre á quien

socorre y continúa hasta que se detiene frente á la empalizada donde trabajaba el hombre llamó y el jóven soltó sus utensilios, de labranza y se acerca á la empalizada donde estaba la jóven recostada, hablan y en su semblante se refleja la expresión de frases cariñosas, la jóven no contesta permanece con la cabeza baja. El campesino insinuante conquistador de repente abraza á la jóven y la besa en los labios, la niña asustada, se resiste, forcejea, se desprende de los brazos que la ataban y huye.

Atraviesa la campiña solitaria y regresa á palacio en cuyo jardín se detiene observando á todos lados y marchando lentamente se encuentra el pobre pajarito en el cesped, mira hacia arriba y vé la ventana por donde lo había lanzado; el pajarito no podía volar y permanecía en el mismo sitio donde había caído; cómo ella regresa á su cárcel, recoje el avecilla, la besa y sube al regio alcázar silenciosa y depositando el pajarito en la jaula, se le acerca su camarera á despojarla de su traje de aldeana. Entanto llega á palacio el príncipe prometido, penetra en el salón del trono con su comitiva, saluda al rey y espera. Sale una dama y sube para anunciar á la princesa que la esperan ya, el príncipe y su padre. Se coloca su manto real, y se dispone á salir, atraviesa la galeria que la separa del salón del trono y aparece bajando las escaleras y sube las del trono, inclina la cabeza frente á su padre y espera, sube el jóven, se coloca frente á ella en idéntica actitud, el rey une sus manos y los bendice entanto la corte aplaude, terminando la ceremonia.

Sale á su habitación y le dice á su pajarito: los dos hemos vuelto á la jaula, la libertad nos molesta.—

Aquel beso que ella recibió en pleno campo libremente, la asustó. el pajarito acostumbrado á encontrar su alimento en la jaula, se sintió débil sin actividad para buscarlo, se asustó al ver la in-

mensa y verde campiña, y permaneció en el sitio·
que cayó. Ella fué en busca de libertad y aquel
beso sin preámbulos ni fórmulas la espantó y regresó para obtenerlo por el rito y el cumplido social.
Fué en busca del amor y la libertad y el choque entre ésta y' la esclavitud fué rudo, venció la costumbre que es la hija mayor de la esclavitud.

* *
*

Después de diarias y detalladas observaciones,·
afirmó que los seres de la tierra, se modifican, cam
bian de aspecto, según el alimento, clima y medios
de vivir.

He observado en los campos de América en
West Tampa, plantas animales y viceversa. Como si un solo molde hubiera sido en el que hubieran
tenido principio todas las cosas.

No dudo en afirmar que la raza humana no tiene derecho de aprisionar á los demás seres vivientes
de la creación que supone bajo su dominio

Habana marzo 22 de 1914.

* *
*

Yo hablo de todo con perfecta comprensión·
de lo que digo, con una profunda intuición que me
orienta; pero nada he podido estudiar de acuerdo·
con los preceptos de los colegios, cátedras o aulas
de enseñanza superior; porque nunca me enviaron
á ellos, mi padre tuvo la santa paciencia de ense-
ñarme á leer y a escribir y conocer las cuadro reglas
de aritmética, luego concurrí á una escuela dirigida
por una profesora isleña, Dª. María Sierra de Soler,
en cuya escuela fuí premiada con varios diplomas,
en los exámenes, de las asignaturas de gramática,
historia sagrada; geografía, lectura etc. etc. Hoy

«que me he presentado como propagandista, periodista y escritora, sin más autorización que mi propia vocación é iniciativa, sin más recomendación
que la mía, ni más ayuda que mi propio esfuerzo importándome poco la crítica de los que han podido cursar un completo estudio general para poder
presentar sus observaciones escritas, protestas ó
narraciones literarias, mejor hechas, alegrándome
de encontrarlas y saborear su expresión correcta
y dispensandola cuando son ramplonas.

Me atrae de un modo irresistible la literatura,
escribir es para mi la más agradable y selecta ocupación, la que más me distrae, la que más se adapta
á mi temperamento, así pues me siento dispuesta á
cultivar este arte y perfeccionarme en el, no por ambición á la gloria, de un renombre, ni por hacer fortuna, ni para establecer distinciones, ni única intención, el móvil único que me ha impulsado á escribir, aparte de el deleite que me proporciona, ha sido decir la verdad, señalar como inútiles ciertas
costumbres, arraigadas por la enseñanza religiosa
convertida en una imposición tradicional; recordar
que las leyes naturales deben obedecerse con preferencia á toda otra legislación y como consecuencia reformar el equivocado concepto que existe sobre la moral, el derecho humano y la igualdad, tratando de que la humanidad sea feliz proporcionando los medios fáciles para su pronta y segura realización.

¿Porque decir, en los anuncios-reclamos para
la venta de sus obras, á Jorge Sand **desordenada**?
protesto de tal calificativo, incorrecto para adjudicarlo á una tan culta dama é inteligente mujer
es indigno de personas educadas.

¿Por qué calificar de prostitutas y viciosas á

mujeres que están á más alto nivel moral que los hombres?

Veo reinas, emperatrices, mujeres inteligentes que piden revindicación, se ha exagerado de un modo abusivo su conducta y procedimiento. Una mujer libre como Ana Bolena porque, acusarla de prostituta y á otras, que no escribo sus nombres porque aún existen familiares.

Los historiadores no han tenido otro motivo para exagerar la conducta de las mujeres, de otras épocas que la preponderancia de los hombres y el ser ellos los legisladores, historiadores y cultivadores de todas las ciencias artes, literatura.

Acostumbran entre ellos, algunos "bombos" exagerados para ensalzar y elevar reputaciones, y con indiferencia para las mujeres cultas, libres e ilustradas creyendo que éstas eran inferiores y no estaban capacitadas para realizar cualquier trabajo intelectual de diferentes índole ó procedimientos.

No acepto como viciosa, ni perversa á mujer alguna conceptuada así, por cualquier historiador que equivocadamente haya creído que la mujer no tiene derecho á usar de su completa libertad, sin ser conceptuada viciosa, liviana etc, entanto el hombre ha podido hacer y realizar, inventar, los más absurdos y ridículos caprichos, sin que pudiese ser mal calificado, despreciado, impedido de concurrir á todas partes sin temor de no ser atendido, respetado y solicitado. La ley del embudo, á la cual nosotros pondremos término para tranquilidad de los justos y para rendir culto á la verdad y á la justicia que merece nuestro sexo.

Marzo 22 de 1914.

VISIONES.

De pronto oí un rumor, como un inmenso clamor de una muchedumbre agitada, á muy lejana distancia....................

No había en realidad en el sitio donde estaba algún disturbio que pudiera justificar aquella percepción; pero yo la oí clara y distintamente en mis oídos, y en aquel momento acudieron á mi mente los recuerdos de la Revolución Francesa; como si hubiera visto las multitudes pasar convulsas en formidable gritería atravesar la calle Rívoli para ir á la Bastilla........¡Ah! que hermoso fué aquel momento!........pero que doloroso para mi cuando recordé en visiones sucesivas el llanto de aquel débil niño, maltratado por Simón........:..¡Pobre Simón cuanto le pesará ahora! que culpa tenía aquel pobre niño, aquella débil criatura?........cuando hasta sus padres eran inocentes: solo tenía la falta, el grave error de la tradición!............¡Oh pueblos! multitudes que os agitais demandando justicia, y no la conoceis! Reclamad! vuestros derechos exigidlos, imponedlos! si quereis, pero respetad los débiles!, los inocentes, que no tienen otra culpa que haber recibido una educación equivocada. Procurad anular su poder, pero no su persona, no teneis derechos de suprimir vidas que no habeis creado. La violencia no puede ser madre de la libertad es su madrasta.

La instrucción es la madre de la libertad; su hija mayor la ciencia y sus hermanas la tolerancia. y la prudencia con el derecho y el deber.

New York 26 agosto 1912.

Vi un gran león que corría rápidamente por la
verde y hermosa campiña, adornada por una límpi-
da almósfera irradiante por los rayos solares, que
llevaba una corona teñida en sangre, y humeada
por el fuego de la hoguera, la corona ladeada, apesar de su pesadez escurríase de la hermosa cabeza, y
al frente de un precipicio que ladeaba rodó la corona por los abismos, insondables, precipitada por
un movimiento que hizo bambolear al león.

Sorprendido el león al encontrarse sin el pesado círculo macizo sacudió sus largas me-
lenas, respiró fuertemente haciendo temblar las
montañas y el llano con su rugido, y trepando en
una roca, se ostentó magestuoso y arrogante desafiando al astro–rey con su melena, y lamiendo sus
ancas redondeadas y brillantes. El león había roto
con la tradición que lo obligaba á llevar la corona
y

Vi un águila que remontando su vuelo, paseaba por el espacio luciendo corona imperial, muy
orgullosa. Una nube que surge formada por un
torbellino de balas, en una ciudad, la aturde, pues
queda envuelta en ella, y cae herida por la bala de
un cañón al caer rueda la corona y golpease y mal-
trecha y sucia una, y moribunda la otra, la condu-
cen á un palacio.

Esta águila se cura de su herida , pero marcha-
rá sin corona. Es el águila imperial de Alemania.

Ví un águila bella que de pié en una roca con-
templaba el precioso panorama de la ciudad de Mos
cow, baja y es aprisionada y conducida al calabozo,
por esbirros armados.

Una nube inmensa oculta la ciudad, las balas
se cruzan y el águila muere.

Es el águila imperial rusa.

Surge otro emblema popular y la tierra es re-
partida o dividida.

*****

Jamás usé carrozas, ni lucí brillantes, ni viví
en palacios, ni arrastré sedas y oropeles, ni deslum
bre la miseria, con el lujo insultante de las joyerias
y de lo superfluo. Desprecié los honores, y rechacé
los privilegios, no atendí las adulaciones, ni admití
los ruegos. Esto, en plena abundancia, y sin haber estudiado la cuestión social, creía que todo el
mundo tenía el derecho de ser limpio, y de estar
calzado, y no entendí porque no lo hacían. Me figuré que todos sabían leer y escribir, y me asombré
cuando ví lo contrario. La ignorancia dueña y Sra.
del mundo, teniendo prisionera las almas, y sin luz
la conciencia. Abismo insondable cuya puerta era
la Iglesia, que ha marcado con su sello las generaciones de veinte siglos!........Protesté de esa deni-
grante marca, porque yo no era esclava, no lle-
vando mis hijos á la infecta pila batismal. Protes-
té, grité, me enronquecí pidiendo justicia para los
pobres, cuando comprendí sus dolores: por calles
y plazas, caminos y aldeas, ciudades y pueblos.
Procedí de acuerdo con mis ideas innatas en mi alma visibles en mi carácter: fuí generosa desinteresada, olvidé las injurias, perdoné las calumnias, dí-
más de lo que podía cuando no alcanzaba para mí,
enjugué lágrimas, consolé aflicciones, comuniqué
alegrías en las tristezas. Prodigué mi alma mi
cuerpo, mis pensamientos, mis ideales, mis aten-
ciones, mis conocimientos, fuí perseverante en la
lucha, y tranquila en la desgracia. Jamás odié, ni
hablé mal de mi prójimo, ni calumnié mis adversa-
rios, ni exploté á nadie para hacer fortuna. Mi alma está díafana y mi conciencia brilla. Jamás me
he revolcado en los vicios, siempre fuí, templada en
mis manifestaciones.

Una estoica de la vida. Ni el placer me enloquece, ni el dolor me mata. Aún así creo que soy muy imperfecta, pero resulta que otros más imperfectos me critican.

He observado desprecios, he visto burlas, he escuchado injurias, he saboreado calumnias, he recibido traiciones, y aún á estos los he ayudado y perdonado, he sentido el beso de judas en mi rostro. Solamente no he rendido culto á las fórmulas sociales, que siempre me parecieron ridículas á hipocritas: y lo son en efecto.

Pues bien después de haber sido injuriada, calumniada, burlada, despreciada, y traicionada, se me quiere obstaculizar mi camino ascendente, colocando á mi paso una piedra; una mentira; no sabia que el Águila sería molestada por el reptil. Pero lo que no sabía yo era que el reptil en vez de arrastrarse, volara, únicamente así se comprende la osadía. Empeño inútil, con el movimiento del águila para cruzar la altura, se desprende una piedra y aplasta el reptil; que espira entre la maleza deshecho, sin, nombre y sin funerales, entanto el águila atraviesa el espacio, á posarse en otra roca y contemplar puede el sol frente á frente.

Llueve y el pobre reptil rueda á impulsos de la corriente desciende de la montaña y de pedazo á pedazo, cae en el abismo, á los piés de la montaña, y rueda al fondo. Pero no desaparece al poco tiempo surge una flor extraña, siniestra rodeada de punzantes espinas, la envidia fué su madre, ella es el odio, y engendrará la traición Pero allí no irán las águilas, otros reptiles se emponzoñarán y herirán con sus espinas. Que quién mal siembra, mal recoge.

Porque la ignorancia es el origen de todos los males.

Debemos pues, contribuir á que todos se ilustren y nadie sea víctima de su ignorancia.

De modo pues que ahora tras largos años de ausencia, yo pregunto, que daño, hice, que yo he hecho para que se me hostigue con tal crueldad? mostradme las heridas que yo haya inferido, decidme las injurias que yo haya pronunciado, repetidme las calumnias que yo haya lanzado, señaladme la miseria que yo haya engendrado; acusadme los dolores que yo haya producido: pronunciad las mentiras que yo haya proferido, y predicado. Contadme las víctimas que yo haya causado. ¿Dónde? Cuando?

¿Que quereís pués? que cuál otro Cristo ascienda al Calvario y muera entre dos infelices? ¿Para redimir á quién? ? á la humanidad? Es inútil no hay redentor, ni redimido de ese modo, donde solo hay una víctima, y aullidos de un pueblo igno rante, y vosotros no necesitais redentores, vosotros mismos podeis serlos, sin víctima que derrame sus sangre, para que caiga sobre vuestras generaciones. Buscad la verdad, no adoreis á nadie, investigad la naturaleza, estudiad sus efectos y vereis la causa. Somos Dioses y pecadores. Procuremos ser Dioses, y desaparecerán los pecadores.

¿Entendeis esto? Seamos Dioses; no aceptando superioridad alguna, y desaparecerán los pecadores, no habiendo débiles, ni cobardes; si estudiosos y valientes.

Cuando no sintais la nostalgia de las fronteras, y si del infinito, cuando jamás profirais una mentira, cuando el temor á los desconocidó no os acobarde, cuando desdeñeis las calumnias, cuando os consagreis al estúdio y al bien, semejareis Dioses terrestres; pero ascenderemos á Dioses Siderales. Es cuestión de tiempo y paciencia Así pues, sí he tenido el valor de mostrar mi debilidad, y luego por medio de la paciencia y el estudio hacerme libre. ¿Qué teneis que reprocharme? ¿Sois mis ju<ces? No hay más juez que la conciencia, es inflexible, y

recta. Si algún mal he podido hacer, ha sido á mi misma, por generosidad. Y la generosidad, no es delito, al menos que la humanidad haya inventado nuevas leyes. ¿Con cuales derechos? Podía ser con el derecho de la perfección la superioridad adquiridad por la perfección. Y la perfección lo es todo, cielo y tierra, abismo, y montañas, sabiduría, amor. ¿Sabeis por qué? por que la sabiduría empezó su jornada, en el átomo, y éste está en los abismos, como en las cimas de las montañas se estremece en las ondas del occeano, como brilla en los rayos del sol. Se agita en las auroras boreales, como vive en las sombras de la noche, bulle en el caliz de las flores, y atraviesa en alas de la brisa en el espacio. Es perfume y es veneno. Está en el fuego y en la nieve. El que ha pasado por todos estos estados tiene necesariamente que ser sabio, justo, poderoso.

¿Quién en la humanidad está en esas condiciones para juzgarme á mí? ¿Quién es el perfecto que puede juzgarme? ¿Quién el superior aquí que pueda humillarme?................

El espacio es infinito, es superior, yo lo he investigado: la tormenta es poderosa, y yo la he desafiado. El abismo es tenebroso, y yo no lo he temido. El mar es peligroso y yo lo he cruzado.

Si la fuerza, deslumbrante de poder, de la voluntad desconocida no temió, darme una chispa de su inteligencia, sin atreverse á juzgarme fuera de yo misma. ¿Quienes sois vosotros que pretendeis penetrar en el interior de mi conciencia, resplandeciente de justicia? ¿No veis que podeis cegaros, si penetrais en el sagrado recinto do se confeccionan el fuego de mis ideales? No, comprendeis que los buhos no necesitan luz: que no pueden marchar frente al sol. Y el sol es belleza y la belleza verdad. No examineis otras almas, estudiad, la vuestra, no trateis de corregir á las demás, sin antes haberos corregido, y después no necesitais corregir, solo dirigir enseñar.

¿A qué perder tiempo, pues en cosas inútiles, que no han de beneficiarnos? Tontos sois. Dejad pues á los demás y correjios vosotros, que si todos hicierais así, no habrían tantos ignorantes en el mundo.

New York, agosto 13 de 1912.

YO...................

(Al artista Manuel García, San Juan).

Soy una equivocada.

Me creo con derecho á disfrutar de todo lo creado por Natura, lo inventado por el hombre, en el arte, la industria, la mecánica, astronomía, etc. y á observar todo lo descubierto por los científicos.

Pero solo utilizo lo necesario y casi siempre desdeño lo superfluo. Desinteresada hasta la exageración. Indiferente ante el vanidoso, espectáculo del lujo y las riquezas.

A veces, para que no olviden que poseo un alma de artista como casi todas las mujeres; engalano mis trajes, sin ostentación. Y si no fuera tan anarquista, es decir tan "cristiana" vestiría espléndidamente, con verdadero arte, y gusto exquisito; pero, y los infelices que carecen de todo lo necesario? los hambrientos y desnudos?............¡Que crueldad! ¡Qué sarcasmo! siendo todos hermanos, que unos se mueran de hambre, y otros derrochen locamente lo superfluo, que cada día invéntase algo nuevo para el lujo: en tanto lo útil, lo necesario se pudre en los depósitos y almacenes, de comestibles, ropa y calzado, habiendo tanto hambriento desnudo y descalzo!...

Yo......imposiblitada para remediar miseria tanta!.................

¡Oh! el problema de la miseria es mi única preocupación.

En tanto, ésta loca propaga, iguales derechos para todos, la fraternidad humana, la derogación de las leyes y los gobiernos.

¡Cosas difíciles!

En vez de cárceles, escuelas, colegios de artes y oficios; libre cambio, amor libre, abolición del matrimonio, sustitución de la propiedad privada por la común.

Un sin fin de **necedades** que se imponen! que lo está exigiendo la época próxima y que ésta se acerca.

Pues apesar de toda ésta franqueza, no he sido comprendida, y además, calumniada y mal interpretada....................................

La opinión de muchos hombres y la mía.

¡La mujer debe ser mujer! ¡la mujer es para el hogar! ¡no debe ser macho! ¡á surcir medias y calzones!, á dormitar al amor de la lumbre tejiendo calceta! ¿Quién la manda á dar opiniones?, ni á meterse en política, ni pretender que la elijan candidata? ¡Eso no se puede soportar! ¿No la hemos permitido ya que ingrese en las cátedras para doctora en leyes ó medicinas? pues no se conforma, ya quiere ser juez, alcalde, jefe de policías, legisladora. Para eso la hemos dejado estudiar, para que quiera echarnos á un lado pretendiendo acapa-

rar nuestros puestos y querer superarnos, no se có--
mo éstas mujeres se olvidan de su debilidad, y de
su indiscreción, no se las puede confiar nada, ni enseñar algo, pues seguida quieren sustituirnos.   ¿Pero como la mujer va á imitar al hombre? si no puede, si es inferior, ¡hasta la naturaleza la condena á
estar recluída durante el parto y la lactancia.

Asi se expresan la mayor parte de los hombres
y ese es el concepto, que le merece la mujer.   Ol-
vidándose de su mujer, su madre y sus hijas.

Pero no hay temor que la sangre llegue á los
rios, ni las discusiones turben la placidez del hogar.
Pues la mujer no deja de serlo, porque haga política
ni exponga su opinión, á si sea legisladora ó detective.
La mujer siempre será mujer, siempre que sea buena madre ó mala tenga esposo ó amante.   Es mujer, y no es ser mujer solamente estando empolvada
y llena de cintas y encajes.   Como no deja de ser
un hombre el que perteneciendo á ese sexo aprenda
á cocinar, á surcir, á barrer y a coser.   Cuantos
hombres lo hacen!............

La mujer no pretende ser superior al hombre
al menos esa no es la intención ni el fin de sus aspiraciones.   Ella superará al hombre por su conducta
y el cumplimiento de su deber.

La inmensa mayoría de las mujeres no fuman,
ni se embriagan.   Y esta es una de las condiciones
que la hará superior en todos los ramos del saber
humano.   De modo no siendo intención de las mujeres el imitar al hombre, en sus defectos si en sus
ventajas y buenas costumbres Como leí en días
pasados que una joven solicitó el oficio de fogonero
de un vapor, y luego dice el patrón—lo hace mejor
y además no bebe wiskey—. Lo que hace suponer
que en el futuro, la mujer será preferida, y el hombre tendrá que dejar sus vicios para conseguir un
empleo.   Y esto beneficiará la especie humana.
La mujer es preferida para enfermera, pues el hom-

bre no puede ni sirve para eso. La mujer será preferida como médica por su cultura y buena fé, pues curará por amor y por no ver sufrir. La mujer será preferida como abogada por su fuerza de penetración y persuación. Será preferida como legisladora porque sus leyes irán á corregir los abusos contra los infelices trabajadores y desheredados. Será preferida en la política porque no se venderá y cumplirá lo que ofrece. Esto en término general con escasos excepciones La mujer no invadirá las casas de juegos, ni ébria maltratará á su marido y á sus hijos. La mujer no quiere invadir el terreno del hombre para adquirir sus vicios y abusos, la mujer, siempre será madre aunque no tenga hijos.

Procurará corregir todo lo que perjudique á las generaciones futuras.

La mujer no será guerrera, aunque sabe morir como cualquier bravo soldado. Si en vez del hombre haber disfrutado de todas las ventajas hasta ahora hubiera sido la mujer hubieran surgido genios guerreros como Napoleón y Alejandro, aunque se llamarían Lucrecia, Cleopatra ó Semiramis, Pero nuestra época fué decadente, ahora empieza. si de aquí en algunos siglos no ha variado el sistema social es probable que la veamos. Aunque apesar de nuestra esclavitud tuvimos Juana de Arco, Agustina de Aragón, y otras más.

En la ciencia tenemos una Mdme. Curie y una Hipatía. En leyes una Concepción Arenal y otras. En medicina muchas empezando. En el foro tenemos infinidad y en literatura varias. En todos los ramos del saber humano tenemos mujeres. Y en arquitectura no debemos olvidar quién hizo construir los magníficos chalets y los famosos jardines flotantes de la Babilonia que hizo variar por completo el estilo de aquella época, fué Semíramis emperatriz del Egipto. Igual en Francia con Diana de Poiters, la Dubarry y otras. De modo idéntico en la música y en la poesía..

En la pintura no debemos olvidar que el hombre se inspira en la Venus, y la mujer no tiene ese recurso, no le gusta inspirarse en ella misma empezando porque dibujaría mal una mujer. Quizá debido á espíritu de rivalidad. Como tampoco hubo Santas Teresa en los hombres, ni María Magdalena. Imitadoras á Jesus las ha habido y las hay sin caer en la exageración. En combinaciones químicas hay muchas aficionadas. Lo que la mujer debe procurar es superar al hombre en su conducta en sus procedimientos. Ser dueña de si misma, empezando por conocer bien sus defectos y debilidades para ir corrigiendo, y así mejorar la especie humana. No dejando de ser madre, y ser madre es atender á sus hijos hasta que anden y lactarlos. Si hubiera un procedimiento que superara á la material lactancia, (y es seguro que se obtendrá) podríamos no recomendar el lacto materno. Pero lo conseguiremos. Esto no estás reñido con aquello.

....

A VARGAS VILA.

¡Oh escritor Poeta:

Cuando escribes,—"este amante de la noche, sueña sobre las ruinas venturosas de su corazón, que no siente ya, la necesidad de las caricias, y muerto para la vergonzosa mendicidad de los besos;" la soledad, única dispensatriz, de caricias sin bajezas, lo ha adormecido con las suyas, y sus labios **sin lujurias**—yo diría sin deseos,—mataron en los suyos, la torpe sed de los ajenos ósculos; y despojado del amor, el solitario, entra libre en el mundo del vuelo, dejando atrás la Vida, como, una

crisálida en pedazos, "libre, como los astros y los
vientos"

"En las sombras demasiado lejanas de la Vida, los recuerdos cantan la canción de los dolores
vencidos;—todos esto, ¡cuánto debió sufrir, y cuanto amó, tu alma fuerte y sincera! Y cuando volviendo á aludir á Amiel, escribes,—"¿fué que no se
conmovió nunca, ante la arcilla luminosa y extática, que es el cuerpo de una mujer?"

Has querido decir **estética,** ó **extática**? si
lo primero belleza, si lo segundo; frialdad, impasi-
bilidad imbecilidad; de cualquier modo que lo digas, lo dices bien,— cada cual, tiene su modo para
decir las cosas, lo esencial es comprenderlo;—pues
hay mujeres muy imbéciles, otras frías, ó perversas.

Tu has deleitado tu alma en la contemplación
de alguna belleza femenina, no encontraste la tuya,
la gemela de tu alma; ah! y cuanto has debido sufrir, si encontraste alguna y no te comprendió.

Cuando te refieres á Nietzsche escribes, "y
no exhibió una querida como un apéndice y no quiso de las mujeres de los otros, despreciando el se-
ducirlas: ¡os dirán que no amaba el amor, ni la mujer y peores cosas os dirán también" y en todo re-
tratas tu alma, tu temperamento y carácter.

¡Oh! si supieras que estoy luchando por entrar
en esa soledad que adoras, estoy en continua rebel-
día con mi temperamento ardiente y apasionado
para el hombre á quien amo, pues yo entiendo el
amor absoluto y no me comprenden!........yo deseo
vivir en todo y por todo para la persona á quién
amo, y que viva para mí; eso lo llaman egoismo de
la mujer para el hombre y del hombre para la mujer, no. Injusticias de la vida; como llora mi alma al saborear los párrafos de "Tristeza Volup-
tuosa" y como deleitome en este alejamiento del
mundo y sus cosas, releyendo tus bellas prosas poe-
ticas: presintiendo que: algún día diré como tú, en

"mis memorias"—"dejadme en el topacio de la tarde, desguanar mi rosario de recuerdos, y resurjan las rosas pensativas, que ornaron mis jardines otro tiempo;"—"es bello, en el crepúsculo sereno, brutal de lo Pasado, alzarse como un monte en el Silencio".

Yo como tú deseo calmar la sed de mis labios, ya tu habrás calmado, dominado los tuyos; aún yo no, estoy en la agonía del amor. Si no consigo hacer tangible mi sueño, sellaré mi alma para el amor, haré enmudecer mis ojos y mis labios para la voluptúosidad del amor, y la pasión no volverá á rugir como tempestad en mi pecho, el silencio y el olvido custodiarán un sepulcro viviente arrastrando un alma en pena que pecó, porque mucho ha amado............y vagaré como un espectro por los lugares solitarios de mi alma tras la huella de un recuerdo, para encender una bujía á Cúpido como se le pone á los muertos. En tanto recorra ese desierto, de cosas tristes ya muertas, verterán mis ojos lágrimas, las últimas, como· sudario cristalino con que se cubre á los muertos; y mi fantasma viviente, alma en pena que revive al calor de los recuerdos; deslizará su amargura entre el rumor de los besos que repercuten fugaces, en el jardin del recuerdo y la paciente jardinera que cultivó aquellos lirios con tal cuidado y esmero los recojerá marchitos por el frío del olvido y los enterrará en su pecho, como vestigios de días y dulces horas de tormento del que amando mucho, mucho, solo le queda el recuerdo. ¡Ah! breves· horas pasadas de dichas nunca olvidadas; lirios de mis amores, marchitos por sinsabores; mis tristes y alegres cantares, ahogados por mis pesares; ya no puedo llorar, ya no puedo cantar; necesito ser insensible á las penas de mi amor.

Siempre estoy y soy contrariada en los deseos que mi mente poética concibe y anhela realizar, para satisfacción de su interno estético romántico.

Ahora comprendo el Amor de Santa Teresa, por Jesus, y como no sentirlo si fué grande, bello, bueno, justo, y santo, si en la tierra lo buscara, fué posible no lo hallará; fué tan grande y tan bueno que en vez de ofenderse por el amor de Magdalena, se dió á ella la regala la misteriosa inocencia de su alma y de su cuerpo........quiero figurarme como estrecharía aquella "pecadora" aquel cuerpo virgen, tranquilo, augusto en el cual las tempetuosas oleajes de la pasión no había salpicado la frente impecable del justo, y con la santa ingenuidad que se daría á las fervientes caricias de su amante enamorada y fiel dicipula.

Habana, Virtudes 32.

Un automóvil pasa, el que lo guía observa á una mujer que va por la calle, se detiene y la pregunta ¿dónde vas?—(ella á la calle 25, 14 Ave:— son amigos se conocen, (él) ¿quieres que te lleve hasta donde vas?—bien, llevame (sube la dama y el automóvil desaparece). Llegaron, (ella) gracias, hasta luego,—(él) no te alejes tan pronto, tu sabes que por mi gusto te retuviera á mi lado y te hubiera llevado........(ella) ¿adonde?—á mi casa— (ella)—¿para qué?—para tenerte bien cerca—(ella) pero y luego?—(él) pues, luego como siempre rendido, á tus pies,—?quiero decir luego?........que vaya á tu casa? (él) pues permaneces el tiempo que quieras, vivo solo, si quieres un mes, hasta que te canses......si quieres menos, pues menos (ella) ¿cuando quieres que vayas? (él) cuando quieras?, cuando puedes ir?—(ella mañana........(indecisa)—(él)— pues mañana; ? a qué hora?—(ella) por la mañana (él) bien sea, me escaparé de mi oficina, vendré á

buscarte te llevaré; y allí, como en tu casa tienes lo
que necesites—(ella) á las 9, frente al Círculo Cu
bano—(él) muy bien—(ella) oye eseplícame eso,
hasta cuando me canse................(él) si, que no sea
por costumbre, que sea por deseo, cuando este se
acaba, entonces........la atracción se vá.........(ella) tu
querrás decir que mientras nos gustemos, (él) des
de luego cuando no te guste más, te vas. (lle ya) si
me gustas tu más, que yo á tí?............(él) lo dudo;
pero probaremos, y de todos modos, nos queda la
amistad y á ella recuriremos cuando veamos en peligro el amor........estás conforme?—(ella) si pero
que hará la amistad?—(éo) pues establecer la cortesía, la consideración vamos, que no pelearemos,
sino nos gustamos........(ella) ya entiendo, muy bien,
muy ingenioso, entonces hasta mañana—adiós.

El jóven se aleja con su auto y la jóven entró
en su casa.

AL SIGUIENTE DÍA.

(Dos curiosos) (uno) que hará Elena en esa esquina?—(el otro) esperará á alguien—(uno) espe-
remos) (un automóvil que llega) el chauffeur saluda
y Elena se acerca. (él) estás lista?—(ella) sí, (él)
pues sube (le abre la portezuela y se alejan, (uno)
no te dije que esperásemos) (el otro) yo me figuré
que esperaba á alguién. pero eso que nos importa?—
(uno), pues conocer con que mujeres se trata, (el
otro) y que precaución hay que tener por eso, (uno)
pues saber lo que hace, que no vengan á hacer creer
lo que no és. (el otro) ¿que puede hacer creer? (uno),
que no conoce hombre alguno.(el otro) y es alguna
cosa mala, conocer á un hombre?—(uno) sí, ¿por-

qué lo niegan?—(el otro), lo niegan, porque nosotros queremos exigirle que no vayan, pero es un cri-
crimen el que esa jóven pasee con su amigo?—(uno)
ellos no van de paseo—(el otro) y que van á hacer?
—(uno) á estar solos, en alguna parte—(el otro) y
eso es algún delito? que hay de perjudicial en eso?
se gustan?, pues se buscan y se retiran para no causar envidias á los demás con su dicha, y que cosa
hay más natural y hermosa que dos que se gusten se
lo digan y se lo demuestren entre sí?—(uno) y después esa jóven pretenderá que otro hombre la haga su mujer?—(el otro) pero nosotros podemos hacer lo que nos plazca y ellas, ¿no?—(uno) porque
nosotros somos responsables de nuestros actos—(el
otro) y ellas no? valiente argumento! es decir que
una mujer no puede ir donde le plazca, dueña de su
voluntad, y ser responsable de lo que haga?—(uno)
y luego querrá ser mujer de otro?—(el otro) pero
ellas nos ponen algún inconveniente, porque hayamos
pertenecido, no á una, sino á muchas mujeres?
—(uno) ellas no, porque no arriesgan nada—(el
otro) ¿y qué arriesgamos nosotros?—(uno) nuestro
dinero—(el otro) hombre vaya con la salida, pero
esos dos que han partido juntos están expuesto á
perder algo?—(uno) ellos no, pero yo que deseaba
esa mujer, después de haber ido con otro?........—(el
otro) y nosotros podemos ir con cualquiera y donde
quiera y ellas nó?—(uno) no perdemos, ni dinero,
ni honra—(el otro) y la mujer con quien vayas pierde?—(uno)no, porque esa no pertenece á nadie—(el
otro) pero nosotros aún después de tener una mujer no hacemos igual?, que perdemos?—(uno) nada, porque nosotros somos los que pagamos y trabajamos—(el otro) pues de igual forma procederá
la mujer, trabajará,—(uno) entonces no se casará,
—(el otro) para qué?—(uno) como!, y quien la
mantiene?—(el otro) su trabajo; o és que te figura
que lo que ella gane, es tuyo también, como el dere-

cho que sobre los esclavos pesaba en épocas pasadas? —(uno) y los hijos, quien carga con ellos?—(el otro) los que lo hicieron, son ambos?, pues á los dos pertenece, excepto durante la época de la lactancia, —(uno) bien, pero yo no estoy conforme, yo quiero una mujer para mi sólo—(el otro) si mientras tu le guste y ella á tí, para ti sólo—(uno) pero no quiero que haya pertenecido a otro antes—(el otro), pero y si ella te exige lo mismo, que tu no hayas pertenecido á nadie?—(uno) no puede exigirlo, porque es una necesidód—(el otro) pues precisamente porque es una necesidad, ella también tiene derecho á satisfarla—(uno) pero yo no pierdo nada,—(el otro) ni ella tampoco, cumple una ley natural, que mal puede haber en que dos se gusten y se lo digan solos?—(uno) no estoy dispuesto a que alguna mujer me engañe,—(el otro) pero si los que engañamos somos nosotros—(uno) pero somos los que trabajamos,—(el otro) ellas también trabajan, de modo que no tienes otro argumento con que defenderte?—(uno) sí, que ellas deben estar contentas con que el hombre trabaje para ellas;—(el otro) pero no lo están, y quieren ser libres é iguales, ante la naturaleza, amigo me retiro, veo que Vd. es la representación de la tiranía contra la mujer. Hasta otro día—Adiós libertador.

En tanto estos, discutían, Elena y Andrés habían llegado á una bella quinta, sencilla, pero cómoda, rodeada de un bosquecillo de árboles, pinos y trepaderas. Habían flores, y aves. Elena bajó, y Andrés le dijo, dándole la mano hasta las 5 que vendré á pasar la tarde contigo, eres libre de estar aquí como te plazca, en el terreno hay un hombre, si deseas algo que no haya en la casa el lo irá á buscar—Bien dijo Elena, hasta la tarde, (Andrés me dás un beso?. Se besaron y el rumor de los labios que se unieron libremente repercutió en la selva, y la brisa pasó y lo llevó más lejos, y las aves

imitaron el sonido extraño, y las flores abrieron sus
corolas al contacto de la brisa que les brindaba el
polen fecundante del amor con armonía de besos.

Llegó la tarde, el crepúsculo anunciaba la apro-
ximación de la noche. Andrés se paseaba con Elena por entre los arbustos, y se ocultaban entre una
sombra de plantas para entonar el himno del amor,
libre de imposiciones tiránicas, en plena selva, á la
luz poética y suave de la tarde que enviaba Febo
oculto tras una nube, despidiéndose de aquella región americana, las avecillas en sus nidos eran testigos del casto himeneo.

Cuentan que pasó algún tiempo y Elena no volvió sola á la ciudad; volvía con un precioso niño á
ver su familia, que había querido recriminarla, pero
que ella decía, soy libre y soy feliz, si no quereis que
vuelva á veros no volveré, pero no quiero otra ga-
rantía que el amor.

Algunos años después tuvieron ocasión los dos
curiosos de ir á cazar y sorprendieron á Elena lac-
tando un niño, y con dos más que jugaban a su lado,
una niña y un niño.   El amor había hecho milagros había convertido á dos en cinco.   El milagro
de los panes y los peces, se habían multiplicado si-
guiendo el consejo del autor de los milagros.

La reproducción és el misterio más hermoso
y encantador de la creación, sembrad un grano de
maiz y tendreis miles; dad un beso y sonarán dos,
producid un sonido y el eco os devolverá otro. U-
nios dos y os convertireis en tres, cuatro...........

Julio 2 de 1913.

.
*

"Al escuchar á un teologo exagerar el acto de
un hombre, que Dios hizo pícaro, al acostarse con
su compañera, que Dios hizo complaciente y her-

mosa, cualquiera diría que ha ocurrido algún cataclismo en el universo. Lector escucha á Marco Aurelio y verás que no ofendes a tu Dios por el frotamiento voluptuoso de dos intestinos.''

"Obras Filosoficas", de Diderot.

EXAGERACIONES.

En diferentes ocasiones he oido hablar refiriéndose á los chinos, calificándolos de gente atrazada, refractaria á la civilización moderna, y no había otro motivo que su cabello largo, y no entender su idioma.   Pero no se han fijado en su laboriosidad en su perseverancia para vencer dificultades, en su higiene personal, y sus diferentes virtudes.

Una infinidad de personas creen que ser civilizado es usar calzado de charol, cuello y corbata nueva, aunque la ropa interior apeste á sudor, y no se bañe ni una vez á la semana y además se hartan como antropofagos, y se desbordan como sátiros. No tienen medida para nada, en todo se exceden en comer, beber, dormir, bailar, no comprenden que todo esceso embrutece el organismo que no se vive para comer y divertirse groseramente, que la vida tiene mas altos fines que el comer y gozar excesivamente.   Que la primera tendencia del hombre que comprende el objeto de la vida y quiere progresar para no ser una bestia, es conocerse á sí mismo, (ya lo dijo Sócrates y en uno de los templos de Grecia estaba esta inscripción: (''Conocete á tí mismo'') para medir sus fuerzas y aumentar sus facultades, moderando sus impetus violentos en todos los órdenes de la vida.

Y estos individuos tan llenos de imperfeccio-
nes, se llaman civilizados, porque se ponen el sombrero de lado, sin lavarse la cabeza al salir del trabajo; se cambian de traje exterior y el interior sucio.   Usan corbata distinta todos los días, y no se
cambian de medias, se perfuman y no se bañan. Se
acerca uno á estas personas y tienen un olor extraño, apesar de su corbata y su cuello alto.   La mezcla de los polvos de la barbería con el sudor, y el
olor especial de la fábrica, combinan una especie
de "perfume" que indigesta.

Se acerca uno á un chino que están trabajando
todo el día y no tienen ese olor desagradable. ¡Oh!
y la boca? esa es un foco de infección, la mezcla de
la comida con el tabaco, es otro "perfume exquisi
to", que marea.   No se lavan la boca, ni la cepi-
llan, ni se les ocurre ir donde el dentista que les examine la dentadura y le diga el modo de conservarla
limpia.   Los que más atrae su atención son las cor-
batas y calzado en la vidriera.

Y las muchachas se ocupan más de las cintas
y encajes que de hacer un poco de gimnasia y bañarse y cambiar de ropa interior frecuentemente,
Estas también, (con valiosa excepciones de igual
modo que en el sexo diferente, las hay notable) se
perfuman sin cambiarse la camisa ó el pantalón, y
se adornan sin lavarse la cabeza y la orejas, y el cuello, y sin haberse bañado.   De modo que para llamarse ó creerse civilizado hay que ser limpio.

La civilización, el progreso moderno descansa
sobre la higiene

Por tanto para estar con el progreso y llamarse
civilizado, es necesario hacer un poco de gimnasia
y bañarse diariamente y además antes de acostarse
volver á lavarse las partes expuestas al aire libre;
sin recomendar que para comer es obligatorio lavarse y desinfectarse las manos bien.   No se debe
comer demasiado, porque eso es faltar á la higiene

del estómago, y cuando el estómago no diluye el
alimento, para nutrir el organismo, fermenta en el
estómago y produce mala digestión, degenera en
dispepsia y luego, produce trastornos en todo el organismo, que originan grandes enfermedades.

Algunos amigos se han extrañado de que durante el día me alimente con algunas frutas y algunas galletitas, ó dos o tres rebanadas de pan, casi
siempre solo, muy pocas veces con queso ó crema de
queso hasta las seis de la tarde hora en que voy á
comer al Restaurant vegetariano del Sr. Argüelles.
Por la mañana me levanto temprano siempre, únicamente cuando me acuesto muy tarde como á la
una ó a las dos, me quedo dormida, nunca me ha
sorprendido en la cama las 9 de la mañana; (me
gusta levantarme temprano porque la mañana es
muy bella y como gran admiradora de la naturaleza, me gusta contemplarla y aspirar la brisa nati-
nal. Y también en altas horas de la noche, contemplar el inmenso espacio iluminado. Pero por no
levantarme tarde, no me ocupo. Si tuviera un obs-
servatorio astronómico entonces dedicaría algunas
horas observando las regiones siderales) Perdonad
la digresión.

Después hago un poco de ejercicio o sea gimnasia sueca, que consiste en abrir y cerrar los brazos varias veces, ladear el cuerpo sosteniéndose en
una sola pierna levantada, los brazos y uniendo
las manos en alto y volverse ya de uno ú otro lado.
Luego, colocar el cuerpo recto, y bajando los brazos hasta tocar la punta de los piés con las puntas
de las manos, manteniendo las piernas unidas sin
doblar las rodillas, esto muy lentamente hasta que
se obtenga hacerlo con facilidad, duración algunos
minutos cada vez hasta llegar á veinte minutos, este ejercicio es muy bueno hasta para el catarro nasal, pues al bajar la cabeza la sangre se agolpa, durante se mantenga bajada la cabezá.

Después de varios ejercicios de esta clase alternados con los anteriores voy al baño, hará algunos años me bañaba el cerebro antes que nada, ahora me mojo los piés primero y con una tohalla mojada enjabonada me fricciono y luego me echo agua encima, si el baño no está escrupulosamente limpio, muy blanco y brillante, que no tenga rayas negras, que son recipientes de sucio y hasta contagiosas; si está limpio entonces me acuesto bajo el agua, sin mojarme la cabeza muchas veces. Luego me fricciono con las manos el cuerpo, y sin enjugarme me visto con una bata ó kimona, sin más ropa que unos pantalones largos para evitar exhibiciones, luego de pié ó sentada al lado de mi ventana (no tengo comedor á mi disposición) para aspirar aire siempre diluyo algunas frutas, con delectación, bien naranjas, mangos, melocotones, manzanas, melón ó piña. Cuando hay naranjas prefiero siempre naranjas y luego tomaba algunas galletas de leche "Uneda" y un vasito de leche, hasta las doce que volvía á comer otras galletitas y el otro vasito de leche, división de un frasco de cinco centavos. Cuando no hay naranjas, utilizo una pera y una manzana otras veces mangos y melocotones. Si no hay manzanas, lo que haya, ahora hay uvas, pues uvas, una pera o dos melocotones si son muy grandes uno, luego tres rebanadas de pan con ó sin queso de crema. Si siento alguna tirantez en el estómago, ó sea vaciedad á las doce vuelvo á comer otra fruta y dos rebanadas de pan. Hace más de un mes que no utilizo leche, porque no me pareció muy limpia y me pasó con las frutas y pan, o galletas. Uno de mis platos favoritos es papas fritas en aceite á la Juliana: estilo francés que mi madre acostumbraba. (1) Son papas cortadas muy delgaditas, y puestas á freir en el aceite herviendo para que no se

---

(1) Mi madre es francesa.

ablanden. Me gusta comerla acabada de freir con aceitunas y un pedacito de pimientos morrones dulces. Este plato con un buen pedazo de pan, y un flan, o un poco de dulce de casquillo de guayaba, es alimento suficiente para mí hasta el otro día por la mañana que vuelvo á emplear la fruta y el pan. Luego me pongo á escribir, á contestar la correspondencia que recibo, y á revisar mis trabajos o a producir nuevos.

He estado escribiendo muchas horas hasta quedarme dormida en la mesa, este sueño de 5 ó 10 minutos debido al cansancio, procuro distraerme leyendo para volver á empezar. Luego salgo.

Para mí el pan constituye mi principal alimento, cuando no puedo, ó no tengo medios de encontrar comida vegetariana hecha.

"LA IGUALDAD HUMANA".

Le hablé á la roca y la roca me contestó........

Observé á los átomos y los átomos me mostraron sus contínuas evoluciones. De el mineral, al vegetal y animal.

Como se desprenden los átomos en solidaridad mútua de un modo contínuo á inimitable. De los árboles, la brisa los transportaba imperceptiblemente á los animales y á los humanos. De los minerales á las plantas, animales y seres humanos.

En continuada ayuda mútua, nunca interrumpida se nutrían todos, sin egoismos, sin interés, sin superioridad. De modo que los átomos en perfecta y contínua evolución cumplían su labor perseverante y triunfadora, de una manera tranquila y ordenada contribuyendo á la formación de los mundos, desde el principio hasta el fin. No se negó la

partícula invisible, á la simple vista, desprendida
de un león ir á formar parte, con otra de un mono
é ir á unirse á la de un perro y alimentar la retina
de una niña ó un anciano.

Las partículas nitrogenadas desprendidas de
un árbol y las oxigenadas yodadas que lanzan en
su contínuo vaivén las olas, jamás se repelieron siguieron unidas á su hermoso destino, á fortificar
los débiles pulmones de un tuberculoso, sin negarse á ser aspiradas por aquel cuerpo enfermo, casi
al borde de la tumba, donde ha de volver á formar
parte del mundo de los átomos y moléculas.

¡Qué belleza y armonía en su contínuo laborar
por la vida y para la vida!

Contemplé las aguas y estas me cantaron en
suavísimas melodías, unas veces, en sordos murmu-
llos otras, en arrogantes y temibles amenazas varias otras, la hermosa canción á la vida en diversas
manifestaciones. alimentando millones y millones
de pecesillos en su inmenso seno, sin distinción de
color, forma, ó costumbres á todos por igual, ''según sus fuerzas, y según sus necesidades'' sin violencia ni restricción.

Besando incesantemente á las rocas, penetrando por sus miles hoyuelos y hendiduras, dando vida á los innumerables caracoles, insectos, é infinidad de animalillos de mar que en ellas moran sin
preferir á la juguetona ''jueyita'', ni al tierno cara-
colito. A todos bañaba por igual.

Penetré en los bosques y **oí** entre sus frondo-
sos y corpulentos árboles, infinidad de preciosas
avecillas, saltando de uno ú otro árbol, de una en
otra rama, trinando alegremente, unas llamando
a sus amados, otras depidiéndolos, otras conduciendo frágiles pajillas para construir sus nidos. Ningún árbol se negó, á recibirlas ni estableció distin

ciones.   Entre ellas tampoco las había, iguales derechos tenían todas.

Partían en numerosas bandadas al acercarse
el invierno de un país á otro, sin rumbo sin pasa-
porte, sin temores, ni recelos, y formaban sus vi-
viendas en otros climas.

Cruzaban el mar rápidamente, y volvian al
terminar la estación alegres y revoltosas á formar
nuevos nidos con nuevos amores............Ni curas!...
ni jueces!...........ni gobiernos!.........ni policías!.........
ni explotadores!......ni usureros!...... ni hambre!......
ni miseria!...... ni tuberculosis!

Ascendí los montes, y **ví** en los valles, diversas
clases de árboles y plantas, grandes y chicas fron-
dosas y raquíticas, fecundas y estériles, ninguna
reprochaba á la otra.   Todas se nutrían de la madre tierra, sin envidias, ni orgullo.   La corpulenta
encima no amenazaba al débil arbolillo de café.
El frondoso árbol de mango, no injuriaba á la humilde malva.   Allí en la montaña aspiré la oxige-
nada brisa, olorosa, por las flores de los valles y el
perfume de las selvas.   Y **ví** que de igual modo uti-
lizaban el aire sutil, la delicada mariposa, como la
veloz golondrina, y la triste gaviota, y el águila caudal.   Subí á otra escarpada cumbre, y **ví** en un lado de ella una como planada agrietada que soste-
nía el nido de una águila!....... con dos aguiluchos
hambrientos, yo tendida sobre la cima, observaba,
la madre como buena, rozó su enorme pico sobre
sus hijuelos movió sus grandes alas y cruzó por sobre mi cabeza, sin verme quizás, la ví descender á
un llano muy cerca, me levanté para seguir la bajada, y no tuve tiempo, pues ella volvía con una ter-
nerita en sus garras; sin moverme esperé á que des-
cendiera, y entonces volví al sitio anterior, y ya
estaba el animalito agonizando, desgarrado, entre
los tres picos corvos de los dos aguiluchos y el águila............¡Pobre ternera!............Cuando estuvo e

hambre saciada de las tres, la madre alzó, el vuelo y posó su arrogante y hermosa figura sobre la cumbre, cerca de donde yo estaba. Me incorporé, sentándome, al borde de la elevada cima, el águila me observaba, yo la miré, y fijas nuestras miradas una en otra, permanecimos. Entonces viendo que la reina de las aves, no cesaba de mirarme como preguntandome................. ¿Qué hacía!................. me decidí á preguntarle: ¿Estás satisfecha?—Mirome de hito en hito, y oí que dijo:-Estoy satisfecha, he cumplido con la ley de conservación. ¿Son así Vdes?—No. Entre mis semejantes, no basta la ley de la conservación, la que domina, es la de la ambición, después de satisfacer todas las necesidades, gustos, caprichos, vanidades, y adornos superfluos amontonan, oro y más oro en las arcas, comestibles en los depósitos, y la gente se muere por falta de comida, calzados y telas en los almacenes, en tanto tiritan desnudos y descalzos infinidad de prójimos de ambos sexos, niños y ancianos, expuestos á mil enfermedades y á miles angustias, y cruentos dolores.....................

–Al águila le centelleaban los ojos, y dijo: Y eso sucede producido por vuestros mismos semejantes, y no le pondreis remedios?—

¿Por cuáles medios pacíficos? por la instrucción. Pero entretanto se mueren de hambre, de miseria, la infeliz clase trabajadora.

—¡Luchad y vencereis! que no es tarde nunca–, díjome—y mirando hácia sus hijos, elevose y se perdió en el horizonte lejano, á buscar nueva presa ....

Bajé al valle, y ví palomas, pavos reales patos, guineas; y en el pequeño lago que noté, se paseaban muy contento varios cisnes, muy magestuosos, cruzando el lago de uno á otro extremos.

Me detuve á contemplar el hermoso conjunto; y seguí para internarme en las selvas....................

Penetré en ella y **ví** una hermosa culebra dormida; seguí, y los lagartos y lagartijos corrían en todas direcciones. Oí silbando otra culebra, y divisé algunos conejos.

Y me dije; en todas partes reina la armoní ɔ, la fraternidad la satisfacción del vivir, y seguí creyendo á todos felices..

Volví á las orillas del mar, me cambié de traje, y me sumergí en las saladas aguas, que parecían, no tener ondas ni olas, tan tranquila estaba su inmensa superficie.

Penetró mi atrevida mano hasta el fondo donde tomé lo que creía ver á tráves del cristalino líquido, era un bello caracol, le observé, y asomaba sus velludas patitas y ojos y me dice vuelve á colocarme donde estaba y sigue indagando que en el sitio donde me encontraste hay un mármol cuadrado, lo levantarás y bajarás por la escalerita que verás.

Así lo hice y llegué á la escalera y bajé, y ante mí, ví, una puerta labrada de mármol también, muy blanco, oprimí un resorte que **ví** y se abrió y ví otra escalera pero más bella, y bajé y penetré en un espacioso vestíbulo de estilo oriental, con lujoso artesonados, y bellísimos adornos, los sillares, eran de mármol labrado, una mesa en un ángulo á cada lado dos columnas con chapiteles corintios, que sostenían artísticas y elegantes ánforas repletas de bellísimas flores que perfumaban la estancia.

Atravesé un gabinete cubierto de colgaduras, y macetas de flores.

Salí y penetré en un bellísimo jardin en el que unas artísticas fuentes, surtían de agua en miles formas juguetonas á las miles de plantas que perfúmaban todo el palacio. El murmullo delicioso del agua mezclábase con el suavísimo susurro de la brisa que jugueteaba, con las encantadoras, rosas, jazmines, nardos, violetas, claveles madreselvas étc. etc., al redor de las fuentes. Lateralmente debajo de magníficos árboles frutales; veíanse bancos de piedra, entre aquellos sombras especialísimas. Tan amplio era todo, que parecía sentirse estar en un bosque, en una gran selva, tal era la diversidad de plantas, árboles y frutas en preciosa confusión

Pasé por una linda calle de árboles simetricamente colocados y regresé al pabellón contíguo al jardín y descansé minutos.

Pasé al amplio y lujoso salón perfumado, me recosté en un sofá de cojines y reconcentrando toda la fuerza mental que pude, dije:—Musa de mi ideal, tanto tiempo soñado, comparece ante mí!............

Cuando terminé mi evocación quedeme abstraída, observando como el salón se iluminaba con suave y blanco resplandor, una brisa sútil como un hálito, como un ténue suspiro me acarició y perfumó todo el ambiente. Ante mí estaba una figura radiante, esplendida, magnífica, envuelta en transparente túnica blanca, con una diadema, en la que se leía en brillantes letras; **"Anarquía"**. Su semblante de un ovalado perfecto, con unos ojos claros, hermosos de un azul delicado, una boca divina, aquel rostro reflejaba la más completa armonía, la más admirable dulzura. ¡Qué magestuosidad en su porte! Qué aspecto más delicado!

Me miraba con una tranquilidad que me sujestionaba.

De pié permanecía, altiva, imperiosa magnífica. Su mirada era una interrogación.—Te he llamado, porque mi tristeza es infinita, mi ansiedad por el bien humano, me consume. Desearía poder transformar los humanos dolores........¡Por piedad!........dime cuando vendrá á ésta humanidad otro Cristo redentor para hacerla feliz? La ví impasíble, levantar un brazo y señalar con su índice, al frente y ví escrito en un cristal de la ancha puerta central: "Los actuales dolores, son consecuencia de pasados errores". Pero pronto finalizará este reinado del oro. El trabajo será la norma de las futuras sociedades. El que no pueda brindar á la comunidad el fruto de algunas horas de labor diaria, de cualquier índole que sea, no será estimado por sus iguales"—Acepto esa explicación, y aquella sentencia. Pero decidme ¿cuando y cómo empezará ese cambio?, pues aún no hay señales. Volví á mirar al cristal y leí: "En la eternidad del tiempo, los siglos son minutos, las generaciones se suceden y al sucederse varían de procedimientos."

EL CAJERO

Por una de esas casualidades de la vida, Ricardo se había encontrado un protector que le había pagado sus estudios de perito mercantil. Nacido en la mayor miseria, su madre lo había criado con miles trabajos.

Ella anémica, como un esqueleto delgada, sin vida, extinguiéndose, como una lámpara sin aceite hacía esfuerzos sobrehumanos por enviar á su hijo limpio á la escuela. La esperanza que le quedaba cuando pensaba en el desamparo del niño, era el padrino, un hombre de alguna edad, austero, sóbrio que había hecho algunas economías, con un comercio al detalle, viudo, sin hijos. ¡Cómo se hubiera alegrado que don Castro, se acordara de su hijo! él era rico podía protegerlo. El día que Ricardo cumplía 12 años, ella esperaba que el padrino llegara con el acostumbrado regalo, ella le habló así:

—Don Castro, éste niño ya es un hombrecito que debía de enviarse á estudiar.

—¿Qué quieres hacer de él mujer?

—Eso Vd. yo que sé.

—Bueno yo lo veré y te avisaré.

—Don Castro Dios lo protegerá,—y Ramona, besándose á su hijo veía como don Castro se alejaba con su lento paso que mecía su cuerpo como un péndulo.

A los pocos días don Castro volvió y le dijo á Ramona prepara á tu hijo para el jueves, toma y le entregó algún dinero hazle alguna ropa interior y mándale á cortar un traje, y me lo envías para tomar el tren y llevarlo á New York.

—¿Vd. va con él?

—No, lo enviaré con un amigo que va para esa ciudad y se encargará, de colocarlo interno en un colegio.

—Gracias don Castro, dijo Ramona.   Cuando venga mi hijo, se lo participaré.

—Bueno, dijo don Castro hasta otro día.

—Que Dios lo conserve bien don Castro profirió Ramona.

Don Castro se alejaba satisfecho creía cumplir con un deber.

Por la tarde cuando llegó Ricardo le dijo Ramona: hijo mío, el jueves de la próxima semana te irás a estudiar y tomando la cabeza del niño entre sus manos la besaba y decía: ¡pobre hijo mío! cuan to me alegro que puedas serte útil mañana que yo falte—enjugándose algunas lágrimas.

— Ricardo le dijo, no te aflijas, que en pocos años será suficiente mi trabajo para los dos.

—Así sea, hijo mío para que ayudes á tu madre que será pronto muy vieja.

—Así lo espero madre mía, y besando á su madre en la frente, sentose á leer en uno de sus libros.

El jueves ya estaba Ricardo esperando que su madre le arreglara la maleta, y lo acompañara á casa de don Castro.   Era la una de la tarde cuando Ramona salió con su hijo á llevarlo á casa del padrino.

Don Castro dormitaba leyendo un periódico

al llegar Ramona, dijo, don Castro, aquí está Ricardo.

Don Castro se levantó y díjoles entren y sientense.

Ramona entró y sentose y Ricardo también.

Don Castro dirigiéndose al niño,—¿y que tal que te parece la marcha?

—Yo voy con gusto, me apena dejar sola á mi mamá; pero yo deseo ayudarla y aminorar sus trabajos.

Don Castro, preparó un cigarro y se puso á fumar.

—A las dos se presentó don Valentin García un comerciante que iba de compras á New York, y saludando á todos dijo á don Castro, ¿éste es el niño?

—Sí, éste es el ahijado, recomiéndolo bien, toma 500 duros, para que pagues el colegio y lo que necesite el niño,

—Muy bien, dijo don Valentin tomando el dinero con billetes que le daba don Castro, y guardándolo en su cartera.

Ahora podemos marchar, pues á las 2 y media está aquí el tren que sigue para New York.

—Si ya pueden irse dijo don Castro

Ricardo y Ramona se levantaron saludaron á don Castro que tomó la cabeza del niño y lo besó en la frente diciéndole—Estudia hijo mío, sé estudioso.

Salieron los tres hácia la estación. A las 2 y media ya estaba el tren en la estación: veinte minutos gritó el conductor.

Ramona abrazó á su hijo y lo besó. Ricardo subió al tren y don Valentin detrás cada uno con su maleta.

Ramona esperó que marchara el tren, y saludar por última vez a Ricardo. El pito del tren sonó y el conductor dió el aviso antes de subir.

El tren empezó á respirar para ponerse en mar-

cha, y Ricardo asomado en la ventanilla saludaba
á su madre.   El tren se alejaba y Ramona aún agi-
taba su pañuelo.

Por fin se perdió el tren de vista en los serpen-
teados raíles de hierros pasando por entre pinos y
palmetos, y follaje áspero que demostraba la tierra seca y árida en la cual crecía, de extensos arena-
les y el mar á la izquierda manso dispuesto á recibir todas las clases de embarcaciones.

Cuando Ramona perdió de vista el humo de la
locomotora, se volvió á su casa y lloró mucho, mucho, cuando volvería á ver á su hijo, y sentose á
orar creyendo que la oración ayudaría á su hijo.

Habían pasado 8 meses y don Castro iba á saludar á Ramona y le dejaba algún billete. Esto
era debido á las palabras que dijo Ricardo antes
de marcharse, y el viejo avaro, egoista que no recordaba otras ternezas en su vida que la de su mujer que se había muerto,   al oir al niño pensar en
ayudar á su madre se le ocurrió que haría bien en
llevarle algo á Ramona aunque fuera para pagar su
casa.   Pero que tarde se había acordado don Castro, cuando ya Ramona extenuada rendida por el
trabajo languidecía huyendo de ella la vida por exceso de trabajo.   La vida huía de Ramona acele-
radamente, había trabajado de día y de noche, y
cuando se encontraba sin recurso, acudía á la tien-
da de don Castro á comprarle al crédito para pagarle luego con miles privaciones, entonces su hijo era
pequeñito, tenía que cuidarlo. ¡cuántas angustias y
desesperaciones! para terminar las costuras de compromiso, tenía que coser de noche hasta la una y las
dos, sin cesar, ahogándose, destruyendo su juven-
tud y su vista perdiéndola, ahora tenía que usar
lentes, y con cuánto trabajo ensaltaba la aguja, ya
le temblaban los dedos, y estaba en la mejor edad
de la vida, en los 35 años y se agotaban sus fuerzas,
y ahora venía aquel señor ? prestarle su ayuda, cuan

do tantas veces con lágrimas en los ojos había ido
á decirle q. no podía pagarle, y nunca le dispensó la
deuda, ¿sería tan ciega la especie humana? el egoismo era tal que hacía perder los más naturales sentimientos.   Su hijo le escribía el progreso que reali-
zaba, y ella satisfecha soñaba con ver á su hijo hecho un hombre útil.

Un día no pudo coser, era tal el dolor que sentía, que tuvo que acostarse á descansar, así pasó
una semana de cama, con fiebre y dolor de cabeza,
una vecina la cuidaba.   Cuando don Castro lo supo, envió el médico. El doctor le dijo á don Castro
que era tiempo perdido, que estaba tuberculosa y
no había remedio.   En esa condición pasó un mes,
se le avisó al hijo que su mamá estaba enferma, pero sin alarma, para no entorpecer al muchacho. Un
día Ramona le dijo á la vecina que le dijera á don
Castro que avisara á su hijo que quería verlo, —Don
Castro le envió un telegrama, para que tomase tren
y llegara á ver á su madre.

El jóven se alarmó y dijo: ¿tanta prisa? extraño és,

—A los tres días llegaba y la madre lo recibió
en sus brazos.

—¡Hijo mío! mi último adiós, se bueno y
estudioso—madre mía me dejas solo! exclamó Ricardo con dolorosa acento, sin observar el rostro de
la enferma, ni darse cuenta que Ramona no respiraba ya al dejarla sobre la almohada notó que estaba inmovil, y gritó ¡Muerta! que desgracia! y ea-
yó de rodillas llorando.

Han pasado algunos años, ya tenemos á Ricardo de cajero en una gran casa comercial de una
gran ciudad de E.U., ganaba un sueldo regular.
Pero era un esclavo, y á veces desesperaba de la vida.   Aquella gente, que venía á efectuar transac-

ciones comerciales no se acordaban ni se ocupaban
del jóven cajero.

El dueño en esa especie de soporífero que proporciona la seguridad de una buena posición, tampoco se ocupaba de su cajero, éste era como el apun-
tador de un teatro, tenía la batuta en la mano y
pasaba desapercibido, la menor distracción en su
trabajo podría ocasionar serias complicaciones y
allí lo veía Vd. doblado sobre su alto escritorio en
su silla giratoria, de la que salía para almorzar y
volver hasta las 5, sin mas descanso, ni más ventaja. Ricardo decía ¡Que vida! allí pasando dinero
de uno á otro lado, millones de dollars sin poder
disponer de un céntimo, acorralado amordazado,
hecho una máquina de contar sin otras aspiraciones
que tener cuidado de no equivocarse. Estar con-
denado á tener en sus manos una fortuna, y no tener nada más que un sueldo mezquino, y con la indiferencia que era tratado, como si no sintiera como si el no tuviera derecho de divertirse como los
demás.

Y para eso había estudiado y su madre había
sufrido tantas privaciones para estar ahora como
estaba. ¡Valiente vida! aquello era un suplicio,
nacer y crecer oyendo llantos y viendo miserias
depender de otro la educación, y por último vivir
entre oro de día y hasta de noche sin aspirar á mas
felicidad que casarse para dejar sola siempre á la
mujer y si quiere ir al teatro ó algún sitio encomen-
darla á un amigo, para que luego suceda lo que le
sucedió al cajero del otro Banco que mientras él
trabajaba, ella iba á pasear al campo con otro que
terminó por ser su amante, y á eso voy yo?—no
de ningún modo, yo tengo derecho á vivir y á ser
feliz, yo no dejaré sola siempre á mi Matilde, nó!...
el hombre que se casa debe llevarse á su mujer ó
permanecer con élla. Esos matrimonios en los que
la mujer hastiada de estar sola se entrega al primer

amigo, es desesperante, ellas no tienen la culpa, somos nosotros los que la exponemos á eso, y si lo hicieran por amor, pero no, sostienen una lucha terrible por permanecer fieles.

Pero aquí pensando no hago algo y es necesario hacerlo, y salir de esta situación.

Cuando regresó á su casa, díjose es necesario que mañana domingo vaya al puerto y revise los barcos que salen á la vela. Pero no, mejor es que vaya á New York, y de allí, embarque á cualquier punto yo avisaré á Matilde para que se prepare.

Al siguiente día fué á ver á Matilde y le dijo es necesario que nos vayamos silenciosamente sabes, preparate para el sábado y á tu tía le dices que le conviene callar y le darás 500 pesos para que se vaya á vivir al campo.—Matilde díjole, que te preocupa, hay algún peligro? No, pero necesito tomar éstas precauciones para evitar algún trastorno—Yo haré lo que me digas.

El sábado siguiente por la noche, hablaba Ricardo con la tía de Matilde explicándole, Vd. no dará informes de su sobrina á nadie dirá que fué á New York a conseguir un empleo, y Vd. se marcha al campo con este dinero que yo le doy.— Tendré cuidado de no comprometerlos.—Si, pero dígame Vd. no se opone á mi enlace con Matilde?— No, ella lo ama á Vd.—Entonces estoy tranquilo despídete Matilde y tomaremos el tren. Ricardo se había disfrazado con bigotes y patillas, y nombre distinto, y de brazo con Matilde parecía un extranjero.

Llegaron á la estación, faltaban diez minutos para llegar el tren, por fin el tren llegó y subieron. Salió el tren. Llegaron y como Ricardo conocía la ciudad se informó de los vapores que salían, el mismo día salía uno para San Peterburgo, y lo tomó. Ya no había peligro, cuando se fijaron que el no estaba en la oficina el lunes por la tarde ya.

era muy tarde, el lunes no había trabajo apenas. De modo que supondrían que iría el martes.

Llegó el martes y la casa comercial envió á preguntar por Ricardo, y los vecinos le dijeron que no lo habían visto. Se pidió informes á los que suponían amigos se informó á la policía para que averiguase, los viajeros que salieron sábado y domingo. Nada se pudo averiguar. Entanto pasaron semanas y meses y no aparecía ni el más leve rastro de Ricardo, y nadie tampoco sabía que se había llevado á Matilde porque la vieja se había ido al campo, y nadie tenía seguridad de aquellas relaciones. Un día fueron de paseo algunos amigos á saludar á la tía y le preguntaron por Matilde y ella dijo que estaba en New York que volvía pronto—Vd. por aquí no se enterará de las noticias y sucesos diarios? ¡Ca! retirada como vivo cuidando mis gallinitas y plantas no me ocupo de otra cosa.—En días pasados hubo el gran conflicto, el cajero de la gran casa comercial de Jacob & Co, se fue llevandose un millón de dollars— Cáspita dijo la vieja y quien era? se llamaba Ricardo— cuando mi hija lo sepa, se asombrará, porque sino equivoco el nombre así se llamaba uno que la enamoraba.—Debe ser el mismo.—Y la vieja disimulaba bien, Se fueron los amigos diciendo: no sabe nada, y mejor era no haberlo dicho, pues ahora se lo dirá á la sobrina y ella si lo quería sufrirá. Pero ya todo era inútil, no averiguaban dónde estaba el jóven; ellos paseaban tranquilamente por los museos, y salieron de San Petersburgo, pasaron á Italia, pasearon por París y se fueron á Granada á comprar una casita ideal á preparar el nido para la cría, pues Matilde daría a luz en dos meses y no podía estar de ese modo. Allí en la bella ciudad dió a luz Matilde una niña á quien llamaron Aurora.

Cuando Ricardo estaba solo en el jardin decía; que vengan ahora á molestarme aquellos majaderos, egoistas que venían á depositar grandes cantidades y no daban á los pobres ni un céntimo, todos eran unos especuladores, con excepción de alguna viuda, pero que importa. ''No hay mal que por bien no venga''. Lo siento por los pobres que habían pero aquellos soberbios y engreídos, que paguen ahora su insolencia, se creían honrados y muy satisfechos de sus combinaciones especulativas.

Cuando preguntaban á la vieja por Matilde decía que se había casado en New York, y que estaba buena. Un día recibió una carta de Matilde, y ella se alegró mucho al saber que su sobrina estaba buena y era feliz.

Ibor City Tampa.

20-25 Mayo 1913.

AMORES.

¡Un socorro, una ayuda para una pobre viuda con un hijo reciennacido!—se atrevió á decir en una esquina de una de las calles de Roma, Gizelda uña mujer que había sido muy admirada en el teatro por su belleza, que había tenido muchos enamorados, algunos que parecieron amantes. Una vez se confió á uno que le agradó y que la dijo que la amaba y se fue con él. Sacrificó su glorioso porvenir, su brillante profesión, para amar, y consagrarse por completo a su amado. Pasaron algunos años y nadie supo de ella. Apareció un día pálida, envejecida con un niño en los brazos solicitando ayuda. Nadie la conoció y nadie la ayudaba como ella necesitaba.

Pasaron días y, semanas, meses y la mujer languidecía, ella se hubiera colocado de sirvienta, pero ¿su hijo? flor de sus amores! no tenía á quien dejarlo para que lo atendiese. Una vez cruzaba la plaza, se cayó al sentarse en un banco, y no pudo levantarse con el niño que llevaba en brazos, el niño se asustó con la sacudida, al caer la madre, pero parece que lo apretó de tal modo en el gran momento de angustia suprema y única, que el niño no se desprendió de sus brazos, solamente gritaba desaforadamente, golpeando con sus manitas el rostro de su madre, y gritaba más y más queriendo abrir la ropa que ocultaba su alimento, para consolarse en aquel seno sin jugo.

Estaba muerta. Un tullido que pasaba al oír los gritos del niño se acercó trató de conocer la madre, como no la conoció se fijó en un medallón, lo examinó y dijo ¡Gizelda! y lo desprendió y se lo llevó. Como no podía levantarla fué todo lo más deprisa que le permitían sus fuerzas á la esquina y llamó con un pito que llevaba al policía de la esquina.

El policía corrió acompañado por el tullido fué al banco, al lado del cual había caído Gizelda, y cogió el niño, y recomendó á "Vigilante" como le llamaban al tullido porque siempre por lo general, era el que avisaba de algo que ocurría, que velara a Gizelda por si despertaba, que el iba por un médico y al mismo tiempo avisara á la ambulancia. El policía fué al teléfono de la esquina y como a dos cuadras más estaba la ambulancia, no tardó en llegar y venía con el médico. El policía corrió para oir que decían de Gizelda. Pero al levantarla se comprendió que estaba muerta, el médico dijo:"Al salón de operaciones, para hacerle la autopsia". To dos subieron al carricoche, y este se alejó á su destino. Vigilante el tullido, se quedó mirando como se alejaba el carro y sacando una botellita con agua azucarada mezclada con ginebra, sorbió un trago y dijo: ¡tan bella como era!, y como yo la conocí; deslumbrando con su lujo y asombrando con sus pro-

digalidades, y embriagando con sus locuras amorosas! Era muy buena!.......y se enjugó dos lágrimas que persistieron en brotar de sus ojos pasando
el brazo derecho por su rostro. En el hospital supo Vigilante que Gizelda había muerto de hambre,
y que el niño había sido enviado á un asilo para niños pobres. Todos los días iba Vigilante á preguntar por el niño, el cual estaba sano y hermoso,
y crecía de un modo singular. Como á la madre no
había podido preguntar que nombre le había puesto a su hijo. En el asilo le habían dado el de Jacinto del Bosque. Ya tenía el niño nombre y apellido. Habían pasado varios años y en su cotidiana
visita un día supo Vigilante que se llevaban a Jacinto a un colegio público interno, para que apren-
diera el inglés, taquigrafía y teneduría de libros. A
los 10 años de estar en el colegio, salió Jacinto con
todos los requisitos para poder vivir de su trabajo.
Era bello como su madre lo había sido, de esbelta
estatura, andar elegante, cualquiera conocía que
era hijo de Gizelda, pero los ojos no se parecían á los
de la madre, ni el tono de voz arrogante á imperativo. Su rostro se contraía muchas veces, cuando
sólo en el café, no tenía con quién cambiar impresiones, con un gesto desesperado: Un día, lo llla-
mó en su distracción el alcalde, que sabía quien era
Jacinto, estando en un grupo de amigos jóvenes y
lo presentó al grupo, invitando á Jacinto á sentarse
entre ellos. Jacinto sentose y continuó conversan-
do de varios asuntos. Hacia una semana que Jacinto había salido del colegio. y obtuvo empleo en
una oficina comercial. Todos las tardes iba al café y encontraba algunos de los jóvenes que le había presentado el Alcalde

Jacinto cuando salía de su oficina por las tardes, habiase fijado que siempre, había una joven
que lo miraba, el la miraba saludaba con el sombrero y seguía hasta el café.

Esta escena repetiase todos los días hasta una noche que se vieron frente á frente en un baile que daba el Alcalde por el cumpleaños de su esposa. Hubo quien los presentara y se invitaron ambos para bailar juntos, él la invitó para un Vals y ella para una Polka. Bailaron el Vals, y Jacinto sintió que era más feliz al lado de ella que el lado de otra que le atraía una simpatía irresistible hacia Alina del Prado.

Cuando bailaron la polka él le dijo á ella, ¿cuando volveremos á hablar y estar cerca otra vez? Alina contestó:

—Es posible que en ni casa celebren mi cumpleaños con un baile.

—¿Cuando?

—El 25 de mayo, yo haré que lo inviten, ó lo invitaré yo.

—Muchas gracias, replicó Jacinto y bailaré con Vd?

—Seguramente dijo Alina, ¿Por qué no?

Y siguieron de brazo por el salón que estaba espléndidamente alumbrado, y se internaron entre los árboles y flores del jardin; por una de las puertas del salón que comunicaba con el. Pasearon un rato, y volvieron al salón, pues las armonías musicales, le avisaban que el baile había empezado otra vez.

El baile terminaba y se despidieron todos. Al siguiente día ál ir á la oficina llevaba un ramo de flores para Alina. Las envolvió bien sin ajarlas y las arrojó al balcón, con ellas también una tarjetita, con estas palabras:

"Srta. Alina

Yo siento por Vd, una gran simpatía, Vd. me atrae de un modo irresistible. Tiemblo ante Vd. como una débil hoja, que el viento meciera.

¿Debo callar ó manifestarlo sin rodeos? Si he sido imprudente ó precipitado no me conteste.

S.S.Q.B.S.P.

Jacinto del BOSQUE.

Alina se levantó aquel día algo tarde por el baile del día anterior. Pero su primer impulso aún con el traje matinal fué ir al balcón, se asomó y vió el paquete que había en el suelo, lo cojió y abrió,eran eran rosas azucenas y violetas. Las colocó en un pequeño búcaro, llevándolas á su tocador, abrió la tarjeta y una alegría, una gran satisfacción refle jose en sus ojos,.. en todo su rostro.

Inmediatamente sentose á escribir contestando la tarjeta, así: ''Amado mío: Que alegría me has enviado con tu tarjeta. ?Por qué callar? Si tu no lo haces hoy, yo lo hubiera hecho pronto. Desde que te ví, te adheriste á mi alma, y vives en mi mente. Te adoro.

Alina.

Luego la selló y la envió al correo. Se amaban sin saber quienes eran, se habían visto era lo suficiente. El era un jóven pobre inteligente y estudioso. Ella rica, bella, con un título de condesa por herencia, aunque sus padres vivían. El vió en ella la mujer que le sugestionaba, su ideal. Ella vió en su tipo arrogante y su gesto imperativo y bello, su soñado deseo, la figura que imaginó su mente artistica; y se le presentaba real y tangible amandola, y anhelándola como ella no esperaba. ?Sería su hado tan benévolo, el que le proporcionó á su amado, que no interrumpiría su felicidad? Eso lo veremos. Alina del Prado hija única de los Condes del Torreón era una niña aún, para los padres preocuparse de su libertad. Era pues su voluntad una orden para todos los de la casa. De modo que

no se imaginó ella que para elegir su amado tendría
que consultar con sus padres.

Jacinto recibió la carta por la tarde, y la satisfacción que sentía, lo demostraba en su rostro.   Salió de su oficina fué al café vió á su Alina en el balcón, saludó con el sombrero y una sonrisa, que ilu-
minó a su amada con ella.   Al ver tan gallarda figura entrar en el café, cualquiera se figuraba era
un gran señor, tenía un porte tan distinguido que
si la madre lo hubiese visto hubiera quedado extasia
da.

En el café, encontró algunos de sus amigos, se
saludaron y él mantuvose reservado en otra mesa,
como rehuyendo formar grupo con ellos, quería
estar solo para saborear el placer sin igual de amar y
ser amado.

Ellos al ver que Jacinto no formaba grupo con
ellos, murmuraron entre sí; el hijo del Alcade que
estaba dijo—Es un orgulloso, no debe olvidar que
mi padre lo recomendó y envió al colegio, otro, el
hijo del marqués de la Villa, dijo y quienes son sus
padres?—porque si no tiene títulos, no debe tener
orgullo alguno—¿Sus padres? no lo sé, oí decir á mi
padre que la madre había sido una gran artista y
que había tenido algunas aventuras amorosas—
¡Bah! dijo alguna prostituta, ni vale la pena men-
cionarla,—Otro agregó,—todo eso no importa, si
el es buen y correcto caballero: éste era heredero de
otro título, sobrino de los Barones del Rio, un muchacho simpático y muy amable con todo el mundo.
De modo que los tres se ocuparon de él, y se entre-
tenían jugando con injurias.   Jacinto leía y releía
la carta de Alina abstraído, no se ocupaba ni se había ocupado nunca de vidas ajenas ni se preocupó
de indagar cual era su familia, ni su rango.

Los tres jóvenes acordaron marcharse y salieron sin poder saludar á Jacinto, pues éste estaba
embebido en la contemplación de la carta: el no sa-

bía quienes eran esos jóvenes, se los habían presentado, pero no sabía que tenían preocúpaciones y jerarquías.

El 25 de mayo por la mañana, al ir á su oficina no vió á su Alina, el sabía que era su cumpleaños, y tenía un precioso regalo para su Alina. Lo envió con un sirviente de la casa, y su tarjeta. El regalo era una bella pluma de oro y nácar, un precioso relojito, con un dije que contenía un pequeño retrato de él.

Jacinto salía más temprano de la oficina, su inteligencia había granjeado el interés mercantil del dueño, y su figura simpática le había obligado á elevar á otro puesto más alto, y aumentándole el sueldo. Iba para su casa muy de prisa, á prepararse para el baile de la noche. Cuando llegó á su casa y abría con llave su habitación; entró precipitadamente un hombre con librea de servicio, y le entregó una esquela.

Jacinto saludó al hombre, entró y abrió el sobre, y leyó la invitación.

A las 10 de la noche, el salón de los Condes del Torreón, espléndidamente iluminado, apenas daba sitio á la concurrencia, que era lo más selecto de la nobleza y lo más notable de la Banca. Entre mil sonidos y ruídos diversos, formaban unos grupos, otros paseaban y aquella multitud se entretejia de un modo desigual. Jacinto no sabía que iba á codearse con la nobleza más antigua, y al mismo tiempo con los mayores usureros. Los había que con mil saltos y maromas habían hecho una millonada para elevar su categoría y pasearse muy orondos entre títulos heredados. Habían intrigantes y prestamistas, enriquecidos improvisadamente, conducidos allí por el azar del juego, en el cual una noche prestó miles de dollars, á un amigo de título y éste lo llevó á lucir su panza y sus bigotes.

Jacinto era el más limpio de todos aquellos señorones y mercaderes. Se paseaba ajeno á los demás con Alina del brazo; ya la música los había enlazados con sus deliciosas armonías.

Jacinto no veía que llamaba la atención á las damas con su bello y arrogante porte, se figuraban era algún príncipe extranjero, presentado por algún embajador. Los caballeros lo miraban y no lo conocían, las señoras le preguntaban á sus esposos, quien era aquel jóven. Nadie lo conocía, pasaba como una bella adquisición de Alina que muy pronto disfrutarían ellas en sus salones. invitándolo á las recepciones últimas.

Se terminó el baile y pasaron al salón del refectorio en donde había Champaingne, licores distintos, dulces verdaderos objetos de arte de la confitería moderna. Alina díjole á Jacinto, mis padres te han mirado mucho, dejame presentarte á ellos, contra todas las reglas, pero es preciso. Fueron á detenerse delante de los padres de Alina ella se dirigió primero y presentó á los padres. Jacinto hizo un saludo respetuoso y dijo su nombre: Jacinto del Bosque. El padre de Alina miraba el rostro todo de Jacinto como recordando y repetía—¿del Bosque?—¿del Bosque?--y agregó, de qué? con la mayor urbanidad ¿Conde, Barón, de que?............

El jóven contestó simplemente: Jacinto del Bosque, y saludando se retiró. El padre dijo á su mujer.

—¿Quién ha presentado ese jóven aquí? y á mi hija?

—No sé, replico, ella, tu sabes que ahora no se puede exigir, muchos requisitos, todos estamos confundidos.

—Es verdad, pero debieron presentarmelo, el Conde quedando pensativo recordaba aquellos ojos y aquel gesto.

—Vamos á la mesa dijo la Condesa, no te preocupes, y se confundieron con los demás.

Alina le extrañó las preguntas de su padre, por
que ella había visto otra gente, allí, que ya esea-
rían ser como Jacinto, tan elegantes y tan hermoso, y le dijo á Jacinto no te preocupes por lo que
diga papá, a la mesa: y sentaronse á tomar alguna
crema, un poco de Chartreuse. Todo había terminado. Jacinto había pasado entre aquellas gentes
como algo luminoso, como la Cenicienta del cuento,
sin haber satisfecho su curiosidad; que quizás en el
coche, en el tocador, en las tiendas, sería objeto
de charla, por averiguar quien era.

Alina recibió mil tarjetas de amigas que pedían
la dirección del jóven para invitarlo á la próxima
fiesta. El siguiente día, ya esperaba Alina en el
balcón que pasara Jacinto, el se detenía con el objeto de verla más tiempo, aquella calle era poco tran-
sitable, el balcón principal de la casa de Alina correspondía á la otra calle, esta era apropósito para
ellos hablar si no hubiera estado tan alto el balcón;
el la envió un beso, y contínuó. Jacinto era muy
estudioso quería graduarse como ingeniero, y hacía sus estudios en su casa, con el fin de examinar-
se, luego.

*
* *

Han pasado muchos meses, el idilio amoroso
continuaba. Alina salía á paseo en su coche, y se
veía con Jacinto, ella bajaba, se internaba entre
plantas y flores á leer y poco después llegaba él,
Un día díjole Jacinto. Es necesario que tu papá
se entere de nuestro amor, para que no crea he venido á sorprenderte en tu ignorancia de niña ¿Quieres? Alina tomando sus manos díjole—si ¿cuándo
vas á ir?—Esta noche si quieres, es jueves y es día
de visita, según me has dicho, pues iré esta noche.
A las 6 se marcharon ella subió en su coche y el se
alejó.

A las 8, estaba ya preparado Jacinto á las 9 es--

taba en el salón esperando que saliera el padre de Alina. Cambiaron saludos y frases corteses. Señor, dijo Jacinto; vengo á pediros la mano de vuestra hija, soy ingeniero y perito mercantil. Caballero, dijo el Conde yo necesito conocer el origen de vuestra familia, y además vuestra posición............ Señor, no soy millonario, ni muy rico, pero estoy en condiciones de casarme. ¿Sabeis dijo el Conde, que me hubiera gustado que tuvierais un título como ella.—Señor no me he ocupado de saber si los tenía ó nó, replicó Jacinto, no los necesito, ni lo deseo, nos amabamos, ni á ella, estoy seguro le preocupa ese detalle, ni se ocupó de saber quién yo era; ni yo indagué ni busqué apariencias, nos amamos y basta, hace un año.

—El Conde exclamó: ¡un año! ¿y por dónde os habeis conocido?

—Muy fácilmente, al salir de mi oficina todos los días nos veíamos, hasta que nos hablamos en el baile del Alcalde.

—Señor necesito conocer vuestra decisión.

—El Conde dijo: yo no puedo contestaros ahora, mi hija es muy jóven: yo os avisaré.

—Jacinto se levantó y con un muy cortés saludo se despidió diciendo: señor no olvideis que nos amamos que los inconvenientes no se han hecho para el amor; decidme ¿puedo visitar vuestra hija?

—No, aún nó: ya lo sabreis.

Saludáronse ambos y se marcharon

En su casa Jacinto daba paseos en su habitación y decía: Pero como yo no estaba enterado de ese detalle, ella no tenía que decirmelo, ¿para qué? acaso los he buscado. ¡Oh! deliciosa niña, cuánta sencillez, mañana la veré y sentose á leer.

En tanto el Conde informa á su esposa el motivo de la visita:— Ese joven ha venido á pedir á nuestra hija.

—¿Se aman?

—Así parece.

—Desinteresada y leal es.

—Estás conforme con ese amor.

—¿Por qué no?

—Es que el no es rico, ni tiene títulos.

—Qué importa.

—Parece Margarita que algún inconveniente ha de haber.

—Yo no lo veo.

—Lo veremos.

—Llamarás á la niña para que ella sepa que ha estado ese jóven aquí, por ella.

—Si vamos á enterarla, el Conde tocó el timbre y apareció un empleado, al que dijo — avise a la Srta. Alina que pase donde sus papás al salón,— volvió el criado diciendo está cerrada y obscura la habitación, supongo esté dormida.

—Dejemoslo para mañana dijo la condesa. Al siguiente día por la mañana después del desayuno, la condesa llamó á su hija y sentándola á su lado, le dijo:

—Por qué no me habías dicho Alina mía que amabas, no merezco tu confianza?

—Me parecía que no era obligación decirlo mamá.

—Muy bien, entonces que esperabas.

—Mamá mía, dijo Alina, abrazando á su mamá, perdoname, esperaba que el lo hiciera.

—Ya él lo hizo anoche, y tu padre le dijo que necesitaba conocer su origen, que le contestaría.

—Pobre amado mío, que triste estará.

—No te ocupes que habrá solución, permiteme que te deje pues necesito ver como arreglan la puerta del jardin, y besándola en ambas mejillas salió dejando á Alina pensativa.

Aquella tarde en el paseo Alina y Jacinto paseaban entre follajes y se prometían amarse a pesar

de todos los inconvenientes, y se despidieron. Jacinto estaba preocupado, donde averiguar quienes
eran sus padres si el mismo no lo sabía,—pero seguramente que alguno los había conocido.   De pron
to se detuvo y dijo ¡qué idea! el Alcalde debe saberlo yo iré á verle —A las 8 estaba en casa del Alcalde esperando que llegara.

—Cuanto gusto tengo en veros dijo el Alcalde
entrando, en que puedo serviros.

—Amigo mío, dijo Jacinto, vengo á solicitar
del amigo me diga quienes eran mis padres.

—Quien pregunta eso hijo mío, porque supongo que tu no serás el que te preocupe, tu sabes que
tu madre se llamaba Gizelda, ''La Divina'' no conozco el apellido.

—Pero mi padre.

—No lo se hijo, pero puedo enterarme con la
policía.

—Con la policía Sr. y que datos podrá daros
ella, ¿han estado mi padre ó mi madre presos al
guna vez?

—No lo creo, hijo, el alcalde estaba indeciso
si declaraba ó no lo que sabía.

—Decidme amigo mío, que parece enmudeceis,
con franqueza decidme lo que sepais.

—Pues bien, replicó el Alcalde, te diré lo
que sé ya, que me lo exiges.   Un día me avisaron
que había un niño, cuya mamá, se había encontrado muerta...............

— ¡Dónde!

—Oye no te impacientes.   Ella te llevaba en
brazos, sufrió algún dolor... y se cayó tu llorabas,
pasó por allí un pobre tullido que avisó á la policía
para que la recojiera..........

—Y ese dónde está? y por que no llevaron á
mi madre á su casa?

¿Por qué?, no lo sé, espera hijo mío en-

viaré á buscar el tullido que te detalle mejor lo que
el refirió al médico.

—Y el médico dónde está?

—El nada sabe, solamente lo que yo te he dicho

—El debe saber de que murió.

—El Alcalde pensó un rato y dijo, de hambre............

¡Madre mía! gritó Jacinto tapándose la boca
con el pañuelo y apoyando su frente sobre sus
manos abiertas con el pañuelo, que crueldad!

—El Alcalde se levantó y cojiendo por nu
brazo díjole, vamos al jardín, que yo envío por el
tullido: el Alcalde envió á buscar el tullido que co-
nocemos por ''Vigilante'' y se llevó á distraer á Jacinto paseando con él en el jardín.—Hijo mío le decía: no desesperes porque haya muerto pobre.

—Señor no pobre: ¡hambrienta! y por qué murió así?

—Ya lo sabremos conformate con ser útil á tí
y honrar donde has nacido con tu inteligencia y pro-
bidad.   —¡Ay! pero que amarga me sabrá la
felicidad, pensando que mi madre murió de hambre! !es horrible!

—Bien pero dime Jacinto á que viene ese interés en saber tu origen; ¿qué ha pasado?

—Estoy enamorado, dijo Jacinto, y después
de un año de relaciones en que hablaba con ella.

—¿Quién es ella?

—Alina del Prado.

—¡Recórcholis!, pues has picado alto muchacho.

—No señor, no lo sabía; la primera vez que hablé con ella fué aquí en el baile que Vd. me invitó
después nos mirabamos por el balcón al ir á mi oficina, nos veíamos en el paseo.

—¿Sólos?—extraño es como la dejan salir sola?

—Ella salía antes a casa de una y otra amiga
sola y otras veces paseaba sola en coche, hasta que
cansados de hablar por señas y cartas, decidió invi-
tarme á sus paseos, y yo la esperaba allá entre bellos ramajes.   Decidí enterar. á su papá y aquí me
teneis con mi desventura.

—Y que te dijo su papá.

—Que deseaba conocer mi familia y mi posición, de ésta le dije lo que era, lo de mi familia vengo á enterarme aquí.

Avisaron al Alcalde que lo procuraban.

—Espera Jacinto, debe ser ''Vigilante'' el tullido

Salió y encontró un empleado que le dijo: ''Vigilante'' está enfermo en el hospital; además hay
un viejo que hace varias semanas quiere verlo, pero
creyendo que era alguna manía, no quisimos molestar á Vd. pero ayer y hoy se ha empeñado de tal
manera diciendo que tiene un encargo para Vd.

—Bien ahora iremos allá.

—Don Eliseo, volvió al jardín á buscar á Jacinto para ir con él al hospital lo encontró pensativo y le dijo: vamos Jacinto, y tomándolo de un
brazo, se lo llevó atravesando el jardín, y la galeg-
ría.

—¿Dónde vamos?, murmuró Jacinto.

—Vamos al hospital dijo don Eliseo, á encon-
trarnos con ''Vigilante''.

—Subieron al coche que esperaba al Alcalde
y se alejaron.

En el hospital pidieron ver a ''Vigilante''
''Vigilante'' estaba en un sillón pálido, tendría como 42 años.   Jacinto fué conducido por un empleado donde estaba ''Vigilante''.

—Buen día, dijo Jacinto.

—Buen día respondió el tullido.

—Dime interrogó Jacinto, podrías informarme
sobre quién era Gizelda, y su marido.

—¿Sois familia de ella?, dijo "Vigilante".

—No te ocupes de eso, contéstame, lo que intereso, saber es quién fué y de que vivió.

—No sé sí hago mal en ello; pero allá voy; yo era un jóven de 16 años cuando el tren me destrozó las piernas, yo creí morir pero me salvaron. Siempre estuve alrededor del teatro: en esa época llegó una muy famosa artista muy bella, yo desesperaba por ir como antes á verla entrar y á veces á serle útil en alguna cosa. Cuando pude salir mi primer paseo fué al teatro, me sentaba en la escalinata de mármol y allí esperaba mientras no hacía sol y luego debajo de los árboles en frente. Un día ví salir una jóven divina, aquello nunca visto por mis ojos y miré que yo había visto, ¡qué elegancia! que ojos! que boca! le digo Sr. que me quedé embobado; y desde aquel día la seguía á todas partes como un bobo y tenía una corte de jóvenes de lo más escojido de la sociedad; la decían primores, se disputaban su mano para subirla al coche de ella, pues apesar de que la ofrecían cada uno el suyo "La Divina" como la deciamos, no aceptaba y subía en su sencillo cochecito. Otro día se formó tal ruído entre ellos por darle la mano que ella dijo, yo la oí que estaba al otro lado de su coche. —Si no sois formales, llamaré á ese tullido, que parece un centinela, siempre lo vereis aquí; para que me de la mano. Con mucho gusto repliqué yo y corri hácia elia que sonreída me miraba y alargándome su mano con una moneda me dijo: "tu no puedes, gracias" con q. dulzura, me lo dijo Sr. si Vd. la hubiera conocido como hubiera admirado su gentileza, su carácter dulce y alegre, de una alegría que parecía que emanaba perfumes de jazmines y rosas. Cuando ella salía á las tiendas, ¡que lujo! que derroche de gracia! ¡cielo santo! no ha venido otra como aquella.

Jacinto estaba emocionado no respiraba, se atrevió á decir en el intérvalo que el "Vigilante" tomaba agua. ¿Y ella de quién era hija? ¿estaba sóla?.

—Siempre sola con una vieja que arreglaba su ropa de teatro.

—De quién era hija?

—Oí decir una vez que se suponía era de alta categoría extranjera y que por disgusto de familia se había dedicado al teatro que le gustába. Ella hablaba correctamente el francés y el italiano, pero no sé si era de uno-ó de otro país. El idioma que élla usaba con más frecuencia era el francés. Después se dijo que la galanteaba el Marqués de la Villa, la acompañaba en su coche. Pero parece que este Sr. la pretendía sin casarse y ella no volvió á dejarlo subir á su coche, pues en la acera le dijo un día cuando el iba á subir; por favor Marqués excuseme, pero no puedo permitirlo más Vd. no quería ser mi amigo: si mí amante, y para ser un amante es necesario que Vd. se dedique á mi y Vd. tiene novia.

....Yo no tengo novia Gizelda, mi familia me la impone.

—Muy bien y si Vd. no tiene valor de rechazar eso, rechace esto otro y terminado.

—No puedo la amo a Vd.

—Pues demuéstrelo.

—Soy único hijo y mi patrimonio está mal, y tengo dos hermanas ¿cómo voy á casarme ahora, si estoy estudiando?

—Pues amigo nada más, y terminemos esto, que me hace daño.

Ella subió a su coche y el otro se quedó en la acera con el sombrero en la mano, pálido. Yo me hice el dormido al ver el dolor de aquel hombre y el se fué. Un día supe por otros, que ella amaba al Conde del Torreón, o por lo menos lo distinguía, este era más independiente tenía un hermano pero aún era jóven: y estaba en el Colegio. La

madre era anciana el padre había muerto. Era el
único que podía agradarle porque era guapo con unos
ojos y un gesto y una presencia sin rival; este señor
había llegado de París, donde había ido á arreglar
asuntos de su herencia. Inmediatamente que ellos
se vieron se amaron. Gizelda me dijo un día, esta noche será la última que vendré á cantar.—¿Por
qué? le pregunté—porque me voy al campo con
mi amante y no vuelvo al teatro por ahora. Eso
me dijo al bajar del coche y entró en el teatro. La
noticia me desconcertó, porque yo adoraba a esa
mujer como á una Diosa. Aquella noche al terminar la función la esperaba en su elegante carrua-
je, el Condesito. Yo la esperaba, porque todas las
noches me daba una moneda. Esa noche me dió
un escudo y me dijo: si necesitas algo me avisarás
con la ayudanta mía, Rogelia, ¿la conoces?

—Sí, señora.

—Adíos eh?, y cuídate.

Se alejó el coche y pasó mucho tiempo sin volver á verla.

La Sra. Rogelia me traía dinero. En los cafés
donde ella había derrochado su dinero y cantado, se
hablaba mal de ella, las mujeres la envidiaban, los
hombres la deseaban y la odiaban. En el teatro el
empresario era otro despechado, el único que la de-
fendía era el Marqués que ella no había aceptado
que luego se casó y tiene hoy un hijo muy jugador
Supe luego que la madre del Conde del Torreón había muerto, y que el hijo, el amante de Gizelda, era
el mayor que se haría cargo de la educación de su
hermano. El venía á la ciudad muchas veces después de la muerte de su madre. Se llevó á su hermano á París, y se llevó á Gizelda oculta. Me lo
contó Rogelia

—¿Dónde está Rogelia?

—Ha muerto, era muy vieja ya. Supe, por cartas que escribía á Rogelia de París, en las que pre-

guntaba por mí, que el Conde se portaba bien: la
llevaba al teatro públicamente y que eran muy felices, porque Gizelda estaba embarazada y soñaban
en ponerle el mismo nombre del padre, Alberto.
Yo estaba muy contento de la dirección que tomaban aquellos amores, porque ella se lo merecía. Un
día vino llorando Rogelia á decirme que había recibido carta de Gizelda en que decía que el Conde se
había muerto en un incidente en un café, provocado por un ébrio y recibió un balazo, dice Gizelda
que era uno que estaba enamorado de ella, y creyó
que matándolo estaría libre. La carta era una manifestación de dolor profundo. Diciendo que volvería aquí, que estaba indispuesta. Al mes recibí noticia que había dado a luz un niño muy bonito y que estaba sin recursos, que volvía á donde Rogelia. Rogelia se enfermó en aquellos días, y no
volvió á salir, yo busqué donde vivía Rogelia y no
encontré. Pasaron meses y un día atravezando
la plaza frente al teatro oí unos gritos de un niño,
miré y era una mujer que se había caído, apresuré
como pude para llegar á ella, y el niño estaba desesperado, me fijo en la mujer y me pareció conocerla ví
un medallón que pendía de su cuello lo abro, lo observo y era ella, no podía ser otra. Le desprendí
el medallón y llamé un policía para que la llevara
al hospital. Luego me enteré que estaba muerta
y de hambre............y se enjugó algunas lágrimas
que se mezclaban entre sus bigotes. Jacinto como si hubiera despertado dijo: y ese medallón, y las
cartas.

—El medallón lo guardo, cartas solamente tengo dos, porque Rogelia era quien las recibía.

Aquel día de su muerte lloré, como yo la había conocido, y como moría, frente al teatro que habíala glorificado como artista y como bella. Luego supe que había recorrido algunas calles pidiendo
en cafés y plazas y nada le daban para su hijo que

estoy seguro que para ella no hubiera pedido, nadie la tendió una mano: ni yo pude verla para ayudarla.

—¿Cómo llegó á ese estado en tan poco tiempo?

—No sé, supuse que al quedar allá sin recursos fué vendiendo sus objetos y luego vendría como pudo, vivió con Rogelia, se murió ésta y la echaron á la calle, porque nadie sabía donde vivía.

—Oye "Vigilante" dijo Jacinto, te puedo pagar lo que pidas por tus revelaciones, y por el medallón y las cartas, yo soy el hijo de Gizelda.

"Vigilante" lo miró de arriba á abajo y díjole: Vd. el hijo de Gizelda que yo dejé un pequeñito en el colegio como ha cambiado con tal expresión de asombro que Jacinto sonrió, y díjole: no me reconocistes?

—No, todos los días iba á preguntar por Vd. en el Asilo. Y si Vd. es su hijo le daré el medallón y las cartas, y sacando una cajita que tenía en el bolsillo: se la entregó.

—¿Qué quieres por eso?

—Señor yo no lo vendo, se lo regalo en nombre de ella. Eso era para Vd.

Al verlo entrar me figuré sería Vd. familia del conde, pues se parece Vd. mucho a él.

—Soy su hijo.

—Ya lo sé, pero no lo sabía.

—Entonces "Vigilante", marcho, gracias, y si me necesitas avísale al Alcalde que el es amigo mío.

—Muchas gracias. Se estrecharon la mano y Jacinto salió, preguntó por el Alcalde y le djeron que se había marchado. Jacinto saludó, y salió, el coche del Alcalde lo esperaba. Dijo al cochero a mi casa y dígale a don Eliseo que luego iré por allá, que tengo que ir a la oficina. Llegó a su casa y entró precipitadamente. Abrió la cajita derramó el contenido sobre la mesa. La medalla y su cadena eran un magnífico trabajo artístico y de un buen oro, tenía algunos brillantes y rubíes, lo abrió y vió el retrato de su madre y del otro lado, un jóven, sería su padre. Lo limpió bien lo lavó y cepilló y después de besar ambos retratos repetidas veces lo guardó en el bolsillo, y se fué a la oficina.

En tanto en la mesa del Alcalde y del Conde se comentaba la resolución de Jacinto de saber quienes eran sus padres. Yo no estaba en esa época aquí, nada sé, pero por el aspecto y natural instinto del chico debe ser de buenos padres,—decía el Alcalde a su familia.

En el comedor del Conde, este decía:

—Vendrá a traer su rango o su fortuna.

—Alina replicó ni una ni otra cosa deseo, lo quiero a él.

—¿Aunque sea un cualquiera?

—¡Cómo un cualquiera! acaso un jóven culto, instruído inteligente, y con su porvenir hecho, es un cualquiera.

—Tú estás enterada de su vida.

—Sí y nó: lo veo salir todos los días de su oficina, todos los días donde supongo que no se juega, ni se bebe, se trabaja: luego á su casa a estudiar,—quereis un ejemplar que mayor prestigio diera a mis hijos.

—Pero hija, eres una niña para hablar así.

—Con 16 años no soy ninguna niña papá.

—Bien si no trae nombre o fortuna, no puedo resolverlo, porque yo no quiero estar a merced de críticas y malas lenguas.

—Me matareis.

—No quieras imposibles.

—Quiero mi felicidad que nadie tiene derecho a discutírmela, ni de buscarla como yo la deseo.

—Eres muy jóven para saber buscar la felicidad, no tienes experiencia.

—La felicidad, y el amor son niños, no viejos.

—Ya lo pensarás luego.

—Tengo mi resolución hecha.

—Muy bien cálmate, dijo la madre.

Terminaron de comer y Alina besó a sus padres
y se retiró a su habitación, pasando por una puerta
al jardin, miró si el coche la esperaba y volvió a su
tocador, para terminar de arreglarse. Se puso un
sombrero a lo Carlota Corday y bajó al jardin; salió
y subió a su coche. Cuando llegó al sitio acostumbrado, ya Jacinto estaba paseándose entre las calles de árboles. Alina, bajó y sentose a leer. Jacinto la vió y se aproximó a ella diciéndole:

—Amada mía, vengo tranquilo y valeroso a
comunicarte, mis impresiones, porque mi alma no
teme encontrarse con la tuya, porque las fórmulas
y vanidades del mundo no pueden separarnos ¡mira si confío en tu amor!

Jacinto había tomado las manos de Alina y
ella lo hizo sentar a su lado y le dijo:

Estoy orgullosa de ti y satisfecha de saber que
me comprendes y me conoces. Ahora dime que
te ha pasado? Jacinto habló así: fuí a ver a tu
papá y me dijo que debía llevar nombre y fortuna,
el que tengo no le basta desea un título para tí. Tu
eres del Prado, yo del Bosque, tu padre cree que
un Bosque es inferior a un Prado. Yo creo que se
equivoca, ahora dime que tu piensa.

Alina mirando con ternura a su amado le dijo:

—A mí no me preocupan esos detalles tontos
de gente a la antigua: a mí no me digas nada de
eso.

—Te lo refiero, para que te enteres de los detalles que puedan interrumpir nuestro enlace.

—Bien, pero para eso tenía pensado reclamar

las leyes, soy libre no esclava y nadie tiene derecho
de obligarme ni contrariar mis aspiraciones.

—¿Tenías pensado algo que resolviera nuestra situación, en caso de una negativa?

—Sí.

—Entonces, mañana tu dirás que resuelves.

—Ya está resuelto: mi padre se opone, proba-
ré su resistencia; si persiste entonces, me valeré de
mis derechos.

—¡Qué valiente eres! déjame besarte sin rodeos,
y estrecharte así entre mis brazos, y Jacinto abra-
zándola fuertemente la besó.

—Alina díjole—me voy, no se les ocurra enviar a buscarme.

—¡Hasta mañana!

—Hasta mañana, Alina mía,

Separaronse y Jacinto se deslizó por el otro lado mientras ella subía al coche. Jacinto llegó á su
casa y se puso a contemplar los retrato del medallón. Dábale vueltas entre sus manos y decidió
abrirlo, desprenderlos del marco para observar si
tenían algo escrito detrás. Empezó por el de su
madre, lo despegó y estaba escrito: ''Para mi
amado Alberto de su Gizelda''. Diciembre, del
año y mes.

Después el de su padre, que decía: ''A mi
amor, á la única mujer que he amado y haré mi esposa.

Alberto del Prado.

Jacinto al ver la firma, se asombró exclamó
¡Cielo Santo! que significa ésto? también Alina se
llama así. Pero yo no puedo ser su hermano, porque el padre de ella vive. ¿Cómo descifro ésto?
a quién puedo pedir informes? Volvió a colocar
los retratos como estaban y fué donde su protector
el Alcalde. Eran las 9 y don Eliseo iba a salir, cuan
do subió Jacinto.

—¡Hóla mi querido jóven, dijo don Eliseo que resultado obtuvo con ''Vigilante''?

—Pues fué intteresante y además este medal!ón dijo Jacinto.

Don Eliseo tomó el medallón que le presenta- ba Jacinto y dijo: magnífica prenda.　¿De su ma- má?

—Sí señor,· pero no es la prenda solamente lo valioso, son los dos retratos de mi padre y de mi madre, y lo abrió enseñándolo a don Eliseo.

—¡Caracoles!, exclamó éste, que bella mujer, y él que guapo que distinguido aspecto.

—Ahora dijo Jacinto debe Vd. leer lo que está escrito en el otro lado y despegó los retratos y dejó que don Eliseo leyera.

Cuando leyó, dijo:

—Muy bien, esto le sirve a Vd. de pruebas, pe- ro este Prado es familia de su novia?

—No lo sé dijo Jacinto y a eso he venido para que Vd. resuelva, o me ayude.

—Bien dijo don Eliseo déjeme el medallón que yo iré donde un amigo mañana y me informaré.

—Gracias don Eliseo, dijo Jacinto, hasta ma- ñana.

Jacinto se fué a su casa a dormir pues eran mu- chas impresiones y tenía necesidad de reposo.

Al siguiente día, después que salió de su ofici- na y fué á su casa se cambió de traje fué á comer, luego marchó á pie hasta el paseo para encontrar á su valiente Alina.—Paseó un rato y luego sentose en un banco á esperar, esperó en vano.　Alina no llegaba.　Pasaron las 6.　Alina no vendría.　Re- gresó a su casa, y no sabía que hacer como averiguar y terminó por decidirse á esperar al siguiente día y sentose á leer.

Entanto ¿qué le había pasado á la Srta. Alina?

La rapidez con que Alina se encerró en su ha- bitación aquella tarde hizo temer á su madre algo y á los pocos minutos la Condesa llamó y como no contestaran entró y no encontró a su hija.

Entonces buscó en el jardín, preguntó á la don cella y nadie la había visto salir, subió y tocó el timbre, presentose el criado, y le dijo: Pregúnte al portero, si la Srta. ha salido.

El criado salió y a los 10 minutos volvió diciendo: No señora, no la ha visto salir por la puerta principal.

—Vaya a buscar el cochero.

—Salió el criado, y la condesa pensativa estaba pálida.

Volvió el criado y dijo:

—Sra. condesa, el cochero no está.

—Entonces, vaya a casa de la Baronesa del Río, y observe si el coche está enfrente.

Salió y la condesa decía: y por qué no habrá salido por la puerta principal, es muy extraño.

Volvió el criado cuando Alina regresaba y bajaba por el jardín.

—Sra. el coche no estaba allí, pero ahora se detenía frente al jardín y bajó de él la Srta, y entró por el jardín.

—Muy bien puede retirarse.

La condesa pasó á la habitación de Alina y díjole:

—Hija mía, te he buscado, y me tenías ansiosa sin saber en donde estabas.

—Salí a dar un paseo para distraerme, dijo Alina besando. á su mamá, ¿me necesitabas?

—No, pero como no salistes por la puerta del frente.

—Me gusta mucho más por el jardín mamá.

—No debes salir sola más, estás expuesta á cualquier accidente y me asusto mucho,—¿sabes? no vuelvas, no quiero.

—Pero mamá, si he regresado seguida.

—No me agrada hija mía.

Alina besó a su mamá y se retiraba, y la madre la detuvo.

—No te vayas leeme algo que me distraíga.

Alina tomó un libro que sobre la mesa había y se puso a leer en alta voz.

A las 9 se levantó para ir a dormir

El conde llegaba y vió a su esposa dormitando y tomando a su hija por la mano la besó en la frente, y le dijo:

—Hasta mañana. Entonces llamó á su esposa y ayudándola á levantar la dijo:

—Vamos al cuarto si tienes sueño.

La condesa se levantó y dijó:

—Vamos al balcón un rato que quiero hablarte.

Ambos se dirigieron al balcón.

—Oye díjole la condesa; nuestra hija es muy crecida, ya es necesario que no salga sola.

—¿Por qué?

—Parece que acostumbra salir sola todos los días, pues ayer fuí a su cuarto, y no la encontré y la busqué por toda la casa, y al fin, se presentó en coche por el jardin.

—¿Sola?

—Si sola.

—¿Sabes si tiene entrevistas con alguién?

—No lo sé.

—Pues hay que averiguarlo,—llamando al cochero y preguntándole:

—¿Vamos a convertir en espía de nuestra hija al cochero?

—De algún modo se ha de saber.

—Bien pero emplea otra forma.

—No hay una más segura que seguirla; pero no me parece correcto.

—Que vas a hacer?

—Mejor ir con ella dijo el Conde y para eso tu.

La condesa exclamó:

—Pero así no irá á donde ella va.

—No importa, así no se establecen sospechas.

—Bueno.

Salieron del balcón y se retiraron a sus habitaciones.

Al siguiente día, Alina como no sabía lo que tramaban, no avisó a Jacinto. Por la tarde a la hora de terminar la comida, díjole la condesa

—Si vas a salir avísame, quiero ir contigo.

—Alina replicó algo sorprendida, pero conteniéndose: Yo no salgo todos los días. Mañana iré mamá.

—La condesa la miró, observando si era contrariarla.

Pero Alina permaneció muda, y muy satisfecha al parecer, pasó al balcón.

Entonces paseándose en el balcón se acordó del cochero que esperaba, ¿cómo hacer?

Entonces silenciosamente pasó por el corredor entró en su habitación y bajó al jardín.

Díjole al cochero, no salgo esta tarde, mañana.

El cochero se alejó y ella siguió paseándose por el jardín y se dijo:

—¿Qué pensará Jacinto? Alma mía, tan bueno como es.

Entonces decidió subir a su cuarto para escribir y decirle que pasara por el jardín.

Veamos que pensó Jacinto, pues esperaba carta de su amada, no podía imaginarse que pasaría.

Él esperaba que Alina resolvería el asunto y deseaba saber que le había ocurrido, que no había acudido a la cita.

Escribiendo en su oficina estaba cuando llegó el cartero y el ayudante le entregó una carta. Era de su Alina la abrió con presteza y leyó:

Amado mío: Ven esta tarde al jardin; para hablar contigo deseo verte, ayer no pude ir al paseo.

Te adora **Ali.na**

Dejemos a Jacinto saboreando la carta y veamos que ha hecho don Eliseo.

Al siguiente día como le había ofrecido a Jacinto fué a ver su amigo, el Marqués de la Villa.

Encontróle fumando y leyendo el diario de la mañana, en su gabinete, de recibir sus visitas.

Al ver al Alcalde se levantó y dijo:

—¡Hola amigo mío! á que debo esta agradable sorpresa.

Don Eliseo le estrechó en sus brazos y exclamó: un asunto muy interesante.

—Vamos a ver, sentaos.

Don Eliseo se acomodó en una butaca, y empezó así:

—Amigo Marqués, hará cerca de 18 años me avisaron, que había sido encontrado en la plaza frente al teatro, una mujer muerta con un niño en los brazos, y que no sabían que hacer con el niño; cuando me lo presentaron, ví el niño más precioso que podía haber visto. Lo envié al Asilo y luego lo recomendé á un colegio, y hoy es un modelo de jóven, estudioso juicioso y muy culto. Pero como no puede haber felicidad completa heaquí que el muchacho se ha enamorado de la hija de los Condes del Torreón y como no tiene nombre resulta que no sabía que hacer.

Pero antes decidme interrumpió el Marqués.

—¿Cómo se llama?

—Le pusimos Jacinto del Bosque. Pero no es un apellido reconocido por su genealogía entre la nobleza, y tampoco es rico. Pero al jóven se le ocurrió preguntarme á mi, y yo le dije lo que sabía, y le recomende fuera donde un tullido que estaba en el Hospital, fué y de allí ha venido con este medallón, que dice fué de su madre, y don Eliseo se lo presentó á su amigo, y le dijo. Abrélo para que me digas si conoces esos señores.

El Marqués abrió el medallón y exclamó:

—¡Gizelda! y Alberto.

—¿Los conocías? díjole el Alcalde.

—Sí y mucho. Me enamoré de esta mujer, y me hubiera casado con ella, pero estaba en pleitos de herencia y no era posible.

A ella le gustó mucho al Conde y este se la llevó a una quinta, y luego que murió la madre se fueron a París. Eramos íntimos amigos, pero nos enfriamos un poco durante su ausencia, pues el sabía que yo estaba enamorado de ella. Después no supe de ellos hasta que el hermano regresó de sus estúdios con luto de Alberto que había muerto de un balazo en un café,—no se supo quien fué. Despuésde ella no he sabido no salía mucho, me casé y ya vez, hasta ahora.

Pero tu dijiste que ella había muerto de hambre, no lo supe yo, pues la hubiese ayudado.

—En la mayor miseria.

—Estraño és, y cuanto no hubiera yo hecho por ella, de haberlo sabido, pobre Gizelda!

—¿Y porqué no trajiste al hijo para verlo?

—Porque yo no sabía si tu conocías á sus padres y creí sería inconveniente.

—Bien traelo cuando quieras.

—De modo que tu ayudarás su proyecto.

—Seguramente, en obsequio al recuerdo de aquella mujer.

—Oye Eliseo, tenía un corazón de oro, tan ¡bella, que la llamaban la "Divina" y sencilla.

—Pero te has olvidado que te dije que Jacinto se había enamorado de Alina del Prado, tu no comprendiste.

—¡Cáspita! no entendí lo que habías dicho, pues bien: son primos y el padre no podrá negarse.

—¿Tú crees?

—Sí, yo iré a hablar personalmente con él padre de Alina.

—Entonces Rafael, me marcho, ya vendré a comunicarte lo que el decida.

—Muy bien Eliseo, a tus órdenes.

—¡Hasta luego!

Don Eliseo salió agradablemente impresionado de saber, que su amigo podría ayudar a su protegido, y que podría complacerlo.

Entanto veamos si Jacinto fué a la cita del jardín. Lo encontramos pasando por frente de la verja, se decidió a empujarla y entrando sentose en el primer banco que vió. Y vemos a Alina que baja la escalera apresuradamente para saludar a Jacinto.

Se levanta Jacinto y recibió a su Alina con los brazos abiertos. Sentaronse y Alina le dijo:

—¿Fuiste ayer al paseo?

—Sí fuí y regresé muy triste, por no haberte visto.

—No pude ir, mamá necesitó llamarme estando fuera y sorprendida de no encontrarme se le ocurrió decirme ayer tarde antes de salir, si vas a salir avísame para ir contigo, yo le dije que no pensaba salir, y te escribí a tí para que vinieras hoy.

—¿Nada más?

—Nada más.

—Pues yo he conseguido que el Alcalde se ocupe de averiguar mis asuntos

—Jacinto mira mi padre, déjalo a ver que me dice.

Al llegar frente a Jacinto y Alina, Jacinto con el bastón hacía dibujos.

—Buenas tardes jóvenes, dijo el Conde, ¿con visitas en el jardín?

—Señor al pasar y ver a vuestra hija he querido saludarla: si es una imprudencia, me retiro.

—Papá dijo Alina, eso es muy natural.

Un criado interrumpió la conversación dicien-

do: Sr. Conde, ahí llegan el Sr. Marqués de la Villa
y el Sr. Alcalde.

—¿Pero aquí en el jardin?

—Sí señor, no quisieron esperar.

Todos miraron y en efecto a pocos pasos ya estaban. Se acercaron y dijeron perdonen que venimos a interrumpir tan bella reunión dijo el Marqués.

Entanto el Alcalde después de saludar a todos
en general se acercó a Jacinto y le dijo:

—Venimos aquí para ocuparnos de tu asunto.
Dice el Conde.

—Vdes. se conocían?

—Si señor replicó el Alcalde es mi protegido.

Y dirigiéndose al Marqués, Sr. permitame que
le presente al jóven Jacinto del Bosque.

—Tanto gusto Sr. dijo Jacinto estrechando
la mano del Marqués.

—Bien dijo el Alcalde, necesitamos al Conde,
si Vdes, no se molestan nos lo llevamos y le dejamos
a Jacinto.

—En lo que pueda ser útil, vamos.

—Con el permiso de Vdes. dijo el Marqués saludando con el sombrero.

Subieron los tres al salón y Jacinto acompañó
á las dos damas paseándose los tres por el jardin.

Asistamos a la entrevista del Marqués, el Alcalde y el Conde. Después de cada cual acomoda-
do, dijo el Alcalde.

—Señor Cónde, hemos venido aquí para aclar-
ar un asunto: ese jóven que dejamos abajo, está
bajo mi tutela, y el me ha referido la negativa de
Vd. respecto de vuestra hija, yo deseo saber que
motivos teneis.

—Amigo mío, únicamente le dije que deseaba
conocer su origen porque no conocía su apellido, y
en qué condiciones estaba para casarse.

—Pues el puede casarse en cuanto a posición,—
replicó el Alcalde, la tiene.—Además dijo el Marqués—yo conocí a su madre, y a su padre; y Vd.
conoce a su padre también, la madre fué una gran
artista, que cuando Vd. estaba en el colegio se la
llevó, antes de morir su mamá, Alberto del Prado.

—¡Mi hermano.!

—Justamente, y luego se fueron a París, si se
casaron allí no conozco la fecha, pero si puedo en-
señaros el retrato de ambos, y dirigiéndose al Alcalde le dijo: mostrad el medallón.

El Alcalde presentó el medallón que el Conde
tomó examinó y abrió lanzando una exclamación
de asombro, ¡Mi hermano, y una mujer!

Una distinguida dama de alto rango que se de
dicó al teatro por disgustos de familia dijo el Marqués.

—Ahora, dijo don Eliseo, debeis observar los
dos retratos por el reverso.

El Conde los sacó del medallón y los miró y
leyó lo escrito.

—De modo Sr. dijo don Eliseo, que ese jóven
se llama Alberto del Prado y por lo tanto os pido
la mano de vuestra hija para él.

—¿Con cual derecho le dais ese nombre?

—Conde dijo el Marqués no podeis negar que
es hijo de vuestro hermano.

—No lo dudo, pero no hizo testamento mi hermano y por tanto yo no puedo responderos en el
acto.

—¿Qué temeis?—dijo el Marqués.

—Estad seguro que si no exigis vos esto él no
se ocupa de eso, él no sabía que vuestra hija tenía
títulos ni que era rica profirió el Alcalde.

—Entonces es muy desinteresado.

—Es un modelo señor repitió don Eliseo.

Yo deseo ser el padrino de la boda, dijo el
Marqués.

—Agradezco el honor que haceis, a nuestra casa, pero bajemos al jardín, y allí acordaremos.

—Mejor es vuestro gusto enviad a llamarlos y lo haremos aquí, o en el salón.

—Muy bien replicó el Conde, tocando el timbre apareció un criado al que dijo que avisara a las señoras y al caballero que estaban en el jardín que subieran.

Habían pasado cinco minutos; cuando entraron en el salón. El Marqués se levanto y habló así: permitime señoras y caballeros que os presente al caballero Alberto del Prado, tomando á Jacinto.... de la mano que no creía lo que oía y el asombro de Alina que dijo, ¡mi primo!—¡sobrino! dijo la condesa, aceptando la mano que le tendía Alberto. Alina preguntó ¿qué habeis resuelto?—pues señorita respondió el Alcalde que os caseis, porque ambos os mereceis.—Gracias proferió Alberto, no esperaba tal solución.—Pues hijos míos dijo el Conde ídos los dos al jardin para que arregleis y decidais cuando os casais.—Salieron ambos sonreídos y las cuatro personas permanecieron hablando, sirvieron refrescos, y el Conde invitó á todos á comer. Me quedaré dijo el Marqués pero permitid que avise á mi mujer que no me espere, y se levantó para avisar por teléfono.

A la hora de sentarse en la mesa avisaron á Alina y Alberto para que subieran. ¿Qué habeis decidido? preguntó el Conde a los dos jóvenes. Que debemos efectuar nuestra unión pronto en este mes. Eso es dijo Alina, estoy de acuerdo.—La Condesa replicó es muy apresurado eso, y no teneis en cuenta las amistades ylas amonestaciones.—Bien ¿y cuando lo haremos? preguntó Alberto.—Dejadlo para el otro mes.—Ya hacen cerca de dos años que estamos enamorados y creo prudente terminar esta situación. Lo entendemos dijo el Conde pero olvidais, que tenemos que cumplir con algunos requisitos, abreviadlo si quereis, pero no os aparteis de ellos tan repentinamente.—Acepto y en este caso dejaré en vuestras manos el asunto.—Eso es dijo el Marqués, el séñor Conde tiene autoridad para hacerlo y lo hará bien.—Terminaron de comer y el Marqués y don Eliseo se despidieron, y Alina y Alberto se fueron al jardin en tanto el conde y la condesa pasaron al balcón. La condesa deseaba saber como era que habían resultado parientes. Muy sencillo dijo el Conde, mi hermano tuvo amores con una artista bonita y ahí tienes el hijo.—Entonces cuando haces las invitaciones?,—mañana contestó el Conde.

Los comentarios en las reuniones y asambleas y fiestas por la boda de Alina, fueron innumerables, ¿de donde, había salido ese novio y ese apresuración por la boda? Eso era faltar contra todo lo correcto y tradicional. Un jóven que llega y no se sabe quien es, desfila en brazos de él la niña y á los pocos días, matrimonio? ¡Qué descaro! decían algunas envidiosas y otras, ¡qué egoista, no lo dejó venir á nuestras fiestas, y le pedimos la dirección para invitarlo y nos dijo que no la conocía.

Entanto Alina se preparaba para su boda importándole las críticas de sus amigas que venían á verla. La noche de la boda llegó y el salón, y el jardín y el comedor estaban iluminados, y con tal profusión de flores que la atmósfera que se respiraba era deliciosa.

Todos estaban desesperados por ver á los novios: al fin los anunció el criado y pasaron al salón de recibo donde habían improvisado un pequeño juzgado, el juez esperaba, los testigos, el Marques de la Villa y el Alcalde, y la numerosa concurrencia que asistía. Alina y Alberto pasaron al salón á saludar a sus admiradores; ya estaban unidos. Y anunciaron que marchaban para Suiza y luego á París.

Toda la concurrencia pasó al comedor y luego

de haber hecho honor á la cena, se despidió. Alberto y Alina permanecieron hasta el final, en compañía de los padres y los testigos, que eran amigos más íntimos. A la una de la mañana se retiraron todos. Al siguiente día Alina y Alberto cruzaban la frontera en dirección a Suiza.

La madre de Alina y el padre decidieron salir á paseo por Venecia y Milán.

EPÍLOGO.

Un año después recibieron los condes noticias de que los jóvenes tenían una niña que le habían puesto Gizelda. Cinco años más tarde el Conde del Torreón había muerto dejando a sus hijos herederos de todo. La Condesa pasó á vivir con sus hijos y dos nietos, una niña Gizelda y un niño Alberto, en recuerdo de aquellos amantes que no conocieron.

Alberto había venido á recoger lo que por derecho le correspondía, y sin recurrir á medios groseros, era dueño de cuantiosos bienes, y además era feliz.

"Vigilante" había muerto en el hospital estando Alberto y Alina en París.

El Márques de la Villa ya era viejo y viudo y el hijo se casó.

El Alcalde paseaba con sus nietos todos los días por el bosque........

CARTAS INTERESANTES DE UN ACRATA DE PANAMÁ.

Mi muy querida hermana Luisa Capetillo.

Después de guardar un silencio de más de un año, hoy te mando una carta para saber de tí;No tengo el propósito de ser muy pesado, pues creo que nada ganamos con diátribas:

Dígame: recibió un retrato de Ferrer que le mandé en el mes de mayo; fué puesto en el correo certificado por mí con el nombre de Juan Chiet:

Con fecha de 28 de este mes dió la Exma. Sra. doña Emilia Serrano Baronesa de Wilson una conferencia en el gran teatro de Panamá, fué un fracaso pues los señores del dinero no les gusta la filosofía

Te mando el recorte del Diario

Contestame: ¿Oye? contestame.

Querida Luisa, tu carta en mi poder hoy, (que dicha la mía y la contesto sin pérdida de momento, no extrañes mi forzado silencio, cuando luchaba en la Zona por la propaganda de nuestras ideas, yo no suponía que el pueblo trabajador me sumiera en la deshonra, y fué así; Discutir con Perez,–jamás– yo reconocía el derecho de atacarme, pero no puedo tomar en cuenta la razon de un canalla.

Para mi vida, gano con mi negocio; cuando me criticaron dejé de ser explotado y me hice comerciante, y esto lo hubiera puesto en práctica mucho antes, pero sufría por propagar en el campo de los trabajadores: ¿Soy yo el canalla, el que sacrificaba mi tranquilidad por la de mis hermanos?

Dejemos esto, y tratemos de tu vida querida hermana mía, se que sufres mucho y que pasas mala vida, yo no tengo fortuna pero si te vienes a Colón de lo que gane comes y vistes como si fueras mi madre, yo no tengo más que una vida y la amo mucho, tu lo sabes; yo te estimo y te quiero como si fueras mi hermana, no pase trabajos yo soy fuerte y puedo ganar para los dos: No te digo más.

Oye, te mando á ''Romeo y Julieta'' soy romántico contigo.

Un abrazo y toma mis consejos.

———

Querida hermana Luisa Capetillo, si no te determinas á venir a ésta y tienes muchos folletos me mandas seis de cada uno, y yo los venderé sí puedo y sino te mandaré su importe a vuelta de un mes contando desde el día que obren en mi poder.

Yo quiero que vengas, pues en esta si no tienes otro medio de vida mejor que el que tienes, cuentas con mi trabajo que dará para los dos.

Tu no me conoces, pero yo soy un amigo que cumplo con lo que prometo.

No dejes de buscar los periódicos que te encargo, son de gran importancia para mí.

———

Querida hermana Luisa. Con fecha 20 de este mes llegaron a mi poder dos periódicos de la U-

nión de Tampa con dos valientes artículos tuyos,
como conozco tu labor en el campo de la lucha, no
dudo que tengas grandes contenedores que reprue-
ben tus trabajos en pró de la emancipación la de
mujer oprimida, los hombres de hoy no aman a la
mujer, aman la carne de Lupanar ó de explotación
para sus apetitos desenfrenados de lujuria.

La humanidad no púede gozar de la libertad
mientras no tenga la mujer libre; una mujer que entrega su cuerpo á los expasmos de un placer esclavo,
jamás dará hijos sanos y fuertes, los senos mater-
nos cuando se dilatan en el placer del coito bajo
la presión del dolor y el miedo que reina en el matrimonio de hoy no pueden congelar el fruto con toda
su libertad porque los músculos de la vida no gozan
de su dominio y expansión para las funciones maternas:

Si un hombre de finas facciones se pone en un
espejo cuando esta poseido de miedo, los músculos
de su cara estarán contraídos de tal manera que
sería difícil conocerlo, esto pasa con la mujer en sus
funciones maternas.

Lucha con valor en el campo de la libertad femenina, la mujer es la que dá la humanidad su vida y su orientación sin mujeres libres no puede el
hombre ser libre.

Sin más por hoy soy tu más cariñoso hermano,
que te quiere...............................

Querida hermana Luisa Capetillo. Tu carta
del 9, fué en mi poder, Gracias por tu puntualidad.
Lamento que mi carta anterior no fuera á tus manos, yo la mandé con fecha 15 certificada con el No.
2911, y contiene dentro una postal un poco román-
tica, pues en su contenido soy para tí muy cariñoso.

La lucha por tí sostenida en defensa de la mujer es grande y te trae gran número de enemigos,
que te darán tus amarguras, si tu en Tampa
hubieras puesto una cantina con muchas **Guapas**
los burgueses fueran tus amigos y los canallas cra-
pulosos te saludarían con amor. Las almas grandes
no buscan el aplauso de la canalla, cuando la crápu-
la Burguesa aplaude á un luchador es para prosti-
uir la santidad de su obra, en luchador es un incom-
prendido, la humanidad cuando no comprende á el
Cristo lo escupe, lo corona de espinas lo viste de pa-
llazo y lo crucifica; cada aplauso de un canalla tiene una gota de cicuta para el Sócrates de la lucha,
son las obrasracines los que expanden en la vida los
títulos, de Muy Grande, Muy Noble Sr.

Cuando el mundo tomó la doctrina de Cristo
fué tan prostituída, que más que el Drama del Gól-
gota, es la comedia de la mofa, huye del vulgo con
tu grandeza y serás grande, en todo dolor está la
gloria del amor y de lucha, la lucha redime á las almas grandes.

¿Cuanto martirio sufres con tus amarguras?—
le preguntó un Rey a Diógenes: "Señor dijo el sabio: mi ropa remendada y mi tonel son fuentes de
esperanzas para mir einado". Cuando tu no puedas
con más dolor en tu corazón, busca el manto de tu
sabiduría y serás reina entre tus verdugos.

Lucha y ama, la lucha, es la vida, el amor es la
esencia de la lucha sin lucha y sin amor la vida fuera un dolor; y cuando tus verdugos estén más en-
diosados en su triunfo les das con tu propaganda la
libertad á sus mujeres y tendrás el consuelo de glori-
ficar lo más santo de la creación, a la mujer redi-
mida de la explotación del hombre prostituído.

Tu hermano que te quiere:

(Oye) mandame si puedes unos folletos de los
tuyos, tengo ganas de conocer tu obra de hoy.

Mi querida hermana Luisa Capetillo.

Cuanto estimo tu carta fecha 27 abril pasado en los dias de soledad y abandono que tengo pasados en mi cama postrado con la fiebre. solo tu y mi madre han tenido para mi un recuerdo: Gracias querida hermana.

La carta tuya fecha 9 de abril llegó el día 15 del mismo y ya me encontraba enfermo, es por lo que esperaba y espero que las fiebres me dejen, para poder luchar en la prensa condenando la brutalidades de tus enemigos gratuitos, Si en Tampa lo pasas mal estimaría qué te vinieras a Colón, con lo que yo gano con mi trabajo puedes comer y vestir hasta que la suerte cambie, yo te estimo en lo que tu vales y supongo que tu no mereces sufrir el desprecio de la burguesía y el canalla abandono de la Gleva prostituída.

Cada día tengo más odio y más desprecio por la masa del pueblo encanallado, son siempre los mismos al través de la Historia. Crucificando á Cristo, dando á Sócrates la cicuta, quemando a Galileo, despreciando a Diógenes, y cortando las cabezas de todos los que descuellan del montón de carne sin ojos que compone el pueblo prostituto.

La ley del humano progreso es tan fatal para los propagadores que solo un espíritu suicida ó un auto-visión de la gloria, puede llevar a las almas nobles y los espíritus exquisito á propagar la libertad, cuando el mundo gana en su perfeccionamiento moral y material, el propagandista pierde su razón y su cerebro, y es lamentable la ley de las compensaciones, pues el que da su alma y su vida en lucha humana, después de perder todos sus atributos y todas sus facultades muere cargado de dolor y de desengaños en el rincón del desprecio público.

Las llamas de los grandes ideales de justicia y redención quema las alas de los Cóndores del pensamiento y cuando no puede traspasar el espacio

con su raúdo vuelo cae al pantano social donde
el escarnio de las zapos destroza las fibras del alma
luminosa, para vengarse de las diferencias que Natura pródiga á sus hijas más queridas.

Querida hermana dispensame que no pueda es-
cribirte ni más, ni mejor, tengo la cabeza muy mala y el pulso muy débil, cuando mejore empe-
zaré mis cartas con largueza: cuando no puedas luchar en Tampa, cuenta que tu hermano esta en Colón y tiene para tí la mitad de lo que gañe con su
trabajo.

Querida hermana Luisa Capetillo.

Desde mi pasada carta, tengo en mi alma el
fantasma del remordimiento: Yo escucho la conciencia que me grita: ¡Desgraciado! el que no puede dar la dicha, no quita la ajena! Cuando un
hombre ama la soledad y el silencio, no busca fuera de su yo el mundo, por que el mundo esta en el
interior de cada uno, y solo en el mundo interior ni
se puede ser traicionado, ni se puede traicionar uno
mismo ¿para que pregonar el dolor en una sociedad de cobardes?, la vida sin su dolor, no es vida, y
el que no puede soportar su dolor, ya puede mar-,
char con paso firme hacia la muerte; es la hora suprema en que el hombre es más grande que Dios.

Cuando un hombre se empeña en buscar la felicidad, tiene que llorar , como un niño que busca
en el vientre de sus muñecas el organismo mecánico de los movimientos ¡Ay! cada muñeca esta cons
truída para un funcionamiento; cada empeño en
buscar la felicidad está impreso por un mecánico
y este mecanismo es la barra de el mecánico estam-
pada en la acción de todo lo creado.

Cuando recuerdo el dolor de mi desengaño amoroso, soymuy desgraciado: ¿por qué? ¡yo amé á Dios
sobre todas las cosas, y el día q. supe q. Dios soy yo,

me dió mucha pena; tanta como la del esclavo de
Elos que se dejó comer de las ratas por no dejar de
ser esclavo; luego amé mucho á los hombres, ylos
encontre esclavos de sus pasiones y luché por la libertad de las oprimidos; y !Ay! dolor, soy traicionado por mis hermanos y comprendí, que cada
uno de los explotados quería explotar mi buena fé, y
me dió miedo tanta cobardía; y amé la mujer: dentro del corazón de la mujer no hay amor, la mujer
ama al que la esclaviza y desprecia al enamorado;
busqué á la hembra como macho y solo dió el fruto
de reproducción y con tanta amargura y con tanto
dolor en el alma, me cargué de desengaños y amé la
soledad.

¿Qué es la soledad?, la más grande representación de la libertad humana, porque en la soledad
ni se puede ser traicionado ni se puede ser traidor:
tu me dirás que para amar la soledad es uno inco-
municativo, no, en la soledad si uno no sabe estar
en ella, le daba miedo, como el que entra por primera vez en un palacio lo admira contemplativa-
mente, pero sí da una grito le da miedo del eco de
su propia voz; y yo cuando entré en la soledad di
muchos gritos de dolor, y no me dió miedo del eco
de mi voz; y con toda la amargura de un niño y la
experiencia de un solitario busqué comunicación
para mi dolor, te busqué á tí, que estas sola en la
cúspide de la amargura, cargada con el dolor de tu
alma y luchando con el desengaño humano.

¿Tú, con estas comunicaciones, quizás com-
prendas que yo soy un fracasado; no, el fracaso esta en no saber vivir la soledad el que busca en su
alma un trono y en su entendimiento un arte, y en
su corazón un escudo, y en su vida una libertad po-
sitiva, y en su dolor un libro; éste no esta fracasado es él, el que hizo fracasar todos los Dioses, todos los perjuicios, todos los falsos ideales, todas las
religiones y todos los falsos amores, para entrar

por su propia voluntad en el reino de la soledad y de la meditación.

El fracaso esta en buscar la comunicación de su alma, y mi alma no es, no puede ser comunicativa.

¿Díme estas molesta por mi carta pasada, no comprendo tu silencio, estoy tan encariñado con tus cartas?

Pronto te mandaré unas postales y unos planos del Canal.

———————

Querida hermana Luisa Capetillo.

Sin ninguna tuya á que poderme referir te mando esta carta. Si me preguntara á mi mismo que porque te escribo, no podría contestar mi pregúnta con toda sastisfacción: Pero si te digo que tengo en mi alma un presentimiento, y este me trae una amargura grande. Comprendo que mi carta confidencia jamás te la debía de mandar, porque tu ni yo somos responsables de que mi alma no esté forjada para mi materia, yo tengo un alma que por su grandeza no cabe en la materia de un triste solitario cargado de desengaños traidores, y como estamos distanciados mi alma y yo de el punto de partida, llegan momentos en que las penas mías tienen que buscar un campo donde expandir su dolor. En este momento supremo, fué que te mandé mi carta, porque la presión de mi amargura tenía 95° grados de atmósfera, y sentía que la cabeza flaqueaba, y que la locura moral reinaba en mí. ¿Qué te decía en mi carta?........Un amor grande que fué traicionado por una ilusión. Una ilusión que muere en el alma cuando ya está el alma muerta de dolor. Un dolor que no cabiendo en mi pecho, estalla en miriadas de átomos y empaña con sus emanaciones todo el mundo interior de mi querida hermana; esta és mí carta; carta de amar-

gura, donde las muertas ilusiones, son la realidad
de una vida que ama y amará, hasta que el
dolor maté la materia y maté el sentir y el pensar.
¡Ah! los que aman y son amados! En la vida solo el Dolor es positivo y el amor una locura en
sí; con mi confidencia hubiera puesto fin á mi amargura, hoy estaría tranquilo pero.... ¡Ay! yo sigo en
puesto del tormento, y tu has tomado parte en mi
dolor para amargar tu alma, sin que la puedas dar
consuelo á mi amargura!

Contestame dime que no estas molesta conmigo, no me odies, y confía en el cariño de tu hermano que te quiere.

Hermana de mi alma.

Tengo en mi corazón una gran amargura: mi
carta última, carta que te mandé y que después me
duele, porque yo hoy comprendo mi poca prudencia y supongo que con mi carta tan **mística** y tan
poco meditada solo conseguí un fin contraproducen-
te, pues como que tu alma, y tu sentimiento como
mujer y como madre están inundados de esta enfermedad materialista que trae conturbado mi entendimiento: ¿Qué puedes tu hacer en mi obsequio para distraer mi dolor? Mi amor desgraciado me trae tan desorientado que hoy no soy ni mi
sombra, toda mi alma tan pura y tan ingenua como
la de un niño, esta tan destrozada y tan rendida de
fatiga que solo con mi fuerza de voluntad puedo
consolar la vida, jamás pude suponer que un amor
sería tan fuerte, que pudiera causar un dolor profundo capaz de causar la muerte.

¿Cómo comprender, que el amor fuente de toda vida humana fuera la fuente de la muerte? Toda mi vida tuve una gran prudencia para el amor,
comprendía que amar á una mujer en la sociedad

presente me traería grandes trastornos, un hombre
que ama la libertad y el arte en la más grandiosa
manifestación de la vida, sin fingimientos ni cobar-
días, jamás encontrará una compañera que dé al
amor su pecho con la natural franqueza de sus sentimientos altruistas.   Es para el comercio del amor
y de la carne, que la mujer esta educada, no para el
amor y la belleza del amor y de la vida.
    Con esta deducción y con esta comprensión de
mi alma y del alma humana en general, voy so-
ñando una vida de amor platónico y como éste a-
mor no tenía en mí una manera de esteriorizarse
fué invadiendo á mi alma una melancolía tan profunda que tuve momentos de soñar con la renun-
ciación de mi yo; en esta época (1910) te comuniqué estas penas de mi alma, y comprendiendo en tí
un gusto artístico de primer orden y una educación
poco común, y un alma superior, puse en tus manos
mi educación y mi alma para que como artísta y
como mujer educada, modelaras mi alma de niño
y mi espíritu de hombre soñador.
    Recuerdo que en una carta me decías con toda
tu ingenuidad que amara á una mujer que buscara
una compañera. ¡Ay!—amar á una mujer es fácil, buscar una compañera es imposible, la mujer
en el amor, es la carne en todas sus atributos, y la
compañera es en la vida, la esposa del **cantar de
los cantares**.   Con toda la fuerza de mi buena voluntad, pretendí armonizar estas dos tendencias
humanas y divinas y busqué los libros, y amé la vida, y busqué la mujer.   En una carta tulla fué para mi la solución de el gran problema: Decías en
tu carta: ''Cuando llegó la tuya salía de una fábrica con el corazón dolorido y el alma destrozada
por todos los grandes dolores de mi vida de amargura.   El doctor me llevó a un Café y me invitó
a bombones y limonada''.
    Este misterio de mi vida triste y solitaria, fué

desterrado de lleno de mi alma. el cuadro de poesía que me pintabas en esta carta fué para mi la clave de un misterio de todo lo misterioso: y amé y amé con toda mi alma porque mi alma estaba enferma de sed de amores. ¿Más. como armonizar estas tendencias tan diametralmente opuestas? por un esfuerzo supremo de mi auto-visión. que matando en mí, toda la parte pura y poetica de mi amor supra-humano pude encontrar una mujer que buscaba con la luz pura de todas mis que ilusiones, fuera tan perfecta, como perfecta era mi amor. Estos mirajes misteriosos fueron tomados de tu vida. Yo me dije: ¡Mi hermana sufré; y en su dolor busca el lenitivo de la vida en la vida misma... No ama; pero la vida es sueño y sueña con el amor: **ilusión del alma** y con el sueño de la vida dialogando con el dolor y con la filosofía goza la más pura esencia de el amor—El dolor............

Fué de este modo que amé; amé con toda la pasión de mi alma: maté el dolor hijo lejítimo de mi alma apasionada y entregué mi corazón a Priori con toda la franqueza de mi alma cándida.

Por esto sufro, por esto lloro; y no dudo que soy amado, la sombra del traidor se puso en mi camino y mató la Gloria de mi amor.

Dispensame estas cartas tan poco agradables.

Querida hermana Luisa.

Tu carta del 18 de agosto obra en mi poder, y no sabes cuanto te agradezco el que tómes tanto empeño en mi dolor; La mujer que amo tanto, esta en Colón, tengo de amores con ella un año; al principio de conocerla tenía miedo de ella dado su temperamento y educación, y solo me limita a ser su amigo y á frecuentar su casa en visita, en estas visitas frecuentes y corteses, exploré su alma y siempre confirmé mi opinión pesimista, opinión sustancial y definida. De que mi adorada estaba tan viciada por los principios educacionistas de este país que mi amor era punto menos que una locura.

Comprendía dentro de mi fuero interno que yo la amaba, pero ponía mi voluntad á mi amor y luché contra mi propio sentir. Este es el epílogo de este Drama tan violento que pudo tener consecuencias fatales.

En el mes de junio del 1912 caí con fiebre en cama, yo vivo solo en mi cuarto y muy distante de su casa, preguntaron por mí á mis conocidos y supieron mi enfermedad y vinieron á mi casa con suma frecuencia y me mandaron medicamentos y me cuidaron como familia.

Con esta manera de obrar, tomé un gran afecto á la familia y después llegué á amar con pasión. ¿Qué es el amor sino un agradecimiento? de esta manera transcurrió un año, no niego que en el año de amores tuve momentos de íntima felicidad y que todo el frío de mi alma para con mi amada se fué trocando en un fuego que consumía mi existencia, este fuego fué en muchas ocasiones causa de grandes trastornos en mi organismo, pues tenía en mi alma una necesidad de amar muy grande, y dado el impetu de mi amor buscaba en mi amada la fuente de el consuelo para mitigar mi sed.

Mujer metalizada y dispuesta á vender su amor y sus favores jamás atendió a una súplica mía, y me propuso como condición definitiva el contrato matrimonial esclesiástico, como la amaba con toda mi alma capitulé á medias y la prometí el matrimonio civil. Jamás—me dijo con un desenfado propio de una mujer empedernida, y está fué la causa de mi rompimiento. ¿Qué puedo yo expirar de una compañera que para darme su amor se transfigura en una Dalila? Un amor que se ofrece cubierto en tanta exigencia, y tan pensado como el de mi amada no puede ser amor, el amor no puede estar pendiente de un cálculo matemático como el libro de caja de un comercio. Mi alma, rebelde á toda especulación no puede transigir con estas mujeres tan metódicas que dan un beso de amor (fingiendo) para proponer un contrato social estipulado en una Vicaria con papel de oficio. Esta es la razón de mi desgracia.

¿Cuanto tiempo tardé en descubrir la traición?

¿Por qué no estudié esta mujer antes de tener amor con ella? Cuando nos pusimos en amores yo dudaba, pero hoy me cuenta una desgracia de familia, mañana una enfermedad que mina su organismo después una amargura que destroza su alma otro día la sorprendo con lágrimas en los ojos, mas tarde conjura amor junto a la tumba de su hermana, y con todas estas manifestaciones de un Dolòr supuesto ó fingido llegué á depositar todo mi amor en su amor, como si lo hubiera puesto en mi misma madre, tanto fué mi amor por esta mujer, que sí no descubro su traición hoy hubiera puesto á sus pies hasta mis creencias, pues estaba dispuesto á casarme canonicamente.

No me critiques hermana mía, un hombre que no tenga corazón pará sufrir con el ajeno dolor esta perdido para la causa de la libertad, y yo tengo dentro de mi alma un lugar muy puro, donde se guardan todos los dolores hermana. Si un hombre me cuenta su vida, vida llena de amarguras y de dolor, lo escucho por cortesía, pero si una mujer me cuenta sus sufrimientos con los ojos llenos de lágrimas y sus brazos rodeando mi cuello y su pecho descansa en mi pecho, yo no tengo corazón para defenderme, si no que le ofrezco todo lo que soy y valgo. Yo tengo una Madre.

A mi no me duele el que no sea mía, yo no amo la materia, lo que me duele es que hoy después de

dar todo mi amor a mi tranquilidad esta mujer goza con mi dolor y mi amargura.

———————   ———

Querida hermana Luisa.

Tu carta 25 de agosto pasado fué en mi poder;
Sabes que lamento en el alma que tomes mi carta
pasada tan fuera de el lugar en que yo la coloqué; yo
no puede negar ˜que tu has comprendido mal mi
carta.

Cuando yo te mandé esa carta tenía un dolor
muy grande. Mi alma de niño, estaba tan amar-
gada, que las visiones más tétricas se engendraban
manchadas de sangre y hiel, con esta manera de
pensar y obrar no dudo que mi carta contenga ex-
presiones poco meditadas; pero en el fondo de mi
carta lejos de buscar una discusión que yo no puedo
sostener, buscaba un consejo sano y prudente uno
tuyo. Comprendo que yo no tengo derecho para
contar mis penas y mis dolores, pero un hombre que
ama mucho sufre mucho, y yo amo tanto y sufro
tanto, que tengo momentos en que me faltan las
fuerzas y el valor para luchar, y en esta diyuntiva
me encontraba cuando te mandé la carta que tanto
te ha molestado.

Me gusta el dolor: amo el dolor, el dolor es tan
necesario como la luz del día, pero soy hombre que
tengo debilidades y flaquezas ó cuando el golpe es
muy rudo no puedo soportarlo; esta debilidad mía
me puso en el caso de confiar en tí mis penas, sin
método, cálculo ni preparación, grandes y
puras cual mi alma las sentía; comprendo que en
el dolor y en las penas prueba uno la grandeza de
su alma y la fuerza de su carácter; pero yo tengo ra-
tos de suprema amargura que supongo que la fuerza de resistencia llega á el máximo de lo posible y

en este caso me encontraba cuando te mandé la carta.

Después de todo tu estás en tu derecho de protestar mi carta, porque la tranquilidad y la dicha de cada uno es su patrimonio exclusivo, y si uno no puede aumentar el patrimonio ó la dicha de los demás, no está en el derecho de disminuirlas, y siendo el derecho de cada uno el primero en el disfrutar de sus dones ó propiedades. ¿Qué derecho tengo yo para amargar tu alma con mis dolores o amargura? en la lucha por la vida cada uno está en el derecho de afianzar su propia tranquilidad y bienestar; y comprendo que el amor es una enfermedad de las que Finon declara en su biología, y comprendo más. ¡Dentro de la lucha procuramos prácticar el principio del más fuerte con toda regularidad por esto el agricultor poda con su brazo las ramas estériles, y cada uno por ley.de conservación matamos los insectos dañinos que encontramos y después con muy buen acuerdo despreciamos á los que no concuerdan con nosotros ó están gastados por sus dolores. Repito que esto es lógico y natural. Digamos lo que nos dé la gana, siempre practicamos estos principios.

¿Cómo puedo negar yo el amor en la mujer? yo conozco la historia de Dalila, de Julieta, de la dama de Las Camelias, de María, de Dora, y la de mi Madre que supera á todos los romanticismos de la historia antigua y moderna, pero esto no es obstáculo para que yo tenga mi alma destrozada por una mujer que la amo más que á mi vida, y que ella me ama, y no podamos estar unidos, nada más que en el dolor que mata nuestras almas; y este es el punto de discusión que podemos buscar en mi carta pasada. Retoca la lectura de mi carta; mira mis ideas emitidas de otro modo más claro, y comprenderás q. mi carta es el reflejo fiel de mi alma q. solo mira su dolor, sin estudiar la causa ni su remedio. Repito que yo no tengo derecho á perturbar tu tranquilidad, pero de esto á que mi carta esté sujeta á un cálculo ó a meditada exposición, hay un mundo de contradicción. Te conté mis penas y mis amarguras porque suponía que tenía derecho á tu consuelo,—y lo tengo—más que tu me lo niegues: ¿Pues que, tu no me has dado implícitamente este derecho con tus consejos de madre cariñosa?

Cada día tengo más dominio sobre mí. El dolor de mi alma está sometido á un estudio profundo, cada día lo amo más (el dolor), pues saco de su fondo un manantial de conocimientos profundos que de otro modo me hubiera sido imposible adquirir, lo que suponía un mundo de amargura es una fuente de placer y de filosofía, lo que pudo ser un suicidio; hoy es la mayor ventura de mi alma, pero de esto á que yo busqué la hembra que no sea Madre. Yo no niego la ley de reproducción, la especie me daría un mentiz solemne en su crecimiento; lo que te digo es justo, mi carta no fué dictada con juicio, salió sin orden ni concierto, como salen las ideas de una frente calenturienta.

Si dudas, busca en tu alma el lugar de la amargura, y el día más desgraciado de tu vida en tus notas ó memorias, y dime con claridad: ¿obrastes en juicio?, ¿tenías dominio de tí? ¿no negastes la fuente de toda razón? no ¿dudastes de la vida? ¿no despreciastes la humanidad? ¿no odiates el mundo?... Hermana mía, para conocer nuestro corazón es menester más ciencia que para conocer el de los demás.. Para perdonar un agravio es menester más valor que para cometer un crimen; y es más oscuro y trabajoso comprender el alma nuestra que la de nuestros hermanos.

Querida hermana Luisa:

Ya me encuentro muy mejorado de mi catarro

tengo más fuerzas y descanso con más tranquilidad, desde el pasado mes como el día 10 estoy en cama y hoy cuento con un poco de más valor y salud.

Cuando tenga más tranquilidad te contestaré á unas cartas tuyas que no están contestadas, tengo en la mano una carta del mes pasado que te la debí mandar y quedó encima de la mesa por falta de quien la llevara al correo. En la noche del día 1 a 2 tuvimos un gran temblor de tierra, las trepidaciones fueron de mucha intensidad y de gran duración, pronto te daré detalles completos.

Tu hermano...........

Querida hermana Luisa:

Tu retrato obra en mi poder, no dejo de comprender que cometí una falta de prudencia al no darte cuenta de su llegada, pero mi vida y mi alma estaban tan conturbadas, que no tenía ánimo para nada, solo tenía como una visión tétrica y sangrienta la fuerza de mi dolor.

Hoy la luz meridiana de la razón á tomado fuerza trasmisiva y puede con su fuerza luminosa desterrar la lobreguez de mi alma.

En el retrato estas muy bien, y te encuentro en la mirada una cosa que no comprendo, no se sí buscas los límites inciertos de la tierra ó si buscas el espacio, ó sí exploras el campo de una nueva filosofía que está en tu mente en estado de gestación. ¿Es tan dura tu mirada. ¿Dígame: ¿con el conjunto de rocas y el siervo crepitando en ellas, que buscas? estos cuadros que son Aguas Fuertes de Goya, yo no los comprendo. Lo demás lo comprendo todo, pero yo no tengo gran fuerza imaginativa para comprender en un cuadro como el de tu retrato todo lo que el arte expresa.

Cuando un alma sueña, y despierta, todas

las conjeturas ó hipótesis son nulas en su emi-
ción, yo no puedo emitir, y no emito mi opinión en
un cuadro que no puedo comprender hoy.

Cuando conozca tu alma y tenga lugar de pensar con más dominio te daré mi opinión definitiva
en el retrato que tengo en mi poder, hoy solo te digo que te doy un millón de gracias por tu obsequio
y que tengo en mi corazón un gran afecto por tí.

Como mi carta consta de muchas cuartillas no
quiero molestar más tu atención, solo te suplico
una gracia especial para mí, por tener la poca dig
nidad de no poder dominar mi dolor y darte el disgusto de todas mis desventuras, confío en tu benevolencia y creo que en tu alma no me guardes rencor por esta franqueza estúpida, y por este amor
salvaje que pudo cortar el hilo de mi vida.

Mi querida hermana.

Cuando salía del correo de poner dos cartas para tí, una de fecha pasada y otra de hoy me dieron
tu deseada carta 26 de septiembre pasado.

En estos días y muy á mi pesar no te he podido mandar cartas ni nada, sufría de un catarro fuerte, y en este clima el catarro es más malo que el pa-
ludismo.

Ya más repuesto de todos mis sufrimientos, (fí-
sico y moral)) tengo ganas de luchar y fuerzas para
la lucha, pues en mi vida pasada no guardo memoria de mi tiempo tan desgraciado y tan cruel para
mi, parece que todas las desgracias se dieran cita
en un día determinado para caer sobre mí como si
yo no tuviera en el mundo ningún fin de justicia ni
ninguna causa de derecho, ni ningún fin de razón
que defender y por quien luchar en el campo de la
vida justipreciando el mérito de toda exposición
social.

Cuando una enfermedad ó desgracia toma posición de una naturaleza, la gran fuerza vital y la despreocupación desaparecen en el individuo y este apocamiento y esta desconfianza que se apodera del cuerpo son los conductores más seguros de una derrota en las luchas por la vida, tengo observado que el triunfo de las cosas que ganamos en una lucha ruda y constante, no está en la mayor ó menor resistencia que ofrecen las cosas mismas si no que está en la fé que uno tiene dentro de su pecho para asegurar su dominio lo que desea para su comodidad ó expansión, toda las cosas están en la categoría de lo posible, el imposible está dentro de nuestra cobardía.

Traigo desde cuatro meses á esta fecha una serie de fracasos que son los que me traen desconcertado de tal manera que no doy un paso con fundamento, cada día saco cuentas nuevas y cálculos definidos, y cada día tengo nuevos fracasos y nuevas contrariedades, este estado tan lastimoso y tan contrario me puso á pensar sobre mi situación y saqué en consecuencia que toda victoria ó todo fracaso está fundamentado dentro de mí mismo, y que cada desilución de mi alma es el producto corriente de una cobardía grande que es la dueña y señora de un alma pequeña.

La casualidad, con este mote tan extraño buscan los tontos y los cobardes la justificación de su propia cobardía, yo tengo otro miraje para mis análisis interiores; no puedo comprender y no comprendo, que si yo tropiezo con una piedra en la calle y caígo y me rompa una pierna, estas cosas están sujetas á meras casualidades; cada cuerpo esta doctado de una fuerza de resistencia propia, y en su marcha evolutiva hacia la finalidad póstuma, todo lo que se pone en su camino es derrotado si es más débil y sí es más fuerte derrota á su contrario, (lucha por la vida), y sentado este principio justo en su fondo y exacto en su forma, yo comprendo que todas mis derrotas están dentro de mí, y que yo soy el que no tengo fé ni fuerza para luchar en mi propio beneficio.

Con tan extraña vida y tan lastimoso estado tengo que luchar para que desaparezcan de lo contrario por ley de evolución dejaría yo de existir; y esto no me gustaria, porque me parece muy poco practico.

Al ilustre letrado y distinguido amigo, Don Herminio Díaz Navarro.

La Corrupción de los Ricos y la de los Pobres

ó

COMO SE PROSTITUYE UNA RICA Y UNA POBRE.

DRAMA SOCIAL EN UN ACTO Y CUATRO CUADROS.

PERSONAJES.

Marina—jóven de 18 años.
Roberto—novio de **Marina.**
Don **Pascual**—(banquero).
Don **Filiberto**—Marqués de Azuria.

Salón elegante—, una mesita con un florero.

Marina—(Entrando con dos estuches de joyas en la mano, que coloca sobre la mesa, siéntase).

Por fin se consumará el sacrificio ésta noche, seré Marquesa de Azuria, y haré rabiar a las hijas de la Duquesa que siempre tratan de herirme con sus títulos.

Yo no amo a ese hombre, pero mi padre me ha deslumbrado con miles ofrecimientos y por fin me decidiré.

Estaba indecisa por Roberto, pero ya se acostumbrará. ¡Pobre Roberto! como se molestará con mi determinación.

Roberto—(Se asoma y viendo a la joven sola, se decide a entrar). ¡Alma mía! por fin vuelvo a verte!

Marina—¡Cómo has podido entrar? no te han visto? (tomándoles las manos).

Roberto—No te preocupes, tu padre rabiará, y luego se calmará. Pero dime cuentame, si has pensado en mí?

Marina—En verdad que has estado ausente algún tiempo ¿qué hacías?

Roberto—En negocios de la casa, comprando en París en Alemania, en Barcelona, no he tenido tiempo para divertirme un día.

Marina—Supongo que mi padre te habrá comunicado la noticia?

Roberto—¿De qué se trata?

Marina—De mi boda, esta noche me caso.

Roberto—¡ Marina!........miserable! para eso me envió al extranjero, ¡y tu también, tu consientes ésta farsa? cobarde eres, é hipócrita!........para eso, sí, apresuró mi marcha para que no me vieras, y poder empujarte a ese abismo de interés, y no te defendiera, para burlarse de mí, y tu lo toleras todo por un título vil......................

Marina—¡Calla! que me ofendes! y además es mi padre, y debo obedecer.

Roberto—¿Qué calle? ¿que es tu padre? y por eso tiene derecho de venderte, pero tú no lo comprendes?, que es la venta de tu cuerpo por un título, y ese es una vileza, una infamia, que realizan con ese hombre; una burla conmigo. ¡Canallas!........

Marina—¡Silencio! que oirán y si yo te soporso, no lo harán de igual modo los demás, te amo y seré tuya pero las circunstancias que me han rodeado me han obligado a proceder de este modo.

Roberto—Y para eso me has dicho tantas veces en el jardín que me amabas, allí debajo de los naranjos en flor que perfumaba el ambiente con sus azahares por entre los cuales se deslizaban los rayos de la Luna, haciendome soñar en un mundo ideal, en una felicidad nunca interrumpida. ¡Ah! sarcasmo del destino, pero que ridiculo soy en creerte, no, yo debo olvidarte! cruel, perjura, me alejaré y te maldeciré has destrozado mis ilusiones, entre ese viejo y tú, me voy; no volveré a verte.

Marina—(Lo retiene). No, si te vas negando mi amor, me envenenaré y mi muerte, será un recuerdo muy triste y doloroso para tí, (lo atrae hasta sentarlo en el sofá con ella) ven mi vida, si soy tuya, si mi alma y mis pensamientos son tuyos (lo acaricia arreglándole el cabello) pasándole la mano por la frente con una sonrisa triunfadora).

Roberto—No puedo resistir a tus palabras, me subyugas, (levantándose) ésta mujer me volverá loco, de ningún modo, yo no debo consentir esta comedia tan infame, si no amas a ese hombre porqué te vas a unir a él, nó! ó él ó yo...............

Marina—Ya apareció el amo, que ordena, me casaré y te amaré a ti, eres mi alma, mi vida...........

Roberto—¡No juegues de ese modo! ¡Marina! no abuses de mi bondad, mi paciencia estallará, ó ireis todos á pasarlo mal! te denunciaré a tí y a tu padre!

Marina—No, tu no harás eso, tu me amas, no es verdad?

Roberto—Pero no comprendes que me trastornas que me irrita que si me lo preguntas otra vez, para demostrartelo seré capaz de matar a tu padre al marqués y de ahogarte á tí entre mis brazos........

Marina—¡Silencio!........he oido ruído en la galeria, vete y vuelve, a las doce te espero.

Roberto—Has dicho que me vaya, no me importa que llegue alguien, si fuese tu padre le arrojaría al rostro su proceder, su bajeza y me dices ¿qué vuelva? á qué?

Marina—Te lo diré, te esperaré en el jardin.

Roberto—Volveré si, pero esta noche resuelves, tu decisión y mi suerte hasta la noche.

SEGUNDA ESCENA.

D. Pascual—Buenas tardes hija mía, aquí tei-nes mi regalo de boda, (entrégale un pliego) una hermosa finca que pertenecía a tu madre.

Marina—Gracias.

Filiberto—A los pies de Vd. señorita, alégrame infinito encontrar a Vdes.

Marina—Beso a Vd. la mano, os invito a ver los regalos de boda, venid.

Filiberto—Con mucho gusto.

Marina—Venid padre mío.

D. Pascual—Vamos hija mía.

TERCERA ESCENA.

Un jardin que da a la calle, una escalinata que comunica con el jardin y la casa de Marina.

Roberto—(Envuelto en su capa, abre la verja, y sientase, aparece Marina cubierta con un velo, bajando la escalera).

Roberto—(Tomándola de la mano). Aquí estoy para que me querías?

Marina—Pero has podido suponer que yo me casaría no si todo era una farsa.

Roberto—Entonces que vas á hacer, cuales son tus proyectos?

Marina—Huir contigo, con mi herencia, he ido anoche donde mi abogado, á quien mi madre recomendó antes de morir y le comuniqué mi propósito, me ha entregado mi herencia y además traigo la escritura de una finca de mi madre, que me entregó mi padre ayer, de modo que si estás de acuerdo marchamos.

Roberto—El automóvil espera, pues mi intención era en caso de que resistieras, llevarte, en mis brazos........(se abrazan y salen) no estaba dispuesto a esperar más.

CUARTA ESCENA.

Comentarios en un café. Varios sentados frente a las mesas de un café.

Uno—(que llega). No sabeis el drama o comedia de anoche, pues muy sencillo, un banquero quiere casar a su hija con un marqués arruinado, la hija acepta la proposición pero ella ama a otro, ó la noche de la boda, cuando todo está preparado, ella recoge su herencia, y huye con su novio dejando a todos esperando.

Otro—Muy bien, por las mujeres valientes!

Uno—Eso es para que los padres no hagan cálculos comerciales con las hijas, eso es una corrupción casar sin amor a dos.

TELÓN.

MATRIMONIO SIN AMOR, CONSECUENCIA, EL ADULTERIO.

PERSONAJES.

ESMERALDA————————
RICARDO --—————————
EDUARDO-————————
UN CRIADO-————————

Esmeralda—(Joven casada con un rico comerciante, al levantar el telón aparece sentada bordando, con calma).

No se lo que me pasa, pero algo me sucede hace un año que estoy casada, poseo cuanto puede imaginar una imaginación artística como la mía, un temperamento soñador, no tengo hijos esto quizás me haga falta, pero lo demás me sobra, criados automóvil, dinero, diverciones, viajes, hace un mes que llegué de Barcelona, estuve en París, visité a

Londres, sus calles sombrías me entristecían, y sa--
limos pronto de allí, pasamos por Italia, encantador
país, soñé en los lagos de Venecia, admiré a Milán y
observé a Génova y Nápoles.

Nada, tengo el alma enferma, me falta amor
yo creo que no se lo que es amor, pues me casé por
salvar a mi padre de un grave empeño, y aquí me
teneis, triste, pero yo necesito distraerme, marcho
a las tiendas, a comtemplar la última moda de París.

2°, ESCENA.

Esmeralda—(En elegante traje que va á las
tiendas.

Eduardo—(Guapo jóven que se cruza con
ella al salir, el jóven la saluda correctamente, vuelven a mirarse mutuamente.

Eduardo—Hermosa mujer, será casada o sol-
tera. Lo sabré mañana.

Esmeralda—Que guapo jóven y que cortés,
qüe fino, parece soltero. Lo averiguaré.

(Suena la sirena del auto).

TELÓN INTERIOR.

Esmeralda—Que regresa de las tiendas con
algunos paquetes, (vuelve a sonar la sirena) se le
cae uno.

Eduardo—(Que estaba en la esquina, corre
y le recoge el paquetito, se miran y se saludan. Ella
entra a su casa, y el dice:) Le he preguntado al
chauffeur y me ha dicho que es casada, pero que no
tiene hijos. Esa mujer será mía.

TELÓN.

Esmeralda—(En su casa). ¿Quién será ese

jóven? como me mira, su mirada me llega al corazón, que culto y delicado.

Ricardo—(El marido) ¿Qué tienes? estas·
triste, quieres venir conmigo? esta noche saldré para New York, volveré ante de fin de mes, me acom-
pañas? (acariciándole las manos y besándoselas).

Esmeralda—No, yo creo que me hace falta un
hijo, no te acompaño, me siento cansada para via-
jar, necesitaría para realizar el viaje un atractivo
poderoso, ese es lo que me hace falta para ir contigo
si puedes brindarmelo te acompañaré.

Ricardo—Que puedo yo ofrecerte? nada conozco que pueda estimular tus nervios, y excitar tu
temperamento, si el deseo de conocer otras costumbres no son suficientes, no sé que decirte, tu dirás.

Esmeralda—Nada, que no voy, que me abu-
rriría sola, en tanto tu acudes a tus negocios.

Ricardo—Entonces hasta la vuelta (la besa).

Esmeralda—Que te diviertas y vuelvas pronto. (sola). Por poco se me escapa y le digo una
impertinencia, pues al decirme que no conocía que
podría excitar mi temperamento que parece dormido, sentí deseos de contestarle, lo hay muy poderoso y tu no puedes ofrecermelo,¡ que mayor estímulo
podría hacer vibrar mis nervios que el amor! eso
ni se pregunta, se adivina.

¿Pero el no comprenderá q. yo necesito sentir
ese natural y expontáneo sentimiento que hace sentir el delirio, cometer las mayores locuras?   ¿Cré-
rán los hombres que no sentimos?

No se les ocurre que sintamos nuestros deseos,
ni se imaginan que podamos cansarnos de hacer una
comedia, en la cual solamente hemos puesto un poco de buen deseo para salvar de un caso apurado a
la familia. Se unen a una mujer sin tener la completa seguridad de ser amados, eso les parece de poca importancia, como si no sintiéramos ni pensara-
mos, como si fueramos un mueble que se compra

sin preguntarle si le gusta uno ú otro dueño, de
igual modo hacen con la mujer, si les gusta, se em-
peñan en poseerla aunque conozcan que no es amado, ni se dedica a conquistarla, nada más que de poseerla.

    Bien, voy á distraerme a casa de la modista.
(sale).

TELON INTERIOR.

3ª. ESCENA.—(en la calle.)

Esmeralda—(Regresa de casa de la modista,
acompañada de Eduardo), suena la bocina del auto
que se aleja).

Esmeralda—Gracias por su cortesía, ha sido
usted muy oportuno encantada de su atención, deseo que sea Vd. mi amigo, mi esposo no está aquí
ahora; Vd. puede venir mañana jueves, me
acompañará en mi paseo diario, ¿no tiene Vd. inconveniente alguno?.

Eduardo—En mi vida tendré mayor placer ni
satisfacción, que en ponerme a sus órdenes, (le da
una tarjeta) mañana estaré a cuál hora?

Esmeralda—De siete a ocho, de la noche, para las reuniones; de 5 a seis el paseo por la Castellana.

Eduardo—Muy bien señora, con el más profundo respeto soy su fiel admirador. Hasta mañana, (se aleja).

Esmeralda—Qué casualidad, al bajar del automóvil se me cae mi portamonedas, un momento
más y la rueda lo aplasta no se como este jóven pudo recogerlo. Como me gusta, que atento, que delicado, que prudente, luego no quería acompañarme
(suspira) ahora a dormir, leeré un poco al observa-
dor de las mujeres Octavio Picón (se retira).

TELÓN.

4ᵃ. ESCENA.—(Esmeralda en su casa.)

Esmeralda—Que día más largo! he procurado distraerme pero de ningún modo he podido evitar que la figura simpática de ese jóven me persiguiese y vuelvo a mirar el reloj y no se apresura, parece que detiene sus minuteros para mortificarme.   Qué largo me parece el día hoy.no se como hacer para no estar pendiente del reloj.   Ya se acerca la hora son las cuatro y cuarto, decidídamente que hoy me parece que en mi vida ocurrirá algo nuevo, no sé el corazón me late con precipitación, (se levanta se contempla frente al espejo).   Estoy bien, elegante, (suena la bocina) ya está aquí, valor, creo que hasta en los ojos sorprenderá la emoción que experimento.

Eduardo—(Haciendo un elegante saludo) señora, mi más entusiasta felicitación, está Vd. encantadora, rindo ferviente homenaje de admiración a la dama como artístista y como mujer....;.perdonadme señora (una reverencia) soy muy franco en mis manifestaciones.

Esmeraldo—No creí conocía Vd. detalles del arte de vestir en la mujer, gracias, por sus elogios.

Eduardo—He dicho la verdad, toda persona de buen gusto sabe apreciar la delicadeza femenina.

Esmeralda—¿Salimos?...........

Eduardo—Es Vd. la que ordena señora yo obedezco.   Salgamos, (salen y suena la sirena del auto).

TELÓN INTERIOR.

Esmeralda—Estoy desesperada, pero tengo que resolver esta noche, o se alejará de mi......no debo dejar que pase la felicidad por mí lado sin ofrecerla un asilo, sin brindarle una oportunidad para.

que me agasaje. Lo dejaré todo, nada me retiene aquí, la consideración a mi esposo......... ...pero que consideración guardó él para mí haciéndome suya sin consultar con mi corazón, sin pedir mi consentimiento, solamente por un compromiso comercial.

Nada, me iré con él lejos de aquí, a formar un nido nuevo de amor, que harta estoy ya de tristezas, y sacrificios, que que se sacrifique otro, ya no puedo más.

Eduardo—Me permite Vd. saludarla señora?..

Esmeralda—Pase Vd. amigo mío, lo esperaba, mi soledad exige una compañía agradable, y mi sentimiento la pide culta y sincera.

Eduardo—Reuniré yo esas condiciones para satisfar, a tan gentilísima dama?

Esmeralda—Seguramente, mi corazón no sabe engañarme. Ha de saber Vd. que he decidido resolver el asunto.

Eduardo—Por favor señora! no me haga Vd. soñar, apiádese de mí, si Vd. no es feliz, si Vd. vive triste, contrariada en sus afectos, en sus aspiraciones, y además me ha robado Vd. mi alma, y si no me equivoco, también Vd. me ama, ¿por qué mortificarnos de este modo?

Esmeralda—Pero cuán precipitado es Vd. no me ha dejado explicar, yo le iba a dar la noticia de mi resolución y se anticipa Vd. y me hace un discurso.

Eduardo—Perdóneme—creí que Vd. me comunicaba una mala noticia.

Esmeralda—Bien, allá vá, ¿está Vd. dispuesto a partir ésta noche?

Eduardo—Ahora mismo, ¿pero es cierto? se decide Vd. la ví y oí anoche tan difícil de convencer, que yo tenía pensado a la negativa de Vd. hoy; marcharme ésta noche para Londres. Era cuestión de vida ó muerte para mí.

Esmeralda—Pues bien, marcharemos juntos.

Eduardo—Entonces, permitidme salir para recoger mi dinero y dar algunas órdenes. Ahora me dejarás tu mano entre las mías, (tomándola su mano y besandola), hasta luego.

Esmeralda—¿Cuando vuelves?

Eduardo—En una hora estaré aquí, y te acompañaré a comer es decir para no provocar la atención de los criados, iremos a un restaurant, ¿quieres?

Esmeralda—Es una cosa nueva para mi, iremos.

Eduardo—(Sale).

Esmeralda—(Sola). Por fin, llegó el momento crítico de mi vida voy a lanzarme tras un ideal desconociendo el mundo y sus condiciones, voy a probar una nueva forma de vida, de acuerdo con mis sentimientos y mis deseos. ¿Cómo saldré en la aventura? No lo sé, pero, el hombre no pregunta se lanza y lucha y la mujer se detiene, recurre a dudas preguntas y a garantías que la aseguren-si va a ser o nó eterna su dicha, yo creo que no debe ser así, también debe arriesgarse suceda lo que suceda, que luche, que invente, que se defienda con sólidos argumentos.

Eduardo—(Se oye la sirena del auto que llega) ¿En qué piensas?...... no te preocupes, ¿ya estas preparada?

Esmeralda—No pienso, y estoy dispuesta.

Eduardo—Marchemos, (salen). El automóvil se despide con su bocina).

Un criado—(Que arregla el salón y recoge algunos papeles, otra vez la bocina se oye) el criado sale).

D. Ricardo—De regreso, y la señora paseando.

D. Ricardo—(Entra) Y la señora?

Criado—Ha salido.

D. Ricardo—No recibió mi telegrama?

Un criado—Se lo entregué en el jardin esta mañana.

D. Ricardo—Muy bien, (se sienta y lée un periódico).

El criado—(sale y vuelve con una carta. (se va).

D. Ricardo—¡Cómo! se ha marchado? yo que había creído conquistar su corazón. Bien, á París, a olvidar la equivocación. (Llama al criado y le dice): preparame otra vez mi equipaje, me marcho, en la estación te espero. A ¡París!...............

TELÓN.

COMO SE PROSTITUYEN LAS POBRES.

SALA sencilla.

Una mujer—(con bata de casa sale a escena, seguida de un hombre bien vestido, que le dá una moneda y la dice: ¿Os agrada ésta vida?

La mujer—No, pero, que recurso me queda?

El jóven—Acudir á la fábrica.

La mujer—No sé oficio, además que ganaría?

El jóven—Lo suficiente para manteneros.

La mujer—Me aconsejas que vaya á ganar un miserable jornal, que respire un aire impuro y que oiga las impertinencias de algún capataz grosero. Con eso no se remedia el mal, siempre seriamos una infinidad sacrificadas en holocausto a una mentira e hipócresía social. Es lo mismo que sea yo que otra, es carne humana q. se humilla ó se desprecia, que se vende y que se atrofia, que se ultraja que se utiliza y pisotea en nombre de la moral cristiana, (con energía) ¿Qué podeis decirme que otra no se merezca? Es igual, dejadme lo mismo yo que otra, sino podemos revindicarnos todas, pues ninguna, yo no soy mejor que ellas.

El jóven—Es verdad, una sola es nada, todas vosotras teneis derecho a ser felices y respetadas.

La mujer—El respeto social, en combinación con las fórmulas estúpidas, es una farsa, decidme de que vale a la pobre niña tuberculosa ser respetada, sino la evitan enfermarse, proporcionándole medios de vivir comodamente? Después se la hace una apología de su virtud y su decoro, cuando ha dejado girones de su alma y de su cuerpo en el taller; ¿por qué ese respeto no garantiza la salud, y ahuyenta las privaciones? Palabras!...............

El jóven—La ignorancia señora encarnada en el egoismo.

La mujer—¿Por qué esa virtud no la hace inaccesible a la pobredumbre en la sepultura? ¿por qué no evita la hediondez de la fermentación en la fosa? Si enterrasen dos niñas de igual tamaño y edad, una virgen inmaculada, otra roída por el vicios y la miseria, ¿la tierra respetará a una más q. a la otra? se librará la virgen de los gusanos?

El jóven—No, la naturaleza no establece distinciones, para ella igual es la virgen, que la prostituta. ella es igualitaria, niveladora por excelencia.

La mujer—Entonces amigo, a que sentir que viva de uno y u otro modo, lo mismo da, las hipocresias sociales no inquietan mi alma ni perturban mi cerebro.

El jóven—Comprendo, pero si eso no os importa, debo recordaros que estais expuestas a miles enfermedades y a prácticar vicios para hacer negocio complaciendo a esa turba de degenerados que os utilizan y luego tratan en despreciaros.

La mujer—Todo eso es muy espléndido para ser dicho pero si Vd. se viera en mis circunstancias seguramente que aceptarias de grado ó por fuerza. Un día llegó un borracho y no le valieron razones, me daba asco acercarme á él pues nada, acostumbra á venir todos los viernes, seguramente que esta noche vendrá. ¿Qué voy a hacerle?......

El jóven—Bien, tengo que marchár, perdonad mi insistencia, hasta otro día, (saluda cortesmente con el sombrero).

La mujer—(sola) Excelente jóven, pero ya es muy tarde, que puedo yo hacer, y además lo mismo da realizarlo con uno solo que con varios, no son todos hermanos según la Biblia y todas las religiones, pues todo ese fárrago de inutilidades me resultan ridículas y tontas, si todo está en venta a que apurarse tanto porque nosotras cobramos? si la que se une a un hombre ya sea por el registro civil o por fórmula religiosa, también se vende, no tiene el marido que atender a todos los gastos? son muy pocas las que van a las fábricas, y eso no es una venta? por que no querran darle ese nombre, pero la es como la nuestra.

Un hombre borracho—¡Buenas noches!

La mujer—Adelante.

El hombre—¿Se puede? muy bien pues date prisa que necesito irme, (tambaleándose).

La mujer—Pues anda, que ya iré............

El hombre—No, sigue tu primero, ¿te quieres marchar verdad? miren Vdes. estas ladronas, que ni pagándoles atienden bien, vamos, que te zurro! (empujándola)

La mujer—Voy, grosero, que te figuras?....valiera más suicidarse........

El hombre—Para lo que sirves, ya podías haberlo hecho, (entran en la habitación contígua, el empujándola hacia delante).

TELÓN.

EN EL CAMPO, AMOR LIBRE.

Aurora—joven campesina..
Victor—jóven obrero.

Es por la mañana, cuando el fresco verdor de los campos lucen los tintes primorosos y poéticos de la primavera. Una jóven con una cofia de lino con las bandas sueltas recorta flores en su huerto, que llamamos Aurora.

Victor—(que pasa con la chaqueta sobre el hombro para el trabajo se detiene a contemplar a la joven) diciendo: Bella ocupación........(recostado de un árbol).

Aurora—(Levanta su cabeza, y dice: Mucho madrugais, eso es muy saludable.

Victor—Para verte antes de ir al trabajo........

Aurora—Ya, ya, si fuera a creeros............

Victor—Creéme niña, el que vive con la naturaleza no miente, vengo a verte porque me atraes como el imán al acero me recuesto de este madero viviente y me parece que estoy unido a él, al menos que este hermano vegetal tenga interés en que te mire, te miro y no quisiera mirar otra cosa, yo no se chiquilla, pero tu me tienes hondamente preocupado porque no se como resolver éste asunto.

Aurora—Pues,.......á mi me sucede lo contrario. cuando te veo........cierro los ojos y corro mucho, hasta no verte.

Victor—Embustera, anda dime que te sucede, que sientes anda! acercate y dame una mano!.........

Aurora—(Acercándose lentamente)   Bueno te voy a contar........pero dejame libre.........me pasa.... ¡qué no te digo!...............

Victor—Empieza tonta ¡qué me haces sufrir!

Aurora—(Dejando su mano en las de Victor) Pues oye, que te ví, la primera vez y luego me asomaba callandita para verte pasar sin que tu me vieras y te miraba; he visto otros pero tu me gustas más, y me siento muy impresionada, y luego me hacía falta verte.

Victor—Ya ves como me quieres tu también y tenías temor de confesarlo. ¡ay!, que alegría, que contento me pones, pues yo no me había detenido antes por temor de. molestarte, y tú, también tú, me deseabas.

Aurora—Ve al trabajo, que es tarde, vuelve a la tarde, cuando la tierra por estos sitios haya dejado atrás al sol, y las aves trinen, y la brisa nos brinda perfumados aromas, cuando habiendo terminado nuestra faena, ya bañados y con ropa limpia estemos descansados; entonces pasearemos juntos debajos de los árboles.

Victor—A las seis estaré aquí. (dame un beso).

TELÓN.

2º. CUADRO.

Aurora—(Paseando en el campo).

Victor—(Acercándose) La hora solemne del crepúsculo vespertino, se aleja, envolviéndonos en sus claridades ténues y melancólicas, dejándonos nostálgicos de ella, por sus encantadoras combinaciones de colores y su elocuente silencio, como si hablara a las almas el lenguaje misterioso del amor, ¡qué bella es la vida!....¿no estás satisfecha de ella, en este sentido?

Aurora—Comprendo esa belleza que nos extasia, pero aun no he disfrutado de ella en todas sus manifestaciones.

Victor—Me permitirás conducirte, por ese
tortuoso camino y evitar que puedas tropezar?

Aurora—Con gran placer. Pero creo que
la mujer debe caminar sola, es decir unidos sí, pero
que haya una protección mútua, que no haga aparecer a la mujer bajo un tutelaje o dirección que al
fin y al cabo resulta odiosa. Que la hace aparecer
inferior siempre y en todas las ocasiones, y no la deja adquirir suficiente confianza en si misma en cualquier caso de urgente necesidad, y además la inuti-
lizan pues no tiene ocasión de usar su inteligecia
y se atrofian sus facultades físicas y morales.

Victor—Muy bien, pero para eso necesita
ilustrarse y prepararse. No ha sido mi intención
tratar de imponer mi voluntad, te ofrecí mi ayuda
para amarnos mutuamente pero sin que se me ocu-
rriese que pudieras imaginar que trataba de cohibir
tus actividades naturales y tus iniciativas personales
En eso no me inmiscuyo, eres completamente libre
de hacer lo que te plazca.

Aurora—Conforme, ahora dime ¿has pensado en mí?

Victor—Sí, todo el día, como si hubiera tenido tu retrato delante. Deseo que me digas si te
gusta la vida del campo.

Aurora—Si, cuidar las flores y las frutas, y a
los animales, contemplar la naturaleza en todo su
esplendor a todas horas.

Victor—¿Y tener hijos?........

Aurora—Si, ¿no es fecunda Natura?, si, re-
producirnos con nuestra carne y nuestros huesos,
que bella es la reproducción, hermosa y sana con
la hermosura de la salud y las buenas costumbres;
como se reproduce la naturaleza toda, observar en
nuestros hijos la naturaleza hecha carne e inteligencia consciente.

Victor—¿Cuántos?........

Aurora—No se, los que vengan, hay tierra suficiente para todos, ¿no és así?

Victor—Entonces no vuelvo á la fábrica, permaneceré contigo aquí, labraré la tierra, e iré a vender mis cosechas al pueblo.

Aurora—¿Buscarás quien te ayude? no te fatigarás?

Victor—Ya tendré un hombre o dos que me ayudarán. Respiraré aire puro y seré feliz, con la tierra libre.

Aurora—Cuando tengamos un hijo sembraremos un huertecillo para él con plantas útiles.

Victor—No lo obligaremos, hará lo que más le guste.

Aurora—Si, y tampoco le enseñaremos ideas religiosas le haremos comprender que el alma es inmortal y que todos somos hermanos.

Victor—Y nosotros que haremos?

Aurora—Complacernos mutuamente con entera libertad, pasearnos cada tarde á la hora del crepúsculo, será una renovación de entusiasmo en nuestra nueva vida.

Victor—Y por las mañanas iré a despertar tu sueño con muchos besos para renovar el recuerdo de la primera mañana.

Aurora—Y cuando contemplemos á nuestros hijos veremos en ellos la reproducción nuestra hecha carne y espíritu por obra y gracia de nuestro amor.

Victor—Y veremos á los hijos de nuestros hijos.

Aurora—(riendo) No estaremos contando los huevos sin haber puesto la galllina?

Victor—No importa, mejor es desearlos que no evitarlos; por supuesto teniendo la seguridad de que estarán bien.

Aurora—Hay muchos que no desean tener hijos porque no pueden mantenerlos.

Victor—También hay muchos que pueden mantenerlos y tenerlos bien y prefieren dejarlos sucios y descalzos por no dejar de vestir á la moda haciendo figuritas y haciendo de la mujer una esclava.

Aurora—Nosotros seremos libres ayudándonos. (Se abrazan y se alejan señalando la Luna que se asoma entre árboles).

Victor—Que bella está la Luna, vamonos, pues a disfrutar de nuestra libertad en el amor ya que no podemos disfrutar de otra por ahora. Pero imaginate que la tierra fuera libre y fueramos a elegir un sitio a nuestro gusto y que él trabajo fuera libre y no percibieramos salario, trabajaríamos para hacer canje de productos, cada semana recojería los frutos de hortaliza y á cada cosecha de cereales marcharían los automóviles de carga repletos de frutos y que orgulloso estaría yo, cuán satisfecho de ver llevar á la ciudad para mis compañeros los frutos puestos á mis cuidados y recibir en cambio todos los objetos necesarios para mis comodidades.

Aurora—Y que feliz sería yo siendo madre de seres libres.

Victor—Vayamos, pues camino de la libertad hacia el trono del amor.

Aurora—Hermosa naturaleza, y asoma la Luna su pálida faz, unidos cantemos un himno de paz.

Victor—Vayamos trás el ideal, deleitémonos con nuestro amor y sembremos gérmenes de libertad en el seno sagrado de Natura q. tu representas, ante el cual yo me inclino en señal de homenaje y admiración. Múltipliquémonos en el templo augusto de la hermosa y libre naturaleza, teniendo por dosel el espléndido espacio estelario iluminando nuestro casto lecho de amores, rindiendole culto a la gran fuerza desconocida que rige el universo. (Hablando se han sentado en el blando cesped y se abrazan).

TELÓN.

El dúo de la **Viuda Alegre.**

A mi excelente amigo el inteligente galeno, culto caballoro y gentil peeta, Dr. Manuel Martínez Rosselló.

DESPUÉS DE MUERTA.

COMEDIA DE LA VIDA REAL.

EN VERSO Y PROSA.

PERSONAJES:-

Lilia—,jóven de 26 años.
Mauly—caballero de 38 años.
Fabio—caballero de 34 años.

La acción pasa en los trópicos en una ciudad de las Antillas.

DECORACIÓN.

Una espléndida selva tropical, una verja que simula un jardin, árboles, guirnaldas, luces de colores, una tumba, formada con una lápida de mármol, rodeada de flores; una lámpara sostenida entre los árboles, pende sobre la tumba.

La tumba será puesta en el lado derecho del esnanario cerca del telón.

1ª. ESCENA.

Lelia—(Entra a la escena con actitud reposada que parezca meditabunda, traje blanco elegante) se dirige a la tumba, recoje una flor que ha caído sobre la blanca lápida, contemplándola.

¡Era una flor que regalaba su perfume, era una perla escondida en el revuelto mar humano!

¡Quién hubiera podido encontrarla y engarzarla cuál un brillante!

¡Pobre flor marchita
a los primeros rayos del sol
humilde violeta escondida
entre tallos sin olor,
brillante perla que un día
lució sin ostentación!

———————

Fué perfume que volaba
en pós de otra mansión,
fué una perla que brillaba
sin provocar la atención;
como flor era divina,
como perla sin igual,
fuera una rosa sin espina
que nunca devolvió mal.

———————

(Hablando con pausa, con delectación, como
quien saborease algún nectar delicioso de un modo
gentil, delicado, expresivo)

La flor con crueldad tronchada
una mañana sin sol,
la perla fué desprendida
de su corona de amor.
Así pasaban los días
contemplando con dolor,
que aquella flor de alegría
se marchitaba de amor.

(Besando la flor que se deshoja en sus manos)

Huíste psiquis hermosa
a la mansión de la luz,
vé con tus ricos aromas
a perfumar otro azul.

———————

Mauly—(Correctamente, vestido, con frac-
chistera, guantes, bastón y capa), abre la verja, se-
mi-oscuridad en escena, relampagos y truenos,
como si tronara entre montañas. Al abrir la verja, y

entrar a escena, lánza una mirada al espacio, frunce las cejas, y exclama: Todo está sombrío como yo, parece que la naturaleza quiere acompañarme en mi dolor, en mi angustia indescriptible........(introduciendo una mano en el bolsillo interior del frac saca una cartera, abréla y dice: Hoy estamos a 25 de diciembre, y (escribe en ella guardándola, sigue hasta la tumba en la que encuentra a Lelia, confundido con este encuentro la hace un galante saludo, y permanece pensativo).

Lelia—Que lejos de mi mente estaba el suponer que Vd. podría venir aquí Mauly...........

Mauly—Hoy es una fecha memorable para mi, tampoco pensé que pudiese encontrar a Vd. aquí....

Lelia—Vivo cerca y cuido de sus flores todos los días, me lo encargó ella...........

Mauly—Un día como hoy la ví por primera vez en su casa, angelical! divina! con un sencillo traje floreado de color rosa-violeta que la hacia sugestiva; fuí presentado en su casa por un abogado amigo de los dos, que también ha muerto.

Cuando entré me pareció que las puertas de lo desconocido se abrían para mi brindándome un mundo de inexplicable delicias!

Al verme junto a ella temblé, aquella niña se había apoderado de mi, me arrebataba la tranquilidad, me trastornaba.

Lelia—Cuanto tiempo hace de esto Mauly?

Mauly—¡18 años!, escucha, cuando por seguir las costumbres me obsequiaron con cerveza, no pude contenerme y le dije, me postraré de rodillas a sus pies si Vd. no bebe primero........humedeció sus labios divinos........y yo apuré el contenido de la finísima copa, como si hubiera querido absorver su aliento.   Tomé una de sus manos la besé entusiasmado.   Aquella chiquilla que empezaba a vivir me tenía desquiciado, al mirarme aprisionó mi alma ·con sus extraños ojos........

Lelia—Ya no existe a que recordarla ahora, todo esto debió Vd. haberselo dicho a ella viva, ahora para que........

Mauly—Dejad que hable permitidme que me expansione aquí frente a su tumba, que me asfixio... a los pocos días prometimos amarnos, todos los días me escribía cartas interminables, muy cariñosas copiaba poesias y me las enviaba, rayaba en frenesí su amor.

Pasaron algunos años, su fidelidad era tal, y su perseverancia era idolatria, llegue a despreocuparme tanto que entre viajes y ausencias pasaron dos años.

Lelia—Pero que hacía Vd? de modo que ahora es que reconoce Vd. que se portó mal? a buena hora.

Mauly—Ignorancia amiga mía, oid; aquella paciencia y dulzura personificada, aquel amor casi locura que sentía ella, —que me llenaba de satisfacción y orgullo y contribuyó a despreocuparme de mi deber,—aquella ignorancia de la vida, fué despertada. El amor esclavo se rebeló. La paciencia huyó para castigar mi descuido.

El entusiasmo amoroso que ella traducía escribiéndome diariamente poesías de autores célebres y cartas delirantes llamándome, terminaba y yo huía.....huía de aquel fuego creyendo se consumiría solo......(enjugándose el sudor).

Lelia—Pero que, ¿era Vd. indiferente a esas manifestaciones? acaso era Vd. insensible ya ¿por qué procedía de ese modo?

Mauly—Amiga mía los excesos anteriores me hacían guardar cierta medida que no podía explicársela ni ella comprenderla. Bien, al regreso de mi viaje a París, apenas fuí a verla, ciertos placeres disfrutados me desviaban de su casa para ir a plagiarlos en las casas de venta pública......

Lelia—Los vicios y las malas costumbres, te-

ner más fuerza que el amor! adonde hemos llegado! que asco! y que vergüenza! para esa moral social............

Mauly—No me interrumpais tanto amigo mía'
oid en silencio, y además y para mayores motivos
estaba enfermo............ ˙ A los pocos meses una noticia me helô la sangre y me enrojeció de vergüenza,
al pensar en la falta que yo había cometido con ella,
descuido q. pagaba con la pérdida de mis mas caras
afecciones e ilusiones; otro hombre la recordaba que
yo no cumplía con mi deber, que el lujo que la rodea-
ba no era aliciente para un alma enamorada........y
ella lo estaba de mí!........y aquel hombre era un a-
migo........ese representó para mi en aquel momento
una aparición del averno!........que me lanzaba al
rostro mi proceder, mi abandono para con aquella
mujer única aquien yo adoraba, en quien había con-
densado todos mis primeros recuerdos de amor, y
que guardaba para el porvenir, para mi vejez triste y desolada, quería reservar aquella pureza encarnada para deleitarme en ella, y me la despertaron.....

Lelia—Pero señor, que egoista erais, queriais
deformar su naturaleza, amoldarla a vuestros caprichos, que crueldad.

Mauly—Dejadme terminar y no me recrimi-
neis, que harto tengo con mi dolor, pues bien, cuando aquella mujer ingénua, con sin igual franqueza,
me confesó su desvío, relatándome la escena....¡qué
culpable me pareció aquel hombre!........si él había
sorprendido algo en su calidad de médico, debió avisarme, requerirme, para evitar mi desgracia, ¿no
era mi amigo?........pero ¡ah! desengaño, la desesperación se apoderó de mi al oir aquella confesión de-
tallada, el cielo de mis ilusiones se oscureció mis
ojos derramaron lagrimas ardientes, (con energía)
en aquel momento yo hubiera triturado a ese hombre! lo hubiera aplastado, como se aplasta a un pre-
til, que espera el momento oportuno para infiltrar

su veneno a traición! ¿qué influyó en aquella mu-
jer-niña para que aquel la despertase? ¿su soledad
mi descuido?..... ¡ni aun así, no la culpo a ella! ¡no!
mil veces no! Ese hombre ha sido un criminal y yo
me dije y en un vértigo de locura lo desafié y en plena plaza lo hubiera abofeteado sino es por los amigos que intervinieron,. porque aquel hombre por un
momento de placer destruyó mi felicidad y lanzó
mi amor de su cuna de ilusiones........ ¡Torpe! in-
sensato! y tantas veces como me utilizó como amigo! pérfido miserable! traidor! cínico!............

Lelia—No debeis culpar a nadie de ese descuido, habeis recibido la justa recompensa de vuestro
proceder.

Mauly—Pero si ella me dijo por muchos años
que no lo había amado a él, que sus pensamientos
eran mios y su alma.

Lelia—Y por qué no la perdonasteis? volvién-
do donde ella.

Mauly—Por preocupaciones sociales que me
obligaban a demostrar una cosa que no sentía.

Lelia—Que cobardía, y la habeis dejado sufrir
sabiendo que os amaba, no teneis corazón y con ella
á esos niños que están privados de vuestras caricias
y protección directa.

Mauly—En verdad no os equivocais me lo han
destrozado he sufrido mucho.

Lelia—Habeis podido evitar lo sucedido, porque no estabais a su lado?

Mauly—Por desconocimiento de las pasiones
humanas, pero dejadme que la implore, (acercándose a la tumba). ¡Perdóname visión azul de mis
ensueños irrealizados! ¡Volaste a otras regiones
mientras yo vegeto con el dolor, dolor de haberte
hecho padecer! perdón........(permanece silencioso
con la frente inclinada).

Lelia—Lo contempla con semblante compasi-
vo, ninguno de los dos ven entrar a un hombre em-

bozado que la oscuridad proteje, este hombre se acerca a la tumba y se arrodilla. Lelia al verlo dice: ¡Un hombre!........

Mauly—(Sorprendido se levanta diciendo): ¡Un hombre! ¿qué buscais aquí? (apuntando con su revólver).

Fabio—A cumplir con un deber! ¿quién sois para pedirme explicaciones?

Mauly—(Acercándose a la luz de la lámpara) ¡Mirad!

Fabio—¡Cielos! que haceis aquí?

Mauly—Y me lo preguntais vos! que sarcasmo! aquí sí, donde debo y puedo estar, en la tumba de la mujer que amé, como no se puede amar dos veces.

Fabio—Me haceis reir, después de muerta ha despertado vuestro amor, por que cuando vivía, bien abandonada la teniais, habeis venido a custodiar sus despojos?

Mauly—No os importa a vos, si la tuve abandonada ó nó, mucho atrevimiento es el vuestro para presentaros a éstas horas y en éste sitio.

Fabio—Esta tumba es vuestra? para que me arrojeis indirectamente de ella? ó es que ha despertado en vos la virilidad que no teniais cuando ella vivia?

Mauly—¡Insolente! ni su tumba respetas, si no te defiendes te mataré como mereces, (apuntándole con el revólver)

Fabio—Hiere, que así proceden los valientes, (presentando el pecho).

Lelia—(Que había permanecido silenciosa corre y se interpone). Qué vais hacer amigos! es así como honrareis su memoria? Después de muerta que beneficio reporta estas discusiones. Permitidme que os recite una composición de nuestra amiga.

A TI.

¿Quién es el que me invoca
en mi tumba solitaria,
y murmura una plegaria
de frases tiernas y locas?
¿Quién es esa triste sombra
que medita silenciosa
y en la noche misteriosa
solo en mi piensa y me nombra?

———————

Oye para que entiendas;
El que ajeno a mi destino
en mi via dolorosa
se cruzó por mi camino
y turbó mi vida hermosa.
Aquel osado que quiso
apagar mi estrella ufana
y en época tan temprana
mi tierno nido deshizo,
El hombre que temerario
profanó el alma mía
penetrando en el santuario
que era toda mi alegría,
¡Ese!...............lo perdono yó
y nadie puede juzgarle
como nadie puede darle
el castigo!..............sino Dios!......

Mauly—¡Lo perdona!......(de la sorpresa se
cae el revólver de las manos, del cual sale un tiro
que va á herir a Fabio, que se bambolea, y cae).

Lelia—(Que al terminar la poesía se alejaba,
al sonido del revólver, vuelve corriendo, y al ver a
Fabio en el suelo, pregunta a Mauly: ¿qué habeis
hecho?....

Mauly—No he sido yo, al caer disparó, sola,

(ambos se dirigen al lado de Fabio, y procuran levantarlo).

Lelia—Como podiamos impedir la hemorragia?

Fabio—Tomad un poco de yerba fina y estrujadla bien y cubrid la herida con ella........

Lelia—(Lo hace, y entre los dos procuran levantar á Fabio, y de pié).

Fabio—(A-Mauly), estais conforme, ahora me perdonais? yo solo no soy culpable, ella quiso vengarse de tu indiferencia y alejamiento! yo sabia que no era amor lo que por mi sintió, yo estaba sugestionado porque era una mujer tentadora, fuí tan débil que no puede resistir a su extraña influencia, en aquella soledad en que la encontraba siempre!

Mauly—Te lo propuso ella?

Fabio—No fué un caso premeditado, fué debilidad de mi parte, exceso de vida en ella, soledad abrumadora que la desesperaba y ansiosa de amor de caricias......se arrojó en mis brazos......perdón!

Mauly—¿Tu la violentaste?....

Fabio—¡Eso nunca! siempre he sido un caballero, tu fuiste culpable por tu abandono......

Mauly—Si eras tan correcto caballero, porque no me avisastes para yo cumplir con mi deber.

Fabio—¿Para cumplir con ella era necesario que yo te avisara?....(con ironía).

Mauly—No estoy conforme, te has tomado atribuciones que no te pertenecían; y eso de que ella quería vengarse de mi alejamiento ¿te lo manifestó ella?....

Fabio—No, pero me lo figuré porque esa mujer deliraba contigo, inmediatamente que llegaba preguntábame si te había visto, si yo sabia donde estabas.

Mauly—¿Qué le decías? porque no me avisaste?

Fabio—Decíale que te había visto en el casino ó en del Café, y no te avisé por que miles cir-' cunstancias lo impidieron.

Mauly—¿Nada más? no la indispusiste conmigo?

Fabio—No había motivo, ella tenía causas suficientes para molestarse......

Mauly—Pues, bien a pesar de todo te creo culpable y no puedo ser tu amigo tu presencia me mortifica, me hiere, me impulsa a matarte!....

Fabio—Mátame acaba de una vez, anda!.... (presentándose frente á Mauly).

Mauly—¡No aléjate!....nadie se enterará de este encuentro inesperado; pues como yo estaba ausente nadie sabrá ésto, marcharé otra vez y nada más.

Lelia—(A Fabio). ¿Sentis dolor?

Fabio—Un poco, acompañadme a la verja. (Lelia lo toma del brazo y lo conduce á la puerta). Gracias, os lo agradezco, adiós!....

Mauly—(Ha quedado pensativo mientras el otro se aleja).

Lelia—Adiós, (vuelve a escena, al lado de Mauly). ¿En que pensais?

Mauly—En ella que sufrió tanto y ha perdonado, no seré yo quien lo castigue, pudisteis creer que yo le había herido?....

Lelia—Una suposición natural, le habiais amenazado primero, luego comprendí que había sido casual.

Mauly—Amiga mía, marcho, aprovecho la oscuridad para irme como un criminal, ya veis los acontecimientos lo requieren, las circunstancias me obligan. Adiós y no me olvideis, orad por mi y por ella. ¡Adiós!....

Lelia Adiós, llevaos una flor de su tumba, (tronchando una flor y dandola, adiós. (permanece algo triste y repite:

Huiste psiquis hermosa
a la mansión de la luz

envía tu ricos aromas
a perfumar éste azul.

FÍN.

Ibor   City,   Florida.

TU RUBIO CABELLO.

En flotantes guedejas por tu espalda
se extiende sin rival tu cabellera rubia
cual perfumada y bella guirnalda
que lucieran al sol perlas de lluvia.

La brisa con ellas juguetea
con desordenada soltura
el sol en ellas se recrea
enviándole luz desde la altura.

¿Por qué te niegas a que yo las una
en bellas trenzas tu cabello de oro?
para que besen los rayos de la Luna
esa gentil cabeza que yo adoro.

Déjame también jugar con ellos
a la placidez de la corriente
para adornar tu blanca frente
con los hilos de oro de tus cabellos.

Ibor City Junio 15, 1913